QUEEN ELIZABETH HOUS
INTERNATION·· DEVELOPMEI

ECONOMICS OF AGRO-CHEMICALS

ECONOMICS OF AGRO-CHEMICALS

An International Overview of Use Patterns, Technical and Institutional Determinants, Policies and Perspectives

SELECTED PAPERS OF THE SYMPOSIUM
OF THE INTERNATIONAL ASSOCIATION
OF AGRICULTURAL ECONOMISTS
HELD AT WAGENINGEN, THE NETHERLANDS, 24–8 APRIL 1996

Edited by
G.A.A. Wossink, Wageningen Agricultural University, The Netherlands
G.C. van Kooten, University of British Columbia, Canada
and
G.H. Peters, University of Oxford, England

Ashgate

Aldershot • Brookfield USA • Singapore • Sydney

Published by
Ashgate Publishing Limited
Gower House
Croft Road
Aldershot
Hants
GU11 3HR
England

Ashgate Publishing Company
Old Post Road
Brookfield
Vermont 05036
USA

British Library Cataloguing in Publication Data
Economics of agro-chemicals : an international overview of use patterns, technical and institutional
    determinants, policies and perspectives : selected papers of the symposium of the International
    Association of Agricultural Economists held at Wageningen, The Netherlands, 24–8 April 1996. –
    (International Association of Agricultural Economists)
    1. Agricultural chemicals – Economic aspects – Congresses
    2. Agricultural chemicals – Environmental aspects – Congresses
    3. Agriculture and state – Congresses
    I. Wossink, G.A.A. (Grada Antonia Arendina)   II. Kooten, G.C. (Gerrit Cornelius) van   III. Peters,
    G.H. (George Henry), 1934–   IV. International Association of Agricultural Economists
    338.1'62

Library of Congress Cataloging-in-Publication Data
IAEE Workshop on Economics of Agro-Chemicals (1996 : Wageningen, Netherlands)
    Economics of agro-chemicals : an international overview of use patterns, technical and institutional
    determinants, policies and perspectives : selected papers of the symposium of the International
    Association of Agricultural Economists held at Wageningen, The Netherlands, 24–8 April 1996 / edited
    by G.A.A. Wossink, G.C. van Kooten, and G.H. Peters.
        p.   cm.
    ISBN 1-84014-084-4 (hard)
    Includes indexes.
        1. Agricultural chemicals – Congresses. 2. Agricultural chemicals – Economic aspects –
    Congresses. 3. Agricultural chemicals industry – Government policy – Congresses. I. Wossink, G.A.A.
    (Grada Antonia Arendina). II. Van Kooten, G.C. (Gerrit Cornelius) III. Peters, G.H. (George Henry).
    1934– . IV. Title.
    S585.I33 1996
    338.1'62—dc21
                                                                                                    97-51287
                                                                                                    CIP

ISBN 1 84014 084 4

Typeset in Sabon by Express Typesetters Ltd, Farnham, Surrey
and printed in Great Britain by Bookcraft (Bath) Limited

Contents

List of Figures   ix
List of Tables   xi

Foreword   xvii
Robert L. Thompson

1   Introduction to Agro-chemicals Use   1
    G.A.A. Wossink, G.H. Peters and G.C. van Kooten

PART I   INVENTORIES AND OVERVIEWS FOR DIFFERENT
         AREAS OF THE WORLD

2   Who Will Feed China? Agro-chemicals and China's Grain
    Strategy to 2010   21
    W. Li

3   Growth and Economics of Pesticide Use in India: Overview
    of the Environment, Patterns and Market Potential   41
    V.P. Gandhi

4   Do Fertilizers Play a Major Role in Sustainable Agricultural
    Development in West Africa?   59
    A. de Jager, A.U. Mokwunye and E.M.A. Smaling

5   Analysis of Intensive Farming Systems in the European
    Union   75
    F.M. Brouwer and P.J.G.J. Hellegers

PART II   AGRO-CHEMICALS USE AND SUSTAINABLE
          AGRICULTURE

6   Agro-chemicals Use and Sustainable Agriculture: Some
    Observations from a Semi-arid Area of India   95
    B.N. Hiremath and K. Singh

7   Use and Abuse of Chemical Fertilizers in a Resource-scarce
    Economy: Karnataka Province, India   107
    H.G. Hanumappa and D. Rajasekhar

8   An Economic Evaluation of Alternative Nutrient Management
    Practices in Sustaining Resource Base Productivity   117
    R.P.S. Malik

9   Economic Evaluation of Low and High External Input
    Agriculture: A Production Function Analysis for Indonesia   127
    R. Ruben, N.B.M. Heerink and E. Mol

10 Evaluating Sustainability of Intensive Farming Systems
    in China   145
    F. Qu, R. Zhang and J. Wu

PART III   EFFICIENCY AND PRODUCERS' KNOWLEDGE
           AND PERCEPTIONS

11 Regional Variation in Efficiency of Fertilizer Use: Food Crop
    Production in Togo   157
    E.M. Koffi-Tessio

12 Environmental and Economic Effects of Spatial Variability in
    Cropping: Nitrogen Fertilization and Site-specific Management 167
    T.J. de Koeijer, G.A.A. Wossink and F.J.H.M. Verhees

13 Farmers' Perceptions of Sustainable Production Techniques:
    Weed Control in Sugarbeet   181
    G.A.A. Wossink, A.J. de Buck and J.H. van Niejenhuis

PART IV   DETERMINANTS OF FERTILIZER AND PESTICIDE
          USE

14 The Effect of Price Changes on the Use of Fertilizer and
    Pesticides in Dutch Wheat Production   195
    J. Dijk and M.W. Hoogeveen

15 The Demand for Fertilizer on Upland Rice in the South-west of
    Burkina Faso: Determinants and Cost and Returns Analysis   207
    A. Sidibé and Y. Sere

16 Farm Management of Fungicide Use in Tulips in the Netherlands 215
    J.S. Buurma and W.H.M. Baltussen

PART V   POLICY INSTRUMENTS AND POLICY ANALYSIS: LDCS

17 Public Policy and Fertilizer Demand in Ghana   225
    K.Y. Fosu

18 Consequences for Agricultural Policies of Analysing Economic
    and Political Factors of Pesticide Use in Developing Countries 237
    G. Fleischer and H. Waibel

19 Financial and Economic Evaluation of Phosphate Rock Use to
    Enhance Soil Fertility in West Africa: Is there a Role for
    Government?   249
    A. Kuyvenhoven, J.A. Becht and R. Ruben

PART VI   POLICY INSTRUMENTS AND POLICY ANALYSIS:
          INDUSTRIALIZED COUNTRIES

20 External Effects of Agro-chemicals: Are they Important and
    How do we Cope with them?   265
    A.J. Oskam

21 Economic Policy and Water Pollution   283
    G. Flichman and D. Jourdain

22 Benefits of Improving Water Quality in South-western British
    Columbia: An Application of Economic Valuation Methods   295
    G.C. van Kooten

23 Policy Instruments to Control Multi-nutrients in an
    Agricultural Watershed   313
    A. Lintner and A.J. Weersink

24 Costs and Benefits of Pesticide Reduction in Agriculture: Best
    Solutions   333
    I. Heinz

PART VII   PERSPECTIVES FOR THE 21st CENTURY

25   Transformation and Environment: Perspectives for Central and
     Eastern European Countries   347
     A. Lütteken and K. Hagedorn

26   Less is More: Why Agro-chemicals Use Will Decline in
     Industrialized Countries   359
     S.M. Swinton

Author Index   373
Subject Index   383

List of Figures

3.1   Elements determining the market environment for pesticide
      policies   43
3.2   Consumption of technical grade pesticides in India   45
3.3   Consumption of pesticides by category in India   47
3.4   Crop consumption of pesticides in India   48
3.5   Pesticide demand by state in India, 1994–5   49
3.6   Scheme of manufacture and distribution in India   50
4.1   Fertilizer use in West Africa, 1970–93   64
5.1   Costs of plant protection products, utilized agricultural area 78
5.2   Nitrogen surplus, by region, 1990–91   79
9.1   Production functions of low- and high-input systems   132
10.1 Hierarchical framework of indicators for evaluating
      sustainability   148
12.1 Effect of soil properties on the relation between plant
      nutrient input and crop output   169
13.1 Efficiency frontiers for weed control in sugarbeet, by
      acreage   186
14.1 Yield of winter wheat in the Northern Clay Area   196
14.2 Moving averages of yield in kg per ha of winter wheat
      (1850–1940: Netherlands; 1945–60: Sea Clay Area;
      1960–95: Northern Clay Area)   197
14.3 Nitrogen fertilizer use in winter wheat, Northern Clay Area   198
14.4 Historical development of the relation between yield and
      nitrogen fertilizer use in winter wheat   199
18.1 Private and social optimum of pesticide use   241
20.1 Deriving socially optimal input use or emission levels   267
20.2 Deriving socially optimal emissions or input use when two
      processes are available   268
20.3 The demand curve for an input   270
20.4 Shadow prices of emissions under different conditions   272
21.1 Income and pollution: non-reformed CAP   291
21.2 Income and pollution: reformed CAP   292

25.1   Spread between input and output prices, Czech Republic   351
25.2   Consumption of commercial fertilizers (NPK) in former
        Czechoslovakia, Hungary and Poland   352
25.3   Reduction in nitrogen and phosphate fertilizers use,
        Hungary   353
25.4   Trends in consumption of pesticides, Hungary   354
25.5   Political development and development of production
        intensity in transition countries   356

List of Tables

1.1   Comparison of world consumption of fertilizers, 1951/52 and 1994/5   2

1.2   Regional shares in total consumption of chemical fertilizers, 1994/5   3

1.3   Development in chemical fertilizer (NPK) use and productivity, by region, 1950–91   4

1.4   Comparison of the world market value of chemical pesticides, by category, 1972 and 1991   7

1.5   Regional market share of pesticides, 1991   7

1.6   Productivity of crop protection for six major food and cash crops, 1988–90   9

1.7   Effectiveness of crop protection in six principal food and cash crops, by region, 1988–90   10

1.8   International results of residue measurements of plant protection products in vegetables and fruit   12

2.1   Chemical fertilizers in China: domestic production, consumption and imports, selected years   22

2.2   Agro-film applied in crop farming, selected years   23

2.3   Contributions of major inputs to growth of grain output in China, by region, 1985–90   24

2.4   Total use of fertilizers and grain and cotton output in China, 1952–95, selected years   26

2.5   Increase of area under some profitable crops in China, 1984 and 1993   27

2.6   Planned production targets for China's three major agricultural products, 1993, 2000 and 2010   30

3.1   Current global pesticides use, selected countries/regions   44

3.2   Percentage share of three groups of pesticides in some national markets and the world as a whole, 1991   46

3.3   Share of various constituents of pesticides industry in consumer's rupee   50

3.4   Progress of production of pesticides in India   51

3.5	Sales of pesticides in India	52
3.6	Global pesticides sales turnover of top 15 companies in India, 1992	53
3.7	Supply-demand balances for grain in India under alternative production and consumption projections for year 2000	55
4.1	Nutrient stocks and other fertility indicators of granitic soils in different agroecological zones in West Africa	61
4.2	NPK budgets in West Africa, selected countries, 1983	62
4.3	Value-cost ratios for maize and cereals in Ghana and Mali, 1981-94	64
4.4	Farm-level nutrient input and output flows	66
4.5	Restoring soil fertility in West Africa: technical options and their impact on nutrient flows	67
4.6	Recommended actions at different intervention levels to facilitate implementation of technology options to restore soil fertility	70
5.1	Total costs of fertilizer and plant protection products, by farming type in the EU, 1992-3	81
5.2	Costs of fertilizer and plant protection products per hectare, by farming type in the EU, 1992-3	82
5.3	Use of plant protection products in The Netherlands, by farming type and the intensity of total use, 1993-4	83
5.4	Cereal farm structure and output characteristics, by utilized agricultural area, central France, 1992-3	84
5.5	Cereal farm structure and output characteristics, Denmark, 1992-3	85
5.6	General characteristics of horticulture, 1992-3	86
5.7	Farm structure and output characteristics on horticultural farms in The Netherlands, 1992-3	87
5.8	Farm structure and output characteristics on horticultural holdings in Andalucia, 1992-3	88
5.9	Structure of farms with at least 75 per cent of UAA used for tomatoes in The Netherlands and in Campania, 1992-3	89
6.1	Trends in fertilizer consumption and food grain production in India	100
7.1	Fertilizer use in Karnataka Province, India	109
7.2	Fertilizer application	110
7.3	Productivity of important crops, by season	111
7.4	Fertilizer application across stages of crop growth	111
7.5	Use of fertilizers, by farm size	113
7.6	Crop fertilizer application response	114
7.7	Changes in crop patterns	115

8.1	Rotation characteristics	120
8.2	Crop yields: experimental results and EPIC estimated	121
8.3	Estimated soil erosion and changes in crop yield	122
8.4	Estimated crop yields: results of regression analysis	123
8.5	Estimate of on-farm and off-farm costs of soil degradation	124
8.6	Economic comparison of conventional and alternative farming practices in sustaining long-term soil productivity in the rice–wheat system	125
9.1	OLS regression results for labour input	135
9.2	Summary statistics for maize farmers in the sample	136
9.3	OLS regression results for LEIA and HEIA systems	138
10.1	Comparison of sustainable agriculture (SA) in developed countries and China	147
10.2	Matrix of indicators for evaluating sustainable farming systems in China	149
10.3	Changes in main ecological–economic indicators of the sustainable farming system in Chuanziying Village, 1982–90	151
10.4	Integrated evaluation of sustainable farming in Chuanziying Village, 1982–90	151
11.1	Yield trends of three major crops in Togo, by region, 1982–93	159
11.2	Fertilizer application rates for food crops in Togo, by region, 1982–90	161
11.3	Value–cost ratios for three food crops in Togo, by region, 1983–94	162
12.1	Data of the two small soil profiles distinguished in the case study	173
12.2	Average annual N-fertilizing, nitrogen–leaching and income effects	175
13.1	Seven strategies for weed control in sugarbeet	185
13.2	Mean Likert scores for weed control attributes, selected strategies	188
13.3	Factor score coefficients for strategies 1 and 2	190
15.1	Fertilization practices in the Hounde area	210
15.2	Rate, yield and area of fertilizer use on upland rice	211
15.3	Determinants of manure application on upland rice	211
15.4	Upland rice budget of different fertilization practices (annual)	212
15.5	Returns to different fertilizer practices over two years	213
16.1	Contribution of fungicide choice, number of sprays and deviations from standard dose rates to the total variance in the use of active ingredients	217

16.2	Relation between *Botrytis* susceptibility and number of sprays	218
16.3	Differences between two farming systems in tulip production	218
16.4	Use of fungicides in two farming systems with tulips, 1994	219
16.5	Contrasts in management between two farming systems	220
17.1	Types of fertilizer imported in Ghana, recent decades	230
17.2	Growth of fertilizer use in Ghana, 1960s–80s	231
17.3	Growth in fertilizer utilization during the 1990s in Ghana	231
17.4	Average annual rate of fertilizer use in Ghana, 1960s–90s	232
17.5	Growth in wholesale prices of agricultural products and fertilizer–crop price ratio in Ghana, 1990–94	234
17.6	Percentage annual share of agriculture in total credit in Ghana, 1990–94	235
18.1	Reasons for institutional failure	240
19.1	Phosphate fertilizer price in Mali, 1994	256
19.2	Financial and economic net present values (in FCFA) and internal rates of return of PR application for different scenarios	258
20.1	Negative external effects of pesticides and minerals in The Netherlands; monetary value and percentage of gross value added in agriculture	272
20.2	Estimated costs of complying with pesticide levels in drinking water and prices of drinking water	273
20.3	Classification of policy instruments to address negative external environmental effects according to situation	274
20.4	Economic incentive policies for pesticides in several OECD countries (circa 1992)	275
20.5	Pesticide policy in three countries with an active volume reduction policy	276
20.6	Type of policies and economic incentive measures with respect to minerals in EU countries	277
20.7	Type of economic incentive policies for three countries with an active policy for fertilizer	278
21.1	CAP reform scenario	292
22.1	Summary of personal and background information	302
22.2	Water quality and sewer maintenance	303
22.3	Regression analysis of willingness to pay for improved water quality	305
22.4	Intensity of preference for fuzzy pairwise ranked items	306
22.5	Regression analysis for intensity of preferences and predicted intensities	307

22.6	Regression analysis of defence expenditures in the Abbotsford region of British Columbia	308
23.1	Farm management practices and pollutant parameters	319
23.2	Effects of instruments on farm management practices, profit and water quality	324
24.1	Water contamination from pesticides, 1995	336
24.2	Costs of current maximum pesticide drinking water guidelines, 1995	339
24.3	Cost of achieving EU pesticide drinking water guidelines, 1995	340
25.1	General economy and agriculture in CEEC10, 1993	348
25.2	Change in real gross agricultural output, 1990 and 1994	350

Foreword

Robert L. Thompson[a]

The economics of agro-chemicals are important and the collection of works from the International Association of Agricultural Economists Symposium on this topic, held in Wageningen, The Netherlands, in April 1996, is very timely. World grain stocks per capita are the lowest they have been in over 20 years, and world market prices have increased significantly. The sustainability of the world's food production system is under intense scrutiny. The farm and agribusiness sectors in many countries have been the target of a barrage of negativism in the media over the last decade. Environmental activists in particular have labelled high-productivity agriculture as part of the problem, not part of the solution. Agro-chemicals have been a particular target of their concern.

In recent years a number of long-term global food supply–demand projections have been made. Among the analysts who have looked at the world food situation recently there is considerable disagreement about the future supply of food but virtual unanimity that demand will double by the year 2025, as a consequence of population and income growth. Yet the growth in world population is moderating more rapidly than many expected, so that even the United Nations' median projections may turn out to be too high.

There has been a widespread loss in confidence in governments' ability to deliver economic development. The dismal record of centrally planned economies in creating employment and economic growth has become widely recognized. Privatization and a broad-based stimulus to the private sector are accelerating economic growth in many low-income countries. This trend has been enhanced by a more open international trading system. It is well documented that the strongest engine of economic growth is international trade. In recent decades, the economies that have performed the best are

[a]President, International Association of Agricultural Economists; President and Chief Executive Officer, Winrock International Institute of Agricultural Development, P.O. Box 376, Morrilton, 72110 Arkansas, USA.

those that pursued an open economy, export-oriented growth strategy, as opposed to an inward-looking, protectionist, import-substituting approach to growth. Full implementation of the World Trade Organization (WTO) agreement and various regional trading arrangements will only reinforce these tendencies. The greatest payoff from these agreements to liberalize international trade is likely to be the faster economic growth that they stimulate in the lower-income countries.

As the purchasing power of tens or hundreds of millions of poor people in third world countries rise, what is the first thing they do? They alter their diets to consume more fresh fruits and vegetables and more animal protein. That, in turn, expands the demand for the inputs necessary to produce these products, such as maize and soybeans. This is the income effect of economic growth on future demand for agricultural products and, in turn, on agricultural inputs. And, in future decades, the income effect on global demand for food may be larger than the effect of population growth.

While the forecasters' crystal balls get cloudier beyond 2025, a number of studies predict that world demand for food will triple before it stabilizes after the middle of the next century. Whether this planet has to grow three times as much food as today or 'only' twice as much, growing it in a manner that protects the quality of the environment will be a challenge of monumental proportions. Can it be done? And what role will agro-chemicals play in the production systems?

The challenge can be met if we make the necessary preparations now. To attain the goal will require a high-technology, science-based agriculture around the globe. We will need far greater investments in research and technology transfer than are made today. Ironically, the United States and Western Europe have been cutting back on public investments in agricultural research for over two decades. They have also reduced their investments in international agricultural research. The contraction in public support for agricultural research has exceeded the expansion in private-sector investments. In addition, achieving the requisite increases in food production calls for a significant change in agricultural policies. The strong anti-rural, anti-farmer bias that is found in many countries' agricultural and rural policies, especially in low income countries, must be abolished. This is not a plea for subsidies for farmers, but for a level playing field.

We cannot double, to say nothing of triple, world food production in an environmentally benign manner by doubling or tripling the area of land in agricultural production. There is only modest opportunity for increasing the area planted on fertile, non-erodible soils. In most countries, expanding cultivated areas will quickly move production onto fragile, highly erodible soils and soils subject to desertification. Of greater environmental concern, an attempt to double the area of land in production would require massive clearing of forests, which would be accompanied by destruction of wildlife habitat and loss of biodiversity. The only way to avoid this environmental disaster is to pursue the path of high productivity, science-based agricultural production.

It should be remembered that farmers were the original environmentalists, committed to protecting their most valuable resource, the soil. Indeed, soil conservation is almost a religion with many farmers. Unfortunately, there have been cases where farmers overfed their crops, permitting excess fertilizer nutrients to leach into the groundwater or to run off into lakes or streams. This has often been in response to public policy incentives that tied subsidies to the volume of farmers' output. In recent years, in many industrialized countries, these subsidies have been reduced and decoupled from the volume of production. This, together with the tough economic conditions of the 1980s, forced farmers to minimize their cost of production and become much more precise in their applications of inputs. To a greater and greater extent, what makes good economics also makes good environmental sense.

In the last 10 to 15 years, crop production in many countries has undergone a quiet revolution that has been little noted in the media or by environmental activists. This is the revolution of low-tillage farming and it is spreading quickly around the world. One observes it in farming systems as different as those in the United States, Australia, Brazil and Indonesia. In addition, the low-tillage revolution is being followed by precision farming in which input applications are tailored to the varying crop and soil conditions as the applicator moves across a field. Slow-release forms of various chemicals are permitting just-in-time delivery of the chemical to the plant to ensure that the plant is adequately treated in a timely manner without leaving excess chemicals that would run off or leach through the soil profile into the groundwater.

This is the golden age of the biological sciences. We are poised for the takeoff of the biotechnology revolution. It will extend the scientific triumphs that began with the advent of hybrid maize and continued through the development of other fertilizer-responsive varieties of the main food crops of the world, including the high-yielding rice and wheat varieties, that appeared in the 1960s and 1970s. Biotechnology will permit continued growth in yields and will provide a broader range of alternatives for controlling the worst crop pests. When taken together with the electronic revolution in agriculture, built upon low-cost sensors, information processing, geopositioning and geographic information systems, we have tremendous potential to continue increasing agricultural productivity while ensuring that the quality of the environment will be protected.

To take full advantage of this potential will require larger investments in agricultural research by both the public and private sectors. Farmers worldwide will need more varieties that are more responsive to fertilizer. They will also need to be able to employ a full range of pest-control strategies, from biological controls to integrated pest management, to biotechnology and chemistry. Advanced modern pesticides will play a key role because they are applied in low doses and have very low, if any, toxicity to mammals and birds. When combined with precision low-tillage agriculture, they are environmentally benign.

To achieve the requisite increases in productivity will require larger applications of nitrogen, phosphate, potash and micronutrients from chemical sources. There certainly is a need in many places for greater application of animal manure and other forms of organic matter to restore and maintain soil structure. However, organic sources simply cannot deliver enough available nitrogen, phosphorous and potash to support the high productivity needed to avoid having agricultural production expand onto lands where great environmental damage would occur. At the same time, we need to see much more attention being paid by public policy around the world to removing the disincentives to farmers, whether those disincentives be in the form of price policy, set-aside policy, or underinvestment in rural roads, schools and agricultural research. Without research results that raise productivity and without ready availability of high-payoff inputs, it will be impossible to avoid adverse environmental consequences.

1   Introduction to Agro-chemicals Use

G.A.A. Wossink[a], G.H. Peters[b] and G.C. van Kooten[c]

Introduction

Efficiency gains in agricultural production as a result of agro-chemicals (chemical pesticides and fertilizers) are reported to be significant. That is obviously important given the projected growth of world population, though in many countries there is an increasing concern about the public health risks and negative environmental effects of agro-chemicals application. These contrary positions – the positive contribution of agro-chemicals to food production versus their real and perceived negative impacts on health and the environment – justify a careful analysis of the role of agro-chemicals within sustainable agriculture. For agriculture to become more sustainable, the relationships between agro-chemical use, crop response and environmental quality and human health need to be studied. Many factors are involved in these interrelationships and their dynamics: agro-ecology and climate, crops and rotations, socioeconomic conditions, farmers' knowledge and their preferences, the influence of research, education and extension, and developments within the chemical industry.

Against this complex background a conference on the economics of agro-chemical use was held under the aegis of the International Association of Agricultural Economists in April 1996 in Wageningen, The Netherlands. The objective was to bring together experts from both industrialized and developing countries to exchange experience and information. This book

[a] Department of Economics and Management, Wageningen Agricultural University, P.O. Box 8130, 6700 EW, Wageningen, The Netherlands.
[b] University of Oxford, Queen Elizabeth House, 21 St. Giles, Oxford, OX1 3LA, UK.
[c] Department of Agricultural Economics, University of British Columbia, Vancouver, Canada.

1

presents a selection of the papers presented at the conference.

This first chapter presents an introduction to agro-chemical use. Information is provided on the growth of fertilizer and pesticide use and on their productivity during recent decades both by region and globally. Environment and health problems related to agro-chemical use are described and their nature is indicated. Finally, we highlight some of the most urgent research questions and major findings emerging from the conference. The text contains many references to the basic literature which readers might find useful as further reading.

Developments in the Use and Productivity of Agro-chemicals

Chemical Fertilizers

The objective of fertilizer use is to limit reductions in crop yield due to shortage (temporal or spatial) of nutrient supply. All crops remove nutrients nitrogen, phosphorus and potassium (NPK) from the soil and, unless these are replaced, the fertility of the soil declines. Nutrients can be produced from different sources: chemical (manufactured or mined), recycling (green manure, animal waste), mineralization in the soil and atmospheric deposition. Here we focus on chemical fertilizers, where average application varies enormously throughout the world (Table 1.1).

Compared with 1951, total use is now almost nine times greater. This is particularly due to increases in the consumption of nitrogen fertilizers. Table 1.2 shows that, in 1994/95, by far the largest share of fertilizers was used in Asia, North and Central America and in Europe. There are differences among these regions in the relative importance of the three types of chemical fertilizers. In Asia, nitrogen fertilizers in particular are important, whereas Europe and NC America have a relatively larger share in the consumption of

Table 1.1　Comparison of world consumption of fertilizers, 1951/52 and 1994/5

| | Volume/share | | | |
	1951/52 (m. tons)	(%)	1994/95 (m. tons)	(%)
Nitrogen (N)	4.2	29.1	73.5	59.7
Phosphate (P_2O_5)	5.7	39.5	29.7	24.1
Potash (K_2O)	4.6	31.4	20.0	16.2
Total	14.5	100.0	123.2	100.0

Source:　FAO Production Yearbook: Fertilizers, several years.

Table 1.2 Regional shares in total consumption of chemical fertilizers, 1994/5

	N/C America	S America	W Europe	Africa	Asia	Oceania	World
			Share in world consumption				
Nitrogen (N)	18	3	16	3	55	1	100
Phosphate (P$_2$O$_5$)	17	8	15	3	50	4	100
Potash (K$_2$O)	26	10	23	2	29	1	100
Total	19	5	17	2	49	1	100

Note: Because of rounding off, row entries might not add up to world total.

Source: *FAO Yearbook: Fertilizers* (1994).

potash. As indicated by Hiremath and Singh and by Li in Chapters 2 and 6, in Asia there has been an emphasis on nitrogen use, enhanced by subsidies. This excessive use of nitrogen has led to distortions in the supply of nutrients in balanced proportions and declining yields. The differences in average application rates per unit of area among the regions are as significant as those with respect to differences in total consumption. In some parts of Western Europe and Asia, application rates exceed 300 kg per hectare (see Chapters 5 and 7). In West Africa average use is less than 10 kg per hectare, which leads to significant soil nutrient depletion (see Chapter 4).

Additional information on aggregate changes in chemical fertilizer use by major regions of the world for a period of four decades is shown in Table 1.3. The huge increase in world use has already been mentioned. Within that, however, there are marked differences. At the beginning of the period the bulk of use was in NC America and Europe, with both areas showing considerable increases to around the mid-1970s. Since then there has been no change in NC America, while European use has marginally declined. Oceania, with its naturally small aggregate use, broadly follows that pattern.

The striking difference is in Asia. There was a steep increase from 1969–71 to 1975–77 (3.87 to 17.60 million tonnes), which has continued. The 1990–92 figure is up by a further 41.22 million tonnes, or by more than three times the 1957–1977 share in the total consumption of N, P$_2$O$_5$ and K$_2$O by region. That experience has not been shared by South America, where use from 1957 to 1977 is only about 50 per cent higher, while Africa lags behind with a much smaller increment of 35 per cent.

Analysis of the productivity of fertilizer use is, of course, a complex exercise which cannot be attempted here. However, attention is drawn to one feature of Table 1.3 which is of interest in the general context. Though fertilizer is used in many farming applications, much of it contributes to cereal production, which is illustrated in the table, along with a figure of

Table 1.3   Development in chemical fertilizer (NPK) use and productivity, by region, 1950-91

Year	N/C America			S America			Europe			Africa		
	Cereal production (1) (m. tonnes)	Chemical fertilizer use (2) (m. tonnes)	Average yield (1)/(2) (tonnes)	Cereal production (1) (m. tonnes)	Chemical fertilizer use (2) (m. tonnes)	Average yield (1)/(2) (tonnes)	Cereal production (1) (m. tonnes)	Chemical fertilizer use (2) (m. tonnes)	Average yield (1)/(2) (tonnes)	Cereal production (1) (m. tonnes)	Chemical fertilizer use (2) (m. tonnes)	Average yield (1)/(2) (tonnes)
1948–52[a]	169.4	4.59	36.9	24.8	0.17	145.9	112.4	6.97	16.0	33.9	0.31	109.4
1954–56	179.2	5.98	29.9	31.2	0.31	100.7	124.9	8.84	14.1	37.3	0.47	78.2
1961–65	210.0	9.25	22.7	40.2	0.55	73.1	158.6	14.62	10.8	51.0	0.82	62.2
1969–71	261.6	17.68	14.8	50.9	1.61	31.6	197.8	24.87	7.9	61.3	1.62	37.8
1975–77	316.9	23.43	13.5	63.0	3.4	19.5	224.1	29.10	7.7	66.8	2.67	25.0
1980–82	391.2	24.11	16.2	72.0	3.67	19.6	257.2	31.66	8.1	74.0	3.55	20.9
1985–87	395.9	23.10	17.1	79.9	5.50	14.5	289.3	32.35	8.9	82.0	3.69	22.2
1990–92	398.7	23.77	16.8	75.3	4.95	15.2	281.4	22.27	12.6	90.2	3.60	25.1

Table 1.3 continued

Year	Asia Cereal production (1) (m. tonnes)	Asia Chemical fertilizer use (2) (m. tonnes)	Asia Average yield (1)/(2) (tonnes)	Oceania Cereal production (1) (m. tonnes)	Oceania Chemical fertilizer use (2) (m. tonnes)	Oceania Average yield (1)/(2) (tonnes)	World total Cereal production (1) (m. tonnes)	World total Chemical fertilizer use (2) (m. tonnes)	World total Average yield (1)/(2) (tonnes)
1948–52[a]	263.3	1.12	235.0	6.8	0.50	13.6	691.9	13.73	50.4
1954–56	353.4	1.66	212.9	6.8	0.71	9.5	732.7	17.98	40.7
1961–65	393.8	3.61	109.0	11.4	1.00	11.4	987.3	32.49	30.4
1969–71	482.8	3.87	124.7	14.6	1.40	10.4	1 237.9	75.32	16.4
1975–77	562.6	17.60	31.9	17.5	1.62	10.8	1 430.3	94.63	15.1
1980–82	654.0	31.36	20.8	18.8	1.69	11.1	1 637.1	115.27	14.2
1985–87	765.2	40.22	19.0	24.0	1.64	14.6	1 832.1	132.25	13.8
1990–92	875.9	58.82	14.9	23.1	1.70	13.5	1 928.4	134.32	14.4

Note: [a]For the yield of cereals, the average of the period was used; fertilizer use indicates the use in the middle year of the period.
Source: FAO, *Yearbook Production*; FAO, *Yearbook Fertilizer*, several years.

'average yield' per unit of fertilizer employed. It hardly needs to be stated that its use is only one factor which may account for changes in production. What the crude 'productivity' measure shows, however, is the importance of deeper study of use within the developing world. In Asia, for example, the marked increase in output, which has more than doubled in the years from the start of the 1960s, has also been accompanied by a change in average yield, which is declining. Production per tonne of fertilizer applied is now relatively low, at 14.9 tonnes. The importance of Asia within the world totals, allied to the fact that the 'average yield' in the developed world and in South America is of broadly similar magnitude, accounts for the lack of major change in the 'world total' average yield over the past two decades.

The outlier is again Africa. Though the production figures may be distorted by drought, its relatively poor performance in raising output, and the apparently higher fertilizer 'yield' (it is about double the Asian figure), could be an indicator of unused potential for agricultural production through additional, more effective, fertilizer use. As stressed by Koffi-Tessio in Chapter 11, there are many features of the African situation, including the need for innovation and extension services to alter cropping systems and optimize application rates and the timing of use, which deserve attention as means of increasing income and food production.

Chemical Pesticides

Whereas fertilizers are used throughout the world and the chemical compounds they contain are easy to define, chemical crop protection is much more complex. There are mechanical, chemical and biological methods of crop protection. Chemical crop protection agents can be defined as substances that protect plants from diseases, pests and weeds, or which are used to secure yields and facilitate harvesting (growth regulators, haulm-killing chemicals).

Pesticides can be classified in many different ways. One might classify them according to intended use: disease and weed control, haulm killing, soil disinfecting, growth regulation, grassland enhancement, and so on. One might also use biological classification: herbicides, nematicides, bactericides and fungicides, herbicides, insecticides and acaricides (to control mites). In practice, usually a mixture of classifications is used. It is common to indicate use figures, by category or in total, in kg of active ingredient (ai); that is, by the weight of the toxic substances.

Since the 1960s, the market for chemical pesticides has increased appreciably, and in this case a value measure can be used (Table 1.4). Sales of chemical pesticides worldwide have doubled since the 1970s, with herbicide sales showing the greatest rate of increase.

Table 1.4   Comparison of the world market value of chemical pesticides by category, 1972 and 1991

	1972 (US$ bn)	(%)	1991 (1972 US$ bn)	(%)
Herbicides	4.5	36	11.9	44
Insecticides	4.5	36	7.8	29
Fungicides	2.7	21	5.6	21
Others	0.9	7	1.6	6
Total	12.6	100	26.9	100

Source: Modified from Dehne and Schönbeck (1994).

The importance of chemical pesticides varies from region to region (Table 1.5). Currently, more than three-quarters of them are used in the USA, Western Europe and Asia. Herbicides are the principal pesticides used in the USA; fungicides are least important in this region. In the temperate regions of Western Europe fungal diseases dominate and fungicides account for about half of chemical pesticide usage. In Asia the main problems are insect pests and fungal disease, so insecticides and fungicides are most important here (see Chapter 3). This use is still rather localized; more than two-thirds of all cropland in the world is not treated with any chemical pesticide at all (Dehne and Schönbeck, 1994).

Since the 1930s, when the first chemical pesticides were introduced (dithiocarbamate fungicides), there have been substantial developments in the synthesized active ingredients, particularly in herbicides and fungicides, though the spectrum of insecticides available is comparatively limited. This increases the chances of the emergence of insects resistant to the active ingredient.

Table 1.5   Regional market share of pesticides, 1991

Product group	USA	Western Europe	Eastern Europe	Latin America	Asia	Others	World total
Herbicides	34	30	6	8	15	7	100
Insecticides	18	20	8	9	31	14	100
Fungicides	9	48	5	6	28	4	100
Total share by region	20	33	6	8	25	8	100

Source: CountyNat West WoodMac, in Dehne and Schönbeck (1994).

Because the chemicals used are so heterogeneous, assessing their productivity is far more difficult than in the case of fertilizers. In Table 1.6, an estimate is presented for six major food and cash crops that are grown worldwide. The intensity of crop protection is best quantified in terms of expenditures on crop protection agents per unit area. However, it must be pointed out that in many parts of the world farmers control weeds by hand or by machine, whereas elsewhere weeds are controlled almost exclusively by herbicides. Direct control of pests and of diseases is impossible without the use of agro-chemicals, however. Table 1.6 shows expenditure per hectare of arable land for the total of herbicides, insecticides and fungicides used. This does not give the total costs of crop protection because the costs of application and the costs of labour and so on are not included, but it does give an overall picture of the intensity of use. On a per unit area basis, use is highest for cotton (US$80.5/ha), followed by potato (US$39.6/ha) and soybean (US$34.3/ha). In cereals the intensity of use is less than US$20/ha on average.

The effectiveness of crop protection is difficult to assess, not least because the concept has both a physical and an economic dimension. Estimates have been made of 'attainable production' and 'production without protection' for each of the crops, on the assumption that they could be either fully protected or not protected at all (Oerke *et al.*, 1994). The difference between the two then measures the full extent of 'potential loss'. Actual production (which always falls between the two limits, as would be expected) is also known, hence it can be presumed that crop protection has limited the losses; the actual size of the limitation is the difference between the 'attainable production' and its observed level. The effectiveness of protection, at least in its physical connotation, is the ratio of the 'potential loss minus the actual loss' to the 'potential loss'. In Table 1.6 (which also has some details for crop loss due to three types of causes, and estimates of the crop saved by the three types of chemical inputs), the overall effectiveness, calculated by the method described, is highest for cotton at 55 per cent, while for soybean and potato, it is around 45 per cent. The other three cases fall in the range 34–38 per cent. On a regional basis (Table 1.7) the figures are high for Western Europe (always greater than 50 per cent) and for North America and Oceania, but the performance is less impressive in other regions of the world except in the case of cotton.

It has to be borne in mind that the level of potential loss rate, and any measure of effectiveness that stems from it, could be misleading. It does have a financial equivalent measured in terms of the value of output that is saved, although the important issue is whether that saving is worth achieving given the cost of the chemicals and the labour and other costs of their application. The goal of crop protection is to prevent economic loss. If the

Table 1.6   Productivity of crop protection for six major food and cash crops, 1988-90

	Rice	Wheat	Potato	Maize	Soybean	Cotton
Use						
Total expenditure (m. US$)	2 400	4 718[a]	704[b]	2 463	1 930	2 722[c]
Per group (%)						
herbicides	36	50.4	31.3	74.3	81.9	18.2
insecticides	38	6.6	36.9	21.9	10.7	64.0
fungicides	24	38.8	31.7	3.1	6.5	3.9
Area harvested (m. ha)	145.8	231.5	17.8	129.1	56.3	33.8
Use ($/ha)	16.5	20.4	39.6	19.1	34.3	80.5
Attainable production,						
world total (m. t)	1047.1	830.7	464.7	728.6	152.0	84.1
Production without crop						
protection (m. t)	184.0	399.6	122.6	294.6	62.9	13.8
Potential yield loss[d] (%) due to						
weeds	34.0	23.9	22.8	28.8	36.3	36.3
animal pests	29.0	11.3	26.4	19.1	12.7	37.0
diseases	20.0	16.7	24.4	11.7	10.5	10.2
Actual production (m. t)	508.9	547.9	272.6	448.8	102.7	52.4
Actual yield loss[d] (%) due to						
weeds	16.0	12.3	8.9	13.1	13.0	11.8
animal pests	21.0	9.3	16.1	14.5	10.4	15.4
diseases	15.0	12.4	16.3	10.9	9.0	10.5
Crop saved (m. t) by the use of						
herbicides	192. 7	68.2	64.7	114.7	33.9	20.6
insecticides	86.5	26.3	47.9	33.5	3.1	18.2
fungicides	51.7	36.9	37.4	6.1	2.3	0.8
Effectiveness of crop protection (%)[e]	38	34	44	36	45	55
Average physical return of crop						
protection						
(crop saved in t/expenditure in US$)						
herbicides	0.23	0.03	0.09	0.06	0.02	0.04
insecticides	0.10	0.08	0.18	0.06	0.02	0.01
fungicides	0.09	0.02	0.17	0.08	0.02	0.01
Average financial return of crop						
protection						
(crop saved in US$/expenditure in US$)[f]						
herbicides	48.1	4.1	11.6	5.9	4.7	19.6
insecticides	10.9	10.9	223.2	5.9	4.7	4.9
fungicides	18.8	2.7	21.9	7.8	4.7	4.9

Notes:
[a] Figure for 1990 (CountyNatWest WoodMac, 1991).
[b] Figure for 1991 (CountyNatWest WoodMac, 1992).
[c] The category 'others' accounts for 13.9%. This category includes defoliants and/or desiccants that are applied before mechanical harvesting.
[d] Loss in % of attainable yield.
[e] Effectiveness potential minus actual loss in per cent of potential loss.
[f] Trade prices used in US$/t: wheat 136.2; rice 209.1; maize 98.1; potato 128.7; cotton 490.6. (See Oerke *et al.*, 1994: 748.)

Source: Own calculation, based on Oerke *et al.* (1994).

Table 1.7   **Effectiveness^a of crop protection in six principal food and cash crops, by region, 1988–90**

Region	Rice	Wheat	Maize	Potato	Soybean	Cotton
Africa	34.0	25.5	26.2	30.7	38.9	49.5
N America	57.3	31.7	45.8	58.9	45.4	64.2
Latin America	36.4	28.6	22.4	44.1	46.6	52.8
Asia	37.5	32.1	30.1	35.8	39.0	51.6
W Europe	51.5	51.3	51.2	54.1	55.2	66.0
E Europe	39.7	24.9	28.9	35.9	37.4	59.0
Oceania	59.3	36.3	52.6	59.6	44.8	66.6

Note: ^{a}In percentage abatement of the potential loss.
Source: Oerke *et al.* (1994).

anticipated physical yield is low, for instance because it is limited by abiotic factors such as shortage of nutrients or water, it might be uneconomical to apply pesticides. There is an economic optimum between the intensity of pesticide used and the remaining crop losses. Therefore the economics of crop protection in different production systems cannot be concluded from the actual loss rates (see, for example, Campbell and Madden, 1990; Carlson and Wetzstein, 1993; Oerke *et al.*, 1994).

Impacts of Agro-chemicals on Environment and Health

The residuals that are generated as by-products of agricultural activity may be dealt with by the environment in two ways: (1) they may be reallocated and/or accumulated, or (2) they may be processed and recycled. Ecological processes exist with category (2) that result in the breakdown and reuse of chemicals, but are not available in (1). Chemical pesticides, phosphorus (P) and potassium (K) belong to the first category. Initially they are diluted and dispersed, but ultimately they will accumulate in some environmental component such as soil or water. Substances in the second category include nitrogen (N) and organic pesticides. Within limits, the environment can receive and process them without any negative effects. This capacity is constrained, firstly, by the environmental transportation mechanisms that carry that substance from the point of release to the environmental component responsible for its breakdown and, secondly, by thresholds that, if exceeded, will induce ecosystem changes. Nitrogen can only be taken up by crops if it is placed close enough to the root system; if that is not the case, it will for example, leach into groundwater.

The major environmental and health effects of nutrients are caused by eutrophication, which occurs when the concentration of nutrients in the environment is so high that it disturbs ecological processes. Nutrient surpluses (organic and inorganic) can lead to a decrease in the quality of groundwater and surface water and to a reduction in the value of nature. It might affect the quality of drinking water, which may lead to health problems. A well known example of the relation between agricultural intensification and human health is the contamination of drinking water by nitrate, which constitutes a hazard mainly for infants (*methaemoglobinaemia*, or blue baby syndrome). Babies may be at risk with nitrogen nitrate levels of 10 mg per litre of water which is easily exceeded in countries with intensive farming systems (see Chapter 2). Other studies mention nitrate as a cause of stomach cancer in adults (see Chapter 2.2).

Environmental problems caused by pesticides are specifically due to the fact that the amount of pesticides coming in direct contact with, or consumed by, the target pest is an extremely small percentage of the total amount applied. In most studies the proportion of pesticides reaching the target pest has been found to be less than 0.3 per cent, with the bulk being emitted into the environment (Pimentel, 1995; van der Werf, 1996). A consensus exists that the environmental impact of a specific pesticide depends on its dispersion, the resulting concentration in the environment and its toxicological properties (van der Werf, 1996).

Apart from environmental and health problems, pesticide use leads also to agricultural or agronomic problems. The most important of these are phytotoxicity (manifested as damaged crops, especially likely to occur when using herbicides), resistance, adaptation (after some years of soil disinfection and other soil treatment the chemicals used are decomposed by micro-organisms before they can become active), the development of secondary pests and changes in quality (Oskam *et al.*, 1992).

Environmental effects of pesticides are caused by emission into groundwater, surface water, air and adjacent fields. The most important routes are evaporation and leaching. Important factors are the characteristics of a pesticide and of the soil and the way in which the pesticide is applied (aerial spraying of crops compared to under-leaf spraying). Natural effects due to pesticide use result indirectly from the environmental effects mentioned. Human health can be affected by the toxic substances in pesticides either in food, drinking water or air.

Notwithstanding the extensive literature on the human and ecotoxicological risks of pesticides (see Chapter 24), data on their actual impact are scanty. At the conference some information was presented on human health risks of pesticide use. An overview of the maximum concentrations of pesticides in shallow and deep groundwater shows that, in

about 30 per cent of water supply in EU countries, the European guidelines
for drinking water (0.1 µg per litre groundwater for individual pesticides and
0.5 µg for total pesticide concentration) are exceeded (see Chapter 24). One
of the few other significant international studies of the human health risks of
pesticides is on residues in fruit and vegetables (van Klaveren, 1997). The
norm used in this assessment is the acceptable daily intake (ADI), which is
the maximum amount of a pesticide that a human being can ingest per
kilogram of body weight during a lifetime without damaging health. There
are significant differences among countries, as indicated in Table 1.8.
Further, it follows that the percentage of vegetables and fruits with a residue
higher than the norm in certain countries is still increasing, particularly for
imported products. Possible effects of pesticides in the air have not been
studied. However, the relative overrepresentation of toxicosis from
pesticides in people working in agriculture indicates that they run greater

Table 1.8   **International results of residue measurements of plant protection products
in vegetables and fruit**

Country	Product group	Year	No residue (%)	Residue < norm (%)	Residue > norm (%)
Denmark	Domestic	1993	90.5	7.4	2.1
		1994	87.8	11.7	0.5
	Imported	1993	74.5	23.9	1.6
		1994	74.7	23.0	2.3
Germany[a]	Domestic	1995	59.4	39.9	0.7
	Imported	1995	43.9	51.1	5.0
Greece	Domestic	1995	81.0	11.3	7.7
Netherlands	Domestic	1993	79.2	19.1	1.7
		1995	61.9	36.1	2.0
	Imported	1993	44.7	49.6	5.7
		1995	46.0	49.6	4.5
Spain	Domestic	1995	61.4	36.0	3.6
Sweden	Domestic	1993	84.6	13.9	1.5
		1995	90.2	9.4	0.4
	Imported	1993	41.2	56.0	2.8
		1995	55.8	38.2	6.0
UK	Domestic	1993	73.3	26.1	0.6
	Imported	1994	57.4	41.0	1.7
USA	Domestic	1993	58.3	40.0	1.7
		1994	56.2	42.5	1.3
	Imported	1993	64.9	31.4	3.7
		1994	64.6	31.3	4.1

Note: [a] Baden–Württenburg.

Source: van Klaveren (1997).

risks of damaging their health than others living in the same areas (Oskam *et al.*, 1992).

Summary Observations

The aim of this book is to assess critically the current status of economic research on agro-chemical use. We seek to answer two questions: what have been the main approaches and limitations in recent research; and what are some of the broader conceptual and methodological developments that are needed to enhance the future perspectives of this type of economic research?

Agro-chemical Use and Sustainable Agriculture

In contrast to conventional inputs (land, labour and capital) agro-chemicals affect output through indirect control mechanisms. These control processes aim to prevent, or reduce, yield loss due to biotic (pests, weeds or diseases) or abiotic (shortage of plant nutrients N, P and K) factors. So yield reduction can be regarded as a function of control actions and the uncontrolled level of the yield-limiting abiotic factors or yield-reducing biotic factors. Inputs that control crop loss act either in a preventive or a curative way. If the limiting or reducing factor is not present, the control input has no effect. This special feature, plus the fact that farmers have limited information on parameters that may vary between and within seasons and plots, makes demand for fertilizers and pesticides more complex than for conventional inputs. Environmental problems have resulted in renewed interest in this topic.

In the economics literature, debates continue about specifications and functional forms to use when studying crop response to pesticides and fertilizer (see Chapter 26). For econometric studies of pesticide use see, for example, Lichtenberg and Zilberman (1986), Babcock *et al.* (1992), Carrasco-Tauber and Moffit (1992), Chambers and Lichtenberg (1994) and Carpentier and Weaver (1995). Literature concerning uncertainty with respect to modelling fertilizer use and crop response includes Ackello-Ogutu *et al.* (1985), Berck and Helfand (1990), Paris and Knapp (1989), Paris (1992) and Chambers and Lichtenberg (1996). Just (1993, pp.11–12) shows that estimates of elasticities vary by more than orders of magnitude for most crops, depending on the functional specifications used.

In Chapter 9, the econometric approach is applied to compare the economics of high and low external input agriculture. Other authors such as Pandey (1989), Blackwell and Pagoulatos (1992) and Fox and Weersink (1995) emphasize that, rather than testing a range of functional specifications and comparing elasticity estimates, the production function should be derived from the biological and ecophysiological processes governing agro-ecosystems. This means that the analysis should start at a disaggregated level – the farm or crop level. By means of crop growth and pesticide and nutrient emission models, crop yields and indicators of pollution can be obtained for different production situations. This information can be used in an ecological–economic farm model to determine impacts of environmental and price policies, and of alternative technologies, on production patterns, farmers' revenue and environmental quality (see Chapters 8 and 21; also Wossink *et al.*, 1992). Both current and innovative production practices can be considered, which is not possible in the econometric approach.

Chapter 10 presents a multiple-criteria method to evaluate and summarize the ecological, economic and social sustainability of different farming systems. Such a method can be used in combination with the econometric or the ecological–economic farm model approach.

Efficiency and Producer Knowledge and Perceptions

All over the world significant differences are found in the efficiency with which farmers use agro-chemicals. Here an important issue is the impact of uncertainty due to limited information given to farmers. For example, Babcock (1992) showed that economically efficient nitrogen application rates for a corn–soybean rotation in the USA are about 35 per cent higher when uncertainty is explicitly taken into account. Risk aversion might further affect the optimal application rate. Chapter 7 discusses interview data for India which show that an increase in fertilizer prices gave a reduction in use and changes in cropping pattern, in line with economic theory, but that total crop production did not decline because of improvements in efficiency. Similar improvements in efficiency of agro-chemical use have been found for European cereal growers after the reduction in EU output prices (Boussemart and Dervaux, 1993). Also a continuing increase in higher-yielding varieties might counteract the expectation of lower yields at higher fertilizer prices (see Chapter 14).

Improvements in efficiency without changing crop varieties or chemical inputs can be achieved by education of farmers to stimulate better use of existing information, or by providing farmers with additional and better information itself. Site specific management or 'precision agriculture', is based on the idea that more detailed information will improve agricultural efficiency. Chapter 12 shows that this innovation can be particularly important as a means of improving the environmental quality of crop production.

Chapters 9 and 26 emphasize that costs and benefits are not the only relevant parameters for the selection of techniques by farmers in developing and developed countries. Utility analysis (farm household modelling) could offer a better methodology to evaluate the impact of agrarian policy instruments on agro-chemical use and land use than estimating crop response elasticities. An alternative would be to use an efficiency frontier approach in combination with a survey of farmers' perceptions and preferences (see Chapter 13).

Policy Instruments and Policy Analysis

If all the ecological and health effects can be measured, an ecological cost-benefit assessment can be made (see Chapter 20). Usually ecological processes have a very different space and time dimension compared with economic processes and often ask for an assessment at a wider spatial level than is common in agricultural economics (see Chapter 23). Health impacts may also take a long time to appear and can be difficult to trace back to a specific polluting source. Not only does the appropriate space and time scale need to be decided on before an economic assessment of pesticide and nutrient use is possible, but indicators of environmental quality have to be defined, particularly for pesticides given their diverse environment and health impacts. As long as ecological costs of agro-chemical use tend to be underestimated because of methodological and data problems in economic research, environmental and economic policy will not be able to signal the right price for pesticide and fertilizer use (see Chapter 18).

Chapter 24 provides an example of an environmental–ecological assessment. The indicator used for policy design and evaluation regarding nitrogen and pesticide use is the concentration in water. With such indicators an economic assessment can be made of the costs imposed by restrictions on drinking water, for example.

In Africa ecological effects of nutrient use are related not to over-application but to the opposite. Nutrient depletion is particularly severe in West Africa when agriculture is intensive. In the Sahelian countries, by contrast, there is little that possibly could be depleted. The economics of the ecological effects can be assessed by various methods (see Chapter 4), but actual data are scarce.

After an ecological–economic assessment of agro-chemical pollution or nutrient depletion, the policy issue is how to curb further environmental harm. There is a multitude of factors that determine agro-chemical use, some internal to the farmer (and his family) and others external, depending on economic and institutional conditions. The average outcome of the total of these factors might be different, even between growers of the same crop in two regions within one country (see Chapter 16).

Main Conclusions

Government agricultural programmes in developed and developing countries have been a major contributor to the overuse and inefficient use of agro-chemicals, especially fertilizers. This has been accomplished by both input and output supports that have distorted land use, crop mixes and applications of agro-chemicals. In developing countries there are many complications. Since public infrastructure can be poor, it is often the case that there has been a slow growth in the marketing of crops (farm gate prices are low). This has reduced the demand for fertilizer available from domestic resources, including manure and phosphate rock, while transport problems have made it difficult to move bulky material easily from supplying areas to the point of use. In other cases cheap food policies, used as a means of placating restless urban populations, have had similar effects, since effectively they reduce the profitability of farming. These features are particularly true for Africa. Elsewhere, notably in parts of Asia, there has been emphasis on encouraging the use of standard NPK fertilizers, which have often been subsidized and drawn from imports. In other cases, export crops are encouraged (cotton is a notable example), with the export crop using fertilizers less efficiently than crops produced for the domestic markets.

For the central and eastern European countries in transition, a special situation applies. Here new rules for economic activities are being institutionalized and agricultural policies are being redefined. Environmental concerns are now considered seriously, which was not the case before the political changes began in 1989/90 (see Chapter 25).

Use of agro-chemicals is often inappropriate (inefficient) because farmers do not apply proper amounts, employ less than optimal crop rotations, and so on. This problem exists in both developed and developing countries, but is most pronounced in the latter. Extension services are poor and many farmers are unable to read labels that give directions as to how to use products. A number of contributors to the present volume recommend that greater emphasis be put on extension, improving farm management and encouraging innovation, instead of limiting policy design to output restrictions, emission limits, price changes, subsidies, and so on (see Chapters 15, 17, 20 and 22). Governments need to reconsider their roles with respect to the agricultural sector, avoiding the application of instruments that distort resource use to the detriment of both people and the environment. This applies as well to developing countries as to the industrialized countries.

This volume contains 26 chapters. The remaining chapters are arranged into seven parts that deal with overviews of agro-chemical use for different parts of the world, agro-chemical use and its relation to a sustainable agriculture, farmers' knowledge, price responses, policy instruments and policy analysis in developing and industrialized countries. After considering inventories for different regions, the presentation moves from the farm to the higher, national or supranational level where policy regulations are the main issue. The volume concludes with some perspectives regarding agro-chemical use in the next century.

References

Ackello-Ogutu, Ch., Q. Paris and W.A. Williams (1985), 'Testing the von Liebig Crop Response Function against Polynomial Specifications', *American Journal of Agricultural Economics*, **67**: 873–80.

Babcock, B.A. (1992), 'The Effects of Uncertainty on Optimal Nitrogen Applications', *Review of Agricultural Economics* **14**(2): 271–80.

Babcock, B.A., E. Lichtenberg and D. Zilberman (1992), 'Impact of Damage Control and Quality of Output: Estimating Pest Control Effectiveness' *American Journal of Agricultural Economics* **74**: 163–72.

Berck, P. and G. Helfand (1990), 'Reconciling the von Liebig and Differentiable Crop Production Functions', *American Journal of Agricultural Economics*, **72**: 985–96.

Blackwell, M. and A. Pagoulatos (1992), 'The Econometrics of Damage Control: Comment', *American Journal of Agricultural Economics*, **74**: 1040–44.

Boussemart, J-Ph. and B. Dervaux (1993), 'Diagnostic de l'efficacité productive par DEA: Une approche complémentaire à l'analyse par les ratios technico-économiques', paper presented at the VIIth Congress of the European Association of Agricultural Economists, Stresa, Italy.

Campbell, C.L. and L.V. Madden (1990), *Introduction to Plant Disease Epidemiology*, Wiley, New York.

Carlson, G.A. and M.E. Wetzstein (1993), 'Pesticides and Pest Management', in G.A. Carlson, D. Zilberman and J.A. Miranowski (eds), *Agricultural and Environmental Resource Economics*, Oxford University Press, New York.

Carpentier, A. and R.D. Weaver (1995), 'Heterogeneity in Production Technologies and Estimation of the Pesticide Productivity', in A.J. Oskam and R.A.N. Vijftigschild (eds), *Proceedings of the Workshop on Pesticides, Concerted Action AIR3 Policy Measures to Control Environmental Impacts from Agriculture*, Wageningen Agricultural University, Wageningen, The Netherlands.

Carrasco-Tauber, C. and L.J. Moffitt (1992), 'Damage Control Econometrics: Functional Specification and Pesticide Productivity', *American Journal of Agricultural Economics*, **74**: 159–62.

Chambers, R.G. and E. Lichtenberg (1994), 'Simple Econometrics of Pesticide Use', *American Journal of Agricultural Economics*, **76**: 406–17.

Chambers, R.G. and E. Lichtenberg (1996), 'Non-Parametric von Liebig–Paris Technology', *American Journal of Agricultural Economics*, **78**: 373–86.

CountyNatWest WoodMac (1991), *Agrochemical Service*, County National West Wood Mackenzie, London.

CountyNatWest WoodMac (1992), *Agrochemical Service*, County National West Wood Mackenzie, London.

Dehne, H-W. and F. Schönbeck (1994), 'Crop Production – past and present, in E-C. Oerke, H-W. Dehne, F. Schönbeck and A. Weber (eds), *Crop Production and Crop Protection; Estimated Losses in Major Food and Cash Crops*, Elsevier, Amsterdam.

Fox, G. and A. Weersink (1995), 'Damage Control and Increasing Returns', *American Journal of Agricultural Economics*, **77**: 33–9.

Just, R.E. (1993), 'Discovering Production and Supply Relationships: Present Status and Future Opportunities', *Review of Marketing and Agricultural Economics*, **61**: 11–39.

Lichtenberg, E. and D. Zilberman (1986), 'The Econometrics of Damage Control: Why specification matters', *American Journal of Agricultural Economics*, **68**: 261–73.

Oerke, E-C., H-W. Dehne, F. Schönbeck and A. Weber (eds) (1994), *Crop Production and Crop Protection; Estimated Losses in Major Food and Cash Crops*, Elsevier, Amsterdam.

Oskam, A.J., H. van Zeijts, G.J. Thijssen, G.A.A. Wossink and R. Vijftigschild (1992), *Pesticide Use and Pesticide Policy in The Netherlands: An Economic Analysis of Regulatory Levies in Agriculture*, Wageningen Economic Studies 26, PUDOC, Wageningen, The Netherlands.

Pandey, S. (1989), 'The Economics of Damage Control: Comment', *American Journal of Agricultural Economics*, **71**: 443–4.

Paris, Q. and K. Knapp (1989), 'Estimation of von Liebig Response Functions', *American Journal of Agricultural Economics*, **71**: 178–86.

Paris, Q. (1992), 'The von Liebig Hypothesis', *American Journal of Agricultural Economics*, **75**: 1019–28.

Pimentel, D. (1995), 'Amounts of Pesticides Reaching Target Pests: Environmental Impacts and Ethics', *Journal of Agricultural and Environmental Ethics*, **8**: 17–29.

van der Werf, H.M.G. (1996), 'Assessing the impact of pesticides on the environment', *Agriculture, Ecosystems & Environment*, **60**: 81–96.

van Klaveren, J.D. (1997), *Resultaten residubewaking in Nederland, Kwaliteitsverslag Agrarische Producten, Verslag 1996*, RIKILT-DLO, Wageningen, The Netherlands.

Wossink, G.A.A., T.J. de Koeijer and J.A. Renkema (1992), 'Environmental policy assessment: a farm economics approach', *Agricultural Systems*, **39**: 421–38.

PART I
INVENTORIES AND OVERVIEWS FOR DIFFERENT AREAS OF THE WORLD

2 Who Will Feed China? Agro-chemicals and China's Grain Strategy to 2010

W. Li [a]

Agro-chemicals and Food Production in China: Overview

Fertilization of soil has a very long history in China. The earliest inscriptions about manuring the fields were found on bones and tortoise shells of the Shang Dynasty (16th–11th century BC). As a result, China has many folk sayings, such as: 'The essence of farming lies in manure' and 'Water determines whether or not we have a harvest, and fertilizer determines whether the harvest is big or small'. The Nobel laureate N.E. Borlaug (1994) noted that 'today China has become the world's largest cereal producer. Her spectacular agricultural progress is due to various factors. Certainly, the development of high-yielding varieties and improved irrigation systems have played major roles. But perhaps even more important has been the efforts to improve and maintain soil fertility'.

Importance of Fertilizers in China

Chemical fertilizers came to China at the beginning of the 20th century, but they were used in large quantities only from the 1960s. In the 1950s, the peasants used mainly farmyard manure and green manure crops with a small proportion of nitrogen fertilizers. Phosphates began to show their effects in the 1960s, but potash fertilizer only in the 1970s, together with other kinds of micronutrients (Lin, 1995). Chinese farmers now recognize that fertilizers are one of the most important factors for increasing agricultural production. The Chinese government has worked out a series of policies and regulations

[a]Institute of Agricultural Economics, Chinese Academy of Agricultural Sciences, 30 Baishiqiao Road, Beijing, 100081, China.

to develop the domestic fertilizer industry, thereby helping China to meet its people's ever-increasing demand for food.

The years of economic reform in China witnessed an unprecedented growth of total agricultural value as well as development of the fertilizer industry. Today China is the second largest fertilizer producer in the world but at the same time, one of the largest importers (Table 2.1). According to the Ministry of Agriculture (MOA), the total output of fertilizers in 1994 was 22.76 mt of nutrients, or 16.3 per cent more than the previous year, 17.17 mt of nitrogen fertilizer (an increase of 11 per cent), 5.32 mt of phosphate (17.8 per cent more), and 0.22 mt of potash (47.8 per cent more). Generally, high-quality fertilizers have often been in short supply. The price of major fertilizers increased remarkably – urea rose to 2020 yuan per ton (US$243) in August 1995, 42.6 per cent higher than the price in January.

The Chinese government lends support in many ways to increase fertilizer production capacity, including preferential taxation and investment. The state invested over 16 billion yuan (about US$2 billion) in 18 large-scale fertilizer projects during the 1990–95 period. Electricity for the medium- and small-sized fertilizer enterprises, for example, is supplied at preferential prices, and small fertilizer products are exempt from value-added taxes. The railway gives priority to transporting fertilizers and the principal raw materials and fuels to the leading fertilizer factories, with discounted fees. Business taxes are not imposed in the case where fertilizers are marketed by the specialized companies (that is, supply and marketing cooperatives), state-owned farms and agricultural technical extension stations. The state fixes the price for fertilizers to support agricultural projects (including reclamation projects, agricultural experiments or demonstrations, poverty-alleviation projects, straw ammoniation for the cattle industry and so on). In

Table 2.1   **Chemical fertilizers in China: domestic production, consumption and imports, selected years**

Year	Production (mt nutrients)	Consumption (mt nutrients)	Imports (mt physical terms)	Retail Price (average mixed price, RMB yuan per 'standard' ton)
1978	8.69	8.84	3.98	231.0
1980	12.32	12.69	5.44	237.0
1985	13.22	17.76	7.61	369.5
1990	18.80	25.90	16.26	630.0
1992	20.48	29.30	18.59	909.9
1994	22.76	33.18	12.66	n.a.

Source: MOA (1995).

addition, the state has established a special fertilizer fund and fertilizer reserve fund for slack seasons (2.5 billion yuan).

Agro-films and Pesticides

Plastic film is used as mulching material to protect soil from frost damage and to retain moisture. Before the 1970s, agro-films were used only in horticulture and nurseries, mostly in the north and in very limited areas. This technique became popular mainly in the early 1980s. Chinese farmers adopted it quickly because of the high returns, and the acreage under agro-film expanded rapidly as an effective way to raise crop yields (Table 2.2); as a result, the acreage approached 4 million ha in the early 1990s. Normally, one hectare of land requires about 75 kg of film, which gives an effect similar to that of 'extending' the cropping zones northward by 2 or 3 degrees of latitude, or 'upward' by a height of 500 to 1000m, and can save 1500–2250 m^3 of water from evaporating. With film mulching, per hectare yield of paddy rice can usually be increased by 450 kg, corn by 750 kg to 2 tons, cotton (lint) by 230–300 kg, peanuts by 4.5 tons, and vegetables by 30 per cent. The major difficulty has been the acute shortage of raw materials from which the agro-film industry suffered. About one half of the facilities were idle in the early 1990s. Total agro-film production was 459700 tons in 1994. Only 81 per cent of the planned production target was met, so it remained unchanged from 1993. China imported 1.38 mt of polyethylene to support the film industry.

China produced 268 400 tons of pesticides in 1994, and imported 31 980 tons. Lu *et al.* (1993) estimated that chemicals prevented losses of about 150 billion yuan in farming in the period 1985–90 by protecting crops from

Table 2.2   Agro-film applied in crop farming, selected years (000s ha)

Item	1981	1984	1988
Paddy rice nursery	1.4	187.3	318.0
Cotton	3.9	857.5	482.3
Corn (maize)	0.0	16.7	482.0
Peanut	2.5	92.0	127.1
Vegetables	7.1	89.3	262.5
Melons, fruits, etc	0.7	91.3	623.7
Total[a]	15.7	1334.3	2295.3

Note: [a] Totals may not match because of rounding.

Source: MOA, *Quan guo nongcun jingji tongji ziliao* (National Statistical Data of Rural Economy), October 1990.

insect pests and diseases; 1 kg of pesticide yielded 49 kg of wheat. Imports of pesticides in 1994 were almost one-third higher than in the preceding year. The quantity of the chemicals can basically meet the demand in the domestic market. The price of chemical pesticides fluctuates only slightly, but a problem remains with quality and variety.

Contributions of Chemicals to Agricultural Growth

China has to double its efforts to raise per hectare crop yields, mainly relying on more physical inputs, such as fertilizers, irrigation, improved seeds and agro-films. Many research groups estimated the contribution of fertilizer to growth of total agricultural output in China during the period 1985–90 and came to similar conclusions. For example, Lu *et al* (1993: 131) suggested that fertilizers contributed about 40 per cent to the output increase in the agricultural sector as a whole. Another source gave a rather lower share: 32 per cent in the case of grain production (MOA, 1995: 167). The latter compared fertilizers with other major production factors: irrigation, agro-films, pesticides, machinery, draught animals and improved seeds. At the national level, the contribution of fertilizers was the highest during the late 1980s (Table 2.3). Agro-chemicals accounted for 40 per cent of the increased output in crop farming during the 1980s if pesticides and agro-films are taken together. An exception was observed only for the west, which is a typically dry region.

According to the National Fertilizer Test Network (Fertnet), a rational combination of NPK fertilizers should increase crop yields dramatically. Based on 5000 field experiments done in various regions of China during

Table 2.3   Contributions of major inputs to growth of grain output in China, by region, 1985–90

Region	Fertilizer	Agro-chemicals		Irrigation	Seeds	Machinery	Draught animals
		Pesticides	Agro-film				
All China	32.1	3.8	2.5	28.2	16.2	11.0	6.2
North	32.1	2.8	2.9	28.8	14.9	11.3	8.7
North-east	33.8	2.8	5.5	16.7	22.5	10.6	8.1
West	19.1	0.7	2.2	43.0	14.8	9.8	14.8
Yangtze[a]	36.5	5.3	2.2	28.0	14.2	8.1	5.5
South	38.2	6.5	1.6	24.6	11.6	6.9	10.5
South-west	35.5	2.6	2.2	26.9	12.3	4.8	15.7

Note: [a] Yangtze refers to the provinces in its middle-lower reaches of the Yangtze River.

Source: Lu et al. (1993).

1981–3, estimates of average yield increases from fertilizer use were as follows: rice 40.8 per cent, wheat 56.6 per cent, corn 46.1 per cent, cotton 48.6 per cent, and rapeseed 64.4 per cent (Lin, 1995). Fertnet reported that, in the early 1980s, 1 kg of nitrogen could increase paddy rice yield by 9.1 kg, wheat by 10 kg and corn by 13.4 kg. Phosphate and potash fertilizers had less important effects on field crops: on average, 4.7 to 4.9 kg, respectively, of paddy rice from 1 kg. From the data collected by the Fertnet, Lin (1995) concluded that 1 kg of chemical fertilizer (nutrient) had a return of 8 kg of grain in the early 1980s, or one-third of total grain output could be attributed to the application of fertilizers.

Efficiency, Returns and Economic Reform

Being a modern input, fertilizer has broken the traditional farming pattern in China. For use to be efficient, farmers must have the required knowledge, and this can be gained from field demonstrations, as well as timely recommendations from extension technicians, especially to those older farmers in landlocked western regions.

Diminishing Returns of Fertilizer

The quantity of fertilizers used in the farm sector rose significantly between 1952 and 1994, but a clear correlation between total use of fertilizers and agricultural output (in our case, grain and cotton) can be seen only before the mid-1980s (Table 2.4). Statistics demonstrate that an additional nine million tons of fertilizers increased grain output by 100 mt and cotton by 4 mt between 1978 and 1984, while over 15 mt of fertilizers contributed only about 44 mt in additional grain and no significant change in cotton output in the period 1984–94, although factors such as pricing policy, government controls and market conditions were not taken into account. While the evidence seems to indicate that the law of diminishing returns of fertilizer use is operating in Chinese agriculture, especially in the case of grain and cotton production, further research is required before a definitive conclusion can be made in this regard.

Changes in Fertilizer Use

There are major changes in fertilizer application patterns that can be summarized as follows. First, more fertilizers were applied to vegetables, fruits and other profitable crops, as predicted by economic theory. The returns of fertilizers from those crops are usually above five to one, whereas

Table 2.4   Total use of fertilizers and grain and cotton output in China, 1952–95, selected years (mt)

Year	Fertilizers	Grain[a]	Cotton[b]
1952	0.08	164	1.30
1957	0.37	195	1.64
1962	0.63	160	0.75
1965	1.94	195	2.10
1970	3.51	240	2.28
1975	5.37	285	2.38
1978	8.84	304	2.17
1980	12.69	321	2.71
1984	17.40	407	6.26
1985	17.76	379	4.15
1990	25.90	446	4.51
1991	28.05	435	5.68
1992	29.30	443	4.51
1993	31.52	456	3.74
1994	33.14	445	4.25
1995	n.a.	465	4.50

Notes:
[a] 'Grain' in Chinese statistics as a rule includes beans and roots.
[b] Ginned cotton (lint).

Source: Lin (1995).

from grains they are only two or three to one. Some of the prosperous south-eastern provinces have become grain importers instead of exporters as they were a decade ago. The acreage under some lucrative crops has more than doubled in the past decade (Table 2.5), which shows that comparative advantage in grain production in many provinces has been declining over time. Some sample surveys have indicated that more than one-fifth of fertilizers went to high-value crops rather than grain crops. Fertilizer also goes to aquaculture, forest nurseries and the feed industry.

Second, returns declined in developed regions. Fertilizer distribution was uneven in China before, but the situation is more serious today. All provinces with application rates of over 520 kg of fertilizers per hectare are located in the relatively developed eastern part of the country, including Fujian (764 kg), Guangdong (703 kg), Jiangsu and Shandong (see Lin, 1995). These levels are comparable to the world's heaviest fertilizer users, such as Japan and The Netherlands, and more than double that in the vast western region of China.

Third, the NPK ratio has been irrational. According to the State Statistical Bureau, China used 18.82 mt of nitrogen fertilizer, 6 mt of P_2O_5, and only

Table 2.5   Increase of area under some profitable crops in China, 1984 and 1993 (m. ha)

Crop	1984	1993	Increase (%)
Vegetables	5.40	9.25	71.5
Mulberry	0.41	0.84	103.7
Orchard	2.22	6.43	189.9
Melons	0.62	1.12	83.3
Total[a]	8.64	17.65	104.2

Note: [a]Totals may not match because of rounding.

Source: Lin (1995).

2.35 mt of K_2O in 1994. That made an imbalanced ratio of 1 : 0.32 : 0.12, because of excessive use of nitrogen and a shortage of potash.

Finally, production cost has risen as organic manure has gone out of favour. Farmyard manure made up 80 per cent of all sources of nutrients in Chinese agriculture in the 1960s; the share was down to about 50 per cent in the 1980s, and continues to decline. Areas under green manure crops (for example, *Astragalus sinicus* L. *Vicia villosa* Roth, *Melilotus* spp, *Sesbania cannabina, Crotalaria juncea* L.) shrank from 12 million ha in 1976 to about 6.5 million ha in the early 1990s, owing to multiple cropping systems and substitution towards manufactured fertilizers. When the Sanjiang Plain in Heilongjiang Province was reclaimed in the early 1950s, the rich black earth contained 6 per cent to 11 per cent humus, but today the figure has dropped to 3 per cent to 5 per cent (Li, 1995a). Farmers have become more dependent on chemical fertilizers, which has resulted in higher production costs and a deterioration of soil texture in some regions.

Efficiency: a Technoeconomic Approach

The Fertnet and other studies provided data that reveal which factors lower the effectiveness of fertilizers, especial nitrogen. In this section, factors that affect the effectiveness of fertilizer are examined.

The first factor affecting fertilizer efficiency relates to subsoil application techniques. This is the focus of one of four key variables which are to be the targets of training programmes launched by the Ministry of Agriculture in 1994. Proper subsoil application is recognized as an effective way to raise crop yields, reduce fertilizer loss and production cost, and improve the environment. As the 1994 experiments in 11 counties showed, per hectare yields of paddy rice could be increased by 427.8 kg, corn by 509.7 kg, cotton lint by 134.7 kg and soybean by 235.5 kg with this technique. In total, 242 counties in 25 provinces had allocated 3.78 million ha for experiments or demonstrations, which resulted in additional revenues of 1.8 billion yuan, coming from 1.09 mt of extra grain and 297 705 tons of cotton (MOA, 1995).

Second is the strategy of optimizing the nutrient composition according to soil type. As mentioned above, improper NPK ratios result in nitrogen loss, suggesting that an improved combination of nitrogen with phosphorous and potassium (or maybe some other micronutrients) is effective in raising crop yields. A farmer can hardly distinguish the exact effect of different fertilizers on individual crops in his village or specific plot. They often consider any application of any kind of fertilizer to raise yields, and especially those that are in short supply.

Combining fertilizers with organic manure or green manure crops (GMCs) is a third method of improving yields. A series of experiments by Chen *et al.* (1989) demonstrate that proper combinations of inorganic fertilizers with organic manure give the highest yields in China and are effective in avoiding soil degradation. Many GMCs respond well to phosphorous and potassium fertilizers, resulting in a much larger amount of biomass. That is a rational way to raise efficiency and reduce soil degradation, as more organic matter returns to soil. Surveys show that soil texture after three years of planting GMCs had more humus than the neighbouring check plots.

It is evident that sound training and extension services are essential in rural areas to give farmers better recommendations with regard to fertilizer applications. The same is true for pesticides. Better education will not only improve the efficiency of agro-chemicals and reduce production cost, but will also benefit the environment.

Fertilizer Management and Marketing

There are many issues related to the production and marketing of fertilizer, with many problems a heritage of the centrally planned economic system. Despite central control over the fertilizer production, different ministries have their own interests in fertilizer management. The retail price of fertilizers (mixed average price per standard ton) increased from 231 yuan in 1978 to 910 yuan in 1992. The inefficient distribution system and high prices discourage farmers from using fertilizers as their use may then no longer be profitable. Corruption is also a problem, often continuing even after it has been reported in the media.

The central and local governments consider it their responsibility to control fertilizer price, but these controls have become more flexible over time. It is the State Planning Commission (SPC) that sets the producer's price ceilings for 'beyond quota' amounts of urea and ammonium nitrate from the state-owned large-scale fertilizer enterprises (for example, 1000 yuan and 700 yuan per ton, respectively, in 1993). The 17 largest state-owned fertilizer enterprises must sell 90 per cent of total output to the state-owned companies or designated stations, at the set price under strict monitoring by the SPC. These enterprises and the Chinese Company of Means of Agricultural Production (CCMAP) have to submit reports on their prices and costs to the SPC every six months. In terms of fertilizer 'beyond planned quotas', price ceilings have been imposed since 1993 (Luo, 1995). The local authorities could adjust only the retail price ceilings according to their own conditions. It was also within the latter's competence to fix the producer's and retail price ceilings for fertilizer produced by local factories. Under the market economy, in 1994 the state permitted a 'floating range' of 15 per cent for prices. The fertilizer producer price could be set by fertilizer factories according to different seasons, regions and supply–demand conditions within the 15 per cent range. The fertilizer retail price could be 10 per cent higher than the 'standard (producer) price' to cover transport fees and leave a profit for the entire business process.

Fertilizer imports are managed only by the China National Chemicals Import and Export Corporation (Sinochem) at the national level, with over 30 branches at province level. The price for imported fertilizers changed in 1994. Governments at the provincial level were responsible for determining the retail prices for imported fertilizers according to their quality as compared to that of domestic fertilizers. The SPC was to check the price of fertilizers imported by Sinochem, while the provincial bureaus would revise the price of the local imports.

The Chinese government has made a series of important changes to improve the efficiency of the fertilizer marketing system in recent years. Three major steps were adopted to reform the fertilizer market structure. First, the marketing process was streamlined. Before 1994, 'planned fertilizer' (domestic plus that imported by the central government) was marketed through the wholesale system at four levels – central, provincial, prefecture and county levels – while retailing was at the grass roots through supply and marketing cooperatives. Wholesale was simplified to two levels in 1994: the national (CCMAP) and provincial. This meant that the previous three-level wholesale system in provinces was reformed significantly.

Second, the competence of fertilizer-producing and marketing enterprises was redefined. As stipulated, the large 17 state-owned enterprises must provide 90 per cent of total output to the state. They can dispose of the remaining 10 per cent by selling to certified companies, often at higher prices. This provided an incentive to these factories to raise their output for extra revenue.

Third, more attention is being paid to a fertilizer reserve. Fertilizers are produced all year round, but demand is seasonal. The Chinese government has set up a two-tier (national and provincial) fertilizer reserve and control system to promote production and stabilize supplies.

China's Food Security Goals: 1996–2010

The Government Goals

Food security is one of the major concerns on the Chinese government's agenda. There will be significant changes in people's diets as their income rises. There is consensus that the basic way to food security is an increase in grain production. According to the Ninth Five-Year Plan (1996–2000), China's GNP in 2010 will be double that of 2000, and population will probably exceed 1.4 billion. That will create a huge demand for high-quality food, notably protein of animal origin. The SPC has worked out targets to produce more food to meet the possible challenge, driven to a larger extent by the growth in income. The figures outlined in the plan are preliminary, or 'desirable': to increase grain by 40–50 mt, cotton by 0.5 mt, meat by 10 mt and fish products by 10 mt. By 2010, China plans to take another large step by producing an additional 60 mt or more of grain, 13 mt of meat and 10 mt of fish. The absolute quantities are impressive, but, if divided by the increased population, these targets do not seem to be high (Table 2.6). The government has no other choice but to mobilize all efforts to realize them.

Food security of such a large and populous country as China is determined by three major factors: domestic food production, imports and grain reserve. The government goals are likely to include a high food self-sufficiency (over 97 per cent since the 1980s), with minimal imports (compared to the population size). It is obvious that fertilizer remains a crucial factor.

Table 2.6   **Planned production targets for China's three major agricultural products, 1993, 2000 and 2010**

Year	Grain Total (mt)	Grain Per capita (kg)	Meat Total (mt)	Meat Per capita (kg)	Aquatic products Total (mt)	Aquatic products Per capita (kg)
1993	456	389	38.42	32.84	18.23	15.58
2000[a]	500	385	48.00	36.90	28.50	21.90
2010[a]	560	400	61.00	43.60	38.50	27.50

Note: [a] Assuming the population will be 1.3 billion in 2000, and 1.4 billion in 2010.

Source: MOA (1995).

Pessimistic v. Optimistic Perspectives

Lester Brown's publication, *Who Will Feed China?*, caused a great stir in Chinese agricultural circles in the winter of 1994, and a heated dispute between pessimists and optimists in the country that continues today. No one denies that there are numerous constraints to agricultural growth in the country, but the majority of scholars believe that 1.2 billion Chinese cannot expect to feed themselves by importing hundreds of millions of tons of food. No country will be able to provide enough food to feed China, even if there are no payment difficulties and political hindrances, and China's trading partners do not impose food embargoes or cause other diplomatic friction.

The pessimists' arguments consist of a number of real and institutional constraints. First, there is a land constraint. China is a typically land-scarce country with only 0.08 ha per capita (about one-third of the world average), and the cropland base continues to decline. The land is intensively used, with a multiple-cropping index of 1.56 (four provinces exceeded 2.3) in 1994. There are many reports of soil erosion, degradation, desertification and humus losses in the rich black soils in the north-east. The area of wasteland is limited and reclamation is costly and ecologically hazardous.

Second, there is a shortage and uneven distribution of water in China. Xin (1996) points out that the Yangtze River basin divides China into two parts: the south is rich in water (81 per cent of the nation's total) but it has less arable land (36 per cent of the country), while the north is just the opposite (19 per cent and 64 per cent, respectively). It caused a sensation throughout China that the Yellow River had no current in its lower reach for four months in 1995, while a decade previous the river was notorious because it caused hundreds of floods. Arable land that suffered from droughts increased from 13 million ha in the 1950s to 30 million ha in 1994. Groundwater resources in the North China Plain are also under threat of depletion. As we know, fertilizer loses its value without irrigation.

Third, there are inadequate funds to support both agricultural research and extension. China's agricultural research intensity (ARI), which expresses expenditures on public-sector agricultural research as a portion of agricultural product, is below 0.3 per cent, one-seventh or less than that in Japan and North America. The result has been an outflow of young research and extension workers to other sectors in expectation of higher earnings. China is short of agrotechnical breakthroughs and 'reserves for tomorrow' of high-yielding varieties of major crops, highly effective but mildly poisonous pesticides, and so on. These shortcomings constitute a serious threat to technological progress in the future.

Fourth, the agricultural price remains distorted (or depressed) as a result of policies biased against agriculture. The agricultural sector has been used to subsidize industrialization, perhaps to the tune of hundreds of billions of yuan. The government is unlikely to be able to make a radical change in this situation in the near future. More importantly, no policy can make grain production as profitable as other business because of the small scale of farms.

However, there are also reasons for optimism. First, there is considerable room to enhance crop yields. The per unit yields of grain crops in many regions of China remain at a relatively low level. So-called 'low-yielding fields' – those fields yielding 10 per cent less than the local average yields – account for about two-thirds of total arable land. For example, the national per hectare output of wheat averaged 3.43 tons in 1994, but there were differences of one ton between neighbouring provinces (for example, 4.78 tons in Shandong and 3.75 and 3.73 tons in its neighbours). The yield differences were affected by inadequate inputs and technologies. Grain production will become profitable when food demand rises, and incentives to raise grain yield improve. Since the 'low-yielding fields' are mainly distributed in the central provinces, the government is shifting priority in grain production geographically, laying greater emphasis on grain production in central China, where the marginal returns to inputs are higher than in the coastal region.

Second, technological innovations will play an increasingly important role. Technical changes in many regions have been slow, and their contribution to agricultural growth remains small. Many typically traditional techniques are dominant in agriculture in the low-yielding regions, while numerous agronomic innovations are already available from labs and experimental stations. The majority of research innovations are promising and will contribute greatly to the increase of output or upgrade of quality in the future.

Third, there is great potential to reduce harvest losses by improving agricultural infrastructure. Most low-yielding regions are located in hilly areas. One way to improve the production performance there is to construct roads and reservoirs, improve the irrigation and drainage network, and so on. According to some reports, about one-fifth to one-fourth of total farm produce is damaged in China as a result of poor infrastructure – a poor transport system and lack of storage and processing facilities. Development of a food processing industry in the rural areas is an effective way to cut down post-harvest losses.

Fourth, it is possible to increase efficient utilization of all agricultural resources. China can feed itself at a relatively low level on only 10 per cent of its territory. The Chinese can produce more food (not only grain) if they use properly all their hills and slopes, water, pasture land, forests and waste lands in the country. China has good climatic conditions to use other agricultural resources to develop a diversified rural economy. Grain production takes only about two months (60 working days) in most provinces; hence farmers' income must be very low if they depend merely on grain production, as they will do nothing for the remaining 10 months of the year. The most important motive for them to plant grain crops is to have enough for their own consumption. There are excess resources in agriculture that can be freed for use elsewhere in the economy or within the agricultural sector itself (for example, food processing, improving agricultural infrastructure, double and inter-cropping).

Finally, there is room to improve yields using more fertilizers and other agro-chemicals.

The Role of Fertilizers

As noted, an effective way to enhance crop yields is to adjust NPK ratios and improve fertilizer use patterns. Under the pressure of the national food security considerations, the central government has decided to speed up construction of some key projects to develop the fertilizer industry and increase output of agro-films and pesticides in the decade to come. The MOA estimated that the demand for three inputs will rise steeply: fertilizer by 150 mt (in physical terms), agro-films by 900 000 tons and pesticides by 210 000 tons.

According to Lin (1995), a general trend in global fertilizer use and NPK ratios is concentrated in the interval of $1 : 0.4/0.5 : 0.4/0.5$. China may be somewhat different if it relies on a larger share of organic manure, as is the intent. However, the NPK ratio must be adjusted at least to $1 : 0.4 : 0.25$ for nitrogen, P_2O_5 and K_2O. This ratio means that China must produce 10.2 mt of P_2O_5 and 6.4 mt of K_2O, which will be difficult to achieve. As the Vice-Minister of Chemical Industry, He Guoqiang, revealed to a newspaper, to increase fertilizer production will occupy first place in the chemical industry during the Ninth Five-Year Plan. China plans to produce 140 mt of fertilizers, so that nitrogen fertilizers will basically meet domestic demand. Self-sufficiency in fertilizers will reach 90 per cent by 2000. The main measures for achieving this target are as follows:

1 Increasing the share of new kinds of fertilizers, including high-concentrate and complex fertilizers. To improve nitrogen efficiency, the focus will be on the development of coated urea and other varieties of slow-release fertilizers.
2 Enlarging production capacity to adjust the $N-P_2O_5$ ratio to $1 : 0.37$. About 50 phosphorous-producing factories will be converted to produce

high-effective ammonium phosphate instead of ordinary super-phosphate.
3   Reconstructing 80 small- or medium-sized factories or re-equipping them with new technologies to optimize their scale and improve the quality of their products.

Philosophy of Environmental Protection

We cannot examine food security (and in general, social security) issues without considering their environmental consequences, and vice versa. Governments of all countries have to weigh trade-offs between the environment, food production and costs. There are two categories of countries with different types of environmental hazards. The main problems of Type 1 (industrialized) countries and regions seem to be characteristic of a post-industrialized society, and include such things as acid rain, pollution of air, water and soils, eutrophication of water, shrinkage of wild habitat and reduced biodiversity, and so on. Type 2 or less-developed countries or regions face a shortage of food. Their pressing problem is to increase food production, while environment issues are mainly associated with soil erosion and degradation (pasture in particular), deforestation, desertification and depletion of many natural resources in general. These countries are doing their utmost to modernize their economies and, as a consequence, pollution becomes a serious industrial problem, *but not because of overuse of fertilizers or pesticides*. The philosophy of Type 2 countries is to duplicate the experience of the industrialized countries: first pollute, later control the pollution. There is a difference, however. Type 2 countries have available to them cleaner technologies for producing industrial outputs than were available to Type 1 countries when these went through the early stages of industrialization. It seems to be a self-evident formula: 'No food security, no environmental protection'.

There are reasons why such a philosophy is adopted. When citizens are starving, the obvious first priority of a country is to increase food production. Meanwhile, backward technologies lead to pollution as much plant and equipment (and technology) in less developed countries is out of date. Many countries do not have the resources to replace old facilities which are prone to creating pollution. Water in many counties in rural China (for example, in the Huaihe River basin and Lake Taihu) is polluted by untreated effluent from industry, rather than from fertilizers or pesticides. A recent source of pollutants is the mushrooming rural township and village enterprises (TVEs). Finally, less-educated people have a poor sense of environment and legality. High illiteracy rates are common in low-income countries or regions. For example, there are many cases of pesticide abuse, destructive mining, overgrazing of pasture and deforestation in China's poverty-stricken regions.

No doubt there are cases where there are detrimental side-effects or externalities from fertilizer use. Zhang *et al.* (1995) report that 37 wells out of 69 sampled in North China exceeded the allowable limit for nitrate content in drinking water. In the overwhelming majority of cases where agrochemical pollution of groundwater occurs, it is observed under vegetable fields, reflecting overuse of nitrogen in suburban areas.

There are two ways to raise food production: to reclaim more land (shift the extensive margin) and/or enhance crop yields (intensive margin). The Chinese government's strategy is to focus on the latter: reclamation was typical of the 1950s, but since the 1980s the top priority is now to increase yields. The acreage sown to grain crops was 120.6 million ha in 1978, with total output 304.77 mt. Thus China would need to reclaim about 60 million ha of land to increase production by 150 mt. In other words, 450 mt of grain (average output in the mid-1990s) would require 180 million ha of cropland at the same level of fertilization, rather than actual acreage of around 100 million ha. China has a very limited area of land suitable for safe reclamation with no erosion hazards, while fertile arable land is being eroded by non-agricultural activities: it is estimated that at least 36 million ha will be taken out of agriculture before 2000. The national plan is to reclaim (or re-reclaim) 24 million ha to offset these losses. Hence the grain area in the future will probably decrease to 90 million ha or less. The effect of substituting fertilizer for land, therefore, is ecologically important in China today.

Most Chinese are sceptical about so-called 'low-input sustainable agriculture' (LISA). With low inputs, China has seen hundreds of famines throughout its history. Some people think LISA is just a trick perpetrated by rich and food-surplus countries for their own interests. But China actually has at least 6000 years of traditional agriculture, which is a kind of LISA. China has to find its own way of promoting food output without causing environmental damage. The major task of Chinese farmers is to increase their input in agriculture: fertilizers, technology, and skill and knowledge.

China's Trade Policy Options: To Import Grains or Fertilizers?

China will likely become a net importer of grains (large in absolute terms, but still quite small on a per capita basis). China's fertilizer imports have been significant in recent years, with the largest import of fertilizers occurring in 1992 (18.6 mt). The reason is that China lacks raw materials to produce some kinds of fertilizers. When China becomes a member of the WTO, changes are likely, as discussed below.

Changing Comparative Advantage and Pressure from Abroad

Grain production requires large-scale management to raise productivity and profitability. China had some comparative advantage in grain production and exported grain two decades ago when the labour cost was neglected as peasants had no choice but to produce grain. The comparative advantage began to decline as the rural economy diversified. More farmers migrated to urban areas or tried to find a job with a TVE. Only some land-abundant provinces (Heilongjiang and Jilin, for example) have kept increasing grain production over these years. The opportunity cost of labour has risen considerably in the past decade, especially in the south-eastern provinces and coastal region. Thus farmers in these provinces are reluctant to increase grain production because of low returns. They would prefer to grow more vegetables, mushrooms, fruits or, more recently, where policy allows, flowers. There is a strong demand for these kinds of perishable commodities in nearby markets.

Comparative advantage in grain production in many provinces is declining because of resource endowments, especially because of the small scale of farms: the national average farm size is half a hectare, but in the densely populated south-eastern provinces may be as small as one-tenth of a hectare. Driven by the goal of grain self-sufficiency, however, the government at all levels pays close attention mainly to cropland improvement, but neglects the use of other natural resources. Farmers in the suburbs of large cities, such as Shanghai and Beijing, also have their 'assigned tasks' in grain production. Some 'large' grain producers with an output of several tons of grain a year were given awards as 'model workers', whose farms might be a little larger (probably 2–3 ha). If such farmers produced vegetables or melons instead of grain, their income would be much higher. Meeting the local leaders' grain self-sufficiency goal results in lower rural incomes due to reduced efficiency.

On the basis of their own studies and experience, many agricultural economists in China disagree with Brown's (1994) forecast. They generally assume that grain consumption per capita is 400 kg and that China's grain production capacity can reach 640 million tons by 2030. However, they hedge the question of what will happen if China's per capita demand exceeds 400 kg or reaches 500 kg in the future. Most Chinese economists tend to study this issue within the framework of domestic production, emphasizing the importance of self-sufficiency. On average, the per capita availability in 1994 of meat was 37.7 kg, eggs 12.4 kg and milk 4.4 kg. Obviously, urban residents consumed much more than their rural counterparts. The urban consumption pattern may extend to rural areas. It is difficult to predict what will happen if the income level of the rural population becomes comparable to the current urban income in two or three decades. It is even more uncertain what will be the impact of income growth on the demand for high-quality food of animal origin, which could be similar to that of Japan or South Korea in the 1980s.

Some grain exporters remain confused as, on the whole, China gives uncertain signals to the world market. China has exported grain irregularly in recent years, mainly as a result of a good harvest and/or insufficient storage facilities. China has also been an irregular food importer if the grain supply was tight or grain prices in the world market were sufficiently low. Domestically, grain prices as well as the sown acreage of grain crops, to some extent, remain under the government's control; hence the state's purchase prices continue to be low. Grain prices in China's free market are approaching or have already (in some seasons) surpassed those in the world market, but world prices must become the signal to producers as well as consumers if the market mechanism is to function properly.

There are two possible choices for policy makers. The government can provide grain producers with large subsidies (for example, supporting output prices, subsidizing fertilizers and other inputs) to keep the current grain acreage unchanged in order to sustain high food sufficiency ratios. However, China's economic growth rates will be adversely affected because more resources will go to the less profitable and less efficient grain sector, and the financial burdens on the central and local governments will become a major hindrance to further development. Alternatively, the government can allow the rural economic structure to change according to comparative advantage and market signals. The income contribution of grain production will then become less important in rural China, because the farmers will tend to shift to profitable crops and animal products, and non-agricultural products and services. The gap between grain supply and demand will grow and China may have to import more grain to meet the demand of its 1.4 to 1.6 billion wealthier people – probably over 40 mt, an amount comparable to that of Japan and the former Soviet Union (taken together) during the 1980s. China will have to accept the role of a large grain importer.

The Chinese are proud that they have been able to feed 22 per cent of the world's population on only 7 per cent of its arable land. The grain sector is looked upon as a 'strategic resource' and food self-sufficiency is associated with national dignity. The dilemma for decision makers is that a slight decline in food self-sufficiency is a definite trend from the economic point of view, in spite of desires to the contrary. Similarly, China was proud that is was not a borrower with debts of any kind (domestic or foreign) in the 1960s and 1970s, but this situation has changed dramatically since reforms began. Under the regulations of the WTO, agricultural protectionism will be sharply reduced, although it prevails in some rich countries. The Chinese government has no reason to prevent less expensive grain from entering China. A simple argument is that the government is simply unable to subsidize farmers (who number in the hundreds of millions) as Japan did. Change will take place as the resources for grain production – land, irrigation water and, probably, labour – become more and more expensive. Of course, there is likely to be an impact on world grain markets, but China's grain imports will be modest even if it readjusts agricultural production in a radical way because grain self-sufficiency in China will remain high – probably more than 90 per cent in the foreseeable future. Government policies will ensure this to whatever extent is possible.

What to Import

Still there are alternatives for China to consider. One of them is to import fertilizers instead of grain. As stated above, the contribution of fertilizers to growth of food output is significant in China's low-yielding regions, which account for about two-thirds of the total arable land. Import of fertilizers or raw materials of the chemical industry will benefit crop farming, and eventually raise farmers' incomes. One obstacle to the economic growth of China is lack of energy resources. Many Chinese medium-size fertilizer factories have to suspend production capacity periodically because of a shortage of raw materials. Efficiency of energy use is often low owing to old techniques and facilities. A precondition for fertilizer imports is good returns to producers. Fertilizers from abroad must not be too expensive. To cut down the cost of production and transport, direct investment of foreign capital in the Chinese fertilizer industry might be feasible, including modern technologies, new types of fertilizers, new machinery for subsoil fertilization, and so on.

Conclusions

Agro-chemicals, including fertilizers, agro-films and pesticides, are essential means to realize China's food security goals. Fertilizer is one of the most important factors for increasing agricultural output and is of fundamental importance for ensuring an adequate food supply in a country with 1.2 billion people. The utilization efficiency of fertilizers in China is not high, partly because of irrational combinations of nutrients and lack of timely application recommendations to farmers. More organic manure and green manure crops should be applied to reduce possible detrimental effects of agro-chemicals, although overuse of fertilizers is not a problem in rural China and is not a significant source of pollutants.

The Chinese government has to make a decision regarding the role that China is to play in world agricultural markets. It is very probable that China will increase grain imports in the coming decades. Under the rules of the WTO, China cannot follow the Japanese example of subsidizing farmers heavily to sustain a high food self-sufficiency ratio, closing the grain market in order to block less expensive grain imports from grain-exporting countries. An alternative is to increase fertilizer imports, which is both a rational production strategy and one that integrates China to a greater extent into the global economy. Such integration can provide benefits to other sectors of the Chinse economy.

References

Borlaug, N.E. (1994), 'Feeding a Human Population That Increasingly Crowds a Fragile Planet', keynote lecture presented at 15th World Congress of Soil Science, Acapulco, Mexico.

Brown, L.R. (1994), 'Who Will Feed China?', *World Watch*, September/October.

Chen, L., Z. Xia and S. Wu (1989), 'Zhongguo youji wuji feiliao peihe shiyong' (Coordinated application of organic and inorganic fertilizers in China), *Proceedings of the International Symposium on Balanced Fertilization*, Nongye Chubanshe.

Li, W. (1995a), 'An assessment of the Agricultural Environment Situation and Policy Implication in China', in K. Hemmi and C.J. Cool (eds.), *Educating New Environmental Leadership for Asia*, Winrock International Institute for Agricultural Development, Los Banos, Philippines.

Lin, B. (1995), 'Zhongguo huafei de shiyong xianzhuang yu xuqiu zhanwang' (The Current Situation of Chemical Fertilizer Use in China and Its Demand in Future) paper presented to a Symposium on Fertilizer Strategy in Agricultural Development in China, 10 October.

Lu, G., S. Fang, K. Chen, X. Ma, and Z. Zhou (1993), 'Nongye wuzhi touru yu nongye zonghe shengchan nengli guanxi yanjiu' (A Study on the Relationships Between Physical Agricultural Inputs and Comprehensive Production Capacity in Agriculture), *Zhongguo nongye zonghe shengchan nengli yanjiu*, Nongye Chubanshe.

Luo, Y. (1995), 'Zhongguo feiliao zhengce yu lifa' (Policies and Laws About Fertilizer in China), paper presented to a Symposium on Fertilizer Strategy in Agricultural Development in China, 10 October.

Ministry of Agriculture (MOA) (1995), *Zhongguo nongye fazhan baogao '95* (Report on Agricultural Development in China, 1995), Zhongguo Nongye Chubanshe.

Xin, Naiquan (1996), 'Dali fazhan jie shui nongye he hanzuo nongye' (To give energetic support to water-saving farming and improve rain-fed agriculture), *Nongmin Ribao*, 1 March.

Zhang, W., Z. Tian, N. Zhang and X. Li (1995), 'Wo guo beifang nongyong danfei zaocheng dixiashui xiaosuanyan wuran de diaocha' (Investigation of Nitrate Pollution in Ground Water Due to Nitrogen Utilization in Agriculture in North China), *Zhiwu yingyang yu feiliao xuebao* (Plant Nutrition and Fertilizer Sciences), **2**, (1).

3 Growth and Economics of Pesticide Use in India: Overview of the Environment, Patterns and Market Potential

V.P. Gandhi [a]

Introduction

The pesticide industry is at once the most complex and the most dynamic agricultural input industry in India. It comprises of over 650 firms of many different sizes and kinds, in thousands of villages and towns, selling over a thousand formulations with about 50 different active ingredients (David, 1995a and 1995b; Srivastava and Patel, 1990). It has shown tremendous development in the last three decades, with growth based primarily in the private sector, unlike other input industries. Nearly 70 per cent of the products sold by the industry go to the agriculture sector where they play a significant role in helping technological transformation, yield increase and growth.

This chapter uses available information to examine the past rate and patterns of growth in the pesticide market in India, identifying major characteristics and important determinants. It examines relevant changes in the macroeconomic environment, and the emerging scenario in which the environment and policies for agriculture will take shape in the future. It analyses, in turn, how the environment and public policies are likely to influence the market for pesticides.

[a] Centre for Management in Agriculture, Indian Institute of Management, Vastrapur, Ahmedabad - 380015, India.

Market Environment for Pesticides

The experiences across developing countries indicate that the growth of input markets is influenced by a large number of price and non-price factors (Desai and Gandhi, 1988; Mellor and Ahmed, 1988). The framework of neoclassical economics is usually unsuitable for explaining this growth because the market is in almost perpetual disequilibrium. For the understanding and analysis of this complex and dynamic market environment, a more comprehensive analytical framework would be useful. Studies explaining the growth and fluctuations of fertilizer consumption in India, China and Sub-Saharan Africa (for example, Desai and Stone, 1987; Gandhi and Desai, 1992) have indicated the relevance of a more comprehensive framework that can be used for understanding the market environment for agricultural inputs in developing countries. Based on this, a framework has been developed here for understanding the market environment for pesticides. The framework, described below, has the following major components: agronomic potential, agroeconomic potential, effective demand and actual consumption. The market environment can be conceptualized as unfolding through the developments within and the interrelationship between these components. Figure 3.1 gives a graphical outline.

Pesticides are primarily yield-saving inputs, although they may also help to improve quality. Pesticides also reduce the uncertainty or risk of obtaining good yields. Research and development work is typically necessary for the creation of new *agronomic potential* for pesticides. However, given the toxic nature of most chemicals, new chemicals have to go through a process of screening and approval by government, and regulations need to be complied with. Pest resistance destroys agronomic potential, while crop susceptibility to pests raises it. If the pest incidence/infestation is low, the potential is low. Expansion of the cropped area also expands the potential. The agronomic potential varies by crop, and cropping patterns influence potential. Expansion of irrigation and adoption of high-yielding varieties, which are susceptible to pests, also raise the agronomic potential.

The existence of agronomic potential is not enough. Pesticides are typically expensive inputs. Unless the output that is lost (or can be saved) is of substantial value, farmers will not use pesticides. The price of the output must be significantly high relative to the price of the pesticide for the agronomic potential to be transformed to *agroeconomic potential*. Thus outputs are important, with pesticide use typically more profitable for high-value cash crops. Commercialization of agriculture expands the potential for pesticides. Output price support programmes and input subsidies also play a significant role in determining profitability. Herbicides save labour and

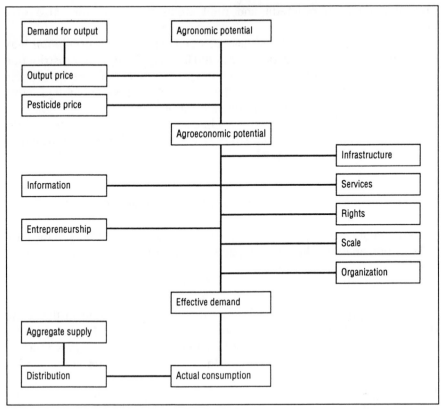

Source: Gandhi and Desai (1992).

Figure 3.1 Elements determining the market environment for pesticide policies

labour shortage or high wage rates enhance the agroeconomic potential of herbicides.

Typically, in a developing country, especially with small farm agriculture, creation of an agroeconomic potential may not be sufficient for there to be real demand. The farmer must know about this opportunity and must exhibit entrepreneurship in responding to this opportunity. Thus dissemination of information through government extension work and company promotions is important. Organization and land tenure can also play a role. Poor infrastructure and lack of transport services can seriously affect the conversion of a good agroeconomic potential into *effective demand*, especially for small farmers. Finally, since subsistence agriculturists lack cash, the provision of credit and rural credit institutions are also very important.

Even when effective demand has been created, *actual consumption* may be restricted if there is inadequate or unreliable supply or a poor distribution system. Supply is affected by the investment in production, the investment climate, government policies, the foreign exchange situation and other factors, such as trade barriers and intellectual property right protection.

The changes and developments within each of these components and the transformations across them can strongly influence the market environment and actual use of agro-chemicals.

The Agrochemical Market: Past Growth and Structure

The growth of pesticide use took place in the market environment of the past. This section analyses the rate and patterns of past growth in pesticide use.

Volume and Growth

India has one of the lowest rates of pesticide use per hectare in the world (Farah, 1994). According to one estimate (Mehrotra and Phokela, 1995), technical grade pesticide use is 10.8 kg/ha in Japan, 6.6 kg/ha in Korea, 1.5 kg/ha in USA and only 0.3 kg/ha in India (Table 3.1). The world market share of India for pesticides is only about 3 per cent (David, 1995a and 1995b). Typically, such low use levels in a country such as India reflect a vast potential for crop yield improvements.

Table 3.1　Current global pesticides use, selected countries/regions

Country	Use level (kg/ha)
Japan	10.8
Korea	6.6
Europe	1.9
USA	1.5
Thailand	1.4
Indonesia	0.6
India	0.3
L America	0.22
Africa	0.13
Oceania	0.2

Source:　Mehrotra and Phokela (1995).

Imports of pesticides are limited in India. Insecticides account for 70 per cent of pesticide production, with benzene hexachloride (BHC) and DDT accounting for 63 per cent (BHC alone accounts for 50 per cent). Thus the use of all other pesticides put together is very low. Notice that both the pesticides identified have been banned for many years in other countries. As yet, only approximately 25 per cent of the crop is treated with pesticides. Coverage is close to 50 per cent for high-yielding varieties and 70–80 per cent for fertilizers. Thus, even on the basis of area, a significant growth potential exists for pesticides.

Figure 3.2 shows the growth of pesticide consumption in India, based on available estimates. The growth rate of pesticide consumption has been estimated to be of the order of 8–9 per cent per annum between 1950/51 and 1992/3, 3–4 per cent between 1970/1 and 1992/3, 3–4 per cent between

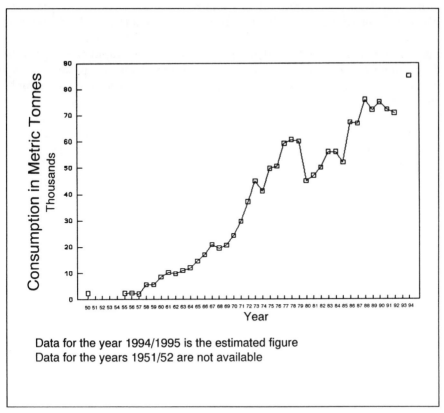

Data for the year 1994/1995 is the estimated figure
Data for the years 1951/52 are not available

Figure 3.2   Consumption of technical grade pesticides in India

1980/81 and 1992/3, and 1–3 per cent between 1986/7 and 1992/3. The fall in the growth rate is in part due to the expanding volume base of pesticide consumption, but also reflects the high concentration of use (continued narrow geographic and crop base of pesticide use).

Products and Patterns

There is a great difference between the structure of pesticide use in India and that in other countries (Table 3.2). International structures and patterns in demand are frequently good indicators of long-term tendencies, and national patterns very often move towards international patterns in the long run as development proceeds. This implies that, even though insecticides would continue to be important (especially in the tropical context), a rapid growth would be seen particularly in herbicides and also in fungicides and other pesticides. Growth rates indicate that this had already begun to happen.

The levels of consumption of pesticides over a set of available years are shown in Figure 3.3. Even though insecticides dominate in the volume of consumption, their growth is much less rapid. On the other hand, fungicides show a more rapid growth, and herbicides an even more rapid rate of growth. Rodenticides also show a rapid rate of growth. Thus the product group composition is undergoing a rapid change and is shifting towards mainly herbicides and fungicides.

Since the discovery of the initial group of inorganic pesticides, a succession of new generations of molecular groups of pesticides has emerged. Detailed figures on pesticide consumption indicate that a very large number of different pesticide molecules are on the market in India – about 34 insecticide, 18 fungicide, 12 herbicide and two rodenticide chemical structures (Mathur, 1993). Among the insecticides, apart from BHC and DDT which have by far the largest volumes, the other chemicals with large volumes are monocrotophos, endosulfan, methyl parathion,

Table 3.2   **Percentage share of three groups of pesticides in some national markets and the world as a whole, 1991**

Pesticide group	USA	China	India	World
Insecticides	23.0	59.0	77.0	29.4
Herbicides	64.0	22.0	10.5	45.4
Fungicides	8.0	19.0	10.0	19.4
Others	5.0	*	2.5	5.8

Note: *included in other sector, not given separately.

Source: Verma (1995).

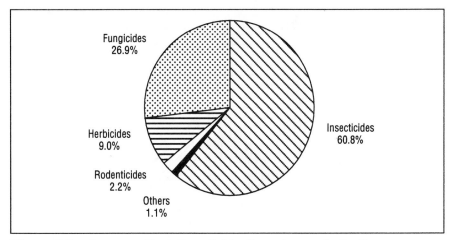

Figure 3.3   Consumption of pesticides by category in India

phorate, phosphamidon and dimethoate. Among the fungicides the largest volumes are seen in sulphur dust, mancozeb, copper sulphate and copper oxychloride. Among the herbicides, the most important by volume are isoproturon, 2,4-D and butachlor. In the rodenticides, aluminium phosphide is relatively more important in volume.

Other chemicals are available elsewhere in the world, which suggests substantial scope for expansion of the product set. One limitation is the Indian Insecticide Act of 1968 which recognizes process and not molecule patent rights, thereby discouraging multinationals from introducing new chemicals.

Crop and Regional Patterns

Crop figures on pesticide consumption are difficult to obtain. Those available (Figure 3.4) indicate a very high concentration in pesticide use (Srivastava and Patel, 1990). Cotton leads, with an enormous 44 per cent share of the pesticide consumption even though only about 4–5 per cent of the gross cropped area is in cotton. Paddy is next, with a share of 22.4 per cent, and has an almost equal share (23 per cent) of the gross cropped area. These are followed by jowar, with 8.9 per cent share, fruit and vegetables with 7.0 per cent and wheat, with 6.4 per cent. Six crops account for almost 90 per cent of pesticide use. These are cotton, rice, jowar, wheat, groundnut and tur. While reflecting the nature of the agroeconomic potential, this also indicates limited efforts in converting potential to effective demand.

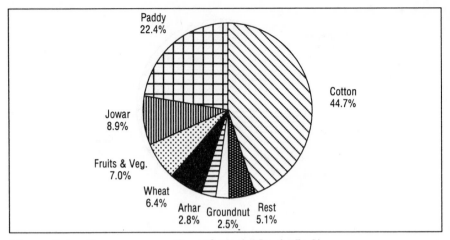

Figure 3.4   Crop consumption of pesticides in India

Geographic concentration of pesticide use is also great. Figure 3.5 indicates that Andhra Pradesh leads in pesticide consumption with a 16.1 per cent share, followed by Uttar Pradesh with a 13.6 per cent share. Five of the 16 states account for almost 60 per cent of pesticide consumption. Studies indicate that, if identification is done by districts, the geographic concentration is much higher. This reflects the limited efforts made by the pesticide companies to develop new markets and spread use to new areas and crops.

Industry Structure and Distribution

Pesticide production in India is carried out by about 650 firms, of which 500 are of small size (David, 1995a and 1995b). Another estimate puts the number of firms at about 850 (Srivastava and Patel, 1991). The small firms only engage in making formulations, whereas the larger firms produce both technical grade material and formulations. The 65 largest firms include both multinationals and Indian corporations. The bulk of the production of DDT and BHC is in the public sector. Except for malathion, ethion, fenvalerate, cypermethrin and aluminium phosphide, most products have a significant market concentration in that one company has a predominant market share. The top 10 companies account for 80 per cent of the production, and the top 16 companies for 94 per cent (David, 1995a and 1995b). Thus there is substantial concentration in the industry. The major reasons are the high investment levels and government intervention.

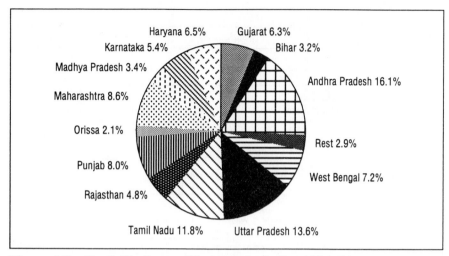

Figure 3.5   Pesticide demand by state in India, 1994–5

The basic industry structure of manufacturing and distribution is depicted in Figure 3.6. Under a scheme introduced by the central government in 1974, manufacturers of certain technical grade pesticides were required to allocate 50 per cent of their production to the state governments. This is made available to non-associated formulators, the objective being to ensure better availability and prices to the farmers. The scheme applies to six important pesticides. However, associated formulators get raw material, credit and other support more easily. In the final analysis, the technical grade manufacturers have about a 60 per cent market share in the formulations market, the non-associated formulators 20 per cent, 15 per cent being with the government and the rest with small distributors or retailers (David, 1995a and 1995b). Technical grade manufactures also collect the lion's share (61.4 per cent) of the customer rupee (Table 3.3). However, the presence of 'me-too' formulators affects quality standards in the market and inhibits market development initiatives and investments of technical grade manufacturers.

The figures on the total production of pesticides over the years by product groups is given in Table 3.4. Insecticides clearly dominate, followed by fungicides and then herbicides. Overall production increased by 33 per cent between 1982/3 and 1992/3. Sales of the members of the Association of Basic Manufactures of Pesticides are given in Table 3.5. In 1991, Rallis, Ciba-Geigy and Bayer were the largest firms. Internationally, the companies ranked by their global sales turnover are given in Table 3.6. Ciba-Geigy, Du Pont and Bayer are the largest.

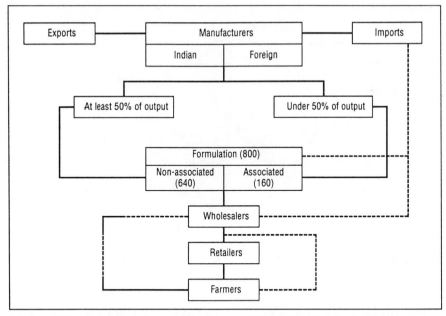

Figure 3.6   Scheme of manufacture and distribution in India

The marketing and distribution of pesticides is done through state departments, cooperatives and private outlets. According to one estimate (Srivastava and Patel, 1990), there are over 77 000 distribution points and retail outlets. The majority are private, followed by cooperatives and then state department outlets. The highest number of outlets is in Andhra Pradesh, followed by Tamil Nadu and then Gujarat. Pesticides fall into the category of an extended problem-solving type of decision making in the buying behaviour of farmers (Venugopal, 1994). Impulsive buying is rare. New

Table 3.3   Share of various constituents of pesticides industry in consumer's rupee (%)

Constituent	Share
1 Technical grade material manufacturers	61.36
2 Formulators	12.00
3 Government	11.68
4 Retailers	10.01
5 Distributors	4.95
Total	100.00

Source: Srivastrava and Patel (1990).

Table 3.4   **Progress of production of pesticides in India**[a]

Year	Insecticides (mt)	Fungicides (mt)	Herbicides (mt)	Rodenticides (mt)	Others (mt)	Total (mt)
1952-53	200	–	–	–	–	200
1953-54	154	–	–	–	–	154
1954-55	432	–	–	–	–	432
1955-56	2 303	–	–	–	–	2 303
1960-61	6 729	598	–	104	11	7 442
1965-66	10 428	1 411	60	269	–	12 168
1970-71	21 722	2 191	14	39	135	24 101
1975-76	32 898	1 906	240	188	15	35 247
1878-79	45 500	3 104	454	144	645	49 847
1979-80	46 115	3 216	417	182	293	50 223
1980-81	39 306	2 552	426	200	778	43 262
1981-82	44 278	2 733	580	260	607	48 458
1982-83	53 922	2 927	1 069	306	702	57 926
1983-84	53 519	2 815	981	340	1 063	58 718
1984-85	51 468	3 946	1 554	355	1 202	58 525
1985-86	47 885	3 828	1 818	283	1 106	54 920
1986-87	47 602	4 552	2 151	429	1 452	56 186
1987-88	49 370	4 030	2 180	460	800	56 840
1988-89	54 480	7 700	3 000	70	–	65 250
1989-90	56 000	6 600	2 860	100	10	65 576
1991-92	n.a.	n.a.	n.a.	n.a.	n.a.	75 000
1992-93	n.a.	n.a.	n.a.	n.a.	n.a.	77 000

Note: [a]Disaggregate data are not available for several years.

Source: David (1995).

pesticides first have to enter into the decision set of the buyer, then they have to win or find a niche within this set. Thus, in a competitive market place, new entrants would not find it easy to enter. Brand equity and brand loyalty are very important.

Studies of the cost of cultivation in major 'green revolution' areas, such as the Punjab, have shown that the expenditure on pesticides has increased very rapidly, far more rapidly than that on any other input (Gandhi, forthcoming). However, its contribution to an increase in the total cost of production has been small, because its share is small. This suggests that farmer sensitivity to pesticide prices in such areas may not be very high. Gandhi (forthcoming) also indicates that labour has a very large share in the cost of production. Thus even small increases in wages would lead to a profit squeeze and a shift towards adoption of labour-saving technology, particularly herbicides. This trend is observed substantially in the labour-intensive crop of rice in the Punjab.

Table 3.5   Sales of pesticides in India (Rs crores)

	Company	1989	1990	1991
1	Ciba-Geigy	65.27	83.2	117
2	Nocil	70.00	78.5	98
3	Bayer	69.00	77.6	115
4	Exel	58.00	79.0	85
5	Hoechst	64.20	68.0	80
6	Sandoz	67.00	80.2	58
7	Shaw Wallace	38.00	44.0	54
8	ICI	36.00	40.0	48
9	Indofil	30.00	33.6	40
10	Cyanamid	28.10	34.2	43
11	BASF	19.47	30.3	37
12	Searle	28.10	27.1	30
13	Rallis	82.00	98.0	140
14	BPM	50.00	55.0	45
15	R.D. Agro	20.00	22.0	20
16	Monsanto	15.00	17.0	15
17	Gharda	48.00	52.8	77
18	HIL	40.00	44.0	44
19	Others	153.00	177.0	186
	Total	981.14	1 141.5	1 332

The rise in wages would be related to opportunities for employment in the agriculture and non-agriculture sector, slowing down of population growth, urbanization and more labour-intensive opportunities in the agriculture sector (such as livestock and vegetable crops). All these factors show considerable changes in recent years which could lead to wage increases and rapid expansion in the potential for herbicides. Herbicide use in rice is found to be lower in traditional rice areas but in non-traditional irrigated rice areas, such as the Punjab and Haryana, substantial expansion in herbicide use has taken place (Naylor, 1994). This is related to the labour intensity of rice and the shortage of labour and the high wages in these areas. Herbicides make rice cultivation possible (and profitable) in some of these areas, but there are environmental costs. However, weeds can reduce yields by up to 33 per cent (Gautam and Mishra, 1995).

For cotton in Andhra Pradesh, the expenditure on pesticides is found to be the highest on large farms (Pandurangadu and Raju, 1990); some 93 per cent of the pesticide expenditure is on insecticides – 56 on conventional and 37 on synthetic pyrethroids. However, studies suggest that use is excessive and indiscriminate. Cost of cultivation of cotton was reported to be rising as a result of such pesticide use, especially of expensive pesticides.

Table 3.6   Global pesticides sales turnover of top 15 companies in India, 1992

	Company	M. US$
1	Ciba-Geigy	2 831
2	Du Pont	1 995
3	Bayer	1 869
4	Rhône-Poulenc	1 842
5	Zeneca	1 716
6	Monsanto	1 647
7	Dow Elanco	1 581
8	Hoechst	1 333
9	BASF	1 142
10	American Cyanamid	1 000
11	Sandoz	841
12	Schering	788
13	Shell	725
14	FMC	455
15	Sumitomo	417

Source: Verma (1995).

Apart from complementary, there is also competition between yield-saving inputs (pesticides) and yield-increasing inputs (fertilizers) (Prabhu, 1987). When faced with yield uncertainty, farmers who are risk-averse tend to use higher than optimal levels of yield-saving inputs and lower than optimal levels of other inputs. The marginal value product of pesticides is often lower than its price. The major motivation for pesticide application is insurance against damage. As a result, more pesticide is used than is economically optimal (in direct terms). Further, large farmers use more pesticide because of their financial capacity. Pesticides do not appear to increase aggregate production (Upender, 1995), while integrated pest management actually reduces pesticide use (Burrows, 1983). Pesticide consumption in India is significantly affected by the price of pesticides and the area under high-yielding varieties (Gopal and Gopal, 1995).

Between 1971/2 and 1988/9, pesticide expenditure in Rs/ha in India shows negative growth rates in the eastern (–2 per cent) and western (–8.7 per cent) regions, but a high positive growth rate in the northern (32.4 per cent) and southern (8.8 per cent) regions (Kumar and Rosegrant, 1994). Between 1971–5 and 1986–8, the share of pesticides in the cost structure rose from 0.3 to 1.2 per cent.

Discussion

The agrochemical industry has substantial micro–macro linkages with many different aspects of the economy. The macro environment has changed substantially in India since the announcement of the new economic policy in mid-1991, leading to increasing liberalization of the economy. A significant and widespread change has taken place in the mind-set of the country (Das, 1995). This is likely to make liberalization practically irreversible.

Liberalization has set the tone for increasing fiscal discipline. The achievements on this front have been somewhat slow to come but the direction has been clear. The popular belief that government funds are unlimited has been broken. Clear signals have been sent to every front that the central government does not have unlimited means to subsidize and bail out inefficient enterprises. Since fiscal deficits remain high (Dholakia, 1995), this fiscal pressure is likely to continue into the future.

The implications for agriculture are that pressures to reduce agricultural subsidies will continue, mainly the major subsidies in irrigation, fertilizers and electricity. Nonetheless, minimum support prices which take into account the cost of cultivation are also likely to be raised, as happened in 1993, in order to protect the profitability of agriculture (Acharya, 1995). This is also because prices of most agricultural commodities in India are lower than world prices, and subsidy levels are lower than in developed countries (Gulati and Sharma, 1991). Politically, agriculture is a sensitive sector (India, Ministry of Finance, 1993; Bhagwati and Srinivasan, 1993).

Liberalization has also ushered in a policy of phased opening of the economy to international trade and foreign investment. The General Agreement on Tariffs and Trade (GATT) and the WTO have added another major dimension to this: a timetable has been set for phased opening up of the economy and a reduction in trade barriers and subsidies, not only in India, but globally. It is believed that this will have a large net positive effect on the agriculture sector of India (Oza, 1995; Nachane, 1995; Gulati, 1995; Gulati and Sharma, 1994). The sector receives many subsidies but, when output side price distortions are taken into account, agriculture is found to be net taxed in India (Gulati and Sharma, 1991). As a result, trade liberalization in the wake of GATT should bring new opportunities to the agriculture sector in India and enhance its profitability.

It has been established that cotton, which is the largest pesticide-using crop in India, has substantial international competitive advantage (Gulati and Sharma, 1991). As a result, trade liberalization will result in enhanced prospects for this crop, increasing pesticide use. Even for food grains this year, there has been a substantial rise in exports that will enhance profitability and increase the use of pesticides.

The improvement in the protection of intellectual property rights (IPR) in the wake of GATT and WTO will result in a better environment for the growth of the agricultural input industry, particularly the pesticide and seed industries, where substantial investment in research and development (R&D) is involved. With better IPR protection, more firms will be encouraged to undertake R&D and introduce new products. In a competitive environment, this will expand the market.

Even though the rate of population growth in India is declining, India's population will continue to grow substantially well into the next century, surpassing one billion people soon after the turn of the century. Feeding such a large population will continue to be a major problem and priority for a long time to come. With reasonable income growth assumptions, the food situation is likely to be one of either near self-sufficiency or of significant deficit in the 2000–2005 time frame (Table 3.7, Sarma and Gandhi, 1990). As a result, agriculture will continue to be a priority. Nearly 70 per cent of the population depends directly or indirectly on agriculture for its livelihood, and this has hardly changed in the past decades. Industry does not yet have the capacity to absorb such a large labour force. Thus, even from the point of view of employment and income, agriculture will continue to be important.

Environmental concerns have emerged over the last decade. The environmental costs of growth are being increasingly questioned (Rao, 1995; Reddy, 1995; Nadkarni, 1994). This will have implications for the pesticide industry since pesticides are toxic and are seen as a major risk to the environment. However, in a country such as India where income levels are low and unemployment is high, employment and income growth are still

Table 3.7 Supply–demand balances for grain in India under alternative production and consumption projections for year 2000 (mt)

Consumption scenario		Total demand	Production scenario (1)	(2)	(3)
Domestic production			219.4	210.7	215.2
1 Consumption of past per	(a)	206.4	13.0	4.3	8.8
capita income growth rate	(b)	214.8	4.6	−4.1	0.4
2 Growth rates envisaged in	(a)	219.7	−0.3	−9.0	−4.5
the perspective plan	(b)	227.3	−7.9	−16.6	−12.1
3 First accelerated growth	(a)	226.3	−6.9	−15.6	−11.1
rate scenario	(b)	233.3	−13.9	−22.6	−18.1
4 Second accelerated	(a)	234.5	−15.1	−23.8	−19.3
growth rate scenario	(b)	240.7	−21.3	−30.0	−25.5

Notes:
[a] Without change in income distribution.
[b] With improvement in income distribution.

Source: Sarma and Gandhi (1990).

major priorities. Since agriculture is needed to feed a huge and growing population, a healthy performance of the sector is important. Agriculture also contributes to export earnings. Thus growth assumes priority, but it must be achieved with protection or minimum damage to the environment (Rao and Gulati, 1994). Further, pesticide use levels in India are among the lowest in the world (Farah, 1994) so environmental problems from this source are unlikely to receive much attention.

Regulations with respect to the introduction of new pesticides and re-evaluation of existing pesticides are already established through the Insecticide Act and will continue to be important. At the same time integrated pest management, more environmentally friendly pesticides and non-chemical remedies and innovations will develop (Pastakia, 1995).

References

Acharya, S.S. (1995), 'Getting the Subsidies Right', *The Economic Times*, 27 March, p.5.

Bhagwati, J. and T.N. Srinivasan (1993), *Economic Reform*, Ministry of Finance, New Delhi.

Burrows, T.M. (1983). 'Pesticide Demand and Integrated Pest Management: A Limited Dependent Variable Analysis', *American Journal of Agricultural Economics* **65**(4): 806–10.

Das, G. (1995), 'A Million Reforms Now', *Business World*, 27 December–9 January.

David, B.V. (1995a), 'Indian Pesticide Industry: An Overview', in B.V. David (ed.), *The Pesticides Industry*, Kothari Desk Book Series, H.C. Kothari Group, Madras.

David, B.V. (ed.) (1995b), *The Pesticides Industry*, H.C. Kothari Group, Madras.

Desai, G.M. and B. Stone (1987), 'Fertiliser Market Development and National Policy in China and India: A Comparative Perspective', paper prepared for IFA–FAIDINAP Southeast Asia and Pacific Regional Fertiliser Conference, Kuala Lumpur, Malaysia, 22–5 July.

Dholakia, B.H. (1995), 'Macroeconomic Analysis of Union Budget 1995–96', *Vikalpa*, **20**(2): 13–26.

Farah, J. (1994), *Pesticide Policies in Developing Countries: Do They Encourage Excessive Use?*, World Bank, Washington, DC.

Gandhi, V.P. (forthcoming), *Technological Change, Prices and Cost Reduction: A Study of Wheat and Rice in Punjab*, Vikalpa.

Gandhi, V.P. and G.M. Desai (1992), 'Converting Potential into Effective Demand for and Use of Fertilisers: A Study of Small Farmers in Gazaland District of Zimbabwe', in S. Wanmali and J.M. Zamchiya (eds), *Service Provision and Its Impact on Agricultural and Rural Development in Zimbabwe: A Case Study of Gazaland District*, IFPRI, Washington, DC.

Gautam, K.C. and J.S. Mishra (1995), 'Problems, Prospects and New Approaches in Weed Management', *Pesticides Information*, **21**(1): 7–19.

Gopal, M. and M. Gopal (1995), 'Multiple Regression Analysis for Quantitative Estimation of Demand for Pesticides in India', *Pesticides Information*, **21**(1): 20-25.

Gulati, A. (1995), 'Rapporteur's Report on New Economic Policy and Indian Agriculture', *Indian Journal of Agricultural Economics*, **50**(3): 570-76.

Gulati, A. and A. Sharma (1994), 'Agriculture Under Gatt: What It Holds for India', *Economic and Political Weekly*, 15 July.

Gulati, A. and P.K. Sharma (1991), 'Government Intervention in Agricultural Markets: Nature, Impact and Implications', *Journal of Indian School of Political Economy*, **3**(2): 205-37.

Kumar, P. and M.W. Rosegrant (1994), 'Productivity and Sources of Growth for Rice in India', *Economic and Political Weekly*, **29**(53): A183-A188.

Mathur, S.C. (1993), 'The Pesticide Industry in India', *Pesticides Information*, **19**(1): 7-15.

Mehrotra, K.N. and A. Phokela (1995), *Resistance in Pests,* in B.V. David (ed.), *The Pesticides Industry*, Kothari Desk Book Series, H.C. Kothari Group, Madras.

Mellor, J.W. and R. Ahmed (1988), 'Agricultural Price Policy for Accelerating Growth', in J.W. Mellor and R. Ahmed (eds), *Agricultural Price Policy for Developing Countries*, IFPRI/Johns Hopkins,Washington, DC.

Ministry of Finance (1993), *Economic Reforms*, Controller of Publications, New Delhi.

Ministry of Finance (various years), *Economic Survey*, Controller of Publications, New Delhi.

Nachane, D.M. (1995), 'Intellectual Property Rights in the Uruguay Round: An Indian Perspective', *Economic and Political Weekly*, **30**(5): 257-68.

Nadkarni, M.V. (1994), 'Agriculture and Environment', *Economic and Political Weekly*, **29**(28): 1021-2.

Naylor, R. (1994), 'Herbicide Use in Asian Rice Production', *World Development*, **22**(1): 55-70.

Oza, A.N. (1995), 'General Agreement on Tariff and Trade, 1994: An Explanatory Note', *Vikalpa*, **20**(3): 27-41.

Pandurangadu, K. and V.T. Raju (1990), 'Economics of Pesticides Use on Cotton Farms in Guntur District of Andhra Pradesh', *Agricultural Situation in India*, **45**(7): 467-70.

Pastakia, A.R. (1995), 'Grassroots Innovations for Sustainable Development: The Case of Agricultural Pest Management', unpublished PhD dissertation, Indian Institute of Management, Ahmedabad.

Prabhu, K.S. (1987), *Pesticide Use in Indian Agriculture*, Himalaya Publishing House, Bombay.

Rao, C.H.H. and A. Gulati (1994), 'Indian Agriculture: Emerging Perspectives and Policy Issues', *Economic and Political Weekly*, **29**(53): A158-A169.

Rao, J.M. (1995), 'Whither India's Environment?', *Economic and Political Weekly*, **30**(13): 677-86.

Reddy, V.R. (1995), 'Environment and Sustainable Agricultural Development: Conflicts and Contradictions', *Economic and Political Weekly*, **30**(12): A12-A27.

Sarma, J.S. and V.P. Gandhi (1990), 'Production and Consumption of Foodgrains in India: Implication of Accelerated Economic Growth and Poverty Alleviation', Research Report No. 81, IFPRI, Washington, DC.

Srivastava, U.K. and N.T. Patel (1990), *Pesticides Industry in India: Issues and Constraints in its Growth*, Oxford & IBH Publishing Co. Pvt. Ltd., New Delhi.

Srivastava, U.K. and N.T. Patel (1991), 'Pesticides Industry in India: Performance and Constraints', *Journal of Indian School of Political Economy*, 3(1): 91–110.

Upender, M. (1995), 'Agricultural Production Function for India: A Macro Time Series Study', *The Indian Journal of Economics* 76(300) (July, Part I): 121–31.

Venugopal, P. (1994), 'Purchase Decision for Branded Agricultural Inputs: A Case of Pesticides', unpublished PhD thesis, Indian Institute of Management, Ahmedabad.

Verma, J.S. (1995), 'The World Scenario', in B.V. David (ed.), *The Pesticides Industry*, Kothari Desk Book Series, H.C. Kothari Group, Madras.

4 Do Fertilizers Play a Major Role in Sustainable Agricultural Development in West Africa?

A. de Jager[a], *A.U. Mokwunye*[b] *and E.M.A. Smaling*[c]

Introduction

The productivity of the agricultural sector in West Africa remains relatively low, mainly because of low and erratic rainfall, the absence of market incentives and increased competition due to trade liberalization, leading to an inability of farmers to replenish sufficiently exported nutrients from the farm. Forced by the need to produce more staple crops for a growing population, farm households abandoned the once stable system of shifting cultivation, reduced fallow and expanded the cultivated area to more fragile soil types. The net effect is that soil fertility levels in the region, are historically low and declining.

The agricultural sector in West Africa is facing a major challenge: satisfying both the short-term demands for food security and income generation and long-term demands for sustainable development and increasing food production. Farm households, as well as intervening agents and policy makers, tend to give priority to short-term production, since this has immediate financial/nutritional (farm household) or political (policy

[a] Agricultural Economics Research Institute (LEI-DLO), P.O. Box 29703, 2502 LS The Hague, The Netherlands.
[b] International Fertiliser Development Centre (IFDC), B.P. 4483, Lomé, Togo.
[c] Winand Staring Centre for Integrated Land, Soil and Water Research (SC-DLO), P.O. Box 125, 6700 AC Wageningen, The Netherlands.

maker) implications. In general, however, farmers are well aware of the negative impacts of current farm management practices, but the socioeconomic environment prevents them from undertaking long-term investments in soil fertility. While international awareness on these issues has increased since the 1992 UN Conference on Environment and Development, well planned, coordinated and integrated implementation of technical and policy instruments at different scale levels is required, with a high level of participation by all stockholders.

This chapter is based on a study conducted for and in collaboration with the International Fertiliser Development Centre (IFDC). The objectives of the study are (1) to collate existing information on farming systems and soil fertility issues in West Africa; (2) to collate existing information on policies, infrastructure and technologies that can directly or indirectly improve soil fertility; and (3) to develop systematically a multidisciplinary, multi-scale framework for action. A multidisciplinary team consisting of agronomists, soil scientists, sociologists, socioeconomists and consultants from the region and The Netherlands reviewed published and unpublished literature and consulted relevant research results and databases. Team sessions were organized to coordinate activities and to develop and fill the framework for interventions. After a description of the major characteristics of farming systems and soil fertility status, the relevant technology and policy tools to address soil fertility problems in West Africa were identified. Specific attention thus focuses on farm-level constraints to adoption of conservation technology and the need for a reorientation of economic valuation in long-term soil fertility restoration. The chapter concludes with a framework for required interventions at different scale levels.

Farming Systems and Soil Fertility

In the agroclimatic or agroecological zones identified by the multidisciplinary team, a wide variety of agricultural production systems exist. The majority of the systems can be classified as rainfed crop production systems. Characteristics of these systems vary by zone: tree crops, tubers and cereals in the Equatorial Forest Zone (EFZ); maize- and cassava-based intercropping systems in the Guinea Savannah Zone (GSZ); and millet/sorghum-based intercrops in the Sudan Savannah Zone (SSZ) and Sahel. In the Sahel and SSZ, livestock-dominated production systems occur, with different degrees of confinement of the animals. Integration between crop and livestock production is increasing in the SSZ and GSZ, although conflicting interests still exist between herders and crop farmers. Increased intensification with production of high-quality fodder and increased confinement systems may lead to a reduction of these conflicts and to an increase in the productivity and sustainability. Intensive periurban production systems are emerging around the growing urban centres in the coastal countries. In terms of area and total production, irrigation is of limited importance in West Africa and there is little scope for further development.

When discussing chemical soil fertility, conceptualized as the sum of the organic and mineral nutrients, a distinction has to be made between the static concept of nutrient stocks with different degrees of nutrient availability to the crops and the dynamic concept of nutrient flows that enhance or decrease the nutrient stocks over time (Smaling *et al.*, 1996). Data on soil fertility stocks at different scale levels – from country to watershed, farm and plot level – are readily available. In Table 4.1, major soil fertility indicators for different Agroecological zones (AEZs) are presented.

There is much variation in soil nutrient stocks at farm level, with farmers, who are resource-poor, risk-averse and pursuing food security, seeing this heterogeneity as an asset (Brouwer *et al.*, 1993; De Steenhuijzen Piters, 1995; Prudencio, 1993). Dynamic nutrient flows can be observed at different scale levels, but currently only data at the country level are available (Table 4.2). It appears that nutrient depletion is relatively severe in densely populated Nigeria and the other coastal countries, such as Ghana and the Ivory Coast, where agriculture is intensive and less than 30 per cent of the land is estimated to be fallow. In the Sahelian countries, nutrient depletion is not severe because there is little in the system in its native state that could be depleted. Low application rates of fertilizers and organic manure and high outflows of nutrients with the harvested crop and considerable losses from

Table 4.1 Nutrient stocks and other fertility indicators of granitic soils in different agroecological zones in West Africa

Agroecol. zone (AEZ)	Depth (cm)	pH water	Organic C (g/kg)	Total N (g/kg)	Total P (mg/kg)	Cation exchange capacity (mmol/kg)	Base saturation (%)
Equatorial	0–20	5.3	24.5	1.60	628	88	21
Forest Zone	20–50	5.1	15.4	1.03	644	86	16
Guinea	0–20	5.7	11.7	1.39	392	63	60
Savannah Zone	20–50	5.5	6.8	0.79	390	56	42
Sudan	0–20	6.8	3.3	0.49	287	93	93
Savannah Zone	20–50	7.1	4.3	0.61	285	87	90

Source: Windmeijer and Andriesse (1993).

Table 4.2   NPK budgets in West Africa, selected countries, 1983

Countries	Arable (in 1 000 hectares)	Fallow (%)	N	P (kg/ha/year)	K
Burkina Faso	6 691	50	−14	−2	−10
Cameroon	7 681	50	−20	−2	−12
Ghana	4 505	24	−30	−3	−17
Guinea	4 128	68	−9	−1	−6
Ivory Coast	6 946	31	−25	−2	−14
Mali	8 015	72	−8	−1	−6
Niger	10 985	47	−16	−2	−11
Nigeria	32 812	18	−34	−4	−24
Senegal	5 235	53	−12	−2	−10
Togo	1 503	49	−18	−2	−12

Source: Stoorvogel and Smaling (1990).

leaching and erosion lead to these negative balances.

In West Africa, data on the impact of cropping systems and farm management practices on soil fertility and nutrient flows are sparse. For southern Mali (van der Pol, 1992) and pasture systems in the SSZ and in the Sahel (Penning de Vries and Djiteye, 1991; Breman and Niangado, 1994), details on nutrient budgets are available, but more comprehensive studies involving different farming systems and focusing on relations between farm household strategies, land tenure, capital availability, market infrastructure, economic performance and gender on soil fertility are lacking.

Economic Incentives, Institutions and Technology

Both policy instruments and technological development can be used to address soil fertility problems in West Africa. *Policy instruments* at different scale levels influence farm household decision making concerning soil conservation. The GATT and structural adjustment programmes (SAPs) initiated by the IMF and World Bank have a great impact on agricultural development and soil fertility in West Africa. But regional policies, like the EU agricultural policy, also have a direct influence on the agricultural sector in West Africa. For instance, increased competition from subsidized beef exported from the EU resulted in lower prices and reduced outlet possibilities for meat produced in the Sahel and eventually discouraged necessary long-term investments in more sustainable and intensive production systems.

The overall effect on the soil fertility of the results of the GATT–Uruguay Round are hard to assess. On the one hand, the agreement is likely to stimulate increased investments in the agricultural sector owing to higher world market prices of some commodities (grains, oil products), but, on the other, increased competition from food crops produced in other regions may lead to short-term reduction in rural income. It is obvious that, in either case, adequate national policies need to be pursued to increase productivity in the agricultural sector.

National governments have different instruments to ensure effective implementation of a certain policy: laws and regulations, financial incentives (subsidies, levies), social regulations and persuasion (extension, research and so on). However, they have to operate within the above-mentioned supranational agreements, and SAPs. A distinction can be made between direct price and market interventions and more indirect facilitating instruments for the development of the agricultural sector (research, extension, transport). Hereafter the following instruments will be reviewed in more detail: SAP-induced instruments (currency devaluation, subsidy removal, deregulation of fertilizer prices); market development of agricultural outputs; and research, extension and development interventions.

Systematic studies on the impact of SAP measures on soil conservation are scarce. The currency devaluation (Franc Communauté Financière d'Agrique (FCFA) in 1994) has largely increased the profitability of the export sector, which may eventually lead to increased fertilizer use and overall investments in soil fertility. In the food crop production sector, however, currency devaluation has not led to an increase in farmers' incomes since the slight increase in food crop prices could not compensate for increased fertilizer prices. The removal of fertilizer subsidies in most West African countries has, at best, resulted in a stagnation of fertilizer use in the food crop subsector and a further reduction of the already low value/cost ratio (VCR) for fertilizer use on cereal crops (Table 4.3). Given these developments, total fertilizer consumption in West Africa has not increased significantly in the past 10 years (Figure 4.1).

In addition to spontaneous developments within the private sector in response to market opportunities, some West African governments have instituted a deliberate policy to transfer fertilizer procurement and distribution functions from the public to the private sector. In Ghana, Senegal and Mali, the state withdrew almost completely, while in Togo and Benin only part of the distribution functions was transferred. In Nigeria, however, the central government maintains a special position in subsidized fertilizer distribution. Since this privatization is often introduced together with other policy measures like devaluation and subsidy removal, short-term market opportunities for the private sector have been limited.

Table 4.3   Value–cost ratios for maize and cereals in Ghana and Mali, 1981–94

Country/fertilizer/crop	1981–90	1990	1991	1992	1993	1994
Ghana						
AS + 15–15–15 (maize)	—	2.6	3.1	1.8	1.6	1.1
AS + 20–20–0 (maize)	—	2.6	3.1	1.7	1.5	1.1
Urea + 20–20–0 (maize)	—	3.0	3.6	2.4	2.2	1.3
Mali						
Imported N-P-K (maize)	2.0	—	—	—	2.3	1.7
Imported N-P-K (rice)	5.1	—	—	—	4.4	4.1
Imported N-P-K (sorghum)	1.7	—	—	—	1.6	1.3

Source: Gerner (1995).

Economies in Sub-Saharan Africa are currently semi-open, with high transfer costs and large non-tradable rural sectors, suggesting that a deliberate commodity approach to supporting agricultural production will be necessary (Delgado, 1995). Since increasing output prices is a key factor in addressing soil nutrient depletion, increasing the performance of food markets, supporting crop diversification and facilitating the development of the processing industry are appropriate policy tools for achieving sustainable agricultural development. The performance of food markets in West Africa can be improved through increased access to credit for farmers and traders, improved storage facilities, increased transport facilities, and adequate and

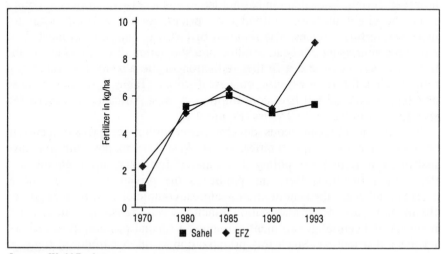

Source: World Bank.

Figure 4.1   Fertilizer use in West Africa, 1970–93

timely market information. Potentials for crop diversification are limited and it is unlikely that non-traditional exports will replace traditional commodities as dominant foreign exchange earners in the coming 10 years.

National research institutes and extension services have addressed soil fertility issues in a rather disciplinary and location-specific way. Attention to soil fertility restoration has also been rather low, with less than 50 per cent of the West African National Agricultural Research Stations having five or more ongoing research and development projects (SPAAR, 1995). Research–extension–farmer (REF) linkages have been rather weak, leading to research activities not focused on farm household needs and problems, research results poorly adapted to local agroecological and socioeconomic conditions, and research not making use of existing indigenous farm management knowledge. A more active role for non-governmental organizations (NGOs) and farmer organizations in the planning and implementation of research and development activities is envisaged, since NGOs appear to be more successful in development of diagnostic methods, innovations in techniques for adopting technologies and participative approaches. Policies have to be developed that (1) facilitate more coherent research activities (such as the ecoregional research approaches of the CGIARs (Consultative Group on International Agricultural Research)); (2) reorient research towards resource-conserving and integrated nutrient management techniques; (3) increase participation in planning and implementation of research; and (4) focus on farm-level extension and increased NGO involvement.

Existing *technologies* to address the problem of soil nutrient depletion can be partitioned into techniques that save nutrients from being lost from the agroecosystem and techniques that add nutrients to the agroecosystem. Since technology is adopted at the farm level, the farm is taken as the focal point. The technology adopted by the farmer can be seen within the context of the manipulation of one or more nutrient inputs, nutrient outputs or internal flows listed in Table 4.4. Options for effecting these flows are provided in Table 4.5.

Fertilizers are not applied to build soil fertility. However, applying fertilizers could mean that (1) farmers get higher yields where fertilizers have been applied; (2) increased biomass production protects the soil surface and may contribute to soil organic matter; (3) there is an increase in area left to recuperate as the desired production has been realized on the fertilized plot; and (4) part of the fertilizer remains in the soil and contributes to soil fertility. Negative effects are that excessive application of certain types of fertilizer (urea, sulphate of ammonia, diammonium phosphate) may pollute the environment and cause soil acidification, and that the application of nutrient A may induce accelerated depletion of nutrients B and C, because

Table 4.4   Farm-level nutrient input and output flows

Nutrient inputs		
IN 1		Mineral fertilizers
IN 2		Organic inputs, subdivided into:
	IN 2a	concentrate for livestock and fish
	IN 2b	other organic feeds for livestock and fish
	IN 2c	urban and agroindustrial waste
	IN 2d	manure obtained from outside the farm
	IN 2e	manure from farm livestock grazing outside the farm during part of the day
	IN 2f	food for the farm family obtained from outside the farm
IN 3		Atmospheric deposition in rain and dust
IN 4		Biological nitrogen fixation in leguminous species (including free-living bacteria and mycorrhiza)
IN 5		Sedimentation as a result of (i) irrigation, (ii) natural flooding or (iii) partial resedimentation of soil materials eroded from upper slopes
IN 6		Subsoil exploitation by trees and other perennial crops

Nutrient outputs	
OUT 1	Harvested crops, meat, milk and fish leaving the farm
OUT 2	Crop residues and manure leaving the farm
OUT 3	Leaching below the root zone
OUT 4	Gaseous losses (including denitrification, ammonia volatilization and losses as a result of burning)
OUT 5	Runoff and erosion
OUT 6	Human faeces ending up in deep pit latrines

Interal flows	
FL 1	Crop residues fed to tethered farm animals or applied to certain plots
FL 2	Biomass from plots under pasture and fallow eaten by roaming farm animals
FL 3	Animal manure from within the farm applied to certain plots
FL 4	Crops, milk, meat and fish obtained from the farm, eaten by the farm family
FL 5	Food remnants and farmyard manure applied to certain plots

Source: Smaling *et al.* (1996).

vigorously growing crops take up more nutrients than crops grown under low-input conditions.

Phosphate rock (PR) seems to play a crucial role in the upgrading of the phosphorous stocks of West African soils. The potential of PR lies in the fact that it redresses phosphorus deficiency, has a strong residual effect, and does

Table 4.5   Restoring soil fertility in West Africa: technical options and their impact on nutrient flows

Technology	Fertility effect	Adding/saving
1 mineral (high-reactive) fertilizer		
increased use	increase of IN 1	adding
more efficient use		saving
2 mineral soil amendments		
rock phosphates	increase in IN 1 (P)	adding
lime and dolomites	increase of pH, increase of IN 1 (Ca, Mg)	adding
3 organic inputs		
from within the farm	reduction of OUT 2	saving
	increased recycling FL 1,3,5	mainly saving
	increase in IN 2a–f from outside the farm	adding
4 improved land use systems		
rotations, green manure	increase in IN 4, reduction of OUT 2–5	adding + saving
fallows, woody species	increase of IN 4,6 reduction of OUT 2–5	adding + saving
5 soil and water conservation	reduction of OUT 3–5	saving
6 integrated nutrient management	combination of IN 1–IN 5	adding + saving

Source: Smaling *et al.* (1996).

not acidify the soil. Farmers, however, are not yet impressed because of the dusty character of the finely ground material, the fact that the material contains only one macronutrient, and its slow reactivity. The major constraint regarding the use of organic inputs is their bulkiness, since large quantities are often required. However, the role of organic materials in maintaining the physical and biological characteristics of the soil is often undervalued.

Techniques of improved land use systems include rotating and intercropping, green manures and cover crops, incorporation of Azolla in wetland rice, agroforestry and related systems, fodder banks and improved pastures, and fallow. Integrated nutrient management attempts to combine these agronomic practices, but adapted to site-specific agronomic and socioeconomic circumstances to redress nutrient imbalances more effectively than by simply considering each nutrient in isolation. This may involve combinations of both low and high external input practices. For instance, combining fertilizers with organic manure increases fertilizer uptake efficiency, reduces acidification risks and supplements nutrients not present in fertilizer with those present in the manure.

Adoption of these technologies at the farm level has been limited, resulting in a similar slow process of technical change in West African agriculture. Several factors influence the adoption of new technologies, including the characteristics of the household, its objectives and the characteristics of the technology (Rogers, 1983). In addition, existing external factors like infrastructure and geophysical conditions will determine the degree of adoption. In the process of technology development and dissemination, so far, relatively limited attention is paid to these processes of innovation, adoption decision behaviour and adaptation of technology to fit local circumstances. Apart from short-term economic profitability, there are other factors influencing adoption decisions: the developed technology may not be appropriate to the specific situation of the farm household; the farm's short-term strategies conflict with long-term effects of restoring soil fertility techniques; farm households are not accustomed to investing money and in most cases do not have the resources to invest; land tenure arrangements prevent long-term investments in the soil; the perception of the problem is not always clear at the farm level; agroecological margins in specific areas are small, so that chances of total crop failure are too high to justify investments in tools, equipment or fertilizers; knowledge at the farm household level is insufficient because of limited access to research results because of ineffective functioning of extension services and the virtual absence of effective research–extension–farmer linkages; limited possibilities of economic development outside agriculture in the region prevent technology developments in the agricultural sector; appropriate supportive infrastructures are lacking; marketing possibilities and market access are limited; the technology conflicts with existing local knowledge, social events or community structures; and fluctuating prices of inputs and agricultural outputs increase farmer risk.

Role of Cost–Benefit Analysis

In cost–benefit analysis, discounting results in lower economic valuation of long-term soil conservation investments. High discount rates lead to preference for none or only very few long-term soil conservation measures. Determination of a realistic discount rate at the farm level is difficult and depends on many factors, such as alternative investment opportunities, the tenure system, commercial bank rates and farm household perceptions. Further, agricultural producers do not always bear the full costs of their decisions to deplete the soil, with the possibility that the true costs of the associated externalities remain hidden, unpriced and ignored until their consequences reach crisis proportions (Gerner, 1995). Use of cost–benefit analysis in these circumstances may be misleading, so a number of other approaches have been developed, such as cost-effectiveness analysis (Bojö, 1990), productivity methods for valuation (Bishop and Allen, 1989; Lutz *et al.*, 1994) and the replacement cost model (Stocking, 1986).

In the productivity method, the effect of yields on, for example, soil loss due to specific management practices is estimated. The variability of the outcome, however, is large and sensitive to prices. For Southern Mali, the results of various studies on valuation of soil degradation showed a variation from 1000 to 25 000 FCFA/ha (Keddeman, 1991). Application of the productivity method in Kenya showed that no soil conservation appears to be the most profitable during the first three years, an intermediate level of conservation is the most profitable during the next six to eight years, whereas intensive physical and biological conservation is only profitable after that period (Ekbom, 1995). In the replacement cost method, the costs incurred to replace damaged productive assets, such as depleted soil, are estimated. The depleted nutrients are considered to have an economic value equal to the market value of an equivalent amount of fertilizer. Implementation of the replacement cost approach and economic indicators such as the economic nutrient depletion income ratio (part of economic return based on soil nutrient depletion) show, for example, considerable soil mining costs in the case of Southern Mali (van der Pol, 1993). In the short term, multiple-goal linear programming models, whereby nutrient balances are included explicitly in the model, may provide insights into the trade-off at the farm level between short-term profit and long-term sustainability objectives (De Koeijer *et al.*, 1995).

While a wide range of technologies is available, adoption of these technologies has been hampered by socioeconomic conditions. A comprehensive, integrated rural development agenda, at the system level, is absent. Rural development efforts are fragmented and ad hoc in nature. Existing policies favour attainment of short-term goals and are not geared towards long-term sustainable agricultural development. Based on observations provided in this chapter, a framework for possible interventions at different scale levels is presented in Table 4.6.

Conclusions

Increased and more efficient use of fertilizers in West African agriculture is essential to attain sustainable agricultural growth. However, resource-conserving technologies are just as essential and in some cases more appropriate and feasible, especially in diverse, complex, resource-poor farming systems. The still existing contradiction between new modernists

Table 4.6   Recommended actions at different intervention levels to facilitate implementation of technology options to restore soil fertility

Level	Mineral fertilizers	Mineral soil amendments (phosphorus and lime)	Organic inputs (crop residues and manure)
	Capital National policies Market development agricultural products/input–output prices	Awareness/R–E–F linkages Perception Pay-back period	Labour Availability
Supranational and regional (West Africa)	Review of SAPs Replacement food aid with fertilizer aid Common regional agricultural policy (increased market protection) Joint fertilizer procurement	Perception of rock phosphate (PR) as capital investment Support for World Bank PR initiative Valuation of unaccounted costs and benefits (internalize externalities) Regional coordination of exploitation of deposits	Valuation of unaccounted costs and benefits Awareness/quantification of international flows of organic matter and nutrients
National and regional	Government support to private fertilizer sector (physical/institutional) Forms of fertilizer subsidies Policy support to agricultural sector Fine-tune fertilizer recommendations for various crops to soil and AEZs Gender-specific extension activities (e.g. more women extension staff)	Formalization/implementation of NARS–Extension/NGO–farmers' linkages Facilitation of exploitation and distribution Establishment of national resource management unit National phosphorus/lime investment policy Extension message and methodology development	Energy conservation policies Waste management policies (recycling of agroindustrial and city waste)
Village/farm household	Financial support services to farmers (selective rates, credit) Development of group-banking systems (Grameen) Development of women banking groups Cash crop development (diversification) Local processing agricultural products Participatory fertilizer trials with farmers and women groups	Participatory on-farm trials Extension message and methodology development	Improved animal husbandy management Measures to reduce/avoid bush burning Maximization of biomass production Increasing quality of organic matter (composting) Improvement of transport facilities and techniques Training in use of green manures

Level	Improved land use systems (LEISA)	Soil conservation	Integrated nutrient management (LEISA+HEIA)
Supranational and regional (West Africa)	Awareness of technology R–E–F linkages Foster international initiative for greening the region Policies to integrate pastoralism and sedentary agriculture Valuation of unaccounted costs and benefits	Labour Payback period Valuation of unaccounted costs of soil erosion and off-site effects	Awareness of technology R–E–F linkages Agronomic performance Awareness/support of international approach Shift in paradigm to ecoregional research and development approach
National and regional	Formalization/implementation of NARS–Extension/NGO–Farmers' linkages NARS research policy shifting from commodity to systems approach Policies to secure land tenure systems Policies addressing gender-sensitive issues in land use	Facilitation of maximum use of indigenous knowledge and materials Development of national soil conservation development scheme (incentives to farmers) Policies to secure land tenure systems	Formalization/implementation of NARS–Extension/NGO–Farmers' linkages Shift from commodity to ecoregional approach Strategy to maximize internal input and optimize external input use Integration of indigenous knowledge with scientific knowledge systems Niche differentiation
Village/farm household	Participatory technology development and demonstration on technical components of improved LUS (AEZ-specific)	Promoting community conservation programmes Development of labour-saving soil conservation technologies Participatory technology development and demonstration	Participatory technology development and demonstration Exploitation of farm heterogeneity

advocating mainly high external input solutions and sustainable production focusing on only generative technologies (Pretty, 1995) should be eliminated (see also Chapter 9 of the present volume). The concept of integrated nutrient management should be the leading principle. In such an approach an agroeconomically optimal mix of nutrient-adding and nutrient-saving techniques has to be available for farm households in different farming systems and agroecological zones. In the process of technology development, the participation of farm households, NGOs and extension needs to be increased considerably in order to make more use of indigenous knowledge and to facilitate adoption at the farm household level. Improved farm management is a key area in technological innovation.

At the policy level, instruments should be geared towards facilitating increased profitability of the agricultural sector through output and input market development and facilitating long-term investment in soil fertility. Both research and policy interventions require a comprehensive national and regional approach, with a high level of participation of all actors.

References

Bishop, J. and J. Allen (1989), 'The On-Site Cost of Soil Erosion in Mali', World Bank Environmental Paper No. 21, World Bank, Washington, DC.

Bojö, J. (1990), *Environment and Development: An Economic Approach*, Kluwer Academic Publishers, Dordrecht/Boston/London.

Breman, H. and O. Niangado (1994), 'Maintien de la production agricole sahélienne. Rapport mi-chemin du projet PPS, Exploitation optimale des éléments nutritifs en élevage', rapport PPS no. 6, IER, Bamako/AB-DLO, Wageningen-Haren/DAN-AUW, Wageningen, The Netherlands.

Brouwer, J., L.K. Fussell and L. Hermann (1993), 'Soil and Crop Growth Micro-Variability in the West African Semi-Arid Tropics: A Possible Risk-Reducing Factor for Subsistence Farmers', *Agriculture, Ecosystems & Environment*, **45**: 229–38.

De Koeijer, T.J., J.A. Renkema and J.J.M. van Mensvoort (1995), 'Environmental-Economic Analysis of Mixed Crop–Livestock Farming', *Agricultural Systems*, **48**: 515–30.

Delgado, C.L. (1995), 'Agricultural Diversification and Export Promotion in Sub-Saharan Africa', *Food Policy*, **20**: 225–43.

De Steenhuijzen Piters, C.B. (1995), 'Diversity of Fields and Farmers', PhD. thesis, Wageningen Agricultural University, The Netherlands.

Ekbom, A. (1995), *The Economics of Soil Conservation in Kenya: A Case Study of the Economic and Agro-Economical Implications of Soil Conservation On Maize Cultivation in Muranga District, Kenya*, IIASA, Vienna.

Gerner, H. (1995), 'Farmers Facing Lower Returns from Fertilizer Use on Food Crops in West Africa', *African Fertiliser Market*, **8**, (3): 4–6.

Keddeman, W. (1991), *Cadre d'évaluation socio-economique et d'environnement au Sahel*, CESES, CILLS/NEI, Rotterdam.

Lutz, E., S. Pagiola and C. Reiche (1994), 'The Cost and Benefits of Soil Conservation: The Farmers' Viewpoint', *The World Bank Observer* **9**: 273-95.

Penning de Vries, F.W.T. and M.A. Djiteye (1991), *La productivité des pâturages sahéliens. Une Étude des sols, des végétations et de l'exploitation de cette ressource naturelle*, Centre for Agricultural Publishing and Documentation (Pudoc-DLO), Wageningen, The Netherlands.

Pretty, J. (1995), 'Integrated Crop Nutrition for Sustainable Agriculture: Technology and Policy Challenges', paper presented at IFPRI/FAO Workshop on Plant Nutrition Management, Food Security and Sustainable Agriculture, Viterbo, Italy, May.

Prudencio, C.Y. (1993), 'Ring Management of Soils and Crops in the West African Semi-Arid Tropics: The Case of the Mossi Farming System in Burkina Faso', *Agriculture, Ecosystems & Environment*, **47**: 237-64.

Rogers, E.M. (1983), *Communication of Innovations*, Free Press, New York.

Smaling, E.M.A., L.O. Fresco and A. de Jager (1996), 'Classifying and Monitoring Soil Nutrient Stocks and Flows in African Agriculture', *Ambio*, **25**, (8): 492-96.

SPAAR (1995), *ASTS Database, Special Program for African Agricultural Research*, World Bank, Washington, DC.

Stocking, M.A. (1986), 'The Cost of Soil Erosion in Terms of Loss of Three Major Elements', FAO Consultants Working Paper 3.

Stoorvogel, J.J. and E.M.A. Smaling (1990), 'Assessment of soil nutrient depletion in sub-Saharan Africa, 1983-2000', Report 28, DLO Winand Staring Centre for Integrated Land, Soil and Water Research (SC-DLO), Wageningen, The Netherlands.

van der Pol, F. (1992), 'Soil Mining: An Unseen Contributor to Farm Income in Southern Mali', Bulletin 325, Royal Tropical Institute (KIT), Amsterdam.

van der Pol, F. (1993), 'Analysis and Evaluation of Options for Sustainable Agriculture: With Special Reference to Southern Mali', in H. Reuler and W.H. Prins (eds), *The Role of Plant Nutrients for Sustainable Food Crop Production in Sub-Saharan Africa*, Reuler, VKP, Leidschendam, The Netherlands.

Windmeijer, P.N. and A. Andriesse (1993), 'Inland Valleys in West Africa: An Agro-Ecological Characterization of Rice-Growing Environments', Publication 52, ILRI, International Institute for Land Reclamation and Improvement, Wageningen, The Netherlands.

5 Analysis of Intensive Farming Systems in the European Union

F.M. Brouwer and P.J.G.J. Hellegers[a]

Introduction

Intensive farming systems with high output levels are generally characterized by high use of agro-chemicals. Rice production in Japan, for example, is characterized by intensive and small-scale farming practice with high input use per hectare. The area planted in Japan in 1991 constituted only 1.4 per cent of global area grown to rice, while share of global rice production was some 2.5 per cent, almost twice the share of planted area. Rice agro-chemical use in Japan, however, was more than 40 per cent of the global total (County NatWest WoodMac, 1992). Similar phenomena are observed in the European Union. The area planted to cereals in Western Europe constitutes approximately 8 per cent of the global total, but share in global cereals production in 1991 was some 18 per cent while share in cereals agro-chemicals use was some 55 per cent. High levels of productivity and input use are largely due to the intensive farming practices employed in this part of the world; land is used rather intensively in the EU compared to other continents. This phenomenon is reflected by a high input of labour or capital, or both. This high intensity of farming in Europe is also reflected by usage patterns of plant protection products and mineral fertilizers. Farming systems in the EU show a diverse pattern, however, with intensive systems that contribute largely to agricultural production. Contrary to this, highly extensive systems contribute largely to the provision of landscape and the maintenance of biodiversity and nature. Dehesas in Spain, for example,

[a] Agricultural Economics Research Institute (LEI-DLO), P.O. Box 29703, 2502 LS, The Hague, The Netherlands.

covers more than three million hectares and includes extensive arable cultivation and complementary silviculture (Brouwer and van Berkum, 1996).

This chapter investigates linkages between the use of agro-chemicals and the characteristics of farming systems in the EU. Issues of environment related to the use of agro-chemicals are briefly summarized as well. The objectives of the chapter are to examine present use of agro-chemicals in the EU on farms with intensive systems, and to relate the use of agro-chemicals to indicators that reflect farm structure and economic characteristics. The use of plant protection products in intensive farming systems is emphasized, as are linkages with mineral fertilizers. An assessment is made of the distribution of agro-chemicals use across intensive farming systems in the EU, which allows us to answer questions such as the following:

1   How is agro-chemicals use distributed among farms?
2   To what extent does high usage of agro-chemicals relate to the economic performance of intensive farming systems and to farm structure characteristics?
3   Is there a positive relationship between expenditures of plant protection products and mineral fertilizers?
4   What is the future scope for reducing use of agro-chemicals in European agriculture?

The assessment is based on the Farm Accountancy Data Network (FADN) of the European Commission, which uses the annual accounting results from a sample of commercial farms in EU member states. Commercial farms are those large enough to provide a farmer with a level of income sufficient to support a family (CEC, 1989). Results are based on the accounting year 1992/3. This sample includes almost 60 000 farms, but is representative of over four million farms in the European Union. The FADN contains farm level data on farm structure, total output and intermediate consumption, and purchases of fertilizers and plant protection products. Costs of plant protection products are an imperfect indicator of agro-chemicals use in terms of active ingredients. It is hypothesized that costs of plant protection products per hectare can be explained by the intensiveness of production and by cultivars.

Environmental Concerns and Use of Agro-chemicals in the EU

Several environmental concerns in Europe relate to the high use of agro-chemicals and the quality of water, air and soils; environmental targets are formulated in the Fifth Environmental Action Programme 'Towards Sustainability' (CEC, 1992). A significant reduction in the use of plant protection products is required and nitrate levels in groundwater need to be reduced through strict application of the nitrates directive. The effects of agro-chemicals on the environment are distinguished between plant protection products and nutrients.

There is empirical evidence that plant protection products pose a threat to the environment (Faasen, 1995). Patterns of agro-chemicals use differ throughout the EU, both among member states and among farming systems. The use of plant protection products across member states ranges from less than 3 kg of active ingredients per hectare (Denmark, Spain, Ireland and Portugal) to over 10 kg of active ingredients per hectare (Belgium and the Netherlands). Use is around the EU average of 4 kg of active ingredients per hectare in Germany and France. Levels are relatively high in Greece and Italy (6-8 kg/ha). Use of plant protection products is highest in areas of intensive farming, because of the risks of the occurrence of pests and diseases. Costs of using plant protection products are highest in regions with intensive horticulture, such as northern Italy, the south coast of France, the south-east coast of Spain and The Netherlands, and regions in France that emphasize specialist cereals and general field cropping (Brouwer *et al.*, 1994). Figure 5.1 gives an overall picture of the costs of plant protection products per hectare of utilized agricultural area (UAA). Costs of plant protection products are highest in regions that have an intensive crop production. On the Spanish plateau and in Wales, regions with a very extensive production system, the costs of plant protection products are rather low (less than 10 ECU/ha). In most regions with high costs of plant protection products, the main farming types are horticulture, fruit and citrus fruit and vineyards. Apart from these farming types, cereals are major crops in eastern England and general cropping is important in the Netherlands and Belgium. In the northern French regions, the high use of plant protection products per hectare is concentrated on specialist cereals and general field cropping (Brouwer *et al.*, 1994).

The quality of water is a major concern in areas of intensive livestock production. Nitrate levels of 50 mg/l (EU drinking water standard) and more may be expected in about 25 per cent of the agricultural soils in the EU, particularly in The Netherlands, Denmark, Belgium, Germany, the southern part of the United Kingdom, the Po Valley area in Italy, and western France (RIVM and RIZA, 1991). This is due to either the high surplus of nitrogen from agriculture or to vulnerability of the soil to leaching, or a combination of these two phenomena. Mineral balances are considered to be an important tool for providing insights into the flows of nitrogen in agriculture. They include input (for example, manure and fertilizers) as well as output

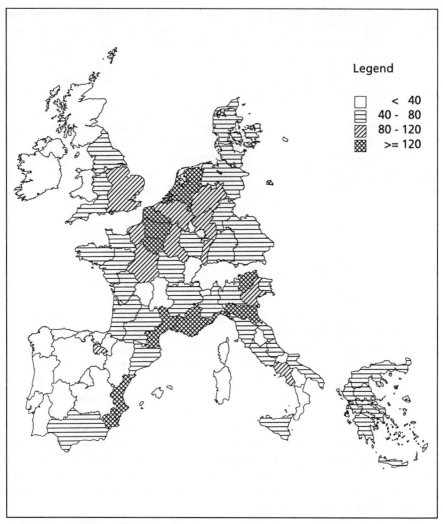

Source: Brouwer *et al.* (1994).

Figure 5.1   Costs of plant protection products, utilized agriculture area (ECU/ha)

components (such as uptake by crops). Nitrogen surplus includes the total amount of nitrogen from mineral fertilizer, animal manure and deposition from the atmosphere, minus the uptake of nitrogen by harvested crops. The nitrogen surplus exceeds 125 kg/ha in Belgium, large areas of Germany (Schleswig-Holstein, Niedersachsen, Nordrhein-Westfalen, Bavaria), France

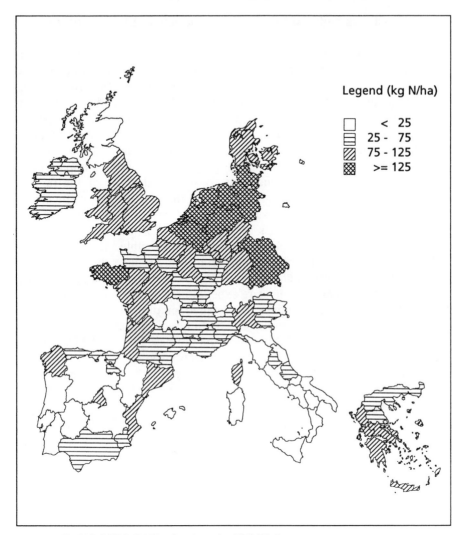

Source: FADN-CCE-DG VI/A-3; adaptation LEI-DLO.

Figure 5.2 Nitrogen surplus, by region, 1990–91 (kg N/ha)

(Brittany) and The Netherlands (Figure 5.2). The input of mineral fertilizers varies between 30 kg/ha (Portugal) and 220 kg/ha (The Netherlands). The supply of nitrogen from animal manure shows a larger variation and ranges between 40 kg/ha (Spain and Portugal) to almost 350 kg/ha (The Netherlands) (Brouwer *et al.*, 1995).

Use of Fertilizers and Plant Protection Products in EU Agriculture

Total costs of plant protection products by agriculture in EU12 in 1992/3 amounted to ECU 5.7 billion (Table 5.1), which is about 7 per cent above the average costs of the three-year period 1988/9–1990/91 (Brouwer *et al.*, 1994). Expenditures decreased during that period by almost 15 per cent, both in Germany and in Spain. Use of inorganic fertilizers also varies across countries and farming systems. Total costs of fertilizers and of plant protection products in the EU are highest for arable farms.

The application of agro-chemicals largely depends on the cropping plan, its intensity, climatological conditions, professional skills of the farmer, market and price supports and regulations on the use of agro-chemicals, as well as availability and price of such products. Costs of agro-chemicals on a per hectare basis in all countries are highest for horticulture farms (Table 5.2), but differences across countries remain considerable.

Expenditures on fertilizers and plant protection products on a per hectare basis are highest in The Netherlands. Differences across farming types are also large in that country. Per hectare expenditures on agro-chemicals are the highest for horticulture holdings. A detailed picture of the use of plant protection products (in kilograms of active ingredients) at the farm level is available by farming type (Table 5.3). Data are based on the FADN of The Netherlands. The average use of plant protection products on arable farms amounts to 16 kg of active ingredients per hectare. It is highest (more than 50 kg/ha) for farms with mushrooms and greenhouse floriculture, and lowest (around 1 kg/ha) for farms with grazing livestock. Average use of plant protection products amounts to 9 kg/ha. This includes all farms represented by the sample in The Netherlands and total size of their utilized agricultural area, including arable crops, permanent crops and forage crops.

The use intensity of plant protection products can be linked to key economic indicators in farming. The ratio between costs of agro-chemicals and total costs reflects the intensity of using this kind of inputs in agriculture. When the ratio of the costs of plant protection products to total costs is high, the incentive to reduce costs in relation to risks is likely to be stronger than in the case when the ratio is low. The use intensity of plant protection products in The Netherlands is highest (7 per cent) for arable farms. Although the use of plant protection products exceeds 30 kg/ha for greenhouse vegetables, greenhouse floriculture and mushrooms, intensity is less than 2 per cent. Among other reasons, this is due to the high costs of energy used to grow crops in greenhouses. Thus the incentive to achieve a reduction on plant protection products is likely to be higher for arable farms than for those with mushrooms, greenhouse vegetables or floriculture.

Farming intensity is related to expenditures on plant protection products,

Table 5.1   Total costs of fertilizer and plant protection products, by farming type in the EU, 1992–3 (m. ECU)

Country	Costs of fertilizers					Costs of plant protection products				
	Arable	Horticulture	Grazing	Other farms	All types	Arable	Horticulture	Grazing	Other farms	All types
Belgium	34	36	85	55	210	43	19	28	50	140
Denmark	142	17	64	71	293	87	9	35	50	180
Germany	260	57	448	289	1 054	249	64	126	204	643
Greece	173	120	12	18	324	119	109	2	5	235
Spain	427	220	53	37	738	136	204	8	12	360
France	1 177	237	768	466	2 649	1 156	452	214	314	2 138
Ireland	40	–	291	33	364	31	–	21	16	68
Italy	606	408	118	109	1 240	381	429	31	50	891
Luxembourg	–	–	10	1	11	–	–	2	1	3
Netherlands	79	153	168	20	420	148	122	25	20	314
Portugal	94	35	34	37	200	42	39	5	10	95
United Kingdom	438	40	425	137	1 040	493	29	55	85	662
EUR 12	3 471	1 324	2 476	1 273	8 543	2 884	1 477	552	816	5 729

Note: All types might differ from total of entries in row because of rounding off.

Source: FADN-CCE-DG VI/A-3; as adapted by LEI-DLO.

Table 5.2   Costs of fertilizer and plant protection products per hectare, by farming type in the EU, 1992–3 (ECU per hectare)

Country	Costs of fertilizers					Costs of plant protection products				
	Arable	Horticulture	Grazing	Other farms	All types	Arable	Horticulture	Grazing	Other farms	All types
Belgium	140	1 140	116	142	151	181	605	38	129	101
Denmark	115	782	96	85	106	70	391	52	59	65
Germany	107	280	93	94	100	102	315	26	66	61
Greece	104	108	61	68	100	71	98	10	20	72
Spain	54	85	19	31	51	17	79	3	10	25
France	123	177	76	102	104	121	338	21	69	84
Ireland	144	–	61	116	69	112	–	4	55	13
Italy	117	154	37	63	98	74	162	10	29	70
Luxembourg	–	–	97	88	96	–	–	20	36	29
Netherlands	134	1 532	143	98	203	251	1 214	21	98	152
Portugal	50	54	24	31	39	22	59	4	8	19
United Kingdom	93	588	39	78	60	105	433	5	48	38
EUR 12	97	151	61	82	85	81	169	14	53	57

Source: FADN-CCE-DG VI/A-3; as adapted by LEI-DLO.

Table 5.3 Use of plant protection products in The Netherlands, by farming type (kg of active ingredients/ha) and the intensity of total use (%), 1993–4

Farming type	Insecticides	Fungicides	Herbicides	Other	Total	Intensity
Arable farms	1.8	4.1	2.7	7.8	16.4	7.2
Grazing livestock	0.3	0.2	0.5	0.0	1.0	0.4
Field vegetables	1.8	5.0	2.0	9.1	17.9	2.9
Greenhouse vegetables	5.1	12.8	0.8	13.0	31.7	1.5
Greenhouse floriculture	10.9	18.5	1.3	27.5	58.2	1.4
Mushrooms	7.8	5.8	1.7	90.2	104.8	0.5
Orchard	2.4	24.1	3.5	3.3	33.2	3.9
Tree nursery	2.2	7.1	2.5	10.2	22.0	1.6
Average	1.3	2.4	1.5	3.7	8.9	1.6

Note: All types might differ from total of entries in row because of rounding off.

Source: Poppe *et al.* (1995).

and crop production is highest in regions that spend the most on plant protection products. This is explained by the fact that intensive cropping techniques may increase the occurrence of pests and diseases. Farmers may respond to this threat through the application of extra dosages of plant protection products in order to avert risks. Research in The Netherlands indicates that differences among farms with the lowest use of plant protection products and those with the highest application levels may be up to a factor of three to six (Vernooy, 1992).

Distribution of Agro-chemicals Use among Farms in the EU

Two farming types are considered in an assessment of the use of agro-chemicals among farms – cereal farms and horticulture farms. Use of plant protection products by cereal farms in the Paris Basin is relatively high compared to the level elsewhere in the European Union (Brouwer *et al.*, 1994). Purchased plant protection products for cereals in this region will be compared with the situation in Denmark, where expenditures on plant protection are below those in the Paris Basin. We also focus on horticulture holdings in the Andalucia region of Spain and in The Netherlands because of high usage levels in these regions.

In the central region of France, the share of costs of plant protection products in total costs increases as plant protection use per hectare rises. Family farm income per hectare is highest for the group of farms with a medium level of plant protection products (Table 5.4). Crop output per hectare of the utilized agricultural area increases with the rise in purchased

Table 5.4   Cereal farm structure and output characteristics, by utilized agricultural area, central France, 1992–3

	Low[a]	Medium[b]	High[c]	All
Purchased plant protection (ECU/ha)	75	121	167	122
Purchased fertilizer (ECU/ha)	105	122	129	119
Crop output (ECU/ha)	770	1 006	1 143	975
Economic size (ESU/ha)[d]	0.5	0.6	0.7	0.6
Family farm income (ECU/ha)	170	246	226	215
Farm net value added (ECU/ha)	301	399	418	374
Share of plant protection costs (%)	11	14	17	14
Utilized agricultural area (ha)	90.0	99.6	93.7	94.7
of which forage crops (%)	18	7	2	9
of which cereals (%)	65	72	77	71
of which other field crops (%)	17	21	21	20

Notes:
[a] One-third of farms with lowest plant protection costs per ha.
[b] One-third of farms with intermediate expenditures on plant protection costs per ha.
[c] One-third of farms with highest per ha UAA expenditures on plant protection.
[d] One ESU equals 1200 ECU of standard gross margin.

Source: FADN-CCE-DG VI/A-3; adaptation by LEI-DLO.

plant protection products. The share of forage crops is highest for the lowest group.

In Denmark, differences in purchased plant protection per hectare are modest across the groups distinguished (Table 5.5). Expenditures of plant protection products for the lowest group are only 1 per cent of total costs. The share of cereals and of other field crops in total UAA increases with the rise in purchased plant protection products, at the expense of forage crops.

Expenditures on plant protection in the EU are highest in regions specializing in horticulture and regions in France that emphasize cereals and general field cropping (Brouwer *et al.*, 1994). For horticulture holdings, costs of plant protection fluctuate from less than ECU 500/ha in Denmark and eastern England to more than ECU 1000/ha in the region of Liguria in Italy and The Netherlands (Table 5.6). The following data are used in Table 5.6.

- Cost of plant protection products per hectare of utilized agricultural area (ECU/ha), which gives an indirect idea of the intensity of production.
- Cost of plant protection products per 100 ECU of output, which presents the share of the costs of plant protection products in the value of output.
- Cost of plant protection products per 100 ECU of farm net value

Table 5.5 Cereal farm structure and output characteristics, Denmark, 1992-3

	Low[a]	Medium[b]	High[c]	All
Purchased plant protection (ECU/ha)	14	48	91	59
Purchased fertilizer (ECU/ha)	107	109	136	120
Crop output (ECU/ha)	471	695	896	730
Economic size (ESU/ha)[d]	0.6	0.7	0.7	0.7
Family farm income (ECU/ha)	−421	−293	−270	−313
Farm net value added (ECU/ha)	−93	158	186	111
Share of plant protection costs (%)	1	4	7	5
Utilized agricultural area (ha)	18.5	25.9	34.4	26.3
of which forage crops (%)	11	4	2	5
of which cereals (%)	82	83	84	83
of which other field crops (%)	6	11	11	10

Notes: As for Table 5.4.

Source: FADN-CCE-DG VI/A-3; adaptation by LEI-DLO.

added (FNVA), which provides information on the share of costs of plant protection products relative to FNVA.

● Cost of plant protection products per 100 ECU of family farm income (FFI), which reflects the share of the costs of plant protection products relative to FFI.

● Cost of plant protection products per 100 ECU of input, which indicates the share of costs of plant protection products in total costs (that is, intermediate consumption, depreciation and external factors).

● Number of represented farms, which reflects the relative importance of a farming type in a region.

● Economic farm size (ESU), which is based on utilized agricultural area (UAA) as well as on the intensity of the cropping plan and the livestock population of the holding. One European size unit (ESU) equals 1200 ECU of standard gross margin.

● Cropping plan (area of different crops in percentage of UAA), which provides the share of crops in total UAA, indicating crops with high or low use of plant protection products.

● Output of crop products per hectare of crop (ECU per hectare) (exclusive of forage crops), which provides information on the intensity of production.

A more detailed investigation of horticulture in The Netherlands and in Andalucia is provided in Tables 5.7 and 5.8. The sample of farms in these two regions is around 15 000. Expenditures on plant protection products range from ECU 550/ha (Andalucia) to almost ECU 1500/ha (The

Table 5.6   General characteristics of horticulture, 1992–3

Country/region	No. of farms	Economic farm size (ESU)	UAA (ha) per farm	Costs of plant protection (ECU/ha)	Costs of plant protection per 100 ECU of			
					output	FNVA	FFI	input
Belgium	5 080	60	3.2	725	2	5	8	3
Denmark	1 670	101	6.4	479	1	3	35	2
Spain								
Andalucia	14 580	17	2.9	546	6	8	13	9
France								
Alpes Côte								
d'Azur	5 580	76	6.4	577	3	7	14	4
Italy								
Liguria	8 330	25	0.9	1 050	2	4	5	5
Netherlands	15 192	145	4.5	1 469	2	6	20	2
United Kingdom								
Eastern								
England	2 280	62	9.4	456	2	5	23	2

Source: FADN-CCE-DG VI/A-3; adaptation by LEI-DLO.

Netherlands), while the average share of plant protection costs in total costs ranges between 2 per cent (The Netherlands) and 9 per cent (Andalucia).

The use of plant protection products on horticulture holdings may differ widely across individual farms. Average use might be high for a specific farming type, but the distribution within a group of farms might be wide as well. In The Netherlands, the distribution ranges from less than ECU 500/ha for the group of farms with the lowest purchases of plant protection products per hectare of UAA to around ECU 5500/ha for the group with the highest plant protection costs per hectare. The share of plant protection costs in The Netherlands is fairly stable (2 per cent) across the groups considered.

The share of market gardening and flowers in the specialist horticulture sector is around 70 per cent, both in The Netherlands and in Andalucia. Market gardening and flowers consist of a large number of heterogeneous products, produced according to different production processes: crops grown in the open or under shelter, irrigated or non-irrigated areas, vegetables or flowers. The share of protected crops within market gardening and flowers varies greatly among the areas considered, from almost 80 per cent in The Netherlands to approximately 50 per cent in Andalucia. The share of sheltered market gardening and flowers in the 'lowest' group is small in The Netherlands, whereas 90 per cent of market gardening and vegetables in the 'highest' group are produced under shelter (Table 5.7).

Farming systems in Andalucia, on average, are much less intensive than

Table 5.7 **Farm structure and output characteristics on horticultural farms in The Netherlands, 1992-3**

	Low[a]	Medium[b]	High[c]	All
Purchased plant protection (ECU/ha)	461	1 595	5 616	1 469
Purchased fertilizer (ECU/ha)	385	2 812	8 604	2 157
Crop output (ECU/ha)	23 958	81 735	293 117	76 197
Economic size (ESU/ha)[d]	11.6	34.1	119.8	32.4
Family farm income (ECU/ha)	4 166	10 908	14 987	7 444
Farm net value added (ECU/ha)	9 735	30 177	92 982	26 577
Share of plant protection costs (%)	2	2	2	2
Utilized agricultural area (ha)	8.1	3.6	1.8	4.5
of which (%)				
open market gardening & flowers	68	61	8	58
sheltered market gardening & flowers	3	15	75	16
forage crops	9	12	14	10
cereals	–	–	–	–
other field crops	–	–	–	–

Notes: As for Table 5.4.

Source: FADN-CCE-DG VI/A-3; adaptation by LEI-DLO.

they are in The Netherlands. Plant protection costs in Andalucia range from less than ECU 150/ha for the group of farms with the lowest purchased plant protection products per hectare of UAA to around ECU 1000/ha for the group of farms with the highest purchased plant protection products per hectare of UAA (Table 5.8). The share of plant protection costs in total costs of specialist horticulture holdings in Andalucia increases from 6 per cent (for the 'low' group) to 11 per cent (for the 'high' group). The share of sheltered market gardening and flowers in total UAA is only 32 per cent for the lowest group but 84 per cent for the highest group (Table 5.8); the share of sheltered market gardening and flowers is only 8 per cent for the 'medium' group. The share of open market gardening and flowers, in total UAA, is around 90 per cent for the group of horticulture farms in Andalucia.

The incentive to achieve a reduction in plant protection expenditures is likely to be highest on farms where these costs are a considerable part of total input costs. These costs exceed 10 per cent in specialist cereal farms in central France and the group of horticulture farms in Andalucia with highest plant protection costs per hectare.

Figures presented so far have focused on specialist cereals and specialist horticultural crops. Some characteristics of horticultural forms specializing in growing specific crops, in this case tomatoes, are provided in Table 5.9. For The Netherlands and Campania (Italy) plant protection costs per hectare of UAA in The Netherlands are some ten times greater than in Campania, but

Table 5.8   **Farm structure and output characteristics on horticultural holdings in Andalucia, 1992–3**

	Low[a]	Medium[b]	High[c]	All
Purchased plant protection (ECU/ha)	146	678	1 065	546
Purchased fertilizer (ECU/ha)	233	743	1 160	628
Crop output (ECU/ha)	6 272	10 993	14 694	9 888
Economic size (ESU/ha)[d]	5.2	4.0	9.8	5.9
Family farm income (ECU/ha)	4 052	3 581	4 757	4 059
Farm net value added (ECU/ha)	5 024	7 297	9 111	6 773
Share of plant protection costs (%)	6	9	11	9
Utilized agricultural area (ha)	4.0	2.7	2.1	2.9
of which (%)				
open market gardening & flowers	4	91	14	36
sheltered market gardening & flowers	32	8	84	36
forage crops	1	1	2	1
cereals	13	–	–	5
other field crops	50	–	–	21

Notes: As for Table 5.4.

Source: FADN-CCE-DG VI/A-3; adaptation by LEI-DLO.

crop output per hectare is about 25 times that of Campania. Farming conditions in both areas largely differ because the share of sheltered market gardening in total UAA is 96 per cent in The Netherlands, but only 2 per cent in Campania. In Campania, more than 90 per cent of production is on open fields.

Scope for Reducing Use of Agro-chemicals

There is a general tendency in the European Union towards a lower use of agro-chemicals. This holds both for mineral fertilizers and for plant protection products (see Chapter 1 of the present volume). Consumption of nitrogen fertilizers in Europe diminished by some 30 per cent over a period of only five years. Similar reduction levels were observed in the use of phosphates (45 per cent) and potassium (45 per cent). Consumption of fertilizers during that period increased mainly in Asia, and was fairly stable in the United States. Mineral fertilizers in The Netherlands, for example, were partly replaced by animal manure, especially in arable crop production. Important factors in reducing reliance on chemical nutrients in The Netherlands included an increasing awareness among farmers of environmental problems due to farming practices. A more rational use of agro-chemicals has been achieved partly in response to this change; at the

Table 5.9   **Structure of farms with at least 75 per cent of UAA used for tomatoes in The Netherlands and in Campania, 1992–3**

	Netherlands	Campania
Purchased plant protection (ECU/ha)	4 260	397
Purchased fertilizer (ECU/ha)	9 037	495
Crop output (ECU/ha)	266 601	9 810
Economic size (ESU/ha)	126.5	10.0
Family farm income (ECU/ha)	− 20 485	6 628
Farm net value added (ECU/ha)	71 829	6 910
Share of plant protection costs (%)	1	13
Utilized agricultural area (ha)	1.9	0.7
of which (%)		
sheltered market gardening	96	2
tomatoes	96	94

Source: FADN-CCE-DG VI/A-3; adaptation by LEI-DLO.

same time, agricultural policy currently aims to promote a move towards less intensive farming practices. The system of milk quotas, for example, has stimulated extensification of dairy production, because of the autonomous increase of productivity. Reliance on fertilizers has also been reduced on dairy farms, while linkages between agricultural production and fertilizers may change in response to stricter regulation on the treatment and application of organic fertilizers.

Annual sales of plant protection products (in kilograms of active ingredients) have been reduced by some 15 per cent since the mid-1980s (Brouwer *et al.*, 1994). There are several plausible reasons for this reduction, including use of dosages that require smaller amounts of chemicals to prevent or treat diseases. For example, sales of herbicides to cereals growers decreased as a result of this chemical substitution process. Climate and weather conditions also affect the use of chemicals to prevent pests and diseases. The use of fungicides, for example, is high in the northern part of Italy, compared to countries like Spain and Portugal. This is due, among others reasons, to the relatively high precipitation levels in that part of Italy, while relatively dry and hot summers in recent years have reduced the use of fungicides in Portugal and Spain.

A third factor is better farm management and employment of modern spraying equipment, which contributes to reductions in the application of agro-chemicals. Further, agricultural policy increasingly encourages less intensive farming practices by subjecting direct payments to conditions regarding the intensity of farming and the treatment of inputs. Council Regulation 2078/92, for example, includes incentives that encourage farmers to use production methods that are more benign with respect to the environment or that conserve the environment and landscape. These measures involve a significant reduction in the use of agro-chemicals in crop production. Finally, consumers are demanding foods that have been grown with fewer pesticides.

Conclusions

Expenditures on fertilizer and plant protection products in the EU vary widely across countries, between farming types within the countries considered and across groups of farms within a farming type in a country. Average expenditures on plant protection products per hectare in the EU12 are lowest for pastures and highest for horticulture, yet 50 per cent of all expenditures on plant protection products are accounted for by arable farms. Structural characteristics of farming practices such as the cropping plan, the production method (sheltered) and the intensity of crop production (number of harvests) determine the distribution of expenditures on plant protection among farms. The use of agro-chemicals depends also on climatological conditions, farm management (skills of farmers), prices and regulations. The share of plant protection costs in total costs serves as an indicator of the incentive to achieve savings by reducing the input of plant protection products. Intensity of use of plant protection products on arable farms in The Netherlands is higher than for horticulture. Finally, there is a tendency towards lower use of agro-chemicals in Europe, induced not only by environmental policy regulations but also by agricultural policy and environmental awareness among farmers. Information about agro-chemicals and improved farm management methods are important in reducing agro-chemical use.

Positive links between expenditures on plant protection and on fertilizers can be detected, with correlation coefficients of 0.98 and 0.86 for horticulture in The Netherlands and Andalucia, respectively. Output of crop production is highest in regions and farming systems with relatively high costs of agro-chemicals. Correlation coefficients among expenditures for plant protection products and crop output are highest in The Netherlands (0.99), although they are also high in Andalucia (0.65).

References

Brouwer, F.M. and S. van Berkum (1996), *CAP and Environment in the European Union: Analysis of the Effects of the CAP on the Environment and Assessment of Existing Environmental Conditions in Policy*, Wageningen Press, Wageningen,

The Netherlands.

Brouwer, F.M., I.J. Terluin and F.E. Godeschalk (1994), 'Pesticides in the EC', *Onderzoekverslag 121*, Agricultural Economics Research Institute (LEI-DLO), The Hague.

Brouwer, F.M., F.E. Godeschalk, P.J.G.J. Hellegers and H.J. Kelholt (1995), 'Mineral Balances at Farm Level in the European Union', *Onderzoekverslag 137*, Agricultural Economics Research Institute (LEI-DLO), The Hague.

Commission of the European Communities (CEC) (1989), *Farm Accountancy Data Network: An A to Z of Methodology*, Commission of the European Communities, Brussels.

Commission of the European Communities (CEC) (1992), *Towards Sustainability: A European Community Programme of Policy and Action in Relation to the Environment and Sustainable Development*, Commission of the European Communities, Brussels.

Council Regulation (EEC) 2078/92 of 30 June 1992 on 'Agricultural Production Methods Compatible with the Requirements of the Protection of the Environment and the Maintenance of the Countryside', *Official Journal of the European Communities*, L215/85.

County NatWest WoodMac (1992), *The Agro-chemical Service: Reference Section, County NatWest Woodmac*, The NatWest Investment Bank Group, Edinburgh.

Faasen, R. (1995), 'Agricultural Pesticide Use a Threat to the European Environment?', *European Water Policy Control*, 5(2): 34–40.

Poppe, K.J., F.M. Brouwer, J.P.P.J. Welten and J.H.M. Wijnands (eds) (1995), 'Landbouw milieu en economie: editie 1995', *Periodieke Rapportage 68–93*, Agricultural Economics Research Institute (LEI-DLO), The Hague.

RIVM and RIZA (1991), 'Sustainable Use of Groundwater Resources: Problems and Threats in the European Communities', Report 600025001, National Institute of Public Health and Environmental Protection, Bilthoven, The Netherlands.

Vernooy, C.J.M. (1992), 'Op weg naar een schonere glastuinbouw 2: het verbruik van gewasbeschermingsmiddelen op praktijkbedrijven', *Publikatie 4.132*, Agricultural Economics Research Institute (LEI-DLO), The Hague.

PART II
AGRO-CHEMICALS USE AND
SUSTAINABLE AGRICULTURE

6 Agro-chemicals Use and Sustainable Agriculture: Some Observations from a Semi-arid Area of India[1]

B.N. Hiremath and K. Singh[a]

Introduction

For crops such as rice and wheat, the introduction and widespread use of high-yielding varieties and associated practices in India gave birth to what is popularly known as the 'green revolution'. The green revolution placed emphasis on the intensive use of agro-chemicals, notably fertilizers and plant protection chemicals in conjunction with irrigation water. It is no surprise that the greatest successes have been in areas with assured irrigation facilities with the green revolution having, in turn, laid the foundation for the socioeconomic development of irrigated areas in rural India. There is less scope for replicating the green revolution technologies in rainfed areas, especially semi-arid areas. Farming systems in such areas are highly location-specific and require new technologies and strategies suited to their micro environments based on indigenous knowledge and skills.

It is estimated that in India by the year 2000 about one billion people will have to be fed and the food requirement will be 240–250 million tonnes (mt). The incremental food production required is estimated to be 1.4 to 2 tonnes per hectare. With limited scope for expanding land under cultivation, it will be necessary to apply modern technologies, including improved seeds,

[a] Institute of Rural Management, P.O. Box 60, Anand 388 001, Gujarat, India.

fertilizers, pesticides and irrigation (Chadha, 1995). Empirical studies reveal that diffusion of fertilizer consumption is widespread. Fertilizer use had been extended to more than 85 per cent of irrigated lands and about 50 per cent of unirrigated lands by 1988–9. Between 1970 and 1989, the rate of diffusion of fertilizers was higher in the unirrigated lands than in the irrigated lands. This narrowed the difference in fertilizer diffusion between the two types of land (Hanumantha and Gulati, 1994).

With an inelastic supply of farmyard manures and the high opportunity cost of growing green manure, increased use of chemical fertilizers is required to increase agricultural production. Already there is mounting evidence that fertilizer response declined through the 1980s (see Vidya, 1995), with excessive use of fertilizers in some areas (Sah and Shah, 1992). The excessive use of nitrogenous fertilizers relative to phosphates and potash fertilizers has resulted in imbalances in the ratio of NPK nutrients (Vidya, 1995).

The need to further increase food production has not lost its urgency, but concerns are emerging over the ecological effects of the new technologies and the sustainability of these technologies. A rapidly increasing population and the consequent need to increase agricultural productivity, on the one hand, and concerns for conservation and sustainable management of natural resources, on the other, are seen as conflicting objectives (Reddy, 1995). Ecological and environmental concerns have necessitated development of technologies that are based on low use of chemical inputs for increasing productivity while protecting natural resources (Shetty, 1995).

Use of chemicals in agriculture is not yet a serious environmental problem in India, particularly in the arid regions, but for the rural population that depends primarily on land for its livelihood the use of agro-chemicals to meet food requirements is unavoidable. The main objective of this chapter is to provide an understanding of the complex factors that determine the use of agro-chemicals in semi-arid areas of India.

Conceptual Framework

By 'sustainable agriculture' we mean a collection of production practices that enable agricultural productivity at a specified level to be continued or 'sustained' over a long time. The key element of sustainable agriculture is non-decreasing productivity in the long run. This involves, among other things, maintenance and improvement of soil fertility while minimizing the undesirable effects on the environment. There are a number of myths about sustainable agriculture, most often unfounded and sometimes partially correct, depending on the situation (Debertin, 1994). These myths include the following: (1) commercial farmers are interested in short-term profits and are least concerned about sustainability; (2) sustainable production practices always reduce farm profitability; (3) sustainable agriculture involves using reduced amounts of agro-chemicals; (4) farming practices that use no purchased inputs are sustainable and will not cause any harm to the environment; (5) most commercial farmers are opposed to sustainable agriculture; and (6) production systems that employ minimum or no tillage production practices are consistent with sustainable agriculture. Reluctance to adopt or slow adoption of sustainable agricultural practices are attributed to some of these myths.

Development experts have recommended a conceptual framework rooted in rural livelihood systems for understanding natural resource management strategies of Indian peasants. The basic premise of the framework is that, in order to reverse the environmental degradation in the semi-arid areas and to attain sustainability, the rural population itself must become the key actor in the development of new approaches. These new approaches, however, have to be understood and promoted in a practical context of the material and mental worlds wherein the farmers live – in the context of the rapidly changing livelihood systems.

The conceptual framework for understanding the rural systems was developed by Hoger (1994). It takes a holistic view of the occupation technology, tradition, cultural cognitive and social structures, and individual, family and societal orientations with reference to the sustainable use of natural resources. Thus the framework is helpful in recognizing the constraints and complexities of the relationship between natural resource management and the factors that influence the livelihoods of rural people. This framework is neither explanatory nor predictive, but it is developed to conceptualize the physical, social and emotional realities that influence decision making with respect to natural resources.

For example, agro-chemicals affect land and water quality and human health adversely but, at the same time, the resulting changes in crops and cropping systems may contribute directly to increases in income and indirectly to improvements in nutrition, education and health, among other things. On the other hand, deforestation has resulted in soil erosion, decreased availability of fodder and fuel, increased use of animal manure as fuel rather than as a soil improver, and increased use of agro-chemicals. Farmer awareness and perception of agro-chemicals, of risks and returns from the use of fertilizers and pesticides, of cultural and emotional attachment to land, water and forests, and of the family preferences for food, cash and social and religious events influence land use and management decisions.

This conceptual framework was used to investigate the following propositions for the tribal village of Mahudi located in a semi-arid region of Gujarat State, India: (1) farmers' different perceptions of the land resource influence their land use decisions; (2) depletion of forests has led to reduced soil fertility and increased use of agro-chemicals; and (3) occupational diversity (migration) has helped reduce the pressure on land, thus reducing the use of agro-chemicals.

Information from a current collaborative research study entitled Rural Livelihood Systems and Sustainable Natural Resource Management in Semi-Arid Areas at the Institute of Rural Management, Anand (IRMA) is employed. Primary data sources include a baseline survey, individual and group discussions, participatory rural appraisal exercises and case studies over a two-year period, 1993/4 to 1994/5. The focus of the data collection was not on use of agro-chemicals, but it did provide qualitative insights gained during the research study. Secondary sources of data on land holdings, fertilizer and pesticide use, food grain production and so on were obtained from the Economic Intelligence Service of the Centre for Monitoring the Indian Economy (CMIE). The data were analysed to establish the relationship among various factors affecting the use of agro-chemicals.

Profile of the Study Area

Mahudi village lies in the Panchamahal district of Gujarat. The village has an area of 797 hectares and comprises 16 hamlets. About 60 per cent of the total area is under cultivation, 34 per cent is covered by forest, and the remaining land is in other uses, including grazing. There are 65 private and 10 public wells used for both domestic consumption and irrigation purposes. About 21 per cent of the total land is irrigated by wells and a checkdam. There are 3470 people living in 528 households. The average family size is 6.6 and the average landholding is 2.46 acres. Approximately 92 per cent of households own some livestock, with an average of 5.5 animals per household (excluding poultry).

Mahudi is dominated by the *Bhil* tribe, which has historically been a nomadic tribe, depending on rudimentary agriculture and forests that together satisfied food, fodder, fuel, housing and other requirements. Today, the land that was once considered relatively fertile has deteriorated as a consequence of deforestation leading to scarcity of fuel, fodder and other forest products. Scarcity of fuelwood in turn has resulted in increasing use of cow dung cakes as fuel that otherwise was used as farmyard manure to maintain soil fertility. At present, subsistence agriculture, supplemented by income generated from seasonal migration, is the mainstay of their livelihoods.

Ruthless cutting of trees and indiscriminate grazing over many decades has accelerated soil erosion through wind and water. To prevent soil and wind erosion, stone bunding is now practised. Two hamlets, Sonasar and Sukimali, have also adopted watershed management and mulching practices to preserve soil fertility and moisture.

The main crops grown during the rainy season are local indigenous varieties of maize, pigeon pea, paddy and millet crops *kuri* and *sama*. During the winter, high-yielding varieties of wheat (*Sonalika* and *Lokvan*) and Bengal gram crops are grown. In most hamlets without irrigation, a second crop is grown utilizing the residual moisture from the rainy season. Thus gram with its deep roots is preferred in winter to shallow rooting wheat. In 1992, the check dam built across the Machchan river facilitated growing three crops a year in Bhorej. With an increase in water availability, wheat is preferred to gram in the winter season. During the summer, the Bhorej farmers grow groundnuts, green gram, soybean and vegetables under irrigation. Owing to multiple cropping, high-yielding varieties of seeds, chemical fertilizers and pesticides are now used, though on a limited scale. However, despite the introduction of new technology, the farmers generally feel that crop yields are now much lower as compared to earlier days. This they attribute mainly to the shortage of farmyard manure.

Study Results: Macro and Micro

National Considerations

India is endowed with 329 million hectares of land of which 142 million hectares are under cultivation. The irrigation potential in India is 114 million hectares, but at present only 70 million hectares are utilized. About 99 million hectares are under rainfed agriculture, accounting for 70 per cent of the total cultivated area. Even when the full irrigation potential is realized, over 50 per cent of the crop area will remain rainfed. The area under high-yielding varieties increased from one million to 55 million hectares between 1951/2 and 1993/4. Over the same period, fertilizer consumption increased from 0.06 million tonnes to 13.8 mt and pesticides from 250 to 82 000 mt (Table 6.1). On a per hectare cropped area basis, fertilizer consumption increased from about 0.6 kilograms to 75.9 kilograms over the same period of time. All these collectively have contributed to the increase in grain production from 55 to 192 mt (Table 6.1) (CMIE, 1994).

Table 6.1   **Trends in fertilizer consumption and food grain production in India**

Years	Fertilizer consumption (Mt of nutrients)				Food grain production Mt
	Nitrogen	Phosphate	Potash	Total	
1950–51	0.059	0.007	–	0.066	5.5
1960–61	0.212	0.053	0.029	0.294	82
1970–71	1.479	0.541	0.236	2.256	108
1980–81	3.678	1.214	0.624	5.516	130
1990–91	7.997	3.221	1.328	12.546	176
1993–94	9.650	3.200	1.000	13.850	192

Source: CMIE (1994).

Fertilizer use decisions of farmers under uncertainty with regard to alternative fertilizer policies have been compared for changes in cropping pattern, input use, sustainability and attitude towards risk for irrigated and dry land farming systems (Babu *et al.*, 1991). The results indicate that farmyard manure is a marginally risk-reducing input in both irrigated and dry land farming systems. Chemical fertilizers and farmyard manure are substituted for each other more in irrigated farming than in dry land farming. Further, the study shows that relaxing the constraint on chemical fertilizers through subsidization policies enabled farmers to invest in the production of risky cash crops. Babu *et al.* (1991) argue that fertilizer policy should consider differences in farming systems and risk attitudes of farmers towards input demand and output supply decisions, and that such considerations would enhance the success of agricultural and price policies.

On the pesticide front, the use of pesticides has shown a steady increasing trend both in terms of quantity and of coverage. Between 1956 and 1984, plant protection coverage increased from 2.4 to 80 million hectares and the quantity from 200 tonnes to 72 000 tonnes (Alagh, 1988). In India, the debate over pesticide use is framed in a dichotomy: prevention of human and environmental poisoning versus increased food grain production and control of insect-borne diseases. Although pesticide consumption in India is only 20 per cent of the world's consumption, indiscriminate use of pesticides led to a higher number of deaths, health hazards, pest resistance and environmental pollution (Vyas, 1994; Chopra, 1994). Analysis of the effects of pesticides reveals that increasing pesticide use does not boost food grain production over the long run, but instead leads to the resurgence of both target and secondary pests (Vishwanathan, 1991). An earlier study by Desai (1970) concludes that the use of yield-increasing inputs, such as fertilizers and water, shifts the demand for pesticides upward because their use on high-value crops generally results in a higher incidence of pests and because it raises yield expectations.

Experience from some of the 46 model dry land watershed development projects in India indicate that such integrated efforts can be successfully replicated to bring about soil and moisture conservation, improved socioeconomic conditions for farmers and ecological benefits. On the basis of a study of a watershed in Karnataka State, Singh (1991) concludes that institutional arrangements and efforts are needed for selecting, screening, releasing technologies, facilitating, coordinating and implementing watershed development programmes. He notes that the project had a positive impact on crop yields, net benefits from crops and availability of water in the project area. The project was financially viable even when the benefits from crops alone were taken into account, and those from horticulture and social forestry activities were not considered. In another study, Singh (1995) found that the watershed management is most appropriate for sustainable agriculture in dry lands.

Results for Mahudi Village

Consider the three propositions put forward earlier in this chapter, and what can be said about them based on the village-level case study.

Proposition 1: farmers' different perceptions of the land resource and themselves as peasants influence their land use decisions. The people of Mahudi perceive land in different ways and at different levels. Perceptions about land are expressed in such common anthropological terms as space, place and commodity. At one level, they view land as the space in which they live, including the pattern of their actions and activities: Mahudi itself is the space. It elicits a community feeling – 'ours'. At another level, land is viewed as place, the location of their home. Unlike most villages of Gujarat, where living places are separate from farms, Mahudi peasants locate their houses on their farms. The place (within the space) is one of the most intimately known parts of the space. Typically, it contains their hut, threshing floor, small yard, garden, fodder storage, animals, cattle shed and manure pit. Place elicits an individual or family feeling of belonging to 'me' or 'us'. Place gives a character to geographical reality by incorporating into it the family unit, the cognitive map of 'things' and the social network of caste, customs and kinship. Place is also a centre of economic activity, whether a market economy is present or not.

Land is seldom seen as a commodity by cultivators in India in general, and in Mahudi in particular. Most cultivators are unwilling to part with their land under any circumstances. Rather than perceiving land as an instrument of production, Mahudians display passionate attachment and loyalty to land since it is the backbone of their livelihoods. When a farmer was asked if he uses land for producing food or for earning profits, he responded, 'Certainly for food; there is no question of profit-oriented agriculture', but he added, '*Kheti paki to taji; nahitar fajeti.*' Literally translated, this means: 'If the crop harvest is good, life is merry; if not, it is melancholy.' Implicitly, one can observe dependency on land and the non-exploitave behaviour towards it. The villagers resent the exploitation of land on purely economic grounds.

Almost all the people of Mahudi, irrespective of their age or occupation, perceive themselves as peasants earning their living through crop and livestock production. The identity of peasant is stronger among the older generation of farmers than among their younger counterparts. Also the bond between land and people appears to be stronger among the older generations as their livelihoods were totally shaped by land-based activities. Access to job opportunities due to migration has resulted in the weakening of that relationship.

The younger generation finds migration more attractive than farming. Living in Mahudi, they are accustomed to putting cash in their pockets by earning Rs 20 to Rs 45 a day for unskilled labour. Cash gives them access to modern goods and amenities, such as clothes, wrist watches, cinemas and restaurants. This gives them a sense of command over their lives. The present generation's dependency on land is becoming partial. Their identity as peasants seems to originate from their belonging to the peasant family rather than from themselves. Increasingly, migration work is becoming a way of life and their perception of themselves as peasants is in turmoil.

Whether land is perceived as space or place determines the ultimate land use. When land is viewed as space, the attitude to land is one of indifference. In Mahudi, forests, grazing lands and other lands belonging to this category are (ab)used, but not cared for, by the people. When asked why they did not take care of the forests, one farmer replied, 'Sir, these trees belong to the forest department. "Ganchi" (oil-miller) took a contract from the government for cutting the trees, so we are outsiders, we can't refuse it.' When viewed as a place, their commitment to land is sincere, leading to its judicious use. It is this perception that inspires them to protect and maintain the productivity of land in the long run (Box 6.1). This behaviour becomes evident in the practices they have been following over the years: land preparation, soil and moisture conservation, choice of crops and varieties, mixed cropping and rotations, green manuring and use of agro-chemicals.

Box 6.1

Cow dung is better for maize, but we do not have a sufficient quantity for our farm. Excessive use of chemical fertilizers 'burns' soil and makes it hard ... Land becomes habituated to fertilizers. We apply both cow dung and chemical fertilizers like diammonium phosphate, urea and phosphate. These modern fertilizers spoil the land; but to get enough maize we have to apply chemical fertilizers. If we apply some chemical fertilizer once, we have to use more of it again the next year. Without it the crop will not be able to produce good yields. When chemical fertilizers are used, more ploughing is required to maintain the quality of land. (Jogi Tita Katara, farmer)

Proposition 2: depletion of forests has led to reduced soil fertility and increased use of agro-chemicals. Elderly farmers like Jwala Badiya Amaliyar (65 years) and Rupa Jokhana Katara (60 years) remember all too well how productive the land was when they were young and when their fathers were cultivating the same land. They remember the land was slightly more rocky and stony than it is today, but the forests were thicker. The availability of organic material for maintaining soil fertility was abundant, thanks to thick forests, availability of grazing lands and a higher cattle population per household. Therefore the average crop harvest from these lands was relatively high. Forests also provided all of the fuelwood necessary for cooking food and keeping them warm in winter, and almost all the cattle dung was available for manuring the fields. Animal manure became a substitute for fuelwood with growing deforestation, and farmers attribute the present low crop harvests mainly to deforestation.

The farming systems and land management practices observed in Mahudi are decisively traditional. To minimize the risks and depend on locally available inputs, farmers diversify their production through mixed cropping, intercropping and livestock husbandry. The value they place on land arises from their concern with the imperative of long-run survival, from their social, symbolic and religious beliefs and activities rather than from short-run economic gains. Therefore their preference is for meeting the family rather than market needs. Nearly 75 per cent of the farm produce is retained for home consumption, with the remainder being kept for seed purposes. Only a few farmers sell cereal grains (wheat and rice) after meeting their consumption requirements. More often than not, legume and oil seed crops are sold in the market for cash.

Over the years, frequent droughts and famines, with consequent poor cropping seasons, and a growing population have all gradually forced farmers to produce two crops a year on the same piece of land. As a consequence of double cropping, farmers have started to use farmyard manure, but the use of cow dung for fuel has resulted in a scarcity of farmyard manure for crop fields. Initially, this deficiency was made good by growing green manure crops, but this required sacrificing a rainy season crop. To avoid the loss of a food crop, farmers started using chemical fertilizers and pesticides to maintain yields (Box 6.2). At present in Mahudi, people use a mixture of manures and fertilizers and compost to maintain soil fertility. In addition, farmers grow shallow-rooted cereals and deep-rooted crops (legumes) in alternate years (crop rotation) and in the same season (intercropping and mixed cropping) to make use of moisture and nutrients from different soil depths. To maintain soil fertility, three plots of land are used, rotating green manure crops, farmyard manure and no manure. Farmers use fertilizers sparingly to supplement the natural fertility so that 'the soil does not become addicted and become hard'.

Box 6.2

Wheat is grown on levelled land and *gram* is grown on unlevelled land. *Gram* is a cash crop and is profitable on selling. We spray liquid pesticide on *gram* and white powder on maize. We do not spray pesticides on wheat and *mung*. Pigeon pea also requires pesticide. *Gram Sevak* (extension worker) advised us to use pesticides. (Rupa Jokhana Katara, farmer)

Proposition 3: occupational diversity (migration) has helped to reduce the pressure on land, thus reducing the use of agro-chemicals in the production process. Close scrutiny of Mahudi's history reveals that, until the late 1960s, Mahudi was a self-contained village with minimal dependence on external sources of income and employment. People were self-sufficient, they grew their food, built their houses, made their agricultural implements, clothes, ropes and so on, all from locally available raw materials. Over the years the population has been increasing steadily, and the animal population per household has declined along with the decline in forest area. The area under farming has now reached its limits, with further expansion of land for agriculture improbable. Land resources are under tremendous pressure to support the livelihoods of the existing households of Mahudi.

For most households, agriculture does not generate enough income to cover household expenditures. Since income from farming is inadequate and landholdings are too small, about 78 per cent of all households sell their surplus labour to augment their agricultural income. Workers migrate to affluent areas of Gujarat during the lean periods and off-seasons because of limited local opportunities. On average, a family earns between Rs 4000 and Rs 10 000 from unskilled migratory (60–90 days) work (Shylendra and Thomas, 1995). The income from non-farm migration work now exceeds 50 per cent of the total income from all sources and the time spent earning it is rising continuously.

Intensification of agriculture in Bhorej hamlet due to the development of irrigation facilities has reduced seasonal migration and high-value crops like legumes, oilseeds and vegetables have entered the cropping system. With the development of irrigation, there has been a noticeable increase in the use of fertilizer. In other hamlets without irrigation, seasonal migration to prosperous areas of Gujarat continues to increase. Income earned from migration is used for the purchase of food and clothes, social and religious events and the construction of houses, but little is invested in agriculture. Seldom does one come across farmers purchasing improved seeds, fertilizers and pesticides with the cash earned from migration. Increasing demand for unskilled and semi-skilled labour in urban areas has resulted in an assured and steady source of income that agriculture under arid conditions is unable to provide. Thus the dependence on land-based activities is on the decline, reducing the pressure on land in arid areas.

On the basis of the macro-level and micro-level evidence about agro-chemicals use in India's agriculture, it appears that there is a multitude of factors affecting their use. Some of the factors are internal to the peasant and others external. It is also evident from the village case study that, in the absence of adequate and balanced use of organic manure and chemical fertilizers, yields have been declining. Sustainable agriculture, therefore, requires adequate and balanced use of organic manures and chemical fertilizers and plant protection chemicals on a long-term basis. In semi-arid areas, the success of agro-chemicals is dependent as much on water management as on other factors.

Note

1   The authors wish to thank Anil Patel for his research assistance and Dr H.S. Shylendra for his helpful comments on an earlier draft.

References

Alagh, Y.K. (1988), 'Pesticides in Indian Agriculture', *Economic and Political*

Weekly, **23**(38): 1959–64.

Babu, Suresh Chandra, S.R. Subramanian and B. Rajasekaran (1991), 'Fertilizer and Organic Manure Use Under Uncertainty: Policy Comparisons for Irrigated and Dryland Farming Systems in South India', *Agricultural Systems*, **35**(1): 89–102.

Centre for Monitoring the Indian Economy (CMIE) (1994), *Basic Statistics*, The Centre, Bombay.

Chadha, K.L. (1995), 'Changing Scenario of Agro-Chemicals in Indian Agriculture', *UNI Agriculture Service,* **20**(33): 731–5.

Chopra, K.L. (1994), 'Pesticide Poisoning' (news reports), *UNI Agriculture Service,* **19**(31): 730.

Debertin, D.L. (1994), 'Sustainable Agriculture: Concepts, Definitions and Myths', mimeo, Department of Agricultural Economics, University of Kentucky, Lexington, Kentucky.

Desai, G.M. (1970), 'Factors Determining Demand for Pesticides', *Economic and Political Weekly*, **5**(52): A181–2.

Hanumantha, R.C.H. and A. Gulati (1994), 'Indian Agriculture: Emerging Perspectives and Policy Issues', *Economic and Political Weekly*, **29**(53): A158–69.

Hoger, R. (1994), 'The Family Universe: Towards a Practical Concept of Rural Livelihood Systems', working paper, Nadel University, Zurich.

Reddy, R.Y. (1995), 'Environment and Sustainable Agriculture Development: Conflicts and Contradictions', *Economic and Political Weekly*, **30**(12), supplement.

Sah, D.C. and A. Shah (1992), 'Efficiency of Fertiliser Use: Demand for Soil Testing Services in Gujarat', *Indian Journal of Agricultural Economics*, **47**(3): 459–67.

Shetty, P.K. (1995), 'Agriculture and Environment', *Ecology Environment, Ecology and Energy Conservation*, **9**(9): 13–17.

Shylendra, H.S. and P. Thomas (1995), 'Non-Farm Employment: Nature and Magnitude and Determinants in a Semi-Arid Village of Western India', *Indian Journal of Agricultural Economics*, **50**(3): 410–16.

Singh, K. (1991), 'Dryland Watershed Development and Management: A Case Study in Karnataka', *Indian Journal of Agricultural Economics*, **46**(2): 121–31.

Singh, K. (1995), 'The Watershed Management Approach to Sustainability of Renewable Common Pool Natural Resources: Lessons from India's Experience', Research Paper 14, Institute of Rural Management, Anand, India.

Vidya, S. (1995)' 'Fertilizer Use Efficiency in Indian Agriculture', *Economic and Political Weekly*, **30**(52): A160–80.

Vishwanathan, A. (1991)' 'Pesticides from Silent Spring to Indian Summer', *Economic and Political Weekly*, **26**(35): 2039–40.

Vyas, S.C. (1994), 'Pesticides Usage Problems and Remedies', *Farmer and Parliament*, **29**(11): 21–2.

7 Use and Abuse of Chemical Fertilizers in a Resource-scarce Economy: Karnataka Province, India

H.G. Hanumappa and D. Rajasekhar[a]

Introduction

The introduction of new agricultural technology in India during the 1960s generated a genuine feeling that small farmers faced difficulties in obtaining fertilizers at market prices, and that subsidies to the fertilizer industry were essential to increase domestic food production and stabilize foodgrains availability (Roy, 1990). A serious crisis in the balance of payments and growing fiscal deficit compelled the Indian government to reduce subsidies to the fertilizer industry, so prices increased dramatically (see Chapter 3 of the present volume).

In this chapter we examine the impact of the fertilizer price rise on efficiency of fertilizer consumption and crop production, using primary data for three villages in two districts of Karnataka Province in India. The districts were chosen after an intensive analysis of secondary data on the level and quality of irrigation, fertilizer consumption and cropping patterns. After averaging the figures on each of these variables for the 1980s, ranks were assigned based on the proportion of area under canals to total irrigated area (an indicator of quality of irrigation), proportion of net area irrigated to net area sown (an indicator of level of irrigation) and fertilizer use per hectare (in kilograms) for all the districts. The percentage area (average for

[a] Agricultural Development and Rural Transformation (ADRT) Unit, Institute for Social and Economic Change, Nagarbhavi, Bangalore – 560 072, India.

the 1980s) under important crops in the districts was also used. We selected districts with extremes in fertilizer consumption per hectare, thus choosing two villages in Bellary district representing (good quality) irrigated and semi-irrigated situations and high per hectare consumption of fertilizers, and a village in Dharwad district with low rainfall and irrigation, and less per hectare consumption of fertilizers. These two districts also differ with respect to crop diversification.

In the irrigated village (Ganikanahal in Bellary district), 90 per cent of the total cultivated area receives assured irrigation from the lower level canal of the Thungabhadra Project (TBP). The semi-irrigated village (Chaganur in Bellary district) also comes under TBP; but as the bulk of the land in this village is located at the tail end of a channel, it does not receive adequate water for cultivation. In the dry village (Huilgol in Dharwar district), most of the land depends upon uncertain and erratic rainfall, with area cultivated fluctuating according to the timing and amount of rainfall.

The methodology adopted for the selection of households for intensive survey was as follows. After obtaining census data on caste and land ownership of households in all the villages and using a stratified random sampling method based on caste and landholding, we selected 60, 76 and 61 households from the irrigated, semi-irrigated and dry villages, respectively. Households were interviewed using a structured questionnaire, which focused specifically on changes in consumption of fertilizers, cropping patterns and crop production for Rabi seasons (November to February) for 1990–91 and 1991–2 and Kharif seasons (June to October) for 1991–2 and 1992–3. In this chapter, we are concentrating solely on the Kharif season, for two reasons: (1) Kharif crops are important for the state (the bulk of the output is from Kharif crops) and (2) the increase in fertilizer prices (especially of phosphorus and potassium) has been most rapid since 1992. For convenience, the Kharif season of 1991–2 is referred to as the first season and that of 1993–4 as the second.

Fertilizer Application Trends in Karnataka

The rise in fertilizer consumption in India during the 1970s and 1980s has been attributed to adoption and spread of HYV seeds (which require and absorb larger quantities of fertilizers), state support to farmers in the form of public investments on rural electrification leading to well irrigation, provision of credit, subsidies to the fertilizer industry (which reduced prices) and popularization of the use of fertilizers through training and extension. The consumption of fertilizers in Karnataka, which was 22 000 tons in 1960–

61, increased from 344 000 tons in 1980–81 to 906 000 tons in 1991–2, but declined following the 1991 price increase to 812 000 tons in 1992–3 and to 805 000 tons in 1993–4 (Table 7.1). Per hectare consumption of fertilizers increased from 32.26 kg in 1980–81 to 76.51 kg in 1991–2, but declined in 1992–3. The increase in fertilizer consumption was due to stable nominal but declining real fertilizer prices during the 1980s, and the increase in irrigation and use of HYVs.

Although per hectare consumption in Karnataka is above the national average, it is nowhere near some of the agriculturally advanced states such as Punjab and Haryana, and per hectare consumption differs across districts in Karnataka. A positive correlation between level of fertilizer consumption and level and quality of irrigation in Karnataka implied that the diffusion rate and intensity are high in irrigated areas. Data from the farm management studies conducted by the Department of Agriculture (Govt of Karnataka) show that, among various crops, fertilizer applied to sugarcane is greatest (342 kg/ha) followed by HYV of maize (207 kg/ha) and of rice (167 kg/ha). These studies also indicate that an estimated 38 per cent of fertilizers were used in irrigated areas (which constituted 22.4 per cent of the gross cropped area in the state) as compared to 61 per cent consumption in the dry areas (constituting 72.6 per cent of gross cropped area). This is further corroborated by the fact that, though the majority of farmers in the dry districts were using fertilizers for dry crops, the consumption was quite low, at 38 kg per hectare, compared to the recommended dosage of 84 kg/ha (AFC, 1991).

Table 7.1 Fertilizer use in Karnataka Province, India

Year	Total (000s tons)	Kg/ha
1980–81	344	32.26
1981–82	384	35.99
1982–83	401	35.75
1983–84	487	42.46
1984–85	591	50.66
1985–86	556	46.65
1986–87	566	47.86
1987–88	558	45.61
1988–89	800	67.68
1989–90	779	64.31
1990–91	833	70.06
1991–92	906	76.51
1992–93	812	65.34

Source: Season and crop reports of Karnataka, for the years shown.

Finally, an overdose of fertilizers was also reported. In the case of irrigated paddy, out of 1161 farmers spread over 12 districts in Karnataka, 29 per cent used more than the recommended dosage of nitrogen, 27 per cent of phosphorus and 20 per cent of potassium during the period 1985–90 (Government of Karnataka, 1993). The ideal NPK ratio aggregated for the country as a whole is 4:2:1, but the current all India consumption ratio is 9.3:3:1. This is due to the continuation of subsidies for nitrogen.

Trends in Fertilizer Use in the Selected Villages

The per hectare consumption of fertilizers declined in all three villages of the study between the two seasons (Table 7.2). While the decline was steep in the irrigated and dry villages, it was marginal in the semi-irrigated village. Concerning the trends in NPK nutrients, the per hectare consumption of nitrogen and phosphorus declined in the irrigated and dry villages, while it increased in the semi-irrigated village. The consumption of potassium declined in the semi-irrigated and dry villages while it increased in the irrigated village. An overall decline in the consumption of fertilizers supports the argument that increased fertilizer prices would adversely affect application rates. But does it also result in a loss of welfare because of a decline in productivity? The productivity levels of important crops in the selected villages did not decline, except in the case of jowar, groundnut and sunflower in the semi-irrigated village (Table 7.3). This suggests that a decline in fertilizer consumption did not result in loss of welfare. On the evidence on fertilizer consumption in different stages of growth across crops, this was to some extent due to an improvement in the efficiency of fertilizer consumption.

Table 7.2   Fertilizer application (kg/acre)

Villages	N	P	K	Total
Irrigated village				
First season	80.06	36.82	19.65	136.53
Second season	77.68	25.57	22.23	125.48
Semi-irrigated village				
First season	39.82	28.29	15.44	83.54
Second season	43.62	29.30	9.27	82.19
Dry village				
First season	6.69	11.76	0.86	19.31
Second season	5.82	11.18	0.38	17.37

Table 7.3 Productivity of important crops, by season

Villages	Paddy	Jowar	Bajra	Groundnut	Sunflower	Cotton
			Per acre production (quintals)			
Irrigated village						
First season	13.08			4.92		
Second season	19.56			3.29		
Semi-irrigated village						
First season	13.41	7.19	3.90		3.00	4.98
Second season	19.95	6.59	5.68		2.58	5.23
Dry village						
First season	1.16		0.33	n.a.		
Second season	6.31		1.23	1.51		

Fertilizer Application across Stages of Crop Growth

Fertilizers are applied at various stages of crop growth. Normally, three stages are popular and the farmers refer to them as the sowing, vegetative and mature stages. In the irrigated village, the overall decline in application of fertilizers was not the same across the stages of crop growth. In general, the consumption of nitrogen and phosphorus declined at the sowing stage, while that of potassium increased. At the vegetative stage, the consumption of nitrogen and potassium increased, while that of phosphorus declined. At the maturity stage, the consumption of nitrogen, phosphorus and potassium declined (Table 7.4).

In the semi-irrigated village, the observed decline in the overall consumption of fertilizers is not true with regard to application of fertilizers across stages of crop growth. The pattern that emerges from this village is that the consumption of nitrogen at the sowing and vegetative stages, and phosphorus at the sowing stage had increased. But consumption of nitrogen

Table 7.4 Fertilizer application across stages of crop growth (kg/acre)

Villages	Sowing stage			Vegetative stage			Maturity stage		
	N	P	K	N	P	K	N	P	K
Irrigated village									
First season	16.23	17.87	7.07	26.20	10.56	6.36	37.64	8.37	6.21
Second season	10.17	9.76	7.71	32.19	9.89	7.54	25.05	5.12	6.19
Semi-irrigated village									
First season	8.92	19.83	7.76	21.61	7.07	6.20	9.29	1.38	1.48
Second season	12.46	23.48	4.27	26.39	3.77	3.58	4.78	2.05	1.42

at maturity stage, phosphorus at vegetative stage and potassium at all stages had declined.

In the dry village of Huilgol, fertilizers are applied only at the time of sowing. Hence an analysis of changes in fertilizer consumption at various stages of crop growth is not attempted for this village.

Fertilizer Applications across Farm Categories

Critics of the withdrawal of fertilizer subsidies argue that marginal and small farmers will be adversely affected by the price rise. With regard to size class, fertilizer use in the irrigated village, one notices a decline in the consumption of fertilizers in all the categories except in the case of large farmers. The decline has been substantial in the case of small and marginal farmers. With regard to per acre consumption of nitrogen, phosphorus and potassium across farm categories, there is no consistent trend. In general, the consumption of nitrogen and phosphorus declined, while that of potassium increased. This is true for all size categories except large farms, where use of nitrogen and potassium increased and that of phosphorus declined (Table 7.5).

In the semi-irrigated village, the observed decline in overall fertilizer use was also not the same across the farm categories. It declined in the case of the middle-size farms but increased in other farms. Such an increase was rapid in the case of small and marginal farmers.

In the dry village, an analysis of the per hectare application of fertilizers by size class shows that a decline in the overall use of fertilizers could be observed only in the case of small, middle and large farmers. There was an increase in the case of marginal farmers. This also holds true, more or less, in the case of fertilizer types (nitrogen, phosphorus or potassium) (Table 7.5).

Fertilizer Use by Crop Type

Those wishing to retain subsidies have also argued that increased fertilizer prices result in a decline in fertilizer use, not so much for irrigated and high-yielding crop varieties, but for dry land crops that are cultivated by the poor. In the irrigated village, the important crops are paddy, jowar, groundnut and cotton. HYVs are used in the case of paddy and cotton and improved varieties of seeds are used in the case of jowar and groundnut. Table 7.6 shows that the per acre application of fertilizers increased in the case of paddy and groundnut, but remained virtually the same in the case of cotton, declining in the case of jowar. The observed decline in the case of paddy is not the same across fertilizer types. Application of nitrogen and potassium

Table 7.5 Use of fertilizers by farm size (kg/acre)

Villages	Size of land (acres)	N	P	K	Total
Irrigated village					
Kharif, 1991–2	0–2.5	82.79	36.38	21.50	140.68
	2.5–5.0	85.95	35.73	17.78	139.46
	5.0–10.0	80.17	37.75	18.73	136.66
	10.0 & above	76.47	36.13	20.70	133.30
	average	**80.86**	**36.82**	**19.65**	**136.53**
Kharif, 1993–4	0–2.5	77.93	25.83	23.83	127.60
	2.5–5.0	71.24	25.39	25.49	122.12
	5.0–10.0	72.27	26.77	19.64	118.67
	10.0 & above	87.21	24.14	23.36	134.71
	average	**77.68**	**25.57**	**22.23**	**125.48**
Semi-irrigated village					
Kharif, 1991–2	0–2.5	25.83	13.42	14.58	53.83
	2.5–5.0	25.77	29.50	9.14	64.41
	5.0–10.0	52.74	45.32	8.09	106.15
	10.0 & above	39.81	25.94	17.41	83.16
	average	**39.82**	**28.94**	**15.44**	**83.54**
Kharif, 1993–4	0–2.5	40.14	22.95	6.50	69.69
	2.5–5.0	50.39	36.88	7.91	95.18
	5.0–10.0	48.54	25.53	0.99	75.06
	10.0 & above	41.60	29.83	12.04	83.46
	average	**43.62**	**29.30**	**9.27**	**82.19**
Dry village					
Kharif, 1991–2	0–5.0	3.48	8.89	0.00	12.37
	5.0–10.0	7.30	14.54	2.64	24.48
	10.0–25.0	5.83	10.50	2.83	19.17
	25.0 & above	7.51	11.95	0.47	19.93
	average	**6.69**	**11.76**	**0.86**	**19.31**
Kharif, 1993–4	0–5.0	5.01	9.90	0.19	15.10
	5.0–10.0	5.59	11.14	0.63	17.36
	10.0–25.0	5.42	8.65	0.88	14.95
	25.0 & above	6.36	12.80	0.05	19.21
	average	**5.82**	**11.18**	**0.38**	**17.37**

increased, while that of phosphorus declined sharply. The case of cotton was the same, but the consumption of nitrogen declined in the case of jowar.

The crop fertilizer application results for the semi-irrigated village are somewhat different from those of the irrigated village. Application rates increased in the case of paddy, cotton and sunflower, but declined in the case of dry crops, notably jowar. There has been no consistent pattern in the changes in the crop–fertilizer application relationship. Regardless of a decline in overall fertilizer use in this village, the application of urea (nitrogen) increased for most of the crops, while that of potassium declined. The pattern in the case of phosphorus was mixed (Table 7.6).

The overall decline in fertilizer use in the dry village was applicable to crops of jowar, sunflower and cotton. In the case of groundnut, there was an increase.

In conclusion, the impact of fertilizer price rise on HYV crops of paddy and cotton was insignificant, while it was adverse in the case of dry crops

Table 7.6   Crop fertilizer application response (kg/acre)

Villages	Crops	N	P	K	Total
Irrigated village					
Kharif, 1991–2	Paddy	84.11	36.29	20.86	141.28
	Jowar	33.55	47.22	6.55	87.33
	Groundnut	25.07	23.84	2.62	51.51
	Cotton	70.23	42.05	16.47	128.76
	All	**80.06**	**36.82**	**19.65**	**136.53**
Kharif, 1993–4	Paddy	85.08	26.55	23.68	135.31
	Jowar	29.08	9.92	9.92	48.92
	Groundnut	74.33	28.33	28.33	131.00
	Cotton	74.91	30.82	22.82	128.55
	All	**77.68**	**25.57**	**22.23**	**125.48**
Semi-irrigated village					
Kharif, 1991–2	Paddy	55.13	24.40	19.27	98.80
	Jowar	19.31	28.59	22.14	70.04
	Bajra	26.98	41.63	2.44	71.05
	Sunflower	23.00	0.00	0.00	23.00
	Cotton	12.94	6.78	3.45	23.17
	All	**39.82**	**28.29**	**15.44**	**83.54**
Kharif, 1993–4	Paddy	72.61	30.94	6.54	110.09
	Jowar	38.46	22.67	8.05	69.18
	Bajra	37.92	29.55	4.25	71.72
	Sunflower	31.15	16.04	6.09	53.28
	Cotton	57.76	50.23	17.72	125.71
	All	**43.62**	**29.30**	**9.27**	**82.19**
Dry village					
Kharif, 1991–2	Jowar	4.92	9.27	2.21	16.30
	Groundnut	4.19	10.70	0.00	14.88
	Sunflower	11.72	26.79	2.03	32.00
	Cotton	9.00	23.00	0.00	32.00
	All	**6.69**	**11.76**	**0.86**	**19.31**
Kharif, 1993–4	Jowar	9.04	5.48	1.48	16.00
	Groundnut	4.48	10.84	0.39	15.70
	Sunflower	4.90	10.47	0.20	15.58
	Cotton	5.49	14.02	0.00	19.51
	All	**5.82**	**11.18**	**0.38**	**17.37**

such as jowar. In other words, the overall decline in fertilizer use between the two seasons did not occur in the case of HYVs of paddy and cotton, which are cultivated under irrigation. Further, the use of nitrogen increased, thus suggesting that distortions in the application pattern will continue.

Changes in Cropping Pattern

An analysis of the effect of the rise in price of fertilizer on cropping pattern is important because of the argument that increased fertilizer prices may force farmers to allocate a smaller area to those crops requiring greater amounts of fertilizer. Crops such as HYVs of paddy and cotton require larger doses of fertilizer inputs. Of the four important crops (paddy, jowar, groundnut and cotton) in the irrigated village, the proportion of area under paddy HYVs requiring larger quantities of fertilizers declined, while that under cotton increased (Table 7.7). The area under groundnut also declined. The decline in the area under paddy was noticeable in the case of all types of farms, except large farms; see Hanumappa and Rajasekhar (1994). In the semi-irrigated village, the proportions of area under paddy and cotton declined (especially in the case of marginal and small farmers), while that under jowar increased and under sunflower decreased. In the dry village, the area under onion, green gram and other crops (notable grains) increased at the expense of jowar. The decline was sharper in the case of marginal farmers.

Thus the evidence on changes in cropping pattern in three villages, although inconsistent, reveals that the area under crops requiring larger amounts of fertilizer declined, after the announcement of a sharp increase in fertilizer prices. Such a decline has been particularly marked in the case of poor farmers. This is as expected by economic theory; see Hanumappa and Rajasekhar (1994).

Table 7.7   Changes in crop patterns (% area in various crops)

Village	Paddy	Jowar	Bajra	Groundnut	Sunflower	Cotton	Total
Irrigated village							
First season	88.68			4.71	0.00	6.61	100
Second season	68.60			1.28	10.58	19.55	100
Semi-irrigated village							
First season	18.05	29.16	12.22	1.10	32.60	6.96	100
Second season	7.25	44.40	9.93	12.93	19.42	6.08	100
Dry village							
First season	35.79		24.82	4.71		34.68	100
Second season		9.65	6.50	34.81		49.04	100

Conclusions

There is some evidence that higher fertilizer prices in India resulted in more efficient use of fertilizers in irrigated areas because, despite an overall decline in fertilizer use in all three villages, crop production did not decline. This implies that farmers are moving towards applying recommended doses of fertilizers. A decline in fertilizer use occurred mainly in the case of phosphorus and potassium during the post-sowing stages. This did not cause any loss of welfare because phosphorus and potassium need not be applied in these stages. Although the use of fertilizers had, in general, declined, application levels were higher than recommended, especially in the irrigated villages. Other things remaining the same, farmers in the irrigated villages can still reduce the use of phosphorus and potassium. Further, the use of nitrogen has increased because of a continuation of subsidies, which are again leading to distortions in the supply of nutrients in balanced proportions. Despite the small sample, we believe that our conclusions apply to India as a whole.

References

Agricultural Finance Corporation (AFC) (1991), *Agricultural Development Project, Supporting Studies III: Sources of Past Growth*, The Corporation, Bangalore.

Chandran, Satish, T.R.S. (1993), *Report of the Expert Committee: Stagnation of Agricultural Productivity in Karnataka in 1980s*, Government of Karnataka, Bangalore.

Hanumappa, H.G. and D. Rajasekhar (1994), *Fertiliser Prices: Impact on Consumption and Cropping Pattern*, ADRT Unit, Institute for Social and Economic Change (ISEC), Bangalore.

Roy, S. (1990), *Agriculture and Technology in Developing Countries: India and Nigeria*, Sage, New Delhi.

8   An Economic Evaluation of Alternative Nutrient Management Practices in Sustaining Resource Base Productivity

R.P.S. Malik[a]

Introduction

The use of chemical fertilizers to replenish nutrient losses and raise crop productivity in intensive farming systems is well known, but there has been growing concern about the widespread use of chemical fertilizers as a means to restore, maintain or build up soil fertility, as some are coming to the conclusion that this does more harm than good and that such farming systems cannot be sustained in the long run. Ways of restoring the drained plant nutrients, which are healthy for the soil as well as the environment, are being increasingly emphasized.

Results from agricultural experiment stations show the long-term physical effects of different ways of restoring drained plant nutrients on crop yields and soil characteristics in intensive farming systems under a variety of agronomic conditions. This information has often not been used to make meaningful economic assessments of these management practices and identify optimal strategies to sustain farm productivity. This chapter demonstrates how an economic evaluation of farm management practices can help arrest land degradation while raising and sustaining the productivity of a given farming system in ways consistent with sustaining the

[a] Agricultural Economics Research Centre, University of Delhi, Delhi 11000, India.

productivity of the resource base. It draws on evidence from the most advanced agricultural region of India, the state of Punjab.

Rice and wheat constitute the staple food that a large majority of the Indian population rely on for their daily caloric requirements. To meet the rising demand for these two commodities by the ever-increasing population, large-scale shifts in cropped area have taken place in favour of these two crops, especially in advanced agricultural regions of the country. Indian farmers have been cultivating rice and wheat for decades and have, over the years, accumulated considerable expertise. As a result of more intensive cultivation of available land, rice and wheat are now grown in sequence with a number of other crops. Rice cultivated in succession with wheat is one of the most important crop sequences. Growing two crops in succession is a relatively new experience for a majority of farmers. While a large amount of research effort has been invested in finding ways to increase the productivity of rice and wheat, relatively little effort has gone into understanding the interactions between the two crops when grown as a system. These interactions are important because of their strong effect on the productivity of the system. For example, because of the very different soil structure and soil mechanical requirements of rice and wheat, land preparation for either crop has implications for the effective establishment of the other. Similarly, nutrients used in one crop of the system have carry-over effects for the succeeding crop.

One of the important challenges that have serious ramifications for the food security of the country is the lack of sustainability of crop yields, as suggested by results from the all India coordinated fertilizer experiments (Nambiar and Abrol, 1989). Evidence from farmers' fields also indicates that, while use of chemical fertilizers and other inputs has been rising over time, crop yields have either remained stagnant or increased only marginally. Yields have not risen in proportion to the increased use of these inputs.

One of the crucial factors contributing to the lack of sustainability of crop yields in the rice–wheat system is the constant degradation of the resource base by repeated cultivation of these two crops year after year. The degradation of the resource base is, in large part, the result of the nutrient-exhausting nature of the farming system and the adoption of 'faulty' cultivation methods. Nutrient management practices generally result in complete reliance on chemical fertilizers as the source of nutrients. Nutrient uptake data indicate that, apart from micronutrient deficiencies, there is a negative balance of nitrogen, phosphorus, and potassium nutrients in the soil, even with recommended levels of fertilizer use (Anon, 1985). The nutrient-depleting nature of the cropping system, coupled with adoption of inappropriate farming practices, which include repeated tillage and intensive irrigation at the time of land preparation, have exacerbated the process of soil degradation and erosion. A fragile resource base, when confronted with the pressure of crop intensification, is likely to accentuate further the pace of degradation. A reversal of this trend, therefore, calls for the development and identification of appropriate farming practices that sustain and even enhance productivity. In this chapter we estimate the impact of conventional and alternative tillage and nutrient management practices in rice–wheat farming systems on soil degradation, and compare the economic efficiency of these management practices in sustaining productivity.

Simulating Crop Yields and Erosion Impacts

The concept of sustainable development implies the endurance of a productivity level through certain agricultural practices over a period of time. Since resource degradation is often a slow process, its impact is generally not discernible immediately or even in the short run. This study employs a 30-year time frame for estimating the magnitude of resource degradation. Estimates of on-farm soil erosion and degradation, and impact on soil productivity, have been derived using the erosion–productivity impact calculator (EPIC) developed by the Agricultural Research Service of the United States Department of Agriculture (Williams *et al.*, 1982). EPIC is a comprehensive crop simulation model that takes into account the complex long-term relationship between soil erosion and soil productivity. It is composed of physically based components for simulating erosion, plant growth and related processes (Williams, 1989). With suitable modifications, EPIC is used to simulate agricultural production in Ludhiana, Punjab. The modified model has then been used to estimate the extent of soil degradation and its impact on long-term soil productivity for alternative management practices.

Apart from the on-farm effects of soil degradation, eroding soils cause certain off-farm effects. While the on-farm costs of soil erosion are borne by the farmer, the off-farm costs are borne by society. The relatively more important off-site effects are surface water pollution, and siltation of irrigation channels, streams and canals. There is a lack of information on the magnitude of this off-site damage, though some of the available estimates suggest that about 75 per cent of sediment deposits in irrigation systems could originate from agricultural lands (Governor's Soil Resources Study Commission, 1984).

For estimating the off-site damage for the study area, we have made some simplified assumptions. The infrastructure of canals and other water conveyance systems in Punjab have been built primarily for irrigation purposes. We assume that all the sediments eroding from croplands are likely to be deposited either in the main canal or other parts of the distribution system, thus interfering with free movement of water through the system, reducing its storage, enhancing the risk of flooding and affecting the quality of water (Malik and Faeth, 1993; Faeth *et al.*, 1994). The off-farm cost of soil erosion has thus been estimated as the cost of dredging sediment from the water conveyance system, transporting it and depositing it back on the fields from where it possibly originated. Transporting the dredged sediment away from the banks of the cleared water channels prevents redeposition in the water channel, and depositing sediments back on the fields may, to some extent, help restore the productivity of the eroded soil.

A brief description of alternative tillage and nutrient management practices analysed in this study is provided in Table 8.1. The conventional tillage practices imply the use of repeated tillage for land preparation, while alternative tillage practices denote reduced or conservation tillage. Both tillage practices have been compared with three different fertilizer strategies: (1) complete reliance on inorganic fertilizers; (2) a mix of inorganic fertilizers and farmyard manure; and (3) a mix of inorganic fertilizers and green manure, using *sesbania*.

The model was validated and calibrated by contrasting the simulated crop yields estimated from EPIC with those realized in the experimental fields of Punjab Agricultural University (PAU), Ludhiana (PAU, 1989). EPIC yields and those actually realized in the experimental plots of PAU show that EPIC could simulate the agricultural conditions of the region fairly closely. Of the various alternative management practices compared, the crop yields estimated from EPIC and those realized in experimental plots differed by a narrow margin (Table 8.2). In fact, eight of the 12 crop yields estimated for

Table 8.1   Rotation characteristics

| | | Source of nutrient supply[a] | |
Code	Tillage practice	Rice[b]	Wheat
CTIF	Conventional	IF	IF
CTFF	Conventional	IF+FYM	IF
CTGF	Conventional	IF+GM	IF
RTIF	Reduced	IF	IF
RTFF	Reduced	IF+FYM	IF
RTGF	Reduced	IF+GM	IF

Notes:
[a] IF = inorganic fertilizer; FYM = farmyard manure; GM = green manure.
[b] The nitrogen sources specified for rice denote: IF = 120kg N through urea; IF + FYM = 60kg N through urea and 20 tonnes of FYM; IF + GM = 80kg of N through urea and 8-week old *sesbania* buried one day before transplanting.

Table 8.2   Crop yields: experimental results and EPIC estimated[a]

Farming practice	Exp.	Rice EPIC	Diff. (%)	Exp.	Wheat EPIC	Diff. (%)
CTIF	4.58	4.74	3.49	4.17	4.28	2.64
CTFF	4.43	4.63	4.51	4.57	4.45	−2.63
CTGF	4.47	4.76	−0.20	4.20	4.31	1.17
RTIF	4.58	4.74	3.49	4.61	4.28	−7.16
RTFF	4.29	4.07	−5.13	4.66	4.67	0.21
RTGF	4.44	4.76	7.21	4.71	4.31	−8.49

Note: [a] Experimental yields are from PAU (1989).

rice and wheat from EPIC differ from experimental yields by a margin of less than 5 per cent, while, in the case of the remaining four, the difference in crop yields varied between 5.1 per cent and 8.5 per cent. The narrow difference between the observed and simulated crop yields provided justification for using EPIC to estimate the extent of soil erosion associated with different agricultural practices and the consequent impact of soil degradation on long-term crop yields. Long-term soil productivity changes have been simulated under identical weather and management conditions. The realized difference in crop yields under such conditions could thus be attributed solely to long-term soil productivity changes.

Soil Erosion and Changes in Soil Productivity

The EPIC estimated extent of soil erosion for different management practices of rice–wheat indicates that, for a given fertilization practice, soil erosion is lower for reduced tillage compared to conventional tillage (Table 8.3). Further, for a given tillage practice, soil erosion is lowest for practices using green manuring and highest for practices relying on use of chemical fertilizers alone as a source of nutrients. The lowest soil erosion rates, estimated to be 0.40 tonnes per hectare per year, are associated with farming practices based on use of green manures and employing reduced tillage practices (RTGF). This is as expected.

The EPIC estimated changes in long-term soil productivity suggest that, for all the farming practices considered, the yield of rice increases, while that of wheat declines over the simulation period (Table 8.3). However, the magnitude of change in crop yields differs between the two crops and between different management practices. Of the various management practices, the rotation relying on the use of a combination of inorganic

Table 8.3   Estimated soil erosion and changes in crop yield

Farming practice	Soil loss (t/ha/year)	Rice yields (tonnes/ha)			Wheat yield (tonnes/ha)		
		Initial[a]	Final	Abs. change	Initial[a]	Final	Abs. change
CTIF	3.24	4.74	4.77	0.03	4.26	4.02	−0.24
CTFF	1.07	4.68	4.79	0.11	4.50	4.28	−0.22
CTGF	0.51	4.75	4.80	0.05	4.28	4.05	−0.23
RTIF	1.42	4.74	4.78	0.04	4.24	4.02	−0.22
RTFF	0.55	4.12	4.67	0.55	4.71	4.52	−0.19
RTGF	0.40	4.76	4.80	0.04	4.28	4.05	−0.23

Note: [a] Initial yield is the average yield of the first three years, while the final yield is the average of the last three years of the simulation period.

fertilizers and farmyard manure (FYM) for the supply of nutrients and using reduced tillage (RTFF) results in the highest increase in rice yield and the lowest decline in wheat yield.

The EPIC crop yield was regressed on time (Table 8.4). The results indicate that, while the regression coefficients for wheat are negative and significant, those of rice are insignificant in all cases except one. Further, while the rate of decline in wheat yield varies marginally across different management practices, it is the lowest for the rotation based on use of FYM. The seemingly small coefficient of rate of decline in wheat yields realized under different management practices should be interpreted carefully. For example, the rate of decline of 0.007 tonnes is only about 0.17 per cent, but in an economy where the long-run trend rate of growth of agricultural output per annum is less than 25 per cent, deceleration in growth by 0.17 per cent in a single crop as the result of soil degradation alone seems to be large enough to merit attention.

The results also suggest that wheat yields decline under all management practices, *ceteris paribus*. If the yield-enhancing effect of technology is more than the loss in soil productivity due to soil degradation, its effect may be masked in the aggregate analysis and the result may still be positive. It is important, however, to note that, had there been no decline in yield due to soil degradation, the realized yield due to technological improvement could have been much higher. The issue is comparing the effect of technology on degraded versus better soils, and what matters is the difference between actual and potential yield.

The estimation of on-farm cost of soil depreciation or an estimate of the economic degradation of soil depends on changes in crop yield, the prices of individual crops in the rotation and the parity between these crop prices. The soil depreciation allowance has been computed as the difference in the net present value of benefits due to changes in crop yields as a result of soil

Table 8.4 Estimated crop yields: results of regression analysis

Farming practice	Crop	Regression coefficient	Standard error	*R* square
CTIF	Rice	−0.00111	0.00150	0.19
	Wheat	−0.00774*	0.00083	0.76
CTFF	Rice	0.00053	0.00171	0.003
	Wheat	−0.00621*	0.00110	0.53
CTGF	Rice	−0.00052	0.00157	0.004
	Wheat	−0.00743*	0.00085	0.73
RTIF	Rice	−0.00082	0.00150	0.011
	Wheat	−0.00776*	0.00083	0.76
RTFF	Rice	0.01786*	0.00178	0.78
	Wheat	−0.00503*	0.00108	0.44
RTGF	Rice	−0.00068	0.00157	0.007
	Wheat	−0.00731*	0.00085	0.72

Note: *Significant at 1% level of significance.

degradation for each of the alternative management practices analysed over the 30-year simulation period. The present values have been derived using three alternative values of discount rates, 6 per cent, 8 per cent and 10 per cent. The prices used to calculate the value of productivity are prices for 1991–2. For estimating the changes in value of productivity at social prices, market prices of crop outputs and inputs have been replaced by their social prices. The results in Table 8.5 suggest that, while the farming practices based on the use of FYM in combination with chemical fertilizers either are resource augmenting (RTFF) or deplete the resource base only marginally (CTFF), all other farming practices are resource depleting.

The off-site cost of soil erosion has been estimated by multiplying the quantity of eroded soil associated with each of the management practices (Table 8.3, col. 2) by the cost per tonne of dredging the sediments from the water conveyance system and transporting it away from its banks. The prevailing cost of removing 100 cubic metres of sediment from water channels and throwing it on the banks of the canal (locally known as *kassi* work) is Rs 525. When converted into per tonne of sediment removal, this works out at Rs 3.28. If we assume that this dredged soil is transported back to the agricultural fields located 10 km away, the cost of loading, transporting and unloading works out at Rs 40 per tonne of sediment. The total off-farm cost of soil erosion is thus Rs 43.28 per tonne. The present values of the off-site cost associated with each of the management practices are presented in Table 8.5. The results indicate that off-site costs associated with conventional tillage are higher than those based on reduced tillage with

Table 8.5   Estimate of on-farm and off-farm costs of soil degradation (Rs/ha)[a]

Farming practice	On-farm costs Market prices discount rate (%)			Social prices discount rate (%)			Off-farm costs Discount rate (%)		
	6%	8%	10%	6%	8%	10%	6%	8%	10%
CTIF	8 972	6 949	5 513	20 476	15 858	12 589	1930	1 579	1 321
CTFF	1 147	642	310	5 087	3 463	2 361	637	521	436
CTGF	8 667	6 727	5 347	19 788	15 356	12 204	304	248	208
RTIF	9 017	6 985	5 541	20 571	15 935	12 640	846	692	579
RTFF	(10 272)	(7 653)	(5 825)	(18 152)	(13 443)	(10 169)	328	268	224
RTGF	8 584	6 645	5 267	19 623	15 194	12 045	238	195	163

Note: [a] Figures in parentheses denote soil appreciation, while all other figures denote soil depreciation.

Table 8.6 **Economic comparison of conventional and alternative farming practices in sustaining long-term soil productivity in the rice–wheat system (Rs/ha)**[a]

Farming practice	Farmer's perspective discount rate (%)			Society's perspective discount rate (%)		
	6%	8%	10%	6%	8%	10%
CTIF	8 972	6 949	5 513	22 406	17 437	13 902
CTFF	1 147	642	310	5 724	3 984	2 797
CTFF	8 667	6 727	5 347	20 092	15 604	12 412
RTIF	9 017	6 985	5 541	21 417	16 627	13 219
RTFF	(10 272)	(7 653)	(5 825)	(17 824)	(13 175)	(9 945)
RTGF	8 584	6 645	5 267	19 861	15 389	12 208

Note: [a] The figures in parentheses denote soil appreciation, while those without parentheses denote soil depreciation. Figures in the last three columns have been derived by adding the on-farm cost of soil depreciation/appreciation at social prices and the off-farm cost of soil erosion.

comparable fertilization levels. The lowest off-site costs are associated with green manuring and reduced tillage (RTGF), while the highest costs are associated with chemical fertilizers and conventional tillage (CTIF) in the current practice.

Finally, consider the comparative economics of different soil and nutrient management practices in sustaining and raising the productivity of the rice–wheat system, both from the farmers' and society's point of view (Table 8.6). The results indicate that the currently widely practiced rice–wheat system using repeated tillage and reliance on chemical fertilizers (CTIF) causes more environmental damage and holds much less economic value for society than the alternative farming systems analysed. In contrast, production systems based on use of FYM and reduced tillage (RTFF), besides averting soil depreciation, add value to the soil. This farming practice enhances the productivity of the rice–wheat system, is most profitable to the farmer and has the largest economic value for society.

Conclusions

The results demonstrate that it is possible to avert soil degradation and not only sustain but raise the productivity of the rice–wheat system through the proper choice of management practices. Integrated nutrient management practices using FYM in combination with chemical fertilizers hold great promise for rice–wheat systems.

The high resource cost associated with current agricultural practices suggests that economic gains could be had through research into resource conservation. So far agricultural research has generally been driven by such considerations as scarcity of land and labour, or increasing profitability, and therefore has become input-intensive. The criteria for evaluating costs and benefits of publicly funded agricultural research are flawed because the economic value of their impact on natural resources has been ignored. Government research funds have supported conventional farming systems to the detriment of alternative systems. Research on sustainable farming practices should, therefore, be given higher priority and higher funding.

References

Anon (1985), *Annual Report: All India Coordinated Research Project on Long-Term Fertiliser Experiments*, Indian Council of Agricultural Research, New Delhi.

Faeth, P., R. Repetto, R.P.S. Malik, K. Kroll and Q. Dai (1994), 'Off-Site Costs of Soil Erosion', in P. Faeth (ed.), *Economic Analysis of Agricultural Sustainability*, United Nations Environment Programme, Geneva, Switzerland.

Governor's Soil Resources Study Commission (1984), *Inland's Erosion and Sedimentation Situation*, Governor's Office, Indianapolis, Indiana.

Malik, R.P.S. and P. Faeth (1993), 'Rice–Wheat Production System in North-West India', in P. Faeth (ed.), *Agricultural Policy and Sustainability: Case Studies from India, Chile, the Philippines and the United States*, World Resources Institute, Washington, DC.

Nambiar, K.K.M. and I.P. Abrol (1989), 'Long-Term Fertiliser Experiments in India: An Overview', *Fertiliser News*, **34**: 4.

PAU (1989), 'Twenty Seventh Annual Report', mimeo, Department of Soils, Punjab Agricultural University, Ludhiana.

Williams, J.R. (1989), 'EPIC – Erosion/Productivity Impact Calculator: 2, User Manual', Technical Bulletin No. 1768, Department of Agriculture, Washington, DC.

Williams, J.R., P.T. Dyke and C.A. Jones (1982), 'EPIC – A Model for Assessing the Effects of Erosion on Soil Productivity', *Proceedings of the Third International Conference on State-of-the-art in Ecological Modelling*, Colorado State University, Fort Collins.

9 Economic Evaluation of Low and High External Input Agriculture: A Production Function Analysis for Indonesia[1]

R. Ruben, N.B.M. Heerink and E. Mol[a]

Introduction

Low external input agriculture (LEIA) is widely acknowledged as a useful perspective for rural development programmes and agricultural research and extension in less developed countries, but suitable methods for economic assessment of LEIA techniques are still poorly developed. A number of practical experiences for making cropping systems less dependent on purchased inputs have been documented (Reijntjes *et al.*, 1992; Hiemstra *et al.*, 1992). Despite wide efforts to promote LEIA farming, actual adoption is still rather limited and unevenly spread among farms (Pretty, 1995).

LEIA farming seeks to optimize the use of locally available resources by combining different farm activities so that they complement each other and give the greatest possible synergistic effects. External inputs are only used to provide elements that are deficient within the ecosystem. Major emphasis is placed on reducing dependency on pesticides and substituting chemical fertilizers for (green) manure. Production systems with high use of (external) inputs (HEIA) are focused on capital intensification through improvement of land and labour productivity. Reliance on external inputs is mostly associated with commercially oriented agricultural production, generally

[a] Department of Development Economics, Wageningen Agricultural University, P.O. Box 8130, 6700 EW, Wageningen, The Netherlands.

with higher levels of specialization. Sustainable resource use is, in principle, possible under both systems, but tends to be accompanied by lower output levels under the LEIA option.[2]

Economic appraisal of LEIA practices receives relatively minor attention, because costs and benefits cannot always be clearly identified (UNDP, 1992). Moreover, a positive cost–benefit relation does not mean that adoption is feasible for all types of farmers. Therefore methods are required that permit the assessment of different technical options from the viewpoint of the farm household economy. Production function estimates can be used to analyse differences in the use of internal and external production factors among farm households (Ali and Byerlee, 1991). Moreover, this procedure permits the analysis of effects of price changes on choices between LEIA and HEIA techniques, and may be useful to indicate policy implications for the diffusion of both types of technique.

The main objective of this research is to demonstrate the usefulness of separate estimates of the production elasticities for primary inputs for HEIA and LEIA systems. Relevant differences in farm household characteristics (such as farm area, tenancy and gender) and cropping systems (such as agroforestry, terracing and intercropping) are included in this analysis to determine their impact on the efficiency of HEIA or LEIA techniques. The results can be used to reveal fundamental differences in the socioeconomic conditions that may enhance the feasibility of LEIA or HEIA systems.

Comparing Low- and High-input Agriculture

Clear definitions for low- and high-input agriculture are not readily available from the literature. On the level of separate cropping or livestock activities, typical LEIA or HEIA operations or techniques used in a particular system can be identified. More difficulties arise when LEIA and HEIA techniques are applied simultaneously to different activities within the farm system. But for an analysis of HEIA and LEIA of a single activity, as in this chapter, it may be sufficient to identify boundaries in the continuum from HEIA to LEIA farming systems. These boundaries are based on the combinations of resources that farmers apply to maintain productivity and soil fertility and to prevent environmental degradation. Starting with a distinction between growth-defining factors (soil and climate conditions and crop characteristics), growth-limiting factors (water and nutrients availability) and growth-reducing factors (weeds, pests and diseases), different production regimes can be distinguished with respect to the ways farmers deal with these factors (Rabbinge and van Ittersum, 1993).

Farming systems that make use of LEIA techniques, mainly rely on fallow (green) manure and recycling of crop residues to maintain soil organic matter content, and use physical measures (terraces, bunds, windbreaks) and cultivation techniques (contour farming, minimum tillage) for soil conservation and soil moisture management (Vereijken, 1992). Moreover, low-input techniques refrain as much as possible from the purchase of chemical herbicides and pesticides. Finally, LEIA is associated with integrated farming systems where synergistic complementary effects among crops become apparent (for example, nutrient fixation, integrated pest management, manure).

Farming systems that make use of high-input techniques rely to a greater extent on chemical fertilizers to balance nutrient requirements and often use mechanical tillage (tractor power or draught animals) for land cleaning, soil preparation to improve water infiltration and root development, and controlling weeds. Plant diseases are more commonly controlled with chemical biocides. For extensive rangelands management, reliance on herbicides is a common feature. High-input farming systems are mostly characterized by a higher level of specialization, but also rely on crop rotations to make use of residual effects of fertilizers and to control diseases.

Important differences between the two farming techniques become apparent when the resource requirements and factor productivities are considered (Ruben and Heerink, 1995). Intensification within low input-oriented farming systems is based on capital-substituting technologies through higher labour intensity. Because part of the family labour and the available land is used to maintain soil fertility, factor productivity of land and labour tends to be relatively low. Moreover, opportunities to be engaged in off-farm employment may diminish, resulting in less income diversification (Reardon and Vosti, 1992). On the other hand, crop diversification may lead to less market risk, but this implies paying a risk premium in terms of the costs of fallowing or lower yield levels.

Farming systems oriented towards high input use are mainly based on capital intensification, giving priority to higher land productivity through the purchase of external inputs (Reardon, 1995). High-input systems rely on measures that enhance input efficiency and select external inputs that are complementary to prevailing soil conditions (pH level, nutrient deficits, carbon balance). Capital-intensive 'precision agriculture' even selects required inputs for each parcel or plot. Both physical capital and human capital (education, information) are considered important, while access to these two resources is strongly enhanced through engagement in off-farm employment.

These differences in resource use can be related to a number of farm household and regional socioeconomic characteristics that will influence technology choice. Farm size, access to markets and off-farm employment are major factors that determine the possibilities of purchasing external inputs. High-input systems probably perform better in high-potential zones (for example, those with sufficient rainfall and adequate topsoil conditions). Low-input systems make stronger demands on family labour and may therefore curtail options for off-farm employment. Both types of technique rely on different mechanisms for income and risk diversification. Maintenance of soil fertility in the long run can be achieved in both systems and has to be reviewed separately (van Keulen and Breman, 1991).

The purpose of this chapter is to derive a method for the socioeconomic evaluation of high- and low-input cropping systems from the viewpoint of the farm household economy. Our central hypothesis is that differences in production conditions, farm household characteristics and socioeconomic settings within the same region will lead to the coexistence of different production technologies. Instead of explaining cropping system choice by the profitability of LEIA and HEIA farming systems (as with cost–benefit analysis), the choice between alternative production systems will be explained by their feasibility under different household-specific circumstances. Some questions to be addressed are the following: (1) what is the economic impact of choice for high-input or low-input systems for the marginal product of the production factors; (2) under which economic conditions are farmers opting for high-input or low-input systems; and (3) which types of farm households typically select high-input or low-input systems? Answers to these questions are helpful in identifying incentives that can be used to influence farmers' choice of production techniques. Moreover, the analysis can be used to improve our understanding of land use systems at the farm household level and how they relate to technology choice, farm household objectives and market structures.

Production under LEIA and HEIA

Quantitative assessment of the attractiveness of low- or high-input techniques is usually realized within a cost–benefit framework. Financial cost–benefit evaluation makes use of market prices to value inputs and outputs.[3] In addition, a suitable interest rate is required for discounting future costs and benefits. For smallholders with limited access to local financial markets and marginal relations with input and output markets, such a financial evaluation based on market prices is less relevant.

Changes towards low-input systems are usually accompanied by adjustments in the cost and benefit structure in the following aspects (UNDP, 1992; Ruben and Heerink, 1995): reduction of external (chemical) input costs; decrease in net (physical) land productivity; increase in labour intensity due to labour demands for manual weeding, maintenance of intercropping and application of manure; and sometimes a (small) increase in market prices (for example, when specific marketing channels exist that offer higher prices for organic produce). In the short run, large-scale adoption of low-input techniques is often only feasible when market prices increase substantially. This supposes the existence of a specific market segment for organic products. Therefore producers need to adjust significantly their farming system before they can benefit from this premium and there may need to be institutions that identify such products (for example, labelling).

Besides these directly measurable items, other aspects should be taken into account as well. A large part of current land productivity is based on soil mining, thus affecting prospects for future harvests.[4] LEIA farming assumes that the benefits of soil mining decrease over time and should be taken into account within a multi-year framework. Sometimes environmental repair is included within a cost–benefit framework, but doing so will generally depress production.

On the other hand, LEIA farming has some additional costs related to the *alternative use value* of land and labour resources. Physical labour productivity (measured in kg/man-day) in most low-input systems is far behind the levels reached in high-input systems. When off-farm employment is an important income source, the increased on-farm labour demand for LEIA may affect farmers' income (Reardon, 1995). This is especially the case when the two activities coincide in time.[5] The same reasoning is valid for land resources, as integrated farming systems may increase effective land use and thus reduce the prospects for renting land to other farmers. Finally, when material inputs represent a small proportion of total production costs, or when cost–benefit ratios are rather small, input prices tend to be of minor importance in producers' decisions. This may severely restrict incentives to adjust input use in these farming systems.

Analysis of the socioeconomic feasibility of LEIA and HEIA methods can be improved by making use of production functions. Cost–benefit analysis only offers partial results from a comparison of a limited number of farmers. It can be used for static comparison of the profitability of alternative production techniques, but not for evaluating dynamic adjustment of farming systems to, say, price changes (Anderson, 1995). The production function approach is a suitable tool for analysing the latter type of questions. For obtaining production function estimates, a consistent data set from a substantial number of farms is required.

Production functions relate physical or monetary output to different input quantities for a given state of technology. They can be represented graphically as a function between production and one input, maintaining all other inputs constant. HEIA and LEIA use different inputs and different techniques for producing agricultural output. The low-input approach emphasizes the use of organic manure, biological pesticides and home-produced seeds and their synergetic effects, while HEIA relies more on chemical fertilizers and pesticides, and purchased (hybrid) seeds. The two techniques are therefore based on different production functions. It would be erroneous to use the same production function with different inputs for the evaluation of two different sets of techniques (Mausolff and Farber, 1995).

In Figure 9.1, the relationship between only one input (for example, nitrogen input from chemical fertilizer or manure) and the quantity of output is depicted for high- and low-input agriculture. At low input levels, LEIA is likely to be more efficient than HEIA. Small input quantities of manure, biological pesticides and indigenous seeds (developed by farmers in a long process of trial and error) are likely to give better results that comparable quantities of external inputs (Hayami and Ruttan, 1985: 133–6). Because of the law of diminishing returns, the LEIA production function is depicted as a concave curve. At a certain point, the LEIA curve will intersect with the HEIA curve. HEIA is more efficient than LEIA when nitrogen input is high, because high-yielding (hybrid) varieties are more responsive to fertilizer (in combination with irrigation water) at high levels of nitrogen input. After the point of intersection, HEIA is likely to produce more output than LEIA

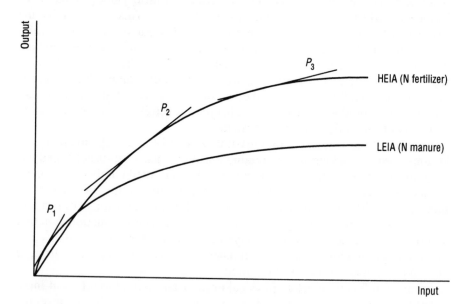

Figure 9.1   Production functions for low- and high-input systems

techniques using the same quantity of nitrogen input. The HEIA function is also assumed to have a concave shape, but the rate of decline of the slope is smaller.

Assuming profit maximization by farmers, the price ratio of nitrogen input and crop output determines the preference for high- or low-input agriculture. At low output market prices and high fertilizer prices, LEIA will be preferred. At relatively high output (and low input) prices HEIA tends to offer better prospects. The price ratio of output to input prices can be shown in the figure by drawing the line that is tangential to the curve.[6] When the ratio of input to output price is high (P_1), LEIA will give the highest profit. When the ratio of input to output price declines, the angle becomes smaller. For one price ratio (P_2), the line that is a tangent to the LEIA curve is also a tangent to the HEIA curve. Marginal output equals marginal input for both techniques, and the two techniques are equally profitable.[7] When the price ratio declines further (P_3), the HEIA technique becomes more profitable than LEIA.

The shape of the production functions may vary for different soil types. On deep, fertile, well-drained soils with fewer acidification risks, the production function will assume a more steep form, as there is a greater crop response to (external) nitrogen input. Therefore the point where the same line is a tangent to both the LEIA and the HEIA production function will be located further to the left (that is, at a lower input level) and at a higher level of output per hectare. This explains why LEIA techniques are assumed to be used mostly in less favourable conditions, mainly to increase soil buffer capacity.

Production function estimates can be used subsequently to evaluate the impact of adjustment in relative prices and marketing conditions on the attractiveness of LEIA or HEIA systems. Reduced output market prices or increases in the prices of external inputs will improve economic prospects for LEIA. Improved transport facilities, better market information and better access to credit services will reduce transaction costs of purchased inputs and tend to increase the farm gate price for crop output, changing relative prices in favour of HEIA techniques.

For peasant producers, financial costs and benefits are not the only relevant parameters for selection of techniques, as profit maximization is not their only goal. Other less tangible benefits that should be included refer to the control of risk[8] guarantees for food security, and dependency on rural financial markets. Objectives of sustainable land use mostly receive a relatively low weight in the farmer's goal function. Prospects for sustainable land use at the farm level depend on the relationship between production and consumption – such as the proportion of the output reserved to offset processes of natural resource degradation. Trade-offs appear when household consumption can only be maintained at the expense of the natural resource base. Agrarian policy instruments may be identified that permit reconciliation of both objectives.

Empirical Analysis

Separate production functions for low and high external input systems have been estimated from household data that were collected in the limestone area south of Malang, East Java, Indonesia, from October 1991 to October 1992. The survey formed part of the Interdisciplinary Research Training (INRES) project in which the Brawijaya University in Malang and Wageningen Agricultural University are working to improve the methodology of farming systems analysis. Farm household data were selected for three different geographical units in order to account for variability in socialeconomic and ecological settings. In general, the Malang area can be characterized as a region of relatively poor soils, with low crop productivity and high levels of soil erosion (van Rheenen, 1995). On the hillsides of Java, most farming systems rely on upland rainfed agriculture with predominantly annual and mixed cropping systems. The major cropping systems consist of maize–sugarcane and maize–cassava intercropping, the latter especially on poorer soils. Moreover, households cultivate home gardens with a variety of annual and perennial crops. Most households possess at least one type of livestock, mostly cattle, with an average of one animal. Owing to population pressures and lack of grazing area, livestock is stall-fed.

Two socioeconomic farm household surveys were held in the Malang region. A multi-visit intensive farm household survey (IFHS) for 36 households was held in two villages in the survey area to gain a better understanding of socioeconomic structures at the micro level. Input and output data of different farming activities were accurately recorded during the period October 1990 to February 1992. Further, an extensive farm household survey (EFHS) of 149 households was conducted in the same two villages in order to improve the representation of the sample. It consisted of two interview rounds of farm household activities for 1990/91 and 1991/2, and one round of farm measurement and land quality assessments. In the extensive survey, no information on labour input was collected.

For the purpose of our analysis, the number of observations in the IFHS is too small. Since the EFHS lacks data on labour input, it was decided to derive a relationship between labour input and other inputs from the IFHS data and use this relationship to estimate labour input for the EFHS. The analysis is limited to maize, the crop that is grown most frequently in the research area.

For the estimation of the labour function from the IFHS data, all labour activities concerning maize production were aggregated per plot. In total, 62 maize plots were included in the regression analysis. Plot size, quantity of maize and quantity of fertilizer were considered relevant explanatory variables. Another relevant variable, maize yield, was not included because it would lead to simultaneity problems.[9] A double-log specification was used to explain labour input:

$$ln\ L = b_0 + b_1\ ln\ A + b_2\ ln\ S + b_3\ ln\ F + e_1 \qquad (9.1)$$

where L is total labour input in maize production (in hours), A is size of maize plot (in hectares), S is total maize seed used (in kilograms), F is total fertilizer used (total nitrogen content of organic and anorganic fertilizers in kilograms), e_1 is a random disturbance term, and the bs are unknown coefficients. The regression results are shown in Table 9.1. All exogenous variables have a significant positive impact on labour input. Around 73 per cent of the total variation in labour input is explained by the three variables.

The coefficient for the labour function is used to specify labour demand in the extensive farm household survey. Summary statistics on the maize farmers in the extensive sample are provided in Table 9.2. The total level of nitrogen input per hectare (derived from dung and urea) was used to distinguish between LEIA and HEIA systems. Based on information provided by INRES project agronomists, a (somewhat arbitrary) level of 45 kg per hectare was used to divide the sample into LEIA and HEIA farmers. Out of the 104 farm households in the EFHS that grow maize, 46 were classified as LEIA and 58 as HEIA farmers.

Major differences between HEIA and LEIA farmers refer to the substantially higher nitrogen input from market-purchased urea and the higher labour and seed input within the HEIA cropping systems. Nitrogen

Table 9.1   OLS regression results for labour input

Variable	Coefficient	*t*-value
Intercept	4.22**	17.6
Ln A	0.38**	4.94
Ln F	0.23**	3.64
Ln S	0.42**	4.80
No. of observations	62	
R^2	0.73	
F–statistic	52.7**	

Note: ** = significant at P < 0.01.

Table 9.2   Summary statistics for maize farmers in the sample (means)

Variable	LEIA	HEIA	Variable	LEIA	HEIA
Yield/ha (kg)	1126**	2117**	Fraction of terraced fields	0.15	0.20
N/ha, urea (kg)	16.6**	95.3**	Fraction agroforestry (trees on field	0.65*	0.47*
N/ha, dung (kg)	6.8	6.7	Fraction owner of land	0.80	0.86
Labour input/ha (hours)	476**	610**	Fraction male household head	0.80	0.88
Seed (kg/ha)	23.3**	33.8**	Farm area (ha)	1.0	1.0
Area maize (ha)	0.25	0.26			

Note: ** = significant difference at $P < 0.01$; * = significant difference at $P < 0.05$.

supply from dung is almost the same for LEIA and HEIA farms. Yields are almost 47 per cent lower on LEIA farms, while labour input is 22 per cent lower. As a result, average labour productivity is 32 per cent lower. The average farm size and maize area are similar in HEIA and LEIA systems, but LEIA farms rely somewhat more on agroforestry practices. Terraced fields, established property rights and male ownership are more frequently found on HEIA farms, but the differences from LEIA farms are not significant.

Separate maize production functions for low and high external input agricultural systems were estimated using a (modified) Cobb–Douglas functional form. The Cobb–Douglas function was chosen for this purpose because of its simplicity, its ease of manipulation and its simple interpretation. An alternative approach is to estimate a production function for all farmers and introduce a dummy variable with value one for LEIA farmers and zero otherwise (for example, Mausolff and Farber, 1995). Such an approach implicitly assumes that output elasticities for land, labour, seed and fertilizer are the same for LEIA and HEIA farmers, and was therefore rejected. Only when the estimated coefficients for the two groups do not differ significantly from each other may the two groups be pooled and a dummy variable added to the equation to allow for differences in disembodied technology between LEIA and HEIA farmers.

The primary inputs in the model are labour, dung and urea.[10] Capital applied by the farmers in the sample is rather rudimentary, and is not included in the regression for that reason. Included production technologies are limited to the percentage of land under terraces (as a fraction of the total maize land) and the use of agroforestry systems (trees mostly planted along the field edges or terrace rims). Socioeconomic characteristics included in the analysis are the status of the maize fields (owned or rented/shared by farm household) and whether the household is headed by a male or a female.[11] This results in the following specification for the farm household production function:

$$\ln Q^A = c_0 + c_1 \ln U^A + c_2 \ln D^A + c_3 \ln L^A + c_4 Terr +$$
$$c_5 Agro + c_6 Stat + c_7 Sex + e_2 \qquad (9.2)$$

in which Q^A is maize yield per hectare (in kilograms), U^A is the nitrogen content of urea per hectare (in kilograms), D^A is the nitrogen content of dung per hectare (in kilograms), L^A is estimated labour input per hectare (in hours), and *Terr* is the fraction of the maize fields that is terraced. The other variables are dummy variables: *Agro* = 1 if agroforestry is used, and = 0 otherwise; *Stat* = 1 if the farmer is the owner of the land, and = 0 otherwise; *Sex* = 1 if the household head is male, and = 0 if the household head is female. In order to avoid problems resulting from the high collinearity between land area and labour input, the variables in (9.2) are expressed on a per hectare basis. The primary input variables U^A, D^A and L^A are expected to have a positive impact on production (c_1, c_2, $c_3 > 0$); the coefficients of the other four variables may have either sign.

As indicated above, labour input is estimated as a linear function of (the natural logarithms of) nitrogen input, seed and land area. Inclusion of all these variables in the equation would create a linear dependency problem. In fact, the correlation coefficient between labour input and maize seed for the present sample equals 0.97. For that reason, seed is not included as an explanatory variable in the production function. Omitting seed input from the equation implies that the resulting coefficient estimate for labour input will reflect the combined impact of labour and seed input (see Dhrymes, 1978: 225–6).

Table 9.3 presents the estimation results for the LEIA and HEIA households, and for the total sample. A Chow test was used to test whether or not the parameter values for the LEIA sample are the same as those for the HEIA sample (Kennedy, 1992: 108). The resulting value for the Chow test (3.99) indicates that the null hypothesis of equal coefficients for the two samples should be rejected. The estimated coefficients for urea, dung and labour in the equation for low-input farming are positive and significantly different from zero (at the 5 per cent testing level). In the equation for high-input farming, these coefficients are also positive, but the coefficient for dung does not differ significantly from zero. As expected, the elasticity of maize production with respect to urea input is much higher for HEIA than for LEIA. For dung, however, the reverse is true. In other words, the responsiveness of maize production to external nitrogen input from urea is highest for high-input systems, while responsiveness of production to internal nitrogen input from dung is higher for low-input systems.

Table 9.3   OLS regression results for LEIA and HEIA systems

| Variable | Coefficient (t-values in parentheses) | | |
	LEIA	HEIA	Total sample
$Ln\ U^A$	0.07**	0.35**	0.08**
	(2.61)	(2.61)	(3.92)
$Ln\ D^A$	0.13**	0.03	0.04*
	(2.95)	(1.09)	(1.88)
$Ln\ L^A$	1.05**	0.86**	1.35**
	(1.27)	(3.78)	(7.70)
Terr	0.57	0.44*	0.47*
	(1.27)	(2.06)	(2.12)
Agro	−0.67**	−0.06	−0.36**
	(2.97)	(−0.46)	(−2.68)
Stat	−0.72**	−0.28	−0.50**
	(2.70)	(−1.43)	(−2.83)
Sex	−0.34	−0.53*	−0.50**
	(1.35)	(−2.50)	(2.80)
No. of observations	46	58	104
R^2	0.69	0.48	0.60
F-statistic	12.3**	6.66**	20.5**
Chow value			3.99*

Note: ** = significant at $P < 0.01$; * = significant at $P > 0.05$.

The elasticity of production with respect to labour input is higher for LEIA farming. So, although the average labour productivity is lower for LEIA than for HEIA, an additional hour of labour input is more productive in LEIA than in HEIA farming, *ceteris paribus*. However, labour represents a combined labour–seed input. Negative coefficients are found for most of the other variables. Only the fraction of the land that is terraced is found to have a positive impact on production, but the estimated coefficient does not differ significantly from zero for both agricultural systems. Interestingly, the dummies for agroforestry and land ownership are negatively related to agricultural production in low-input farming. The latter finding may be explained by the fact that farmers that sharecrop or rent land have to produce more in order to pay the rent for the land they are using. Agroforestry practices within LEIA systems imply a sacrifice in terms of available land for cropping, and apparently do not supply sufficient nutrients in the short run to substitute for organic fertilizers. Finally, female-headed households are found to have a higher yield in high-input systems than male-headed households.

Conclusions

Separate estimates of the production function reveal fundamental differences between HEIA and LEIA cropping systems. Production elasticity for high-input agriculture is strongly dependent on nitrogen input from urea, while for low-input agriculture nitrogen input from dung is far more important. Average land and labour productivity levels in the latter system stay above those reached under HEIA, possibly owing to the lower input efficiency of dung compared to urea and the higher labour requirements for dung application. Moreover, LEIA systems partly compensate lower nitrogen input with relative higher labour use; for each kilogram of maize output, LEIA farmers apply 0.42 working days, against 0.28 for HEIA farmers (Table 9.2). This is because of labour demands for soil maintenance activities (such as tree cultivation) and labour use for transport and application of manure. The regression results indicate, however, that the marginal labour productivity in LEIA and HEIA systems is similar, and any differences are not significant.

Both high- and low input systems are characterized by increasing returns to changes in factor proportions ($c_1 + c_2 + c_3 > 1$), so that margins for improvement of crop productivity are present. Within HEIA systems, major productivity growth is reached through higher use of external inputs, while for LEIA systems reliance on higher labour intensity seems to be more likely. The latter tendency implies that substitution between labour and nutrient inputs is feasible, thus considering the nutrient status as a function of the quantity of labour invested in soil fertility-building activities (Dommen, 1992). Labour is traditionally executed by women, so the higher yield reached by households with a female head could be related to the gender division of labour.

For policy purposes, attention could be dedicated to the economic and institutional conditions that may enhance the feasibility of LEIA or HEIA systems. Relative prices of nitrogen input (from urea or dung) compared to crop output determine the selection of each technique. Increasing of the price of urea will make LEIA systems somewhat more attractive. Otherwise, progress in (transport) infrastructure, information availability, access to credit and other improvements in the functioning of markets will usually reduce the costs of purchasing inputs and increase the farm gate price received for crop output. Small peasant producers who are only marginally incorporated into the market will be induced to produce for the market (De Janvry and Sadoulet, 1994) and, after the input–output price ratio has passed a certain critical level, to adopt high external input production techniques. As a consequence, low-input agriculture tends to be restricted to an environment with low market development; in the long run this may limit the opportunities to improve its economic performance.[12]

Small farmers with limited land resources will give priority to high land productivity at lowest possible risk. Moreover, the effects on labour demand and internal division of labour should be analysed seriously. If LEIA requires more labour, the sacrifice of farm households in terms of *leisure* or external wage income may limit its adoption. In case of limited market development or missing markets, technology choice in basic food crop production may be extremely restricted (De Janvry *et al.*, 1991).

The *access* to resources and/or markets may also influence resource allocation and technology choice. In the case of a limited development of local factor markets (for capital and land), small farmers depend on informal sources for access to credit to purchase inputs, and on landlords to acquire access to land. In these circumstances, prices are fixed within the framework of a contractual arrangement (Hayami and Otsuka, 1993). In order to induce these farmers towards LEIA, household savings behaviour and the propensity to invest in soil maintenance activities are of primary importance. The high labour input that is needed for soil conservation implies that it is a feasible option only when labour opportunity costs are low.

Most LEIA experiences can be found at individual farms and within externally financed rural development projects. Extension towards a (sub)regional scale takes place through farmer-to-farmer communication and supporting activities of local NGOs. As most LEIA techniques offer locally specific solutions, diffusion will remain limited to their specific *recommendation domain*. But in order to reach some minimum scale in marketing of organic products (and thus creating a separate market segment), broader adoption remains an important perspective. Therefore, *'farmers-pull'* instruments that reinforce the socioeconomic environment of peasants' demands for internal inputs may be even more important than the supply of appropriate technology.

Incorporation of a LEIA orientation in agrarian policies for regional development therefore requires the identification of suitable incentives that influence technology choice at the farm level. As discussed above, costs and benefits are not the only relevant parameters for the selection of techniques by peasant producers, as profit maximization is usually not the only goal. Moreover, sustainable land use is not always an explicit priority at the farm level and has to be made consistent with other household objectives. This will offer valuable insights into the conditions that could be favourable for HEIA or LEIA. Farm household modelling may offer a feasible methodology to evaluate the impact of agrarian policy instruments on land use (Ruben *et al.*, 1994).

Further empirical analysis of the economic rationality of LEIA farming is urgently needed. This should be based on detailed data sets describing farmers' behaviour. Concise registration and analysis of variable input use, labour use and output level, their prices and relative scarcity, will offer valuable insights into the conditions that could be favourable for HEIA or LEIA.

Notes

1 Data used for this research are derived from farm surveys conducted within the framework of the INRES Project with Brawijaya University in Malang. Theunis van Rheenen is acknowledged for his support to make this database accessible, and Marja van der Lubbe for her assistance with the statistical processing. The authors wish to thank Arie Kuyvenhoven (WAU) and Max Merbis (SOW-VU) for their comments on a previous draft.

2 While HEIA systems can become more easily sustainable with respect to nutrients, LEIA systems mostly reach better results for reduced emission of chemical residues.

3 With appropriate policies to correct for market imperfections, environmental off-site effects could be incorporated into input costs or output prices.

4 Evaluations of income streams based on nutrient depletion, and valued against market prices for fertilizers, indicate that in Southern Mali up to 40 per cent of farmers' incomes proceed from soil mining (van der Pol, 1992).

5 The valuation of labour cost is debatable. For on-farm labour, a *reservation wage* can be determined as the minimum remuneration required to mobilize labour resources. Furthermore, *leisure* time also has to be valued, as it clearly contributes to household utility. In the case that additional labour demands are met by family labour, leisure decreases. This may be compensated by relying on hired labour, but only at the cost of an increased marketing rate of output (in order to guarantee wage payment), reinforcing the influence of market risks. Consequently, while natural risk is avoided in LEIA systems, market risks may increase.

6 For simplicity, it is assumed that the prices of nitrogen input in fertilizer and dung are the same. The analysis can easily be extended, preferably in a three-dimensional framework, to the case of different prices for the two sources of nitrogen input.

7 Assuming the costs of complementary inputs are equal for the two techniques.

8 The assessment of risk is based on reduced yield variance due to improved soil management (soil moisture and organic matter contents). Moreover, price risk depends on yield covariance among farmers in the same region. Small peasant producers are considered to be *risk-averse*, thus willing to sacrifice part of their income for risk diversification. This trade-off should be included in the cost–benefit framework.

9 The resulting estimation procedure for the production functions is a variant of two-stage least squares. In the first stage, labour input is regressed on some relevant exogenous variables for the small (IFHS) sample. The result is used to derive an instrumental variable estimator of labour input for the large (EFHS) sample. In the second stage, production is regressed on the instrumental variable estimator of labour input and a number of exogenous variables.

10 Urea and dung were the only nutrient sources that were measured in the survey. Another nitrogen source, often used by households in the survey area, is the presence of gliricidia trees at the border of the fields. This potential nitrogen source is taken into account as a dummy variable.

11 Some additional variables were included in the initial analyses. These include the age of

the head of household, total family size, whether the household produces only for own consumption or also for sale, the average slope of the tilled maize land, village dummies, whether maize is intercropped with cassava or not, and land quality (good, regular or less suitable for agriculture). Forward as well as backward elimination methods within multiple regression analyses indicated that these variables do not contribute significantly to explaining the variation in maize production. For that reason, these variables were excluded from subsequent regression analyses.

12   It should be noted, however, that the picture may change when prices of important external inputs are such that they reflect external (off-site) environmental costs. The incorporation of environmental costs related to high chemical input use will raise the ratio of input to output prices for high external input agriculture. As a result, profitability of HEIA techniques will decline and LEIA techniques are likely to be preferred by more farmers.

References

Ali, M. and D. Byerlee (1991), 'Economic Efficiency of Small Farmers in a Changing World: a Survey of Recent Evidence', *Journal of International Development*, **3**: 1–27.

Anderson, J.R. (ed.) (1995), *Agricultural Technology: Policy Issues for the International Community*, CAB International, Wallingford, UK.

Byerlee, D. (1995), 'Technology Transfer Systems for Improved Crop Management: "Lessons for The Future"', in J.R. Anderson (ed.), *Agricultural Technology*.

De Janvry, A. and E. Sadoulet (1994), 'Structural adjustment under transaction costs', in F. Heidhues and B. Knerr (eds), *Food and Agricultural Policies Under Structural Adjustment*, Peter Lang, Frankfurt.

De Janvry, A., M. Fafchamps and E. Sadoulet (1991), 'Peasant Household Behaviour with Missing Markets: Some Paradoxes Explained', *Economic Journal*, **101**: 1400–1417.

Dhrymes, P.J. (1978), *Introductory Econometrics*, Springer, New York.

Dommen, A.J. (1992), *Physical and Economic Interactions in African Traditional Agriculture: Implications for Resource Conservation*, UNCTAD, Geneva.

Hayami, Y. and K. Otsuka (1993), *The Economics of Contract Choice: An Agrarian Perspective*, Clarendon Press, Oxford.

Hayami, Y. and V.W. Ruttan (1985), *Agricultural Development: An International Perspective*, Johns Hopkins University Press, Baltimore.

Hiemstra, W., C. Reijntjes and E. van der Werf (1992). *Let Farmers Judge: Experiences in Assessing the Sustainability of Agriculture*, Intermediate Technology Publications, London.

Kennedy, P. (1992). *A Guide To Econometrics*, 3rd edn, Blackwell, Oxford.

Mausolff, C. and S. Farber (1995), 'An Economic Analysis of Ecological Agricultural Technologies among Peasant Farmers in Honduras', *Ecological Economics*, **12**: 237–48.

Pretty, J.N. (1995), *Regenerating Agriculture: Policies and Practices for Sustainability and Self-Reliance*, Earthscan, London.

Rabbinge, R. and M.K. van Ittersum (1993), 'Tension between Aggregation Levels', in L. Fresco, L. Stroosnijder, J. Bouma and H. van Keulen (eds), *The Future of the Land: Mobilising and Integrating Knowledge for Land Use Options*, John Wiley & Sons, Chichester, UK.

Reardon, T. (1995), 'Sustainability Issues for Agricultural Research Strategies in the Semi-Arid Tropics: Focus on the Sahel', *Agricultural Systems*, **48**: 345-59.

Reardon, T. and S. Vosti (1992), 'Issues in the Analysis of Policy on Soil Conservation and Productivity at the Household Level in Developing Countries', *Quarterly Journal of International Agriculture*, **31**: 380-96.

Reijntjes, C., B. Haverkort and A. Waters-Bayer (1992), *Farming for the Future: An Introduction into Low-External-Input and Sustainable Agriculture*, Macmillan, London.

Ruben, R. and N. Heerink (1995), 'Economic Evaluation of LEISA Farming', *ILEIA Newsletter*, **11**(2): 18-20.

Ruben, R., G. Kruseman and H. Hengsdijk (1994), 'Farm Household Modelling for Estimating the Effectiveness of Price Instruments on Sustainable Land Use', DLV Report No. 4, AB-DLO/DE-WAU, Wageningen, The Netherlands.

UNDP (1992), *Benefits of Diversity: An Incentive Toward Sustainable Agriculture*, New York.

van Keulen, H. and H. Breman (1991), 'Agricultural Development in the West African Sahelian Region: A Cure Against Land Hunger?', *Agriculture, Ecosystems & Environment*, **32**: 177-97.

van der Pol, F. (1992), 'Soil Mining: An Unseen Contributor to Farm Income in Southern Mali', Bulletin 325, Royal Tropical Institute, Amsterdam.

van Rheenen, T. (1995), 'Farm Household Level Optimal Resource Allocation: An Explorative Study in the Limestone Area of East Java', PhD study, Wageningen Agricultural University, The Netherlands.

Vereijken, P. (1992), 'A Methodic Way to More Sustainable Farming Systems', *Netherlands Journal of Agricultural Science*, **40**: 209-23.

10 Evaluating Sustainability of Intensive Farming Systems in China[1]

F. Qu[a], R. Zhang[b] and J. Wu[c]

Introduction

China is the largest developing country, with only 0.09 hectare of arable land per capita. In 1991, grain output and GNP of per capita were 378.3 kg and US$390, respectively. China's efforts to increase food production and to meet other socioeconomic objectives have had destructive impacts on the environment, including soil erosion, increasing land desertification and intensifying environmental pollution. To address these problems, since the early 1980s China has paid increasing attention to alternative farming practices or a system of sustainable agriculture that suits its own national conditions.[2] By the early 1990s, some 29 sustainable agriculture pilot units had been set up at the county level, 138 at the township level and more than 1200 at the village or farm levels. These pilot projects, whose purpose is to carry out experiments and demonstrate sustainable agriculture programmes, are scattered over all provinces and municipalities in mainland China, except for the Tibet Autonomous Region. It is likely that more and more areas at different levels will be incorporated into sustainable agriculture in the future.

After a relatively long term of sustainable agricultural development, it is necessary to examine its effects on the environment and the rural economy. This chapter evaluates the sustainability of alternative farming systems in China, using multi-criteria evaluation. First of all, the main features of sustainable agriculture development are identified which affect the

[a] Resource Economics Division, Nanjing Agricultural University, Nanjing, 210095, PRC.
[b] Institute of Environmental Protection, The Ministry of Agriculture, Tianjin 300191, PRC.
[c] Institute of Agricultural Ecology, Zhejiang Agricultural University, Hanghou 31000, PRC.

framework of evaluation indicators and models. Then a multi-criteria evaluation model of a sustainable farming system is developed, followed by a case study. Brief conclusions then follow.

Main Features of Sustainable Agriculture in China: Background to Evaluating Sustainability

Although a generally accepted definition of sustainable development exists (that found in the Brundtland report), defining a workable definition of sustainable agriculture is complicated. After more than 10 years of experience, more and more agricultural scientists and economists characterize China's sustainable agriculture as a comprehensive agroecosystem based on a multi-tier and multi-purpose intensive management system and on successful agricultural practices, especially those of China's traditional organic farming (see Chapter 2 of the present volume). This agroecosystem is designed and managed in accordance with ecological economic principles and systematic engineering methodology, through the application of advanced science and technology. Three principles are stressed: (1) the protection and conservation of natural resources and environment are the foundation for sustainable agricultural productivity; meanwhile food security and income increase are prerequisites for reducing pressure on the environment; (2) sustainable agriculture emphasizes the relationships of components within the agroecosystem and the relationship between it and the socioeconomic environment; and (3) sustainable agriculture stresses that agricultural resources should be recycled and saved within the production system in order to reduce the negative impacts of external inputs and production wastes on the environment, and to lower the production costs of agricultural products (Luo and Han, 1990).

As an important alternative to petroleum-based agriculture, the concept of sustainable agriculture was proposed first in the United States in the early 1980s (Harwood, 1990). According to Parr *et al.* (1990), a workable concept of sustainable agriculture is the low-input farming system that seeks to optimize the management and use of internal production inputs (that is, on-farm resources) in ways that provide acceptable levels of sustainable crop yields and livestock output, and that result in economically profitable returns. In fact, sustainable agriculture in North America is mainly a low-input farming system, while biodynamic agriculture is the dominant form of sustainable agriculture in Western Europe. Many aspects of sustainable agriculture in China, especially the overall goals and basic means of achieving the goals, are similar to those of sustainable agriculture in developed countries. Both types have a very definite holistic orientation.

Both are concerned with long-term environmental and economic sustainability of agricultural production, placing major emphasis on crop rotations and other soil-building practices. Both emphasize man as an ally of nature, rather than man trying to conquer nature (Cheng and Taylor, 1992).

In some aspects, however, China's sustainable agriculture differs from that which has been practised in developed countries, especially in terms of goal setting, the levels of external inputs and agricultural instruments, which are to a large extent determined by basic physical and socioeconomic conditions of the country. A comparison of sustainable agriculture in China and developed countries is provided in Table 10.1. From this table we find that the most important feature of sustainable agriculture in China is the emphasis on increasing output and intensive external input. Thus, in China, sustainable agriculture is also called intensive sustainable agriculture or high external input sustainable agriculture (HEISA) (Qu *et al.*, 1994).

Table 10.1 Comparison of sustainable agriculture (SA) in developed countries and China

Item		SA in developed countries	SA in China
1	Emphasis of goals	Protecting environment and maintaining resource base with acceptable yield or return	Integration of increasing output and income, and improving ecological and social impacts
2	Strategic options	Environmental protection planning, project programming and legislation	Integrated development of resources and diversified structure of ecological economy
3	Industrial organization	Cropping and breeding related to soil use and water resource protection	Cropping, forestry, animal husbandry, fishery, processing and environmental engineering industries
4	Input system	Low-input, self-maintaining and greater emphasis on reduced chemical use	Intensive input of techniques and labour, less emphasis on reduced chemicals use
5	Development and organization	Spontaneous and scattered activities of researchers and farmers; sluggish advocation by government	Government initiates, supports and directly intervenes

A Conceptual Model of Sustainability: Evaluation of Alternative Farming Systems

A sustainable farming system is one that maximizes the net (discounted) economic benefits of farming subject to the maintenance of the services and quality of agriculture's natural resource base over time. Therefore sustainability is related to the ecological and economic functions, the effect on society of farming systems and the harmonization of the ecological-economic functions and their impact. Thus multi-criteria evaluation is necessary to measure sustainability.

For the main features of sustainable farming in China, Figure 10.1 provides a basic system of evaluation indicators that are used to measure the sustainability of the system. The evaluation indicators are divided into three hierarchical levels. The top level (V) is the integrated benefit index that measures the sustainability of the farming system. The indicators in the second layer (B) are different benefit indices that measure the different ecological, economic and social benefits of the farming system. Ecological benefits are defined in terms of the efficiency of the material-balance cycle, energy consumption and appropriate impacts on the environment. Economic benefits include a measure of the ratio of economic outputs to factor inputs in the farming system: that is, a benefit–cost ratio. Social benefits are related to the impacts of the farming system on society, such as income distribution changes and the commodity rate of products (Qu, 1987). The bottom layer (X) includes all individual indicators that belong to different benefit groups (X_l, X_e and X_s) and supply basic information for indicator index evaluation of

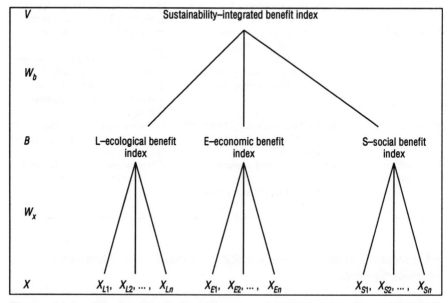

Figure 10.1   Hierarchical framework of indicators for evaluating sustainability

the intermediate and top layers. The basic procedure of evaluating the sustainability of alternative farming systems from X to V using weights W_x and W_b is also displayed in Figure 10.1.

The forgoing indicators provide only a basic framework for analysis. The choice of and the weights for specific indicators for the second and third layers depend on land types and the evaluation units themselves, because different land types and farming system levels (e.g., household farm or village farm) result in different structures and functions within a farming system. Therefore, the matrix of X-level evaluation indicators can be defined as $A = \{X_{kij}\}$, where k refers to the type of benefit (L, E or S); i to the land type and j to the farming system (village, household and so on). As illustrated in Table 10.2, indicators are available for six land types and four farming levels. If the evaluation is to be carried out in the wetland area and at the village level (X_{33}), for example, all necessary individual indicators chosen according to the characteristics of wetland farming system at the village level should be taken into account in the development of indicators for evaluating the farming system.

The Multi-criteria Evaluation Model of a Sustainable Farming System (MEMSFS)

In China, a sustainable farming system emphasizes the integration and improvement of ecological, economic and social benefits of agriculture. Sustainability is thus evaluated by a measure of the integrated benefit that is derived from the ecological, economic and social benefits. For this purpose, two methods are employed in MEMSFS: an integrated index method and a fuzzy evaluation method. Let the integrated evaluation index V (top layer in Figure 10.1) be defined as

$$V = \sum_{i=1}^{n} W_i B_i ,$$

Table 10.2 **Matrix of indicators for evaluating sustainable farming systems in China[a]**

	Plain area	Hill & mountain	Wetland	Inland water	Grassland	Suburban area
County	X_{11}	X_{12}	X_{13}	X_{14}	X_{15}	X_{16}
Township	X_{21}	X_{22}	X_{23}	X_{24}	X_{25}	X_{26}
Village	X_{31}	X_{32}	X_{33}	X_{34}	X_{35}	X_{36}
Family farm	X_{41}	X_{42}	X_{43}	X_{44}	X_{45}	X_{46}

Note: [a] In this table, the k subscript (for benefit index) is ignored for convenience where B_i is the intermediate level value of indicator i; W_i is the adjusted weight of indicator B_i in determining V; and n is the number of intermediate-level indicators (L, E, S). The indicator V measures the sustainability of alternative farming system, with a higher value of V indicative of a more sustainable system. The B-level indices are constructed in a similar fashion to those of the top level.

The difficulty is to determine the weights to be applied in constructing the upper level indexes of sustainability. In this study, the weights assigned to I-level indicators, which are then used to obtain the $I+1$-level indicators, are determined from specialists' pairwise judgments of the importance of two I-level indicators. A fuzzy approach similar to that described by van Kooten (Chapter 22) is used. However, when there is more then one land type in the evaluation area or unit, each indicator will have several different weights in different land types: the relative importance (weights) of the same indicator will vary with different land types. In this case, several weights of the same indicator U_i, should be adjusted to integrated weight according to the proportion r of each land type area to the total area of evaluation unit. Adjusted indicator weights will become

$$W_i^* = \sum_{r=1}^{n} U_{ir} K_r$$

where K_r is the proportion of the area of land type r to the total area of evaluation unit, and n is the number of land types involved in the given evaluation unit.

Application of MEMSFS to the Evaluation of Sustainable Agriculture[3]

The case study is of Chuanziying, a typical plain village located to the south of Tianjin's suburb. Dryland farming is carried out, with grain, vegetables, pork, eggs and milk being the main products of the agroecosystem. Until 1982, the ecological–economic benefits were low and unstable, as manifested in low outputs of grain and low net per capita income (Table 10.3). The main problems included (1) alkaline soil and insufficient water resources; (2) a serious deficit of soil nutrients, partly as a result of the burning of most crop residues; and (3) sole reliance on grain production. Since 1982, the village has carried out a sustainable agriculture programme (a village-level pilot project) as directed by the Institute of Environmental Protection (i.e. Ministry of Agriculture) and local government. Priority has been given to energy resource development, soil improvement and income enhancement. As can be seen from Table 10.3, major achievements included (1) cropping and structural adjustments to improve soil quality and increase

Table 10.3 Changes in main ecological-economic indicators of the sustainable farming system in Chuanziying Village, 1982-90

Indicator	1982	1984	1986	1988	1990
Grain output (kg/ha)	3 600	4 215	5 003	5 738	6 375
Rate of use of solar light (%)	0.237	0.303	0.408	0.264	0.308
Output-input ratio of energy in cropping	1.575	2.264	3.107	2.378	2.788
Input-output ratio of nitrogen	1.552	1.496	1.137	1.543	0.893
Ratio of organic to inorganic	0.253	0.849	1.144	1.281	2.134
Coefficient of forage use (%)	17.93	18.39	20.82	21.41	22.74
Bioenergy as % of total energy consumption	28.22	31.23	89.80	58.59	61.88
Forest cover (%)	6.0	6.5	7.0	8.5	10.0
Changes of improved soil (%)	4.8	5.0	5.3	6.4	7.4
Benefit-cost ratio in farming	1.69	1.84	3.14	2.48	3.07
Land productivity (yuan/ha)[a]	3 797	5 860	4 901	5 132	5 933
Labour productivity (yuan/person)[a]	680	1 850	4 503	4 777	3 539
Net income per capita (yuan)[a]	46	49	134	139	352
Commodity rate of products (%)	34.99	45.87	56.85	62.31	84.33

Note: [a] not deflated.

Source: Zhang *et al.* (1992).

farm income; (2) increasing fertilizer use, with a 'reasonable' blend between organic and inorganic fertilizers; (3) biogas energy resource development to replace fossil fuels and provide organic fertilizer; and (4) agricultural product processing to increase product value and to retain more residues within the agroecosystem.

During the last decade, China's sustainable agriculture programme appears to have been a success. With cropping strategies that improve nutrient balances in the soil, biogas development that reduces the burning of crop residues, and livestock production that increases the supply of organic fertilizers, soil quality has improved, as has the potential for an increase in economic benefits. In 1990, grain output per hectare had increased to 6375

Table 10.4 Integrated evaluation of sustainable farming in Chuanziying Village, 1982-90

Benefit Index	1982	1984	1986	1988	1990
Ecological	0.1066	0.3024	0.5256	0.5888	0.6890
Economic	0.0000	0.1671	0.4668	0.5416	0.8814
Social	0.0000	0.2116	0.4921	0.7350	0.9764
Integrated	0.0460	0.2522	0.4738	0.5796	0.8315

kg (from 3600 kg in 1982), and net income per capita, at 352 yuan, was some eight times greater than that in 1982, albeit in nominal terms. The changes in the lower level indicators are provided in Table 10.3, while changes in the intermediate and top level indicators are provided in Table 10.4.

Conclusions

In this chapter, a multicriteria evaluation model for sustainable farming systems (MEMSFS) was developed, and applied at the village level near Tianjin, China. The results indicate that China's sustainable agriculture programme has a significant positive effect on both the agricultural environment and the rural economy, especially with regard to food security, alleviation of poverty, rural employment and soil conservation. The case study provides evidence to indicate that ecological and socioeconomic goals are not competitive, but that ecological, economic and social benefits can be simultaneously improved – farming systems in China can be sustainable.

Notes

1 This chapter is part of the research project, 'Methodology and Application of Ecological Agriculture Evaluation in China', which was sponsored by the Ministry of Agriculture PRC. An earlier version of the chapter was presented at the Third Asian Farming System Symposium. The authors are grateful to N. Heerink, P.G. Pardey and R. Ruben for helpful comments on a previous draft.
2 From the late 1970s, the alternative to the existing farming system was originally called 'ecological agriculture' in China. Because its concept and contents are different from those of ecological agriculture in developed countries, but somewhat related to what 'sustainable agriculture' involves in developed countries, most agricultural scientists and economists have denoted 'ecological agriculture' in China as 'sustainable agriculture' (see Cheng and Taylor, 1992; Lu, 1992).
3 The main work in this section was carried out at the Institute of Environmental Protection of the Ministry of Agriculture PRC, Tianjin.

References

Cheng, X. and D.C. Taylor (1992), 'Sustainable Agriculture Development in China', *World Development*, **8**(2).
Harwood, R.R. (1990), 'A History of Sustainable Agriculture', in C.A. Edwards, R. Lal and P. Madden (eds), *Sustainable Agricultural System*, Soil and Water Conservation Society, Ankeny, Iowa.

Lu, L. (1992), 'Development and Perspectives of Sustainable Agriculture', *Agricultural Tech-Economics* **2**.

Luo, S. and C. Han (1990), 'Ecological Agriculture in China', in C.A. Edwards, R. Lal and P. Madden (eds), *Sustainable Agricultural System*, Soil and Water Conservation Society, Ankeny, Iowa.

Parr, J.F., R.I. Papendick, I.G. Youngberg and R.E. Meyer (1990), 'Sustainable Agriculture in the United States', in C.A. Edwards, R. Lal and P. Madden (eds), *Sustainable Agricultural System*, Soil and Water Conservation Society, Ankeny, Iowa.

Qu, F. (1987), 'The Eco-Economic Evaluation in Agriculture: A Conceptual Approach', *Agricultural Economic Problems*, **4**.

Qu, F., N. Heerink and W. Wang (1994), 'Land administration reform in China: benefits, shortcomings, and options for further reform', *Wageningen Economic Papers*, 1994-4, Wageningen Agricultural University, The Netherlands.

Zhang, R., S. Liu, Z. Wang and F. Qu (1992), 'Theory and Methodology of the Evaluation of Sustainable Agriculture', *Jiangsu Rural Economics*, special issue.

PART III
EFFICIENCY AND
PRODUCERS' KNOWLEDGE
AND PERCEPTIONS

11 Regional Variation in Efficiency of Fertilizer Use: Food Crop Production in Togo

E.M. Koffi-Tessio[a]

Introduction

Food production per capita in Sub-Saharan Africa is decreasing and the natural resource base is degrading. Already there is evidence that soil degradation has reduced crop yields in West Africa. This is due mainly to rapid population growth rate accompanied by salinity of lands, reduced fallowing, deforestation and erosion. Most countries in Sub-Saharan Africa, including Togo, are experiencing declining levels of food self-sufficiency. In 1965, for example, these countries were 107 per cent self-sufficient, but self-sufficiency declined to 103 per cent in 1975 and to only 93 per cent in 1985 (Rask, 1992). The population growth rate ranged between 2.5 per cent and 4.4 per cent between 1970 and 1975, for example, while crop production grew at a rate of only 1.7 per cent on average. Loss of self-sufficiency coincided with a period of declining per capita incomes and stable per capita food consumption. Hence poverty is the main cause of food insecurity in Africa, with the small subsistence farmers experiencing the lowest labour productivity. To ensure sustainable agricultural production and increase in incomes (and agricultural labour productivity), at least in the short run, it is important to improve soil fertility through the use of external nutrients such as fertilizers (Teboh, 1994).

In Togo, soil fertility is declining at an alarming annual rate of 18 kg/ha

---

[a] Université Du Bénin, E.S.A., B.P. 1515, Lomé, Togo.

for nitrogen (N), 5 kg/ha for phosphorus (P) and 15 kg/ha for potassium (K), although these values hide large regional disparities. It is anticipated that soil nutrient deficits of N, P and K will reach 21 kg, 7 kg and 19 kg per hectare by the year 2000 if appropriate measures are not taken (IFDC, 1990). This chapter examines the regional variation in efficiency of fertilizer use in Togo. It is hypothesized that existing comparative advantages of producing food crops among the five regions of Togo results in differential efficiency of fertilizer use, which is important for the formulation of food policy.

Food Production and Security in Togo

Food security can be defined as: 'the ability of a country, a region or a household to assure, on a long-term basis, that its food system provides the total population access to a timely, reliable and nutritionally adequate supply of food' (Eicher and Staatz, 1986; World Bank, 1986). Food security involves both adequacy of and accessibility to food, with the latter accomplished by increasing effective demand by increasing incomes. In this regard, micro and macro factors are important, and include technology innovation and adoption, institutions that support small farmers and merchants (for example, extension services and guaranteed access to credit) and monetary, fiscal and trade policies that affect the overall rate of growth and distribution of income (Coetzee and Van Zyl, 1990). Increased use of fertilizers is one partial and legitimate solution that can improve food security in developing countries, but it should be accompanied by innovation and extension regarding the way fertilizers can best contribute to an increase in incomes (for example, cropping systems, optimal application rates and timing of applications).

As noted, food security is important to West African countries, and the situation has worsened in the last several decades. Trends in the yields of the major food crops in Togo are provided by region in Table 11.1. Comparing the regions with identical major crops, the 'Plateaux' and 'Maritime' regions have a comparative advantage in producing cassava and maize, whereas the 'Kara' and 'Savanes' regions specialize in producing millet. Though sorghum consumption is more important in the northern part of Togo (Central, Kara and Savanes regions), the 'Plateaux' region appears to have a comparative advantage in producing sorghum. Since food yields can be increased by improved applications of fertilizer, *ceteris paribus*, it is important to understand the determinants of fertilizer use in relation to food security.

At the farm level, decisions to use fertilizers in Togo depend on crop mix choice, farm size, availability of extension services, income, access to

Table 11.1   Yield trends of three major crops in Togo, by region, 1983–93 (kg/ha)

Region	Major crops	1983	1984	1985	1986	1987	1988	1989	1990	1991	1992	1993
Maritime	Maize	634	818	929	220	443	910	720	651	593	500	964
	Cassava	5 950	8 200	9 261	10 343	9 384	8 409	8 367	8 615	7 811	9 566	8 597
	Groundnuts	506	416	554	432	274	468	252	340	309	318	311
Plateaux	Maize	889	1 069	893	1 090	1 078	1 505	1 408	1 417	1 186	1 355	1 450
	Sorghum	680	784	772	2 307	1 319	1 345	925	1 215	1 413	1 559	1 280
	Cassava	5 054	10 963	7 987	7 398	9 520	10 996	8 845	7 824	11 937	7 399	9 822
Central	Sorghum	611	1 399	770	1 052	775	790	716	766	769	776	773
	Maize	772	1 305	1 211	1 574	1 558	1 549	1 447	1 634	1 602	1 989	1 598
	Yams	9 736	12 558	13 576	11 669	10 115	11 898	11 937	11 934	11 666	11 974	11 310
Kara	Sorghum	647	832	627	766	759	805	791	762	549	531	823
	Beans	256	416	436	183	296	194	422	328	235	275	193
	Millet	528	478	520	485	580	354	379	472	359	389	345
Savanes	Millet	643	783	712	825	645	572	1 007	437	391	698	635
	Maize	461	619	912	—	626	1 172	2 016	630	1 734	1 906	1 776
	Sorghum	508	624	723	820	584	399	883	450	555	888	478

Source: Calculated from data 'Direction des Enquêtes et Statistiques Agricoles' (DESA, 1996).

fertilizers and risk (Akakpo-Drah, 1992). Other factors such as rainfall and soil quality are also important (IFDC, 1990), as are (lack of) credit, transport networks and seasonal price variations.

Value–Cost Ratio Approach: Analytical Framework and Results

Economic activities should be efficient, with improvements in efficiency assumed to be good and declines in efficiency taken to be bad. Economic efficiency consists of technical efficiency and price efficiency. Technical efficiency is purely an engineering concept. A production unit is said to be more technically efficient than another if it consistently produces larger quantities of output from the same quantity of measurable inputs. Price or allocative efficiency, on the other hand, is purely a behavioural concept that depends on the device used to measure value of marginal product and opportunity cost. A production unit is said to be price-efficient if it maximizes profits or minimizes cost. The value–cost Ratio (VCR) is an efficiency indicator that is used in partial economic analysis. In the case of fertilizer, VCR compares the value of increased yield due to the use of fertilizer with the per unit cost of fertilizers used. It is defined as follows:

$$VCR = FRR \frac{PUP}{FUP}$$

where FRR is the fertilizer response rate, PUP is the product unit price and FUP is the fertilizer unit price. Various studies by the Food and Agriculture Organisation (FAO) and the International Fertiliser Development Centre (IFDC) in Africa suggest that the minimum VCR should be two in order to account for handling, transport, opportunity cost, and so on (Pouzet and Harris, 1992), although a more recent study by the IFDC (1990) suggests that VCR must be greater than four to take account of various risks related to prices and weather. Field investigations provide various VCRs, varying from one researcher to another, and with the date of the study, region and crop. But VCR also varies as a result of food and fertilizer prices and, more importantly, the fertilizer response rate, which is influenced by material and sociological factors at the regional and local levels (Pouzet and Harris, 1992).

As noted above, there are regional disparities in soil degradation and extant soil condition. Deficits in nitrogen are almost the same in all regions, but northern regions have higher deficits in phosphorus while southern

Table 11.2 Fertilizer application rates for food crops in Togo, by region, 1982–90[a]

Region	Food crops	1982	1983	1984	1985	1986	1987	1988	1989	1990
Maritime	Maize	8.2	1.4	2.0	2.9	2.6	1.3	1.3	2.4	2.7/2.8
	Cassava	0	0	0	0	0	0	0	0	0
	Groundnuts	6.6	0	0	0	17.0	0	0	0	0
Plateaux	Maize	2.4	1.9	0.6	0.9	0.9	0.8	0.7	2.0	1.9/1.2
	Sorghum	0	0	0.2	0.3	0.6	0	0	0.2	0
	Cassava	0	0	0	0	0	0	0	0	0
Central	Sorghum	8.0	6.5	2.5	1.8	0.05	0.03	0.07	0.05	0.2
	Maize	18.4	23.0	10.9	10.3	9.5	9.8	9.3	6.8	8.4/11.8
	Yams	0	0	0	0	0	0	0	0	0
Kara	Sorghum	3.4	4.5	4.0	4.0	0.5	1.4	0.8	1.4	0.6
	Beans	0.7	0.01	0.1	0.4	0	0	0.5	0.4	0.4
	Millet	—	—	—	—	—	—	—	—	—
Savanes	Millet	—	—	—	—	—	—	—	—	—
	Maize	—	—	7.3	8.1	—	5.4	9.6	26.4	12.1/11.5
	Sorghum	21.3	13.1	6.7	4.4	6.6	3.7	1.8	4.7	4.0

Note: [a]Fertilizer application rate = area fertilized/total cultivated area × 100 (expressed as %); 0 means no fertilizer is applied to the crops, while a dash means data are not available.

Table 11.3   Value–cost ratios for three food crops in Togo, by region, 1983–94

Region	Food crops	1983	1984	1985	1986	1987	1988	1989	1990	1991	1992	1993	1994
Maritime	Maize	7.8	4.8	2.3	3.7	3.8	4.0	3.0	3.4	2.8	3.0	1.8	1.8
	Cassava	15.8	16.2	11.3	9.7	9.7	8.4	7.3	8.7	9.5	9.2	9.7	4.2
	Groundnuts	–	–	–	–	–	6.6	8.1	7.4	7.7	8.6	7.1	4.8
Plateaux	Maize	16.5	8.2	5.8	6.9	6.6	7.1	4.9	5.7	4.2	5.5	3.3	2.8
	Sorghum	14.5	7.4	4.8	6.0	4.7	6.6	4.4	4.8	3.0	7.2	5.4	2.4
Central	Maize	10.1	5.4	3.7	4.0	4.0	4.5	3.3	3.5	3.2	4.5	2.3	1.8
	Yams	11.3	9.6	7.0	5.2	5.2	5.2	5.3	5.5	4.8	4.7	4.1	2.3
	Sorghum	5.9	4.3	2.5	2.3	3.1	3.3	2.5	2.1	2.2	3.0	2.1	1.1
Kara	Sorghum	5.9	4.3	2.5	2.3	3.1	3.3	2.5	2.1	2.2	3.0	2.1	1.1
Savanes	Millet	9.0	7.2	6.2	3.5	3.6	6.1	5.0	3.5	–	–	–	–
	Maize	–	–	–	–	–	5.3	4.3	3.5	3.5	4.9	5.4	3.6
	Sorghum	6.4	5.5	4.3	3.0	2.8	4.4	3.5	2.6	3.8	4.5	3.2	–

Source: Calculation.

regions have greater potassium deficits (Stoorvogel and Smaling, 1990; Mokwunye and Pint-Toyi, 1991). Fertilizer application rates are 15 per cent of recommended levels for domestic food crops, but 100 per cent of recommended levels for cotton, an export crop. During the agricultural campaign of 1993–4, less than 20 per cent of farmers used fertilizers on food crops. Regional comparative analysis indicates that almost 50 per cent of farmers used fertilizers in the 'Savanes' region, but less than 5 per cent used then in the 'Maritime' region; the share of farmers using fertilizers in the 'Plateaux', 'Centrale' and 'Kara' regions was 18.6 per cent, 23.9 per cent and 29.6 per cent, respectively (DESA, 1996). As we move from the forest zone to the savannah zone, fertilizer use intensifies for poor-quality soils (Table 11.2). This was true of maize between 1982 and 1990, though the 'Plateaux' region, with a low fertilizer rate of application, has the highest yield, compared to the 'Savanes' region with a high fertilizer rate of application.

Based on 12 years of data (1983–94) for three main food crops in each region of Togo and the fertilizer response rates obtained from field trials, value–cost ratios were calculated (Table 11.3). As the data are from specific field locations within regions, prices are specific to that location. The results indicate a downward trend for all crops and regions. For example, the VCR for maize in the 'Maritime' region decreased from 7.8 in 1983 to 1.8 in 1994. The same trends were observed in the 'Plateaux' and the 'Centrale' regions. Maize became an important food crop in the 'Savanes' region in 1988, and the VCR was evaluated at 5.3. By 1993, it had fallen to 3.6. These downward trends in VCRs clearly threaten food security in Togo as farmers' incomes and maize availability are decreasing. Except for the period before 1988, and the 'Plateaux' region after 1988, the VCRs for maize are lower than four in all other regions.

Recent FCFA devaluation (January 1994) increased the price of fertilizers by almost 100 per cent, leading to a sharp decrease of VCR for all food crops in all regions in Togo. Togo embarked on a Structural Adjustment Programme from 1983, with subsidies on fertilizers being gradually removed over the period 1983–7. This also contributed to the decrease of the VCRs.

In the 'Kara' and 'Savanes' regions, identical downward trends for VCRs for sorghum were observed. The 'Savanes' region has a comparative advantage in production of sorghum using fertilizers. Since soils in the region are poor, fertilizer response is good. Except for 1994, tubers such as cassava in the 'Maritime' region and yam in the 'Central' region had VCRs greater than four. Farmers are likely to be better off investing in these crops. Prospects for groundnuts production using fertilizers in the 'Maritime' region are favourable, though the VCR decreases as a result of devaluation.

Conclusions

Overall, fertilizer use provides significant returns to the farmers and can contribute to food security in Togo. Unfortunately, the average rate of fertilizer application to food crop remains low compared to that for export crops. Farmers growing export crops usually have easier access to fertilizers than those growing food crops, and this is a primary determinant of the different application rates. If food security is to be improved, it is important to improve delivery systems in order to increase access to fertilizer by farmers. Togo is a producer of natural phosphate. The use of natural phosphate as a substitute for imported fertilizers is now gaining national attention because it is cheap and more accessible to farmers, and because of its potential contribution to food security. Although use of phosphate might raise additional environmental concerns, it is clear that fertilizers play an important role in future food security in Togo. However, government policies need to focus more on both technical and economic considerations in order to improve fertilizer use efficiency in Togo.

References

Akakpo-Drah, A. (1992), 'Analyse socio-économique de l'adoption des innovations au Sud-Est du Togo: Cas des engrais, semences améliorées et pesticides', Rapport No 91/01/AE, ESA-UB, Lomé.

Coetzee, G.K. and J. Van Zyl (1990), *An Assessment of Food Security in South Africa*, IIAE/AGRECONA, Windhoek.

Direction des Enquêtes et Statistiques Agricoles (DESA) (1996), *Productions et Superficies des principales cultures vivrières au Togo*, MDR/DESA, Togo.

Eicher, C.K. and J.M. Staatz (1986), 'Food Security Policy in Sub-Saharan Africa', in A. Maunder and U. Renborg (eds), *Agriculture in a Turbulent World Economy*, Allen Gower, Brookfield, Vermont.

IFDC Africa (1990), *Etude des secteurs des Engrais en Afrique: Approvisionnement, commercialisation et demande des engrais en République du Togo*, LEI-DLO, Institut de Recherche Agro-Economique.

Mokwunye, A.U. and A.K. Pinto-Toyi (1991), 'Efficient fertiliser use for increased crop production: The IFDC–AFRICA experience in Togo in Alleviating Soil Fertility Constraints to Increased Crop Production in West Africa', *Fertilizer Research*, **29**(1): 235–44

Pouzet, D. and G. Harris (1992), *Economic Analysis of On-Farm Fertiliser Use Options at Village Level in three West African Agroecologies (III) The Village of Naki-Est (Guinea Savanna Zone) in Dapaong Region of Togo: Soil Fertility Restoration Project Report Lomé*, IFDC, Africa.

Rask, N. (1992), *Dynamics of Food Self-Sufficiency and Economic Growth: A Challenge to Southern African Agriculture*, IIAE, Windhoek.

Stoorvogel, J.J. and E.M.A. Smaling (1990), 'Assessment of Soil Nutrient Depletion in Sub-Saharan Africa: 1983–2000. Vol. I: Main Report, The Winand Staring Centre for Integrated Soil and Water Research (SC-DLO)', Wageningen, The Netherlands.

Teboh, J.F. (1994), 'Le Phosphate naturel en tant qu'amendement du sol: Qui doit en assurer le financement? Etudes diverses sur les engrais', No. 12, IFDC-Africa, Lomé, Togo.

World Bank (1986), *Poverty and Hunger: Issues and Options for Food Security in Developing Countries*, World Bank, Washington, DC.

12 Environmental and Economic Effects of Spatial Variability in Cropping: Nitrogen Fertilization and Site-specific Management[1]

T.J. de Koeijer, G.A.A. Wossink and F.J.H.M. Verhees[a]

Introduction

For sustainable agriculture, efficient input use is crucial. Therefore insight into the relation between inputs and outputs is needed, but the functional form and empirical estimates of production functions are still a matter of debate. Following von Liebig, it is assumed in production ecology that the production function for the single nutrient input, that is, nitrogen (N), phosphate (P) or potassium (K), can be characterized by a linear relation with a plateau (LRP) (de Wit, 1992; Paris, 1994). For any given nutrient, the threshold yield is the yield in the absence of the nutrient. As the level of nutrient is increased, yield is assumed to increase until a plateau is reached, when no further increases in yield can be obtained by additional doses of the nutrient. Of course, the level of the threshold yield, the slope of the response curve and the height of the plateau depend on the applications of other nutrients. Agronomists argue that the LRP for any one nutrient should be estimated under conditions where none of the other major nutrients is limiting (Perrin, 1976). Economists generally assume functional forms with

[a] Departments of Ecological Agriculture, Economics & Management and Marketing & Marketing Research, Wageningen Agricultural University, P.O. Box 8130, 6700 EW, Wageningen, The Netherlands.

decreasing returns for nutrients, but recent economic research points to the superiority of LRP models (Kuhlmann, 1992; Ackello-Ogutu *et al.*, 1985; Berck and Helfand, 1990; Frank *et al.*, 1990; Paris, 1992, 1994).

According to Goudriaan (1979), relations where an output no longer diminishes continuously as the input increases can be described as a non-orthogonal hyperbola. The general form of this function is:

$$y = (-(b + x) + ((b + x)^2 - 4acx)^{0.5})/(-2a) \qquad (12.1)$$

where *y* refers to output and *x* to input. Parameter *c* gives the maximum level of the output. The initial efficiency between input and output is defined by *c*/*b* and *ac*/*b* determines whether the output reaches the maximum gradually (0<*ac*/*b*<1, curve with decreasing returns) or abruptly (*ac*/*b* = 1, Blackman curve (Schröder *et al.*, 1993).

The major issue in the discussion about production functions is the value of *ac*/*b*. As Berck and Helfand (1990) point out, the variation in *ac*/*b* can be explained by the aggregation level on which the experiments are based. In production ecology, production functions are often derived from experimental plot data. However, the estimation of production functions at the field, farm or country level is a completely different matter. Across any large area, variation within agro-ecosystems occurs as a result of environmental variation and agricultural activity (Almekinders *et al.*, 1995). Therefore variability in agro-ecosystems plays a far more important role at the farm level than in controlled experiments. Sources of variation are the environment, genetic resources and management (Almekinders *et al.*, 1995). Under conditions of variation, plants in different areas of the field will be limited by different limiting values of inputs. By accounting for the heterogeneity of input levels in a crop, Berck and Helfand (1990) achieved a reconciliation between the von Liebig and the smooth aggregate production functions. They showed that, even if a crop operates according to the limiting nutrient principle on homogeneous plots, the addition of heterogeneity of one or more inputs or residual fertility results in a smooth aggregate production function for the whole field. This is illustrated in Figure 12.1.

Since functional form depends on the amount of variation, and on the level of aggregation, decreasing the aggregation levels results in different functional forms and optimal input levels. This means that the efficiency of inputs can be improved by decreasing the aggregation level. This happens when site-specific management is used. Site-specific management means that the use of inputs is attuned to differing circumstances within a plot. As the result of increasingly stringent environmental legislation, site-specific management is currently getting greater attention.

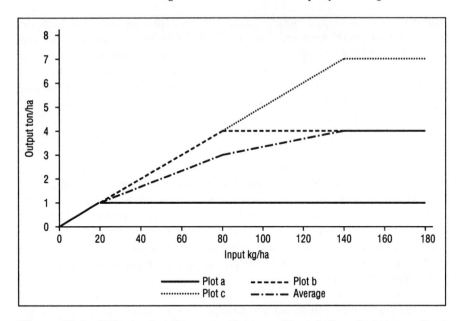

Figure 12.1   **Effect of soil properties on the relation between plant nutrient input (kg per ha) and crop output (kg per ha)**

This chapter highlights soil fertility as a source of environmental variation and the use of site-specific management. Schueller (1992) provides an overview, arguing that, although field variability is important, it is not studied as much as would be expected. For the Dutch situation, which is characterized by very small fields compared to the case of North America, the economic and environmental effects of site-specific fertilizing have been tested on hypothetical soils (van Noordwijk and Wadman, 1992) and for only one crop (Booltink and Verhagen, 1997). In this chapter we present the results for an existing field and a whole crop rotation, thereby gaining more insights into the practical relevance of site-specific fertilization management. The objectives of the remaining sections of this chapter are to explain the importance of variability for input–output relation assessment and to present a case study for the economic and environmental effects of site-specific fertilizing.

Nitrogen Model: Methodology

To analyse the relation between physical yield, nitrogen input, heterogeneity and nitrogen leaching, a model is used that simulates the nitrogen dynamics in a crop rotation (Habets and Oomen, 1994). The nitrogen-Dicea model uses relatively simple data which can either be provided by farmers or are easy to estimate using historical information. The model enables the assessment of the amount of nitrogen leaching in a certain crop rotation, thereby providing a better indication of the environmental damage of fertilizing compared to only calculating the nitrogen surplus. In the nitrogen-Dicea model the mineralization of organic matter and the water balance are central processes. Inputs in the model are the initial level of organic matter, the level of nitrogen-input, the deposition of nitrogen, nitrogen-fixation, the crop rotation and weekly weather data. The weather data include weekly soil temperatures at a depth of 10 centimetres, weekly precipitation and evaporation. Other data include the pH, ground water fluctuation during the summer, the thickness of soil layers in the profile, soil type, date of sowing, date of maximum evaporation, nitrogen-assimilation of the crop, maximum evaporation factor, amount of fertilizer, soil tillage, initial organic matter and data about crop residues.

For each week during the growing season the water balance, mineralization, nitrogen intake and nitrogen loss are calculated by the model. Model outcomes include the amount of mineral nitrogen, the amount of organic matter and the water balance of the preceding week and these serve as starting-points for the calculations of the following week. The amount of water leaching, nitrogen leaching and nitrogen available are the outcomes of the weekly calculations. Crop growth is not simulated in the nitrogen-Dicea model. If the relation between available nitrogen and crop yield is known, however, the effects of lower nitrogen fertilization can be calculated. If the amount of nitrogen uptake needed for optimal growth is not available, the resulting yield loss will be calculated.

For the experimental field, only the yield is known, not the nitrogen uptake, but we start by assuming there is no nitrogen shortage. Nitrogen uptake is calculated using functions derived from Greenwood et al. (1990). These functions represent the relation between total dry weight yield and the percentage of nitrogen in the total crop when nitrogen is not a limiting factor.

$$TN_p = ((5.697 \ W_p^{-0.53})/100)W_p \qquad (12.2)$$

$$TN_w = ((3.857 \ W_w^{-0.33})/100)W_w \qquad (12.3)$$

TN_p = total nitrogen uptake of potato in ton/ha^{-1}
TN_w = total nitrogen uptake of winter wheat in ton/ha^{-1}
W_p = total production of potato (main product plus crop residue) in d.wts ton/ha^{-1}

W_w = total production of winter wheat (main product plus crop residue) in d.wts ton/ha^{-1}

Functions (12.2) and (12.3) are only available for winter wheat and potatoes. Hence we use the following formulas, derived from Stouthart and Leferink (1992), for sugar beet and barley:

$$TN_b = 15 \, G_b + 3.5 \, R_b \qquad (12.4)$$

$$TN_s = 1.5 \, B_s + 3.0 \, R_s \qquad (12.5)$$

TN_b = total nitrogen uptake of summer barley in kg/ha^{-1}
TN_s = total nitrogen uptake of sugar beet in kg/ha^{-1}
G_b = grain production of summer barley in fresh product ton/ha^{-1}
R_b = residue production of summer barley in fresh product ton/ha^{-1}
B_s = beet production of sugar beets in fresh product ton/ha^{-1}
R_s = residue production of sugar beets in fresh product ton/ha^{-1}

It is assumed that half the straw remains on the land. The amounts of crop residue for barley and sugar beet are derived from Stouthart and Leferink (1992), and Smit and van der Werf (1992). If in the simulations there is less nitrogen available than needed according to functions (12.2)–(12.5), the yield effects of lower nitrogen fertilization can be calculated with the relation between available nitrogen and crop yield if nitrogen is a limiting factor. The following formulas, derived from Schröder *et al.* (1993), are used:[2]

$$N_P = (13.93 \, y_p{}^2 - 173 \, y_p)/(y_p - 11.9) \qquad (12.6)$$

$$N_W = (21.67 \, y_w{}^2 - 207 \, y_w)/(y_w - 9.4) \qquad (12.7)$$

$$N_S = (8.34 \, y_s{}^2 - 150 \, y_s)/(y_s - 16.7) \qquad (12.8)$$

N_P = the total nitrogen uptake by potatoes in kg N/ha^{-1}
N_W = the total nitrogen uptake by winter wheat in kg N/ha^{-1}
N_S = the total nitrogen uptake by sugar beet in kg N/ha^{-1}
y_p = the production of main product of potato in kg d.wts/ha^{-1}
y_w = the production of main product of winter wheat in kg d.wts/ha^{-1}
y_s = the production of main product of sugar beet in kg d.wts/ha^{-1}

These functions are characterized by diminishing returns. Therefore nitrogen uptake increases significantly when the maximum yield is approached. The amount of nitrogen uptake by the crop residues must be known because it plays an important role in the nitrogen cycle. These relations are also derived from Schröder *et al.* (1993):

$$DM_p = (-(173 + x_p) + ((173 + x_p)^2 - 4 \cdot 41.09 \cdot 4x_a)^{0.5})/(-2 \cdot 41.09) \quad (12.9)$$

$$DM_w = (-(126 + x_w) + ((126 + x_w)^2 - 4 \cdot 12.9 \cdot 9 \cdot x_w)^{0.5})/(-2 \cdot 12.9) \quad (12.10)$$

$$DM_s = (-(216 + x_s) + ((216 + x_s)^2 - 4 \cdot 33.37 \cdot 6.3 \cdot x_s)^{0.5})/(-2 \cdot 33.37) \quad (12.11)$$

DM_p = the amount of potato crop residue in kg d.wts/ha^{-1}
DM_w = the amount of winter wheat crop residue in kg d.wts/ha^{-1}
DM_s = the amount of sugar beet crop residue in kg d.wts/ha^{-1}
x_p = the total nitrogen uptake by potato in kg/ha^{-1}
x_w = the total nitrogen uptake by winter wheat in kg/ha^{-1}
x_s = the total nitrogen uptake by sugar beet in kg/ha^{-1}

The foregoing functions have to be adjusted in order to predict the same nitrogen-uptake as the functions of Greenwood *et al.* (1990) for the situation where there is no nitrogen deficiency. The ratio of the second and the third coefficient were kept the same, which implies that the initial nitrogen efficiency remains unchanged as required by the LRP theory. This correction is done only for potatoes and sugar beet. For winter wheat, no nitrogen deficiency occurred in the simulations.

$$N_{Pclay} = (13.93 \, y_{Pclay}^2 - 83.01 \, y_{Pclay})/(y_{Pclay} - 5.71) \quad (12.12)$$

$$N_{Psand} = (13.93 \, y_{Psand}^2 - 154.10 \, y_{Psand})/(y_{Psand} - 10.60) \quad (12.13)$$

$$N_{Sclay} = (8.34 \, y_{Sclay}^2 - 145.96 \, y_{Sclay})/(y_{Sclay} - 16.25) \quad (12.14)$$

$$N_{Ssand} = (8.34 \, y_{Ssand}^2 - 176.50 \, y_{Ssand})/(y_{Ssand} - 19.65) \quad (12.15)$$

The model is applied to farmland situated in a polder (reclaimed around 1930) in the north-west of the Netherlands. The plot is 300 by 200 metres and part of the 'Van Bemmelen' experimental farm. The soil is marine clay, with soil characteristics described on 65 points of the plot. In the plot, four different soil profiles can be distinguished. Three of these react in the same way to nitrogen. For this research, it was sufficient to divide the plot into only two different zones. Roughly, the field consists of one-third sand and two-thirds clay. The most important characteristics of the two profiles are represented in Table 12.1.

In the simulations of the different fertilization strategies, weather data of one year, 1985, are used. This year can be characterized as relatively wet (so water was not a limiting factor) and with normal temperatures. The four-year crop rotation in the case study included potato, winter wheat, sugar beet and summer barley. The model was validated by simulating for 1994 and 1995,

Table 12.1   Data of the two small soil profiles distinguished in the case study

	Zone 1	Zone 2
Type of soil	sand	clay
pH	7	7
Groundwater level (cm)	145	145
Thickness layers (cm)	25/35	40/80
Organic matter (kg d.wts/ha)	59 200	78 000
Yield winter wheat (kg/ha) (1995)	8 000	10 000
Yield potato (kg/ha) (1994)	25 000	45 000

Source: Verhagen *et al.* (1995).

for which the yields and nitrogen input were registered on the experimental field, Van Bemmelenhoeve. As the data show, the variation in crop yield is considerable, especially for potatoes, where the yield level in clay is almost double that of sand. The yield ratio between zones 1 and 2 for sugar beet and summer barley is assumed to be equal to the yield ratio between zones 1 and 2 for winter wheat. Sugar beet and summer barley, like winter wheat, have an intensive root system, in contrast to potato. The prices used in the model calculations were based on KWIN (PAGV, 1994) which gives average prices for 1989–93 of Dfl. 0.1955 for potato, Dfl. 0.3768 for wheat, Dfl. 0.1067 for sugar beet and Dfl. 0.4322 for barley, per kg product.

Scenarios

The following nitrogen fertilizing strategies were simulated:

1   a constant rate of fertilizer application according to the nitrogen recommendations (IKC-at, 1993). In this strategy the field is regarded as a homogeneous clay soil. Although one-third of the field consists of sand, the nitrogen residue in the soil is taken into account as an average value for the whole;

2   location-specific also according to the nitrogen fertilizer recommendations (IKC-at, 1993). In this strategy, the soil is fertilized differently depending on whether it is clay or sand and the nitrogen residue in the soil is distinguished for both zones;

3   a constant rate of fertilizer application according to the environmental restriction that drinking water not exceed 50 mg nitrate per litre groundwater;

4   location-specific according to the previously mentioned environmental restriction;

5   potential nitrogen efficiency, location-specific but without yield reduction. Here there is enough nitrogen available for the plant throughout the growing season, while the residue of nitrogen is minimized. This strategy is highly theoretical because it is based on a priory knowledge of the weather data over the cropping season.

For the simulations of the environmental scenarios, the restriction of 50 mg nitrate per litre groundwater is converted into the amount of allowed nitrogen loss per hectare. The amount of allowed nitrogen loss depends on soil characteristics and the crop. The calculated amount of tolerated nitrogen loss is the starting-point for the simulations of the environmental scenarios. With this knowledge, the maximum amount of nitrogen input is found, after which possible yield reductions can be calculated. In the scenario with a constant rate of fertilizer application, the average amount of allowed nitrogen loss per crop is used. In the site-specific scenario, the allowed nitrogen loss is calculated per zone.

Simulation

In Table 12.2, the average quantities of applied nitrogen fertilizer, nitrogen leaching annual and income effects are presented for the complete crop rotation of four years. In the traditional strategy (constant rate of application according to fertilizer recommendations for clay) there is no shortage of nitrogen although the amount of nitrogen residue, especially in the fourth year, is very low. Nitrogen-leaching on sand is higher than nitrogen-leaching on clay. In the location-specific fertilizing strategy, the quantity of applied fertilizer is higher for sand than for clay. This is caused by the nitrogen residue which, in sand, leaches to a greater extent than in clay. In the spring the nitrogen supply in the sand is lower, resulting in higher fertilizer application.
Within the crop rotation, there are also differences in the leaching of nitrogen. Leaching of nitrogen is significantly higher for potato. This is caused by higher fertilizer applications for potato, which has a relative inefficient root system.
Insights into the effect of location-specific fertilization can be gained by comparing the strategies according to the fertilizer recommendations for the total field with location-specific fertilization. According to the model results, location-specific fertilization does not lead to a decrease in average nitrogen input or nitrogen-leaching. The distribution of nitrogen fertilizer between the clay and sand zones differs; in spring there is hardly any nitrogen in sand, so more nitrogen has to be administered. On clay less nitrogen leaches, there is

Table 12.2   Average annual N-fertilizing, nitrogen-leaching and income effects

Fertilizing strategy	Zone[a]	N-input kg/ha	N-leaching kg/ha	Income-effect Dfl./ha
Constant at	S	166	112	0[b]
recommended rate	C	166	92	0
		166	**99**	**0**
Location-specific at	S	183	131	−18
recommended rate	C	157	83	9
		166	**99**	**0**
Constant rate within	S	88	59	−164
environmental norm	C	88	27	−81
		88	**38**	**−109**
Location-specific rate within	S	49	43	−365
environmental norm	C	111	36	42
		90	**38**	**−93**
Rate based on potential	S	106	53	60
N-efficiency	C	94	16	76
		98	**28**	**71**

Notes: [a] Zone S is characterized by soil type sand. Zone C is characterized by soil type clay.
[b] The N-uptake was sufficient for non-limiting growth.
Figures in bold indicate the acreage weighted average.

more nitrogen available in spring, and hence the fertilizer input is lower. The distribution of nitrogen-leaching under a site-specific regime differs greatly when compared to the traditional scenario. The leaching of nitrogen on sand is higher because of the higher nitrogen input, but this effect is compensated by lower nitrogen-leaching on clay. The economic effect is nil.

To meet the drinking water norm of 50 mg nitrate per litre in groundwater, nitrogen input must be reduced by 47 per cent. This reduces nitrogen-leaching by 62 per cent. In the crops potato and sugar beet, this restriction results in considerable yield reductions for both zones. For summer barley, yield reduction only occurs in zone 1. The yield reduction for potato is bigger on clay than on sand, while for sugar beet the biggest yield reduction occurs on sand. The yield reduction is 191 Dfl./ha. The yield loss is not compensated for by lower input costs of 74 Dfl./ha.

Sugar beets are especially sensitive to a lower nitrogen input. Nitrogen is applied early in the season and, therefore, a great part leaches, especially on sand; in winter wheat, this problem is less important because nitrogen is applied in three portions.

Where nitrogen-leaching needs to be curtailed in any year or zone, there is growth inhibition due to nitrogen deficiency. This happens especially on sand with potato, sugar beet and to a lesser extent with barley. On clay, a small yield reduction occurs only with potato. Comparison of the two environmentally restricted strategies provides insight into the economic effects of site-specific fertilizing when nitrogen input has to comply with environmental restrictions. Location-specific nitrogen application has a small positive economic effect of about 20 Dfl. per hectare.

The last strategy represents the search for the most efficient fertilizing strategy; according to the nitrogen-Dicea model, there is no nitrogen deficiency and, at the same time, the nitrogen residue is kept as small as possible. To determine the optimal amount of nitrogen, the weather over the coming season is taken into account, although this is not possible in reality. On sand, more nitrogen is supplied in spite of the lower need of the crop in order to compensate for leaching on sand. The strategy complies with the drinking water norm. A 42 per cent reduction in nitrogen input is possible in this strategy. The nitrogen leaching is only 28 per cent of the leaching in the traditional strategy. For potato especially, a strong reduction of nitrogen input occurs, as the last kilogram of nitrogen cannot be extracted from the ground by a crop, and certainly not by potato.

Discussion

It is clear that fertilizer recommendations are for farmers who are risk-averse. They are not so much based on the maximum yield level and nitrogen uptake as on the soil and weather characteristics in which expected losses are already taken into account. The form of the current nitrogen recommendations is a fixed amount of nitrogen fertilizer minus an estimate of the mineral nitrogen supply of the soil (van Noordwijk and Wadman, 1992). Therefore the site-specific distribution of nitrogen does not result in higher yields. The risk that too much nitrogen leaches during bad weather conditions for optimal crop growth is smaller with site-specific management. This means that site-specific management has a positive effect by reducing the risk that there is not enough nitrogen available on sand. Even though, in this research, the calculations were done for relatively wet weather conditions, no positive yield effect was found. However, the simulations indicate that the available nitrogen would not have been sufficient for optimal crop growth if the weather conditions had been rather worse.

Like the economic effects, the effects on groundwater quality were also nil. According to the explanation presented above, site-specific management can lead to more leaching of nitrogen in very bad weather conditions. The scenarios for the environmental restrictions can have smaller negative economic effects if higher leaching in the crops with high economic returns can be compensated for by lower leaching of nitrogen in winter wheat and barley. The economic effect of location-specific fertilization could be improved by compensating for the high leaching level of nitrogen on sand by the lower leaching level of nitrogen on clay.

The theoretical scenario shows how much nitrogen should be applied to avoid risk. Even for the relatively unfavourable weather conditions (wet) in the simulations, the amount of nitrogen can be reduced by 40 per cent without yield losses. This scenario indicates the importance of not only site-specific management but also weather and, therefore, time-specific management. In fact, the theoretical scenario could be partly realized by dividing the fertilizer input into many doses spread over the growing season.

In this research, the two differing soil types in the experimental field are treated as more or less homogeneous. In practice, however, the exact location of these differing soil types is not known and more zones may exist. Furthermore, the border between two zones is gradual. This means that the simulation results indicate the maximum differences because, in practice, location-specific fertilizing cannot be as accurate as is assumed in this study.

If site-specific management was extended to include phosphate and potassium, the economic effect in the case of environmental restrictions could be more significant. Furthermore, as regards environmental and economic effects, the effects, not only on inputs of nutrients and their emissions, but also on the use of pesticides, are of interest. Because there are interactions between fertilizing and chemical crop protection, the calculated economic and environmental effects of site-specific management could be more significant when applied to both types of inputs. However, further research into these interactions is required.

Notes

1   The authors are grateful to G.J.M. Oomen for comments on an earlier draft.
2   On the experimental field the production of winter wheat exceeded the maximum production according to the theoretical function. Therefore the function is adapted as follows: maximum dry matter yield per hectare is increased by 11.3 per cent to 9.4 tonnes. The ratio between the second and the third parameter should be constant to get the same initial nitrogen efficiency. Therefore, the second parameter is increased by 11.3 per cent as well. The formula then becomes as indicated in the text.

References

Ackello-Ogutu, C., Q. Paris and W.A. Williams (1985), 'Testing a von Liebig Crop Response Function against Polynomial Specifications', *American Journal of Agricultural Economics*, **67**: 873–80.

Almekinders, C.J.M., L.O. Fresco and P.C. Struik (1995), 'The Need to Study and Manage Variation in Agro-Ecosystems', *Netherlands Journal of Agricultural Science*, **43**: 127–42.

Berck, P. and G. Helfand (1990), 'Reconciling the von Liebig and Differentiable Crop Production Functions', *American Journal of Agricultural Economics*, **72**: 985–96.

Booltink, H.W.G. and J. Verhagen (1997), 'Using decision support systems to optimize barley management on spatial variable soil', in M.J. Kropff, P.S. Teng, P.K. Aggarwal, J. Bouma, B.A.M. Bouman, J.W. Jones and H.H. van Laar (eds), *Applications of Systems Approaches at the Field Level. Volume 2*, proceedings of the Second International Symposium on Systems Approaches for Agricultural Development, held at IRRI, Los Baños, Philippines, 6–8 December 1995.

de Wit, C.T. (1992), 'Resource Use Efficiency in Agriculture', *Agricultural Systems*, **40**: 125–51.

Frank, D.F., B.R. Beattie and M.E. Embleton (1990), 'A Comparison of Alternative Crop Response Models', *American Journal of Agricultural Economics*, **72**: 597–603.

Goudriaan, J. (1979), 'A Family of Saturation Type Curves, Especially in Relation to Photosynthesis', *Annals of Botany*, **43**: 783–85.

Greenwood, D.J., G. Lemaire, G. Gosse, P. Cruz, A. Draycott and J.J. Neeteson (1990), 'Decline in Percentage of N of C3 and C4 Crops with Increasing Plant Mass', *Annals of Botany*, **66**: 425–36.

Habets, A.S.J. and G.J.M. Oomen (1994), 'Modelling Nitrogen Dynamics in Crop Rotations in Ecological Agriculture', in J.J. Neeteson and J. Hassink (eds), *Nitrogen Mineralization in Agricultural Soils: Proceedings of a Symposium Held at the Institute for Soil Fertility Research Haren*, AB-DLO, Haren, The Netherlands.

IKC-at (1993), Stikstofbemestingsrichtlijnen voor de akkerbouw en de groenteteelt in volle grond, IKC-at, Lelystad, The Netherlands.

Kuhlmann, F. (1992), 'Zum 50. Todestag van Friedrich Aereboe: Einige Gedanken zu seiner Intensitätslehre', *Agrarwirtschaft*, **41**: 222–30.

PAGV (1994), *Kwantitatieve informatie voor de akkerbouw en groenteteelt in de vollegrond 1995*, PAGV, Lelystad, The Netherlands.

Paris, Q. (1992)' 'The von Liebig Hypothesis', *American Journal of Agricultural Economics*, **74**: 1019–28.

Paris, Q. (1994), 'Von Liebig's Law of the Minimum and Low-Input Technologies', in P.C. Struik, W.J. Vredenberg, J.A. Renkema and J.E. Parlevliet (eds), *Plant Production on the Threshold of a New Century*, Kluwer Academic Publishers, Dordrecht/Boston/London.

Perrin, R.K. (1976), 'The Value of Information and the Value of Theoretical Models in Crop Response Research', *American Journal of Agricultural Economics*, **58**: 54–60.

Schröder, J.J., P. van Asperen and G.J.M. van Dongen (1993), 'Nutriëntenbenutting en -verlies bij akkerbouwgewassen: een theoretische verkenning: Deelstudie voor het project "Geïntegreerde Akkerbouw"', CABO-DLO, Wageningen, The Netherlands.

Schueller, J.K. (1992), 'A Review and Integrating Analysis of Spatially-Variable Control of Crop Production', *Fertilizer Research*, **33**: 1–34.

Smit, A.L. and A. van der Werf (1992), 'Fysiologie en stikstofopname en-benutting: Gewas- en bewortelingskarakteristieken', in: H.G. van der Meer and J.H.J. Spiertz (eds), *Stikstofstromen in Agro-ecosystemen*, CABO-DLO, Wageningen, The Netherlands.

Stouthart, F. and J. Leferink (1992), *Akkerbouw: Mineralenboekhouding*, CLM, Utrecht, The Netherlands.

van Noordwijk, M. and W.P. Wadman (1992), 'Effects of Spatial Variability of Nitrogen Supply on Environmentally Acceptable Nitrogen Fertiliser Application Rates to Arable Crops', *Netherlands Journal of Agricultural Science*, **40**: 51–72.

Verhagen, A., H.W.G. Booltink and J. Bouma (1995), 'Site-Specific Management: Balancing Production and Environmental Requirements at Farm Level', *Agricultural Systems*, **49**: 369–84.

13   Farmers' Perceptions of Sustainable Production Techniques: Weed Control in Sugarbeet

G.A.A. Wossink, A.J. de Buck and J.H. van Niejenhuis[a]

Introduction

Given recent policy regulations, arable farmers in the Netherlands have to integrate environmental quality as an objective along with the conventional objectives of income and employment. Integrated Arable Farming Systems (IAFS) are considered an effective way to achieve a competitive, safe and more sustainable agriculture. In IAFS, pesticides and fertilizer inputs are replaced by measures requiring greater management skills, such as multifunctional crop rotation and integrated crop protection. Since 1979, IAFS prototypes have been developed and tested on experimental farms (Wijnands and Vereijken, 1992). In 1990, a project set up to disseminate IAFS prototypes included a pilot group of 38 innovator farms. These farms easily attained the governmental targets of diminishing inputs and also achieved attractive financial results (Wossink, 1994). As a follow-up in 1993, a second project included 500 arable farmers who intend to convert to integrated farming. These 500 farmers can be seen as potential early adopters. Despite these encouraging figures, there has been limited progress in the conversion towards IAFS (Schoorlemmer *et al.*, 1994).

Given that adoption of new agricultural technologies is a greater problem than increasing the stock of such technologies (Reichelderfer, 1989), a

[a] Department of Economics & Management, Wageningen Agricultural University, P.O. Box 8130, 5700 EW, Wageningen, The Netherlands.

fruitful research endeavour is to examine factors determining adoption. A crucial factor is the economic advantage to be gained. For IAFS techniques, the relative financial advantage is usually small, with such techniques frequently not in step with the prevailing values and norms of farmers. Further implementation efforts are considerable because of labour requirements and a high degree of complexity. This implies that, in the case of IAFS techniques, the well-known innovation characteristics suggested by Rogers (1983) are not fulfilled. In particular, because the financial benefits of IAFS techniques are small and uncertain, subjective aspects might be decisive in the adoption progress. This chapter focuses on the assessment of these subjective aspects.

Behavioural economics (Gilad and Kaish, 1986) emphasizes the relevance of psychological variables in explaining economic behaviour: motives, perceptions, attitudes and expectations – not the objective character of goods/actions or stimuli matter but the subjective characteristics as perceived by the decision maker. Hence perception plays an important role in selection processes. Adoption of a technology will depend on an agent's (farmer's) perception of the technology's bundle of associated characteristics. This approach is used in marketing research, but few studies have examined adoption factors in the context of farm management (for example, Adesina and Zinnah, 1993; Adesina and Baidu-Forsu, 1995; van der Meulen *et al.*, 1996).

The first objective of this chapter is to determine to what extent farmers' subjective perceptions of cost and risk differs from normative costs and risk – whether a lack of knowledge may explain the signalled delay in adoption of IAFS techniques. A second objective is to assess the characteristics perceived by farmers as important in adoption of IAFS techniques. Adoption of environmentally friendly weed control techniques in sugarbeet is the focus of this study, with economic aspects assessed by a normative analysis of costs and risks and behavioural aspects by perception analysis of survey data.

Data Use and Methods

The empirical analysis presented in this chapter is based on a survey of sugarbeet growers on the sandy soils in the region of North Limburg. In the study region there are about 700 sugarbeet growers, of whom 100 were approached, and 74 filled in the questionnaire.

Normative Analysis

Technological development has brought different possibilities for reducing the input of chemicals for weed control in sugarbeet. The farmer may choose 'low dosage systems', spraying a low quantity of chemicals just after emergence, or row spraying with additional mechanical control between the rows. Electronically operated mechanical control between the sugarbeet plants is a further way of reducing chemical use. In total, seven strategies of weed control in sugarbeet were analysed in the normative analysis.

Normative data from 'Kwantitatieve akkerbouw informatie' (Ippel and Noordam, 1991) were used to calculate the average costs per hectare of each weed control strategy. Only the variable costs are taken into account in this assessment at the crop level: namely, the costs of herbicides, fuel and lubricants and costs of machines used only for weed control in sugarbeet. All weed control strategies are equally effective.

In addition, risk and the opportunity costs of the equipment and labour were taken into account. In the risk assessment, a weed control treatment is considered successful if an application is followed by a long enough dry period. When postponement is necessary, spraying with a higher quantity of chemicals is required. At failure, the treatment is repeated if possible. Otherwise, a higher quantity is used one week later. Probabilities for postponement due to inappropriate weather conditions and probabilities for failure due to insufficiently prolonged dry period were determined using weather data for the period 1954–88. Adding the costs of the extra treatments, combined with their probabilities, yielded total costs for each of the seven weed control options, averaged over the year.

At the farm level, an 'efficiency line' can be constructed if the opportunity costs of labour and tractor use and the acreage of sugarbeet are known. This convex function consists of the points of lowest costs given a certain use of active ingredients; points dominated by a linear combination of other points are not taken into consideration. As opportunity costs of equipment and labour depend on the farming system, the acreage of sugarbeet, the capacity of the equipment and the cropping plan, a sensitivity analysis was carried out to gain insight into the influence of these costs on the optimal choice of strategy.

Perception Analysis

For the seven weed control strategies, the individual scores on prespecified features were measured. Respondents to a survey were asked to indicate, on a five-point Likert scale, their degree of agreement or disagreement with each of various features. The perception scores were used to explain the farmers' preference for one of the strategies. Factor analysis was used to construct scaled scores (Hair *et al.*, 1987).

Empirical Results

Seven strategies of weed control in sugarbeet are identified in Table 13.1, along with the outcomes of the normative analysis. Strategies 1 to 4 are used in practice; strategies 5 to 7 are based on a prototype of an experimental, electronically steered thinning machine that destroys the weeds *in* the row and can spray some chemicals around the sugarbeet plant. In calculating the costs, risk was accounted for by means of the probabilities of failure or postponement of the treatments and the costs of the extra operation required. The treatment can be repeated in the case of failure of strategies 1–4. In the case of failure of strategies 5–7, an emergency chemical treatment for weed control within the row is necessary.

Figure 13.1 presents efficiency frontiers for four different acreages of sugarbeet (2, 4, 6 and 10 hectares), and four different levels of costs for labour and tractor (0/0, 18/13 and 32/18 Dfl. per hour and costs of contract work).[1] The figure shows that new control systems enable a reduction in the use of active ingredients combined with some lower costs. Particularly for small acreage and in the case of contractor work, the strategies are financially similar, but vary significantly in herbicide use. The outcomes of Table 13.1 and Figure 13.1 were used to judge farmers' subjective perceptions of labour requirements, risk of failure and herbicide use.

The questionnaire indicated that 60 per cent of the 74 farmers applied strategy 2 ('spraying full field with low dose'). This system is most common in the Netherlands. Strategy 1 ('spraying full field with high dose') was used by 30 per cent of the respondents. Of the others, 8 per cent performed the weed control by using strategy 4 ('spraying row with low dose'). The average area of sugarbeet for farms in the survey was 3 hectares, which corresponds with the average area in the region. Cropping is a secondary activity for most farms, with the majority earning their main income from hogs or poultry (53 per cent) and horticulture (27 per cent).

Table 13.2 presents the mean scores on a five-point scale of 15 attributes that distinguish among the strategies of weed control. Only a few respondents were familiar with strategies 5–7; these are not included in Table 13.2. The attributes relating to agronomy, farm equipment and the social environment of the farmer are based on van Niejenhuis and Haverkamp (1992), Jorritsma (1985) and on expert advice. The mean scores are used to derive a ranking of the weed control options with respect to the features 'high weather risk', 'much labour required' and 'environmentally friendly', which are then compared with the results in Table 13.1. The subjective ranking of the features is in line with the normative ranking from Table 13.1. For each of the three features, the first four positions in the ranking were identical. Lack of knowledge of the features is apparently not an explanation

Table 13.1 Seven strategies for weed control in sugarbeet[a]

Strategy	Costs Dfl.ha⁻¹ Contractor	Costs Dfl.ha⁻¹ Own machinery	Costs due to risk[b] Dfl.ha⁻¹	Herbicides Active ingredients kg/ha⁻¹	Herbicides Costs Dfl.ha⁻¹	Labour requirements hour ha⁻¹
1 Spraying full field with high dose (twice)	653	518	—	5.18	473	1.0
2 Spraying full field with low dose (4 times)	636	366	—	2.02	275	2.0
3 Spraying rows with high dose (twice), mechanical treatment between the rows (3 times)	734	809	33	2.59	237	6.5
4 Spraying rows with low dose (4 times), mechanical treatment between the rows (3 times)	816	647	23	1.01	138	7.7
5 Spraying rows with high dose (once), 'electronic harrowing' in the row (once) and mechanical treatment between the rows (3 times)	827	1 715	45	1.52	118	7.9
6 Spraying rows with low dose (twice), 'electronic harrowing' in the row (twice) and mechanical treatment between the rows (3 times)	1 141	1 648	38	0.59	69	10.5
7 'Electronic harrowing' (3 times) and mechanical treatment between the rows (3 times)	1 158	1 409	72	0.50	45	11.3

Notes: [a] Area per farm 4 ha; opportunity costs for labour 32 Dfl.hr⁻¹, and for machinery 13 Dfl.hr⁻¹.
[b] Own mechanization.

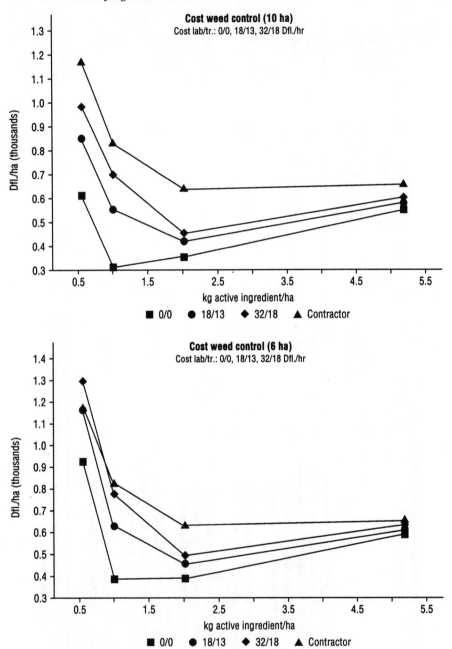

Figure 13.1　Efficiency frontiers for weed control in sugarbeet, by acreage

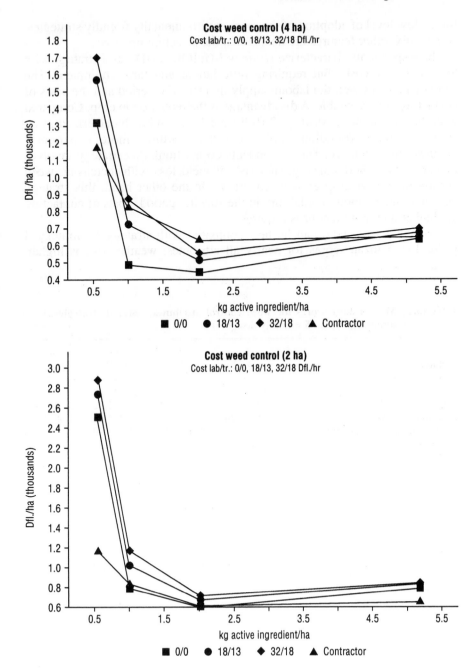

Figure 13.1 (continued)

for the low level of adoption of the more environmentally friendly strategies. Apparently, other features are decisive in the selection process.

The respondents characterize *strategy 1* (full field HD²) as a strategy with high herbicide costs, but requiring little labour and farm equipment. The strategy matches well the labour supply in a specific period and the costs of contacting are acceptable. A disadvantage is the reduction in crop. Compared with the first strategy, *strategy 2* (full field LD) can be characterized as an environmentally friendlier application that requires more experience, alertness and guidance. The respondents do not think this strategy involves higher costs of herbicides, greater risk of yield loss with increasing weed density or greater crop-growth reduction. On the other hand, this strategy does not match labour availability in the specific period, costs of contacting are higher and more labour is required.

Strategy 3 (row HD) can be best compared with strategy 1. Strategy 3 yields lower mean scores for nearly all attributes: weather risk is higher,

Table 13.2   Mean Likert scores for weed control attributes, selected strategies, (1 = totally agree, ... , 5 = totally disagree)[a]

Features	1 n = 52		2 n = 15		3 n = 7		4 n = 7	
	av.	s.d.	av.	s.d.	av.	s.d.	av.	s.d.
High cost of herbicides	1.97	1.31	3.82	1.31	4.38	1.02	3.75	1.49
High weather risk	2.57	1.34	2.10	1.37	1.94	1.48	1.38	0.52
Extra farm equipment required	4.64	0.89	4.40	1.14	2.00	1.10	2.00	1.31
Much experience required	3.04	1.48	1.97	1.26	1.75	0.86	1.88	1.13
High costs of the contractor	4.22	1.33	3.12	1.68	2.19	1.56	2.25	1.58
Great risk of yield loss with increasing weed density	2.95	1.34	4.36	1.00	3.94	1.39	3.38	1.51
Great uncertainty about effectiveness of herbicides	3.39	1.31	3.59	1.30	3.40	1.24	3.14	1.21
Great carry-over effects on subsequent crops	4.09	1.27	4.05	1.18	4.13	1.02	3.87	0.99
Much labour required	4.26	1.11	4.21	1.39	2.31	1.35	1.25	0.46
Good guidance required	2.82	1.59	3.31	1.25	1.94	1.24	1.75	0.89
Strong growth reduction	2.60	1.21	2.07	0.88	4.19	0.98	3.25	1.28
Does not match labour supply in specific period	4.21	1.04	4.47	1.37	2.44	1.31	1.13	0.36
Much alertness required	2.25	1.35	3.35	1.15	1.63	1.02	1.38	0.74
Many hours manually removing weeds required	3.82	1.20	4.05	1.07	3.56	1.31	2.00	1.51
Environmentally friendly	3.84	1.36	1.90	1.19	1.25	0.45	1.88	1.13

Note: [a] av. = average score; s.d. = standard deviation, n = number of respondents.

more labour and farm equipment are required, the costs of contracting are higher, the strategy does not match labour supply, and more experience and alertness are required. On the other hand, this strategy can be typified as environmentally friendly, with lower costs of herbicides.

Strategy 4 (row LD) can be best compared with strategy 2. Just like strategy 3, mean scores on strategy 4 are lower for nearly all attributes, but the margin between them is smaller. The major characteristic of this strategy is that it requires extra farm equipment. As this strategy requires more labour, it does not match labour supply in a specific period and the costs of contracting are higher. Just like strategy 3, it can be typified as environmentally friendly, with lower costs of herbicides.

Only a few respondents are familiar with *strategy 5* (row HD + mech.), *strategy 6* (row LD + mech.) and *strategy 7* (mechanical). In comparison with strategies 3 and 4, the respondents indicate higher weather risks, which require good guidance and alertness. These strategies also require more labour, which does not match labour availability in the specific period. According to the respondents, it also requires an increase in hours of manually removing weeds.

Factor analysis was applied to the perception scores. Factor analysis enables one to distinguish the most relevant underlying attributes and their interrelations, as perceived by the farmers. Factor analysis was only conducted for strategies 1–4, since the other strategies are currently not in use. Table 13.3 presents the results for strategies 1 and 2, although the factor patterns are similar to those for strategies 3 and 4. Considered are the four main factors (with an eigenvalue greater than 1).

Factor 1 may be characterized as 'knowledge'. Experience, guidance and alertness are the main 'explanatory' variables. There is also a relation with weather risk[3] and, to a lesser extent with labour requirements, costs of herbicides and the environmental friendliness. Only for strategy 1 is there a relation with high costs of the contractor. In practice, many farmers using this strategy will have it done by a contractor.

Factor 2 concentrates around 'manual labour'. It concerns that part of the farm organization connected with the use of labour for manually removing weeds. There is a strong relation with uncertainty about the effectiveness of herbicides and a weaker one with the extra farm equipment required, variable tractor costs and high costs of the contractor. For strategy 1, there is also a strong relation with carry-over effects.

Factor 3 might be called 'risk of yield loss'. The potential yield loss due to growth reduction is positively related to the costs of herbicides, negatively to environmental friendliness and positively to weather risk. For the second strategy there is also a strong connection to carry-over effects. So the farmer might have the perception that greater use of herbicides is less

Table 13.3   Factor score coefficients for strategies 1 and 2

Variable	Strategy 1: full field wigh high dose Factor					Strategy 2: full field with low dose Factor				
	1	2	3	4	comm.	1	2	3	4	comm.
Much experience required	0.76		0.34		0.73	0.73			0.28	0.63
Good guidance required	0.72				0.64	0.63	0.29			0.55
Much alertness required	0.66		−0.33		0.60	0.79				0.66
High weather risk	0.63		0.43	0.20	0.70	0.43		0.29	0.47	0.59
Much labour required	0.20	0.73		0.21	0.63	0.25	0.78		0.17	0.70
Many hours manually removing weeds required		0.61	0.39	0.34	0.68		0.36		0.70	0.62
Uncertainty effectiveness of herbicides	0.33	0.74	0.19		0.70		0.24		0.77	0.70
Strong growth reduction			0.82		0.70	−0.35	−0.20	0.62	0.42	0.82
Great risk of yield loss	0.23	0.25	0.75		0.77	−0.45			0.72	0.74
High cost of herbicides	0.19	−0.31	0.18		0.72	0.17			0.74	0.69
Does not match labour supply in specific period	0.29			0.74	0.65	−0.18	0.55	0.25	0.36	0.53
Extra farm equipment required		0.23		0.70	0.70		0.65		0.33	0.54
Variable tractor costs	0.24		0.75		0.64		0.77			0.70
Environmentally friendly	0.33		−0.15		0.82	0.70	−0.24	−0.30	0.21	0.75
High costs of the contractor	0.67	0.23		0.15	0.53		0.17			0.76
Great carry-over effects on subsequent crops		0.77		0.23	0.71	0.30		0.63		0.60

Note: comm. = communality.

environmentally friendly, causes growth reduction and yield losses, and has high weather risks.

Factor 4 has to do with the farm 'labour balance' in the spring: the necessity to get a balance between demand and supply of labour in total in a certain period. Weather risk, labour required, hours manually removing weeds and extra farm equipment are also related.

The main conclusion of the foregoing analysis is that costs are not important as a distinguishing feature among the different weed control techniques. This is in line with the normative assessment. According to the outcomes of the perception analysis, knowledge, labour aspects and risk are decisive in the choice of a specific control technique. Further, farmers have a generally high perception of risks, both for the conventional and for the more environmentally friendly techniques, and this may be a barrier to adoption of the latter.

Conclusions

Farmers' subjective preferences for characteristics of new weed control techniques are important determinants of adoption behaviour. An important advantage of the approach used in this chapter is that it identifies the key characteristics of the techniques that need to be concentrated upon for improvement if adoption is to be achieved. The results indicate that the conventional focus in technology development on agronomic characteristics is much too narrow. Farm organizational (labour requirements and labour balance), management (knowledge) and risk characteristics appear to be decisive in the adoption decision. This suggests that the focus needs to be changed to include such characteristics.

In The Netherlands, row spraying (strategies 3–4) is often promoted as an appropriate IAFS method to achieve a reduction in herbicide use. From the perception analysis it appeared, however, that row spraying involves a considerable adjustment in the business organization and is considered risky compared with conventional practices. For farmers such as those in North Limburg where sugarbeet is not a main source of income, it is doubtful whether labour-intensive environmentally friendlier methods are the best alternative. Methods based on less damaging herbicides might offer a better perspective.

Further research is needed to determine whether the perceptions and preferences of sugarbeet growers are also important with regard to adoption of environmentally preferred management practices in other arable farming regions. Furthermore, following a group of farmers over several years could yield interesting information on changing preferences over time, focusing in particular on learning processes. In this way it could be verified whether a changeover to environmentally friendlier farming might be expected.

This research must be seen as a first step in examining how behavioural economics approaches can be applied in farm management research.

Notes

1   1 Dfl. = 0.5 US$.
2   HD refers to high dose spray, LD to low dose.
3   Our analysis of weather risks showed that these are low. Farmers might have a risk perception higher than the normative outcomes presented in Table 13.1.

References

Adesina, A.A. and J. Baidu-Forson (1995)' 'Farmers' Perceptions and Adoption of New Agricultural Technology: Evidence from Analysis in Burkina Faso and Guinea, West Africa', *Agricultural Economics*, **13**: 1-9.

Adesina, A.A. and M.M. Zinnah (1993), 'Technology Characteristics, Farmers' Perceptions and Adoptions Decisions: A Tobit Model Application in Sierra Leone', *Agricultural Economics*, **9**: 297-311.

Gilad, B. and S. Kaish (eds) (1986), *Handbook of Behavioral Economics*, J.A. Press, Greenwich, Conn.

Hair, J.F., R.E. Anderson and R.L. Tatham (1987), *Multivariate Data Analysis with Readings*, Macmillan, New York.

Ippel, B.M. and W.P. Noordam (1991), 'Kwantitatieve informatie voor de akkerbouw en de groente-teelt in de Vollegrond 1990-1991', Publicatienummer 53, PAGV/IKC, Lelystad, The Netherlands.

Jorritsma, J. (1985), 'De teelt van suikerbieten, Terra (Groene Reeks), Zutphen, The Netherlands.

Reichelderfer, K.H. (1989), 'Externalities and the Return to Agricultural Research: Discussion', *American Journal of Agricultural Economics*, **71**: 464-5.

Rogers, E.M. (1983), *Diffusion of Innovations*, The Free Press, New York.

Schoorlemmer, H.B., A.J. de Buck and G.A.A. Wossink (1994), 'Risk and Risk Perception in the Conversion to Sustainable Production Methods in Arable Farming', proceedings 38th EAAE Seminar, Copenhagen, 3-5 October.

van der Meulen, H.A.B., G.R. de Snoo and G.A.A. Wossink (1996), 'Farmers' Perception of Unsprayed Crop Edges in the Netherlands', *Journal of Environmental Management*, **47**: 241-55.

van Niejenhuis, J.H. and H.C.M. Haverkamp (1992), 'Economic View on the Reduction of the Use of Herbicides in Sugarbeet', *Med. Fac. Landbouww. Univ. Gent*, **57**, (3b): 1013-20.

Wijnands, F.G. and P. Vereijken (1992), 'Region-Wise Development of Prototypes of Integrated Arable Farming and Outdoor Horticulture', *Netherlands' Journal of Agricultural Science*, **40**: 225-38.

Wossink, G.A.A. (1994), 'Farm Economic Modelling of Integrated Plant Production', in P.C. Struik, W.J. Vredenberg, J.A. Renkema and J.E. Parlevliet (eds), *Plant Production on the Threshold of a New Century*, Kluwer Academic Publishers, Dordrecht/Boston/London.

PART IV
DETERMINANTS OF
FERTILIZER
AND PESTICIDE USE

PART IV

14 The Effect of Price Changes on the Use of Fertilizer and Pesticides in Dutch Wheat Production

J. Dijk and M.W. Hoogeveen[a]

Introduction

Although the EU agricultural policy reform in 1992 was not primarily directed at reducing the environmental pollution caused by agricultural production, it will have an impact on the environment. In this chapter, the effects of a reduction in the grain price on the input levels of nitrogen fertilizer and pesticides and on yields in Dutch winter wheat production are investigated. First, a description of long-term developments in yield and nitrogen and pesticide use is given. The effects of lower grain prices on these long-term developments are discussed. This serves as a background for the analysis of the short-term effects of lower grain prices on inputs and outputs. A crop level relation between inputs and yield is estimated for the South West Clay Area in the Netherlands for the period 1981–90. Optimal input and output levels are determined on the basis of this relation. This is done for the historical period and for situations with changing price ratios.

Long-term Trends in Wheat Yields, Fertilizer Use and Pesticide Inputs

The yield level of wheat is increasing from year to year. The Dutch yield level of winter wheat has been changing from about 1500 kg/ha in 1850 to

[a] Agricultural Economics Research Institute (LEI-DLO), P.O. Box 29703, 2502 LS, The Hague, The Netherlands.

3000 kg/ha in 1925, 5000 kg/ha in 1970 and 8500 kg/ha in recent years (Dijk *et al.*, 1995). Series of yield figures should be interpreted with care. Because of the dynamics in agriculture they do not always refer to the same area.

Figure 14.1 shows yield levels for the Northern Clay Area in the Netherlands for the period 1945–95. Figure 14.2 shows moving averages for the yield levels for the Netherlands (1850–1935), the clay areas in the Netherlands (1935–63) and the Northern Clay Area (1963–95). Because of the aggregation level of the available data it is not always possible to construct a long-term series for separate regions, but even when a series is available for a rather homogeneous region (for example, with respect to soil type) one cannot draw conclusions on the trend in the yield level without knowing something about the dynamics in agriculture. The area of winter wheat has been increasing over the course of time, whereas in recent years there was also an opposite tendency because of an increasing 'set-aside' area. So the average yield level in different years does not refer to the same area or the same group of farms. The introduction of set-aside will probably result in an increase in average yield because the less yielding hectares will be set aside first.

Weber and Ehlers (1987) present a logistic model (S-shaped curve) for the description of the yield increase in the course of time. After a period of

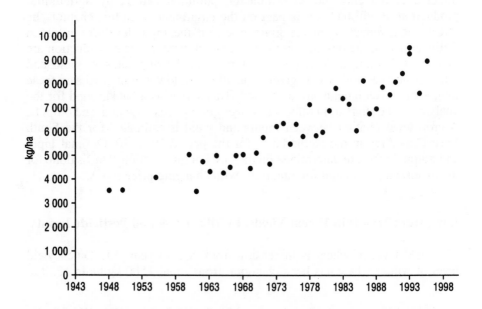

Figure 14.1   Yield of winter wheat in the Northern Clay Area

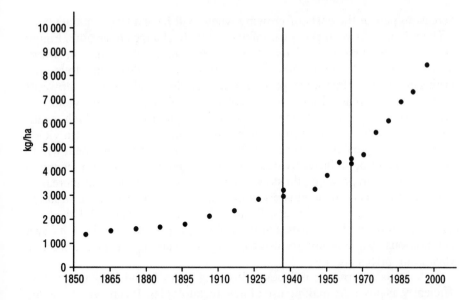

Figure 14.2   Moving averages of yield in kg per ha of winter wheat (1850–1940: Netherlands; 1945–60: Sea Clay Area; 1960–95: Northern Clay Area)

exponential growth, a turning-point will be reached, and after that the yield increase will be diminishing because the potential attainable yield is being approached. Figures 14.1 and 14.2 do not give the impression that the point of return has already been reached in the Netherlands, although Weber and Ehlers estimate the maximum attainable yield at about 13 tons per hectare.

There are a number of factors which have been playing a role in the continuous increase in yield. In the 19th century there was only a moderate increase connected with the use of manure, rotation and set-aside. In the first part of the 20th century, new varieties were developed and artificial fertilizers were introduced, but it was to be several decades before the use of fertilizer increased considerably. The introduction of short straw varieties accelerated the use of fertilizer. Also herbicides were used in increasing amounts. From the 1970s the use of pesticides increased enormously. The introduction of new varieties and inputs was accompanied by the emergence of experimental farms, educational facilities, extension services, mechanisation, reallotments, cooperatives, and so on (Hutten and Rutten, 1990). So the yield-increasing use of fertilizer and pesticides should be seen as part of a complex of factors. De Veer (1986) argues that in the future the main factors behind yield growth will be automatization and biotechnology. An increasing part of the costs of growing wheat will have a fixed character.

The relation between chemical inputs and yield changes over time. Figure 14.3 gives an overview of the developments in fertilizer use in wheat growing. After a steady increase from 1970 onwards, 1986 seems to mark a turning-point, but after some years of decrease the trend has been upwards again in recent years. Figure 14.4 depicts the relation between yield and fertilizer over the course of time. This relation is roughly linear, which means that the extra amounts of nitrogen do not result in a decrease in extra yield.

The technological developments behind the yield increase of wheat will to a certain extent be induced by economic developments. This implies that a reduction in grain prices could slow down the growth rate of yield increases. However, there is no strong historical evidence that a bad economic situation decreases the yield growth significantly. Figures 14.1 and 14.2 describe periods of high and low prices, but the yield growth seems to follow its own 'autonomous' path. Many yield-increasing innovations are also attractive when grain prices are low.

As long as a farmer continues cultivating grain he will try to do it as efficiently as possible, making use of new technologies. It can even be stated that price decreases result in an accelerated introduction of new production

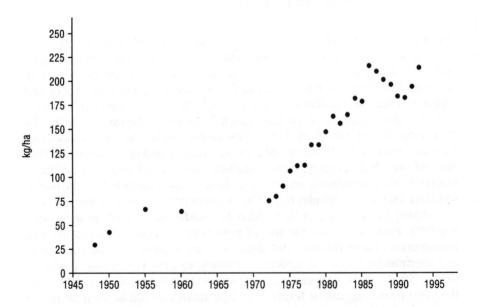

Figure 14.3   Nitrogen fertilizer use in winter wheat, Northern Clay Area

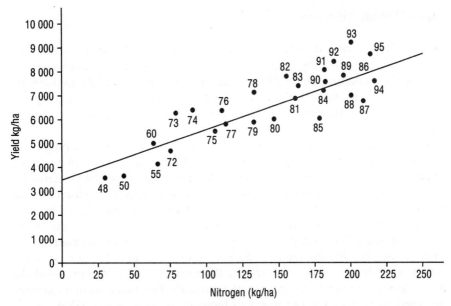

Figure 14.4   Historical development of the relation between yield and nitrogen fertilizer use in winter wheat (48 = 1948, etc)

techniques, because farmers are stimulated to do everything possible to survive. Also the takeover of inefficient farms by efficient farms results in a more rapid yield growth.

Assuming that in the longer term the acreage of grain will not be reduced drastically on a worldwide scale, because an increasing number of mouths have to be fed, it remains profitable to invest in research and development directed at yield increases. Also in the Netherlands grain will cover a considerable area in the future because of lack of economically attractive alternative crops which suit the cropping pattern. However, the direction of yield-increasing technologies may change in the course of time. In the present period of increasing environmental regulation, yield increases will not be sought in an increased use of chemical inputs. But it may take a considerable number of years before technological changes become effective and are available at farm level.

In any case, a reduction in the growth rate of wheat yield as a consequence of lower grain prices since 1983 cannot yet be observed. Following the peak in wheat prices in 1983 (Dfl. 574 per ton), prices decreased to Dfl. 414 per ton in 1990 and Dfl. 324 in 1994 (Jager, 1995) (1 Dfl. = 0.5 US$). But, at the same time, yields kept growing at high rates, despite a decrease in input use.

Input–Output Relations

In the short term, decreasing marginal returns will be present. The possibilities of producing a certain amount of wheat with the help of fixed and variable inputs are limited by the state of technology, and the knowledge and management capabilities of the farmers. Given the decision to grow wheat, and given the prices of inputs and output, the farmer has to choose input levels.

The production possibilities can be described with the help of a crop level production function. These production functions are in general not available or are only available for experimental situations (Janssens and Groenwold, 1993). For the Netherlands farm level, panel data on winter wheat production are available from the Dutch Farm Account Data Network (FADN). One of the main regions where winter wheat is grown is the South West Clay Area. For each year in the period 1981–90, about 70 observations were available. Input–output relations were estimated to link variable inputs to yield. Equation 14.1 relates the nitrogen fertilizer input and the pesticide input to yield, making use of a quadratic functional form. Dummies are used to correct for (weather) differences between years (Dijk *et al.*, 1995).

$$Y = 4005 + 17.08 * N - 0.0323 * N^2 + 7.15 * P - 0.0081 * P^2 +$$
$$(12.1)\ (5.9)\qquad (4.6)\qquad (4.6)\qquad (3.4)$$

$$780 * D82 - 158 * D83 + 1232 * D84 - 449 * D85 + 1124 * D86 +$$
$$(5.6)\qquad\quad (1.1)\qquad\ \ (8.6)\qquad\quad (3.1)\qquad\quad (7.7)$$

$$294 * D87 + 712 * D88 + 497 * D89 + 778 * D90 \qquad\qquad (14.1)$$
$$(2.0)\qquad\quad (4.6)\qquad (3.3)\qquad\quad (5.3)$$

$R^2 = 0.41$ $n = 691$ period: 1981–90

Y = yield of winter wheat (kg/ha)
N = nitrogen fertilizer input (kg N/ha)
P = pesticide input (guilders (value 1980)/ha)
D = year dummy

About 40 per cent of the variation in yield per hectare could be explained by the variation in input levels. When the equation is estimated on a yearly basis, the R^2 is slightly lower. The coefficients have the expected sign. An alternative specification with an extra interaction term $N * P$ does not result in satisfactory estimation results, because of the high correlation of such a term with the other variables. Splitting the observations in groups with a large and a small share of grain in the cropping pattern, or in groups with a large and a small share in the use of manure on the farm, did not result in a better explanation of the variation in yields. Manure is seldom applied for the cultivation of grain, but the application of manure in previous years on other arable crops could have some effects on the grain yield in this year.

From 1990 on, the input of pesticides is also available in kilograms of active ingredients. Estimation for 1990 with amounts instead of guilders results in a deterioration of the estimation results. This may be explained by the fact that the input 'pesticides' is a collection of many different types of pesticides. The price that is paid for a kilogram of active ingredients is an indication of the effect the application of pesticides has. A certain effect can be reached with a large amount of cheap pesticide or with a small amount of expensive pesticide.

Optimal Input and Output Levels

Given the input and output price levels, optimal input levels were calculated. The actual nitrogen fertilizer use was about 10 per cent lower than the optimal input level in the period 1980–90. For another region, the Northern Clay Area, nitrogen input was also below the calculated optimum. Apparently, farmers do not apply nitrogen abundantly, as is sometimes assumed (Janssens and Groenwold, 1993). Too large amounts of nitrogen have a negative effect on the production level and on the quality of the wheat. It is not easy to model these quality effects in an input–output relation.

Pesticide use, on the other hand, was 25 per cent higher than the calculated optimal level. This supports the idea that pesticides are used rather abundantly to reduce the risk of bad harvests. The difference between the actual and the calculated level has been increased in the second half of the 1980s. This may be explained by increasing pressure of diseases and a more intensive cropping pattern.

A maximum yield (8273 kg/ha) is reached with input levels of 265 kg N and Dfl. 444 of pesticides; the optimum level is 216 kg N and Dfl. 277 of pesticides. The difference in yield between the optimum and the maximum level is only 300 kg.

Effects of Price Changes

A reduction of the wheat price by 30 per cent from Dfl. 390 (price level

1991) to Dfl. 270 per ton results in a decrease of the fertilizer input by 11 per cent, of the pesticide input by 38 per cent, and a decrease in yield by 6 per cent. So a lower wheat price has much stronger effects on the variable inputs than on the yield level. The effect on the yield level is also small when compared to the long-term increases (see the second section above). For the farmer, decreasing grain prices is a very expensive way to come to a reduction in input and output levels. Increasing input prices could have the same effect with much less reduction in profits. A doubling of the price of nitrogen fertilizer gives a decrease of 22 per cent in the nitrogen input and a 3 per cent decrease in yield. Because of the absence of any inter-action between fertilizer and pesticides in equation (14.1), the calculated pesticide input level does not change when the fertilizer price changes. In practice, pesticide input will also be reduced when nitrogen input is being reduced.

The reduction of grain prices was directed towards a reduction of the grain yields. From the point of view of environmental policy, there is the side-effect of a reduction in chemical inputs. Besides that, lower grain prices make levies on chemical inputs much more effective. A 30 per cent reduction in grain price and a levy of 100 per cent on the nitrogen price result in a decrease of nitrogen use by 43 per cent, considerably more than the 22 per cent that would result in the situation with the higher grain prices. More detailed information on the results can be found in Dijk *et al.* (1995).

A point of discussion is that the level of nitrogen input also affects the wheat quality. A lower nitrogen input may result in a lower nitrogen content of the harvested product, which will result in a lower price. In that case it may be more profitable to maintain a higher nitrogen input (Zeddies *et al.* 1994).

Discussion

The 30 per cent reduction in grain prices as a consequence of the EU agricultural policy reform will have a stronger effect on the use of chemical inputs than on wheat yield. Farmers will 'move down' on the input–output relation because of decreasing marginal returns. According to model calculations for the South West Clay Area of the Netherlands, nitrogen use will decrease by some 10 per cent and pesticide use by some 40 per cent. Yield decreases will be 6 per cent.

But at the same time the input–output relation is continually shifting upwards, resulting in an increased input use and yield. In the course of time there is an almost linear relation between nitrogen input and yield. The reduction in yield and input use that results from lower grain prices will interrupt the steady growth in input and yield growth; but, starting from a somewhat lower level, the growth will continue.

Figure 14.3 shows developments in nitrogen use in the Northern Clay Area. Between 1986 and 1990, nitrogen use per hectare was reduced by 10 per cent. This may be due to the grain price decrease from Dfl. 550 to 400 per ton between 1983 and 1990, but an increased environmental consciousness may also have contributed to it. From 1992 onwards, nitrogen use increased again. For the South West Clay Area, the same tendency has been found. This is surprising because in 1992 grain prices fell considerably. Perhaps the set-aside of a part of the area with low input use contributes to this result, but the main explanation will be the decrease in the price of nitrogen fertilizer by about 20 per cent between 1990 and 1993.

For pesticides there is a steady decrease in input use. Between 1983 and 1993, the pesticide input (constant value) for wheat cultivation decreased by some 25 per cent. Between 1989 and 1993, the amount of active ingredients decreased by some 35 per cent from 8.3 kg to 5.3 kg (Jager, 1995). Part of this reduction should be ascribed to new types of pesticides which contain a lower amount of active ingredients.

Of course, the decrease in chemical input use as a result of changes in agricultural policy is attractive from the point of view of environmental policy. However, a reduced input use can be achieved with considerably lower costs for the farmer by levies or regulations with respect to polluting inputs. A positive effect of low grain prices is that environmental measures are much more effective, because a reduced input will decrease profits less when output prices are low.

This chapter only analyses the partial effects of a lower grain price on the input of nitrogen and fertilizer and the wheat yield. Of course other effects will also occur, such as changes in cropping pattern, set-aside and so on. Substitution between chemical inputs and, for example, labour and machinery is also omitted from the analysis. On experimental farms in the Netherlands, large reductions in fertilizer and pesticide use were realized by so-called 'integrated farming systems'. Mechanical weeding, increased observation and measurement, and so on, result in lower inputs but also in lower outputs. The decrease in financial returns is not fully compensated for by the decrease in costs. Research on these experimental farms but also on 'real' farms indicates that the grain price would have to fall below Dfl. 250 per ton before such a drastic reduction in chemical inputs would be profitable for the farmer.

In this chapter attention is focused on chemical *inputs*. From the point of view of environmental policy, the *emissions* into the environment are more relevant. For nitrogen, this means that the difference between input and crop uptake is a more relevant variable than the input itself. For winter wheat, the nitrogen surplus is not very high (some 50 or 75 kg/ha). A 10 per cent reduction in input will result in a much higher relative reduction in surplus. The absolute reduction in the surplus, however, will be lower than the reduction in the input because the crop uptake of nitrogen also decreases. When talking about emissions it is important to distinguish between the emissions per hectare and the emissions per kilogram of wheat. Lower input levels generally result in lower emissions per hectare, and mostly also in lower emissions per kilogram of wheat, but the two do not necessarily move in the same direction.

That lower input levels also result in a higher yield per kilogram of nitrogen seems contrary to the conclusions of de Wit (1992). He argues that, from the point of view of what is called resource use efficiency, high yield and input levels are favourable. But his perspective is the long-term perspective (see the second section above) in which the circumstances under which the conversion of nitrogen and other inputs into wheat become gradually more favourable. In theory, production circumstances with high yields and high input levels could be preferable from the point of view of resource use efficiency. But Figure 14.4 does not support this hypothesis.

So, even in the long term, it is not certain whether resource use efficiency is highest in intensive cropping systems. Also, even if this is the case, resource use efficiency is no guarantee of environmental efficiency. In the short term, resource use efficiency may be increased by reducing the input level from the level that is perceived by the farmer as economically efficient. However, the question remains whether resource use efficiency should be striven after.

References

de Veer, J. (1986), 'National Agricultural Policies, Surplus Problems and International Instability', *Tijdschrift voor Sociaalwetenschappelijk onderzoek van de Landbouw*, (1): 4–21.
de Wit, C.T. (1992), 'Resource Use Efficiency in Agriculture', *Agricultural Systems*, **40**: 125–51.
Dijk, J., M.W. Hoogeveen and T. de Haan (1995), 'EU-landbouwbeleid en milieubelasting in graan- en grasteelt', *Onderzoekverslag 132*, LEI-DLO, The Hague.
Hutten, T. and H. Rutten (1990), 'De druk der omstandigheden; technologische trajecten in de Nederlandse landbouw', in A.L.G.M. Bauwens, M.N. de Groot and K.J. Poppe (eds), *Agrarisch Bestaan: beschouwingen bij vijftig jaar Landbouw-Economisch Instituut*, Van Gorcum, Assen, The Netherlands.
Jager, J.H. (1995), 'Saldi van akkerbouwgewassen', *Periodieke Rapportage 10-93*, LEI-DLO, The Hague.

Janssens, S.R.M. and J.G. Groenwold (1993), 'Effect van heffingen op stikstof op de bedrijfsvoering in de akkerbouw', *Mededeling 478*, LEI-DLO, The Hague.

Weber, A. and H. Ehlers (1987), 'Langfristige Entwicklung der Getreideerträge in der Welt', *Agrarwirtschaft*, **37**(11): 338–44.

Zeddies, J., C. Fuchs, J. Hufnagel and J. Walther (1994)', 'Qualitätsweizen-produktion nach der EG-Agrarreform', *Berichte über Landwirtschaft*, **72**: 1–35.

15 The Demand for Fertilizer on Upland Rice in the South-west of Burkina Faso: Determinants and Cost and Returns Analysis

A. Sidibé and Y. Sere[a]

Introduction

Soil fertility is generally low in Burkina Faso as a result of natural degradation of soils during cultivation and a failure to take steps to restore fertility and improve crop productivity. Fallowing has been the traditional way to restore fertility and is attractive because it requires no effort or expense other than the cost of clearing the land when it is returned to cultivation. However, owing to increasing demographic pressure and declining productivity, there is a shortage of arable land and, consequently, a reluctance to leave land uncultivated for the time required to restore fertility. Thus fallow length has decreased significantly.

African farmers have also traditionally used animal manure to maintain and enhance fertility and productivity on fields located close to the living area of the family farm. In recent years, farmers in Burkina Faso as elsewhere in Africa have begun to use chemical fertilizers, such as urea and combinations of nitrogen, phosphate and potassium (NPK), especially on cash crops such as cotton and peanuts (see Chapter 4). Farmers are now developing strategies for choosing optimal amounts and combinations

[a] Institut d'Etudes et de Recherches Agricoles, FASO Western Zone BP 910, Bobo Dioulasso, West Africa.

of chemical, organic and natural methods for enhancing soil fertility.

This chapter reports on fertilization practices of upland rice farmers in the south-west of Burkina Faso. Between 1993 and 1996 researchers at the national agricultural research institution, INERA (Institut d'Etudes et de Recherches Agricoles), have demonstrated that upland rice is a suitable crop in the agroclimatic zone where cotton has been grown for many years as the major cash crop. Increased rice production is important in Burkina Faso because the country continues to import 77 per cent of its rice needs, and opportunities for expanding the irrigated rice area are limited. A main reason for introducing upland rice production is the recent currency devaluation in Burkina, as in other countries in the franc zone, that has doubled the price of rice (which is imported), while reducing that of cotton (which is exported). Farmers are responding to relative prices and adopting upland rice production. However, there is a need to find the optimal fertilization strategies that maximize returns and reduce soil degradation. Therefore the objectives of this study are to identify and characterize the principal types of fertilization practice and identify the best ones, and to assist in making these practices available to farmers.

Methodology and Assumptions

Data used in this study come from experiments on rice fertilization carried out in Hounde, a region about 100km north-east of Bobo-Dioulasso and located in the Soudano-Sahelian zone. The rainfall pattern is unimodal, with the rainfall season lasting 120 to 170 days, from mid-May to mid-November. Mean annual rainfall is 700 to 1000mm, with a variation of 20–30 per cent: precipitation of some 450 to 800mm occurs during a low rainfall season.

The important crops are cotton, maize and sorghum. Upland rice is a secondary crop known to farmers but seldom produced owing to the profitability of cotton as a cash crop. Cultivation of upland rice has increased in the past three years as a result of the factors mentioned above. Two improved varieties of rice that INERA considers promising are FKR 33 and FKR 44-18, whose yields have averaged 3–4 tonnes/ha. The adoption rate of the new varieties is about 65 per cent (Sere and Sidibé, 1996). However, cultural practices are applied in various ways, some of which are not as profitable, owing to lack of proper extension. It is necessary to characterize, identify and evaluate the economic benefits of farmer fertilization practices to improve upland rice production in the Hounde region. A simple linear regression model is used to asses determinants of fertilizer use. The chemical fertilizers used are NPK and urea, and animal manure is also used.

NPK and Urea Use

It is assumed that NPK and urea use are both determined by the following function:

$$NPK = f(NPK_{cotton}, NPK_{maize}, area_{maize}, manure_{rice}, area_{rice}, urea_{rice}), \quad (15.1)$$

where NPK_{cotton} refers to the NPK rate on cotton fields, NPK_{maize} to the rate on maize fields, $area_{maize}$ to maize area, $manure_{rice}$ to the application rate of manure on upland rice fields, $area_{rice}$ to upland rice area, and $urea_{rice}$ to the rate of application of urea on upland rice.

NPK and urea are provided by the cotton board (Sofitex) as credit conditional on the farmer planting cotton. In this way, the quantities of fertilizers are directly related to cotton area, assuming that the recommended rate of fertilizer is applied. However, farmers applied fertilizer at lower rates, moving the surplus to other crops, such as maize. With the introduction of upland rice, the fertilizer designated for cotton was diverted to both upland rice and maize. Hence we can assume that the quantity of NPK applied on cotton fields is inversely related to its use on upland rice, and that the upland rice area is inversely related to the amount of NPK and urea applied on rice. Finally, since manure can substitute for mineral fertilizers, its use is inversely related to NPK and urea use on upland rice.

Manure Use

The manure used in the Hounde region may or may not include kitchen wastes and crop residues. Farmers who use manure carry it from home to their fields using animal carts at the beginning of the rainy season. It is assumed that manure use is determined by the following function:

$$manure_{rice} = F(cart, labour, age, bov, area_{rice}, urea_{rice}, NPK_{rice}), \quad (15.2)$$

where *cart* refers to the number of carts in the household, *labour* is the number of workers in the household, *age* is the age of the head of the household, *bov* is the number of cattle, and the other variables are as defined earlier. The number of cattle is positively related to the rate of manure use on upland rice. Manure use is likely limited by the lack of labour and means of transport, so the number of the workers and animal carts will be positively related to the rate of manure use on upland rice. Owing to the possibility of substituting chemical fertilizers for manure, an increase in chemical fertilizer use results in a decrease in manure use on upland rice. An increase in upland rice area results in a decrease in the *rate* of manure application.

Determinants of Fertilizer Use: Regression Results

The study employs a random sample of 29 farmers who have adopted upland rice. Fertilizer practices of these farmers are provided in Table 15.1. Two practices appear most common, one based on combining urea and farmyard manure (sometimes with NPK) and the other on NPK only. Hence our analysis is based on the NPK and urea–manure practices. Researchers recommend:

1   ploughing and levelling at the start of the season, with an injection of manure;
2   a single application of NPK at the rate of 200 kg/ha; and
3   spreading urea twice – on the 15th and the 45th days after seeding – at the rate of 50 kg/ha each time.

Those who used only NPK as fertilizer, applied NPK once at the rate of 192 kg/ha (Table 15.2).

Results of the ordinary least squares (OLS) regressions for NPK and urea applications contradict the model suggested above. None of the explanatory variables is statistically significant. R^2 values are 0.46 and 0.23 for the NPK and urea regressions, respectively, while the associated F statistics are 0.25 and 0.55. Regression results for manure application on upland rice are provided in Table 15.3. These indicate that manure use is highly dependent on the upland rice area, the rate of urea use on upland rice and the number of on-farm workers, carts and cattle. NPK is not included in the regression because farmers in the sample, with one exception, associate NPK with manure as an upland rice fertilizer (see Table 15.1). Upland rice area, the number of carts and the urea application rate on upland rice had signs opposite to what was expected.

An important question that this analysis raises is: why does the manure application rate increase proportionately with area in upland rice? Upland rice production with manual traction is difficult and has a high labour

Table 15.1   Fertilization practices in the Hounde area

	Number of farmers	%
NPK + urea	1	3.4
NPK + urea + manure	2	6.9
Urea + manure	11	37.9
NPK	15	51.7

Table 15.2   Rate, yield and area of fertilizer use on upland rice

	Urea + manure	NPK
NPK rate (kg/ha)	–	192
Urea rate (kg/ha)	111	–
Manure rate (kg/ha)	2 248	–
Yield (kg)	2 250	2 050
Area (ha)	0.39	0.25

requirement, so the upland rice area is extended using animal traction. This increases the amount of manure availability, as each animal provides enough manure to fertilize 0.5–0.7 ha. Surprisingly, an increase in the number of animal-drawn carts does not lead to an increase in manure application rates, as originally hypothesized. One reason for this is that animals pulling carts are some distance from the fields and manure is not picked up as the carts are moving, at least not by the owner of the cart.

Table 15.3   Determinants of manure application on upland rice

Variable	Coefficient	t statistic
On-farm workers	1.2556	6.470
Age of household head	−0.6279	−3.409
Number of cattle	0.2624	2.697
Number of carts	−0.3274	−3.075
Area planted to rice	0.4756	4.529
Urea rate on upland rice	0.2152	1.802
Constant	0.3865	1.011

Notes: $R^2 = 0.980$; adjusted $R^2 = 0.940$; $F = 24.394$; significant $F = 0.0122$.

Originally, it was assumed that the urea application rate on upland rice would be negatively related to manure use, but the current analysis shows that the opposite is true. As indicated in Table 15.1, many farmers use manure together with urea, perhaps because their use may be complementary in production.

Economic Efficiency and Fertilizer Use

Revenues from the sale of upland rice and associated agricultural production costs for two fertilizer schemes – NPK and urea plus manure (Table 15.1) – are provided in Table 15.4. An on-farm economic analysis of the two

Table 15.4   Upland rice budget of different fertilization practices (annual)

Item	Urea + manure	NPK
Revenue		
Output (kg/ha)	2 250	2 050
Price/kg (fcfa)	105	105
Total revenue per hectare (fcfa)	236 250	215 250
Costs		
Seeds		
Quantity (kg/ha)	77	96
Price (fcfa)	105	105
Value (fcfa)	8 085	10 080
NPK		
Quantity (kg/ha)	0	192
Price (fcfa)	165	165
Value (fcfa)	0	31 680
Urea		
Quantity (kg/ha)	110	0
Price (fcfa)	165	165
Value (fcfa)	18 150	0
Manure		
Quantity (kg/ha)	2 300	0
Price (fcfa)	7	7
Value (fcfa)	16 100	0
Agricultural equipment depreciation (fcfa)	10 000	10 000
Family labour		
Quantity (hours/ha)	1 440	1 430
Cost/hour	100	100
Total cost (fcfa/ha)	144 000	143 000
Net benefits		
Net cash benefit (fcfa)	210 015	173 490
Net cash benefit (fcfa) with buying manure	193 915	173 490
Total net benefit (fcfa)	39 866	20 490
Total net benefit (fcfa) with buying manure	23 766	20 490
Return to fertilizer (%)	566	548

fertilizer systems over a two-year period is provided in Table 15.5. A two-year time frame is employed because the benefits of manure applications last for a period of two years. (There may also be some carry-over effects from NPK and urea, but these are not taken into account.) The results indicate that the net cash benefits of urea plus manure are some 20 per cent higher than those of NPK. This is linked to the differences in yields (average yield of urea plus manure is 9 per cent higher than NPK only), lower seed requirements (77 kg/ha for urea plus manure versus 96 kg/ha for NPK) and lower fertilizer costs (75 per cent lower for manure plus urea). These savings more than offset the increase in other costs. When all costs are taken into

Table 15.5   Returns to different fertilizer practices over two years[a]

Item	Urea + manure	NPK
Net cash benefit (fcfa/ha)	38 153	33 734
Total net benefit (fcfa/ha)	9 199	3 984
Fertilizer cost (fcfa/ha)	6 213	6 160
Return to fertilizer (%)	614	548

Note: [a] assumes no discounting.

account – both cash costs and costs associated with feeding of cattle, the opportunity costs of carts, and so on – the benefits of the urea plus manure practice are more than double those of NPK use (Table 15.5). This is true even though the true costs of urea plus manure (taking into account opportunity and cattle-feeding costs) are greater than the costs of purchasing NPK (Table 15.5).

Conclusion

For upland rice production, it has been demonstrated that a fertilization strategy of manure plus urea, which relies on nutrients produced on the farm, yields higher net cash and total net economic benefits than does use of chemical fertilizers. Not included in the analysis were the benefits to the soil of the former practice. Further research into both the agronomic practices and the economic benefits will be needed to study the long-term profitability and effect on sustainable development, however. It is recommended that greater emphasis be placed on farm management and extension in the future.

Bibliography

Sere, Y. and A. Sidibé (1996), *Suivi Evaluation de l'impact des actions pilotes: Analyse socio-économique des déterminants de l'adoption du riz pluvial dans le Sud Ouest du Burkina*, INERA/Programme Riz; farakoba, Bobo-Dioulasso.

Sidibé, A. and Y. Sere (1995), *Analyse comparée de la rentabilité économique du riz pluvial dans le Sud Ouest du Burkina*, INERA/Programme Riz; farakoba, Bobo-Dioulasso.

Sidibé, A., M. Bertelsen and S. Ouedraogo (1993), 'Analyse Économique de la production du Compost dans le Sud Ouest du Burkina', INERA/Programme RSP; farakoba, Bobo-Dioulasso.

16 Farm Management of Fungicide Use in Tulips in the Netherlands

J.S. Buurma and W.H.M. Baltussen[a]

Introduction

This chapter concerns the differences among growers of ways of controlling the fungus *Botrytis tulipae* in tulips. The differences are first attributed to technical factors like fungicide choice, number of sprays and deviations from standard dose rates, with differences in the technical factors attributable to risk perception, knowledge configuration, farm circumstances, cultivar choice and so on.

In 1990, the Dutch Ministry of Agriculture, Nature Management and Fisheries (MANF) formed the Multi-Year Crop Protection Plan. One of the targets of this plan is a 35 per cent reduction in fungicide use over the period 1984/8–2000. Monitoring results show that to date almost no reduction in fungicide use has been achieved (Plant Protection Service, 1995). Other studies show that the differences among growers in pesticide use (and also in fungicide use) are large. In flower bulb production, for example, the use of active ingredients varied from about 30 kg/ha to almost 200 kg/ha in 1993 (Poppe *et al.*, 1995).

The objective of this study is to obtain insight into the factors that result in differences in fungicide use among growers. Special attention is given to the management behaviour of growers. These insights may provide new perspectives for the reduction of fungicide use. The study focused on control of *Botrytis tulipae* in tulips, with attention further limited to fungicide use

[a] Agricultural Economics Research Institute (LEI-DLO), P.O. Box 29703, 2502 LS, The Hague, The Netherlands.

during the field period. The use of fungicides for disinfection of planting material was not included.

Method

In theory the use of pesticides strongly depends on the risk perception of the grower. Risk perception is connected with the farmer's knowledge and with physical and economic farm circumstances. In theory, the grower's goals (risk perception, disease resistance, externalities) will influence his or her knowledge about pesticides, cultivars and environmental effects. More knowledge will result in improved farm circumstances and in enhanced preventive measures. The combination of better farm circumstances and preventive measures will reduce the infection pressure and/or the susceptibility of the crop. The sequence of perceptions and reactions will finally result in a reduced use of pesticides.

Starting from the theoretical framework, a workshop was organized with four experts on pest management in tulips (one grower, two extension workers and a researcher). The results of the workshop in combination with the theoretical framework were the starting-point for the design of a questionnaire. The draft of the questionnaire was discussed with the experts. After improvement of the questionnaire, a pre-test was conducted. The target was to survey the situation at the bulb farm in 1994. A stratified random sample of 40 tulip growers was drawn. Two subgroups of 20 growers were considered: growers in sandy soils and growers in silt/clay soils. If a farmer refused to cooperate, a similar replacement farm was selected at random. All selected farms specialized in bulb production.

The contribution of the technical factors (fungicide choice, number of sprays and deviation from standard dose rate) to the total variance in fungicide use was computed with stepwise linear regression. The answers to the management-related questions (risk perception, farm circumstances, preventive measures) were valued on the basis of a scaled score. A correlation matrix was computed from the technical and management-related variables. The correlation matrix was used to associate the technical factors with the management-related factors.

Results

Technical Factors

The differences in fungicide use among tulip growers for controlling *Botrytis*

Table 16.1 Contribution (R^2) of fungicide choice, number of sprays and deviations from standard dose rates to the total variance in the use of active ingredients (kg/ha)

Technical factor	Minimum	Maximum	Average
Fungicide choice	0.38	0.72	0.55
Number of sprays	0.20	0.46	0.33
Deviation from standard	0.02	0.08	0.05

tulipae are significant. Within the survey the amounts of active ingredients varied from 2 kg/ha to 37 kg/ha. Regression analysis with the technical factors shows that about 55 per cent of the variance can be attributed to differences in fungicide choice (Table 16.1). Another 33 per cent can be attributed to differences in the number of sprays. The deviations from the standard dose rates explain about 5 per cent of the differences in use of active ingredients per hectare.

The factor fungicide choice corresponds to a complex of factors that take in production region, cropping frequency, cultivar choice and pesticide registration policy. This complex of factors comprises the 'farming system'. The characteristics of the farming system are further elaborated upon in the next section.

The number of sprays is strongly related to the most *Botrytis*-susceptible cultivars at the farm, as indicated in Table 16.2. On the other hand, there is almost no correlation ($R^2 = 0.08$) between the number of sprays and the average susceptibility of the cultivars at the farm (Table 16.1). This implies that the grower adjusts his spray scheme to the most susceptible cultivars.

Farming Systems

The survey results made clear that two farming systems for tulips can be distinguished: one system for coastal areas and one for inland areas. The two farming systems differ at several points (Table 16.3). On the coast, tulips are grown in a 1:3 rotation. The basal infection pressure of *Botrytis tulipae* will be high because of the 1:3 rotation and the many tulips grown in the immediate environment. On the other hand, the conditions in the field are relatively unfavourable for *Botrytis tulipae* because of a fairly dry microclimate and moderately susceptible cultivars.

For inland farming systems, tulips are grown on rented land in a 1:6 rotation. The infection pressure of *Botrytis tulipae* is low because of the 1:6 rotation and the few tulips growing in the immediate environment. On the other hand, the conditions in the field are relatively favourable for *Botrytis*

Table 16.2   Relation between *Botrytis* susceptibility and number of sprays (respondents)

Number of sprays	Moderate	High	Very high
7	2		
8	1	2	
9	2	6	
10	2	1	
11		2	2
12	1	2	3
13			3
14		1	3
15			2
16			1

tulipae because of a fairly humid microclimate and the highly susceptible cultivars.

The fungicide choice is strongly correlated with the farming system. Differences between the two farming systems and the impact of fungicide use and fungicide costs are provided in Table 16.4. An initial factor is the use of modern fungicides (with low standard dose rates). The modern fungicides (Shirlan and Allure) are used by 20 per cent of the growers on the coast, but are not used inland. The difference is caused by legal restrictions on the use of the classic fungicides, Mancozeb and Zineb-Maneb, in parts of the coastal area. A second factor is the composition of the fungicide cocktail. On the coast combinations of basic fungicides are exceptional, while such combinations are quite common inland (1.1 compounds versus 1.6 compounds). The difference is probably caused by the higher risk perception inland. As a result, the inland farming system has a 60 per cent higher

Table 16.3   Differences between two farming systems in tulip production

Characteristic	Coastal farming system	Inland farming system
Type of product	bulbs for dry sales	bulbs for cut flowers
Type of soil	sandy	silt/clay
Evaporation	low	high
Planting system	beds	ridges
Type of habitus	slender leaves	luxurious leaves
Cropping pattern	tulips 1:3	tulips 1:6
Type of rotation	flower bulbs	arable crops
Infection environment	many tulips around	few tulips around
Botrytis susceptibility	moderate	high

Table 16.4 Use of fungicides in two farming systems with tulips, 1994

Key figure	Coastal farming system	Inland farming system
Growers using Shirlan/allure (%)	20	0
Number of basic fungicides in cocktail (n)	1.1	1.6
Dose rates (kg ai/ha/spray)[a]	1.2	1.8
Number of fungicidal sprays (n)	11	12
Fungicide use (kg ai/ha)	13	21
Fungicide costs (Dfl./ha)	603	818

Note: [a] ai refers to active ingredient.

average dose rate (kg ai/ha/spray) than the coastal farming system.

The difference between the two farming systems is just slightly increased by the number of sprays. In physical terms (kg ai/ha), inland fungicide use is about 60 per cent higher than on the coast. Expressed in financial terms (Dfl./ha), the difference between the two farming systems is about 35 per cent. The financial difference is smaller owing to both the higher costs of the modern fungicides and price differences among the classic fungicides.

Management Factors

Some management-related matters, such as risk perception and *Botrytis* susceptibility, have already been mentioned in the previous sections. In this section growers' management in the two farming systems is considered in more detail. Table 16.5 provides an impression of the contrasts between the two farming systems.

The inland growers perceive *Botrytis tulipae* to be more risky than do their coastal colleagues. The perception corresponds to the *Botrytis* susceptibility of the cultivars, which is relatively low on the coast. This means that cultivar choice determines risk perception and not the other way around. The knowledge of cultivars is in line with this finding. The growers in the farming system with *Botrytis*-susceptible cultivars have more knowledge about *Botrytis* susceptibility than their colleagues on the coast. However, the time spent on reading and learning contradicts the previous story. Coastal growers are more active in gathering plant protection information than those inland. They are also more active in keeping records of fungicide use and in making field observations. These activities seem necessary in the inland farming system rather than in the coastal one.

The higher fungicide input in the inland farming system again corresponds

Table 16.5   Contrasts in management between two farming systems

Management factor	Coastal farming system	Inland farming system
Risk perception	lower	higher
Susceptibility	lower	higher
Knowledge of cultivars	less	more
Reading and learning	more	less
Pest control logbook	more common	less common
Fungicide input	lower	higher
Opinion on reduction	less positive	more positive

to the higher susceptibility and risk perception in that farming system. On the other hand, it is striking that the inland growers see more possibilities for reduction of fungicide use than their coastal colleagues. This contradicts the risk perceptions in the two farming systems.

Discussion

It was noted above that risk perception appeared to depend on cultivar choice and not the other way round, and that knowledge gathering and field observation did not correspond to *Botrytis* problems. Further to this, opinions on reduction in fungicide use contradict the risk perceptions in the two farming systems. On the coast the growers' behaviour is determined by public concern over pesticide pollution in the area. Public concern is the result of high annual rates of pesticide application and the presence of pesticide residues in surface water and groundwater. As a short-run tactical measure, the growers defend themselves by arguing that risks are exaggerated and by ignoring the problem. Long-term strategic behaviour is one of giving much attention to acquiring knowledge about environmental effects and plant protection.

Inland growers' behaviour is determined by the risk of crop losses from *Botrytis tulipae*. The risk is caused by the coincidence of susceptible cultivars and a humid microclimate. In the short run, they react with preventive and protective measures such as a 1:6 rotation and a stiff spray scheme. In the long run their strategic behaviour is to focus attention on effective fungicides and resistant cultivars. Consequently, they have much knowledge on these matters.

Growers gather knowledge to meet the public concern, but with respect to implementation they try to play down the public concern. Inland growers gather knowledge to reduce the *Botrytis* problem but, pending implementation, they try to combat the problem as much as possible. The models make clear that strategic behaviour has to be sustained for several production cycles to achieve changes in the tactical behaviour.

The results of this study are important for policy makers. They show that fungicide use can be reduced by pushing the bulb growers in the direction of modern fungicides, although the transition to such fungicides is hampered by the higher costs. Another option is to replace susceptible cultivars with less susceptible ones, but this option is hampered by consumer preferences: the grower will not adopt less susceptible cultivars that might result in a weak position for him in the market. The results also indicate that coastal and inland growers react differently to policy instruments: coastal growers are eager to invest in knowledge regarding externalities and supervised control, while inland ones are eager to invest in knowledge regarding less susceptible cultivars and more effective fungicides.

The results expected from this study do not support the relation between growers' goals, growers' knowledge, farm circumstances, preventive measures and use of pesticides. Rather, differences in use of pesticides are strongly related to the two distinct farming systems. Furthermore, the theoretical assumption that knowledge about pesticides would reduce their use appears false. Knowledge was assumed to be an exogenous factor that would lower risk perceptions and consequently the use of pesticides but, the opposite seems true.

Development of less susceptible cultivars has no point as long as susceptible cultivars are still grown. The use of pesticides is determined by the most susceptible cultivar and not by the mean susceptibility at the farm. However, development of fungicides can decrease overall use. At the farm level, more attention should be paid to the dose rate per hectare and per spray, rather than to the number of sprays.

References

Ministry of Agriculture, Nature Management and Fisheries (1990), *Multi-Year Crop Protection Plan* (in Dutch), Ministry of Agriculture, Nature Management and Fisheries, The Hague.

Plant Protection Service (1995), 'State of Affairs Implementation Multi-Year Crop Protection Plan in Practice 1994' (in Dutch), *Verslagen en Mededelingen nr. 178.*, Plant Protection Service, Wageningen, The Netherlands.

Poppe, K.J., F.M. Brouwer, J.P.P.J. Welten and J.H.M. Wijnands (1995), 'Agriculture, Environment and Economics; Edition 1995' (in Dutch), *Periodieke Rapportage 68-93*, Agricultural Economics Research Institute (LEI-DLO), The Hague.

PART V
POLICY INSTRUMENTS AND
POLICY ANALYSIS: LDCS

17 Public Policy and Fertilizer Demand in Ghana[1]

K.Y. Fosu[a]

Introduction

Continuous cropping of a given piece of agricultural land tends to result in excessive decrease of plant nutrients. One way of restoring soil fertility or increasing land productivity is to use fertilizer. In Ghana, in an attempt to increase land productivity, successive post-independence governments have implemented policies geared towards increasing and sustaining the use of fertilizer by farmers. This raises the issue as to the nature of such policies and the extent to which the policies have influenced the demand for fertilizer by farmers.

In April 1983, Ghana joined the group of developing countries implementing an IMF–World Bank-supported Structural Adjustment Programme. This programme comprised macroeconomic reforms including restrictive monetary and fiscal policies, foreign trade liberalization and large nominal exchange rate depreciation (World Bank, 1984). The programme also included sectoral reforms. With reference to agriculture, most product markets were deregulated, with most agricultural product prices subsequently largely determined by the competitive market mechanism. Similarly, agricultural input markets including the fertilizer market were deregulated. Fertilizer delivery was privatized and the subsidies on fertilizer and other inputs were gradually withdrawn. In the context of these recent economic policy reforms, an important question is whether fertilizer demand has changed during the Structural Adjustment period and what policies, if any, should be implemented to stimulate sustained increased demand for fertilizer in Ghana. This study addresses these issues: they are important to

[a] Institute for Research on Macroeconomics of Food, Agriculture Industry and the Environment (IFROMEFAIDE), P.O. Box 323, Legon, Accra, Ghana.

225

the development process in Ghana, but to date they have not been the subject of research.

Fertilizer Policies

The determinants of the formulation and implementation of the fertilizer policies of each post-independence government in Ghana are ascertained in this section.

Policies of the 1960s

During the immediate post independence period, the Nkrumah government observed that domestic agriculture could not satisfy Ghana's domestic food and raw material requirements. In view of this, the levels of imports of food and industrial raw materials increased rapidly, creating serious imbalances (deficits) in Ghana's balance of payments. In addition, the shortage in domestic food production tended to result in high food prices that increased the cost of living. The poor performance of domestic agriculture was due to low productivity in the sector, which was the result of a low level of soil fertility. In order to reverse the trend of low soil fertility and to sustain adequate levels of soil fertility, the government encouraged farmer use of chemical fertilizers, emphasizing that the benefit of fertilizer use in terms of increased yield should exceed the cost.

The instruments employed to step up the supply and farmer utilization of fertilizer included the following. First, research on the economic feasibility of importing fertilizer for use on crop land was encouraged, and fertilizer trials were promoted. Second, the government planned to make fertilizer available within reasonable purchase distances through marketing organizations at various points in the country; this was to reduce the transaction cost and increase farmer access to fertilizer. Third, agricultural credit was provided to farmers, and farmer utilization of fertilizer continued to be subsidized by the government at a very high rate (almost 100 per cent). Finally, the government lifted the restrictions on the importing of spare parts of vehicles, improved the coverage and quality of feeder roads, and authorized the extension service to help in the distribution of fertilizer.

Policies of the 1970s

During the period 1967–9, agricultural production grew at less than the target 5.5 per cent per annum. Food demand continued to outstrip food supply and food prices increased significantly. In view of the poor performance of domestic agriculture, food and industrial raw material imports increased, exerting adverse pressure on the trade balance. The Busia government thus desired, among other things, that Ghana would be self-sufficient in rice and possibly a net exporter of the crop. The government identified low levels of land and labour productivity as the major determinants of the poor performance of domestic agriculture. It was recognized that state-controlled agricultural product markets as well as investment in major irrigation and agricultural mechanical schemes had been unprofitable. The Busia government conceded that the use of fertilizer was still relatively insignificant and that this continued as a major cause of the low productivity of land. To deal with the problem, the government imported and distributed 5800 tons of fertilizer to farmers during 1970–71. This level of imports was greater than the average annual level of fertilizer utilization at the time; however, the government argued that this was to stimulate fertilizer use so as to increase crop yields.

The Busia government employed a number of fertilizer policy instruments. First, it set up a revolving fund into which the proceeds from fertilizer sales went; the fund financed the purchase and delivery of more fertilizer. Second, the government subsidized small-farmer use of fertilizer, at a rate of 80 per cent. Large-scale farmers were not eligible for this subsidy: these large companies and institutions were to purchase fertilizer at full cost. Finally, the government authorized the extension unit of the Ministry of Agriculture to collaborate with the United Nations FAO and UNDP on fertilizer trials and dissemination in the Ajumako, Swedru, Kpandu and Ho districts so as to increase crop output through fertilizer use.

During the period 1972–9, the NRC–SMC government proposed to increase agricultural output by putting more land under cultivation and by increasing crop yield per acre by 1980. For example, the yield of maize was to be increased from 100 to 1200 kg per hectare by 1980. Domestic agriculture was expected to produce enough food to feed the people in Ghana at affordable prices so as to satisfy basic nutritional requirements. Domestic agriculture was also expected to supply the resources (specifically, basic raw materials) for a sustained industrial revolution. Moreover, agriculture was to play a major role in Ghana's quest for balance of payments improvement, and this was to be achieved through exports of cocoa and non-traditional commodities such as cashew, pineapple, yam, chillies and ginger. The government further recognized the need to increase the levels of output of small-scale farmers so as to increase farmer income. The government noted that an important way of improving land productivity was through increased farmer use of fertilizer. However, fertilizer was often not available at the right time and in the right quantities. Hence the government stimulated sustained increased levels of utilization of inorganic fertilizers by farmers, particularly those cultivating maize, ginger and sorghum (Naga White variety).

The policy instruments for achieving these targets included the following. First, the department of agriculture was mandated to distribute fertilizer to ginger farmers. Second, the Ghana Grains Development Board was authorized to distribute fertilizer to farmers in the major grain-growing areas. Generally, the Ministry of Agriculture was empowered to assist farmers in their procurement and utilization of fertilizer. Finally, the use of fertilizer by farmers was subsidized at an annual rate of 80 per cent.

Policies of the 1980s

The Limann government noted that, during the 1979 cropping season, there were shortfalls in the supply of all crops except cassava. To reverse this trend, area under cultivation was to be increased to 1.1 million acres. In view of the low level of productivity in the agricultural sector, there was the need to increase agricultural productivity. For example, maize yield was to be increased by at least 50 per cent. The government proposed to focus on the small-scale peasant farmer. In order to increase yields, it followed the goals of its predecessors by concentrating on increased farmer adoption of fertilizer. In this regard, the government set a minimum target of 120 000 tons during 1980–81. The policy instruments employed by the government included programming the importing of fertilizer to ensure that fertilizer distribution was undertaken before the planting period of March–April in each year, mandating farm supply centres to provide fertilizer at the right time, and subsidizing fertilizer use at rates of 65 per cent and 45 per cent in 1980 and 1981, respectively.

The PNDC government came to power in December 1981. Just as the previous government had done, the PNDC government noted the poor yields of all staples. In addition, agricultural output was observed to be falling whereas food prices and the cost of living were high. Fosu (1989a) observed that the share of food in consumer price inflation was high at the time. In addition, Ghana's food self-sufficiency fell from 71–83 per cent in 1964/6 to 60 per cent in 1982. By 1984–6, domestic food production satisfied 80 per cent of the minimum requirements of maize. Thus there was a need to step up agricultural productivity, particularly productivity in the food subsector, in order to reduce the levels of food prices and ultimately reduce inflation in the whole economy. In order to accomplish this, farmers were to be encouraged to adopt and apply standard fertilizer application rates of 250kg per hectare of sulphate of ammonia, compound fertilizer and 20-20-0 (NPK fertilizer with a 20 weight percentage of pure nitrogen and a 20 weight percentage of phosphorus) for maize and 200kg per hectare for yam.

The policy instruments employed by the government included the following. First, the Ministry of Agriculture was to continue to import fertilizer on behalf of the government. Second, Commodity Boards and the Ministry of Agriculture were to distribute fertilizer at subsidized rates to farmers. However, the government gradually reduced the annual rate of subsidy, from 45 per cent in 1983 to 15 per cent in 1989, and completely withdrew the subsidy in 1990/91. Third, the importation, wholesaling and retailing of fertilizer were privatized under the World Bank–IMF-supported Structural Adjustment Programme launched in April 1983. However, the public stores were to be kept until the private sector demonstrated adequate capacity to take over fertilizer supply completely. Finally, in order to foster efficient use, fertilizer delivery was to be effected through farmer groups. Financial institutions were to channel 60 per cent of loans to maize, cassava, rice, poultry and pig production.

Policies of the 1990s

The privatization of fertilizer importation, wholesaling and retailing was continued during the 1990s by the PNDC/NDC government. The delivery and use of fertilizer have not been subsidized in the 1990s. Farmers have had to purchase and use fertilizer at full cost. Agriculture has had to compete with non-agricultural activities for credit, and credit has had to be used at full cost. Farmers have also had to employ irrigation services at near full cost.

Fertilizer Use

Various types of fertilizer have been imported and used in Ghana during the post-independence period. These include various straight fertilizer types and compound or complex fertilizer types. Table 17.1 details the specific nitrogen, phosphate and potash fertilizer types employed by farmers in Ghana. The most popular fertilizer types employed by farmers from the 1960s to the 1990s include sulphate of ammonia, muriate of potash, urea, 15-15-15 NPK and 20-20-0 NPK.

The average utilization growth rates of nitrogen and potash fertilizers increased steeply between the 1960s and 1970s (Table 17.2). However, utilization growth rates for nitrogen and potash fertilizers declined steeply between the 1970s and 1980s. In contrast, the utilization of phosphate fertilizer, which averaged 33.64 per cent per annum during the 1960s, declined slightly to 33.5 per cent per annum during the 1970s, but increased to 67 per cent during the 1980s.

The growth in the utilization of various types of fertilizer during the 1990s

Table 17.1   Types of fertilizer imported in Ghana, recent decades[a]

Fertilizer type	1960s	1970s	1980s	1990s
Sulphate of ammonia	+	+	+	+
Single superphosphate	+	+	+	0
Triple superphosphate	+	+	+	0
Muriate of potash	+	+	+	+
Sulphate of potash	+	+	0	+ (1993–4)
Magnesium sulphate	0	+	0	0
Urea	+	+	+	+
15-15-15	+	+	+	+
20-20-20	+	+	+	+
5-20-15	0	+	+	0
10-20-12	0	+	+	0
DAP/CAN[b]	0	+	+ (1980, 82)	0
3-25-18	0	+	0	0
2-24-11	0	+	0	0
Other mixtures	+	+ (1978)	+ (1989)	+ (1993–4)

Notes:
[a] + = imported; 0 = not imported; years in parentheses indicate date the type was imported if limited to one or several years.
[b] Denotes diammonium phosphate/calcium ammonium nitrate.

Source: Own calculation.

is detailed in Table 17.3. For all fertilizers combined, the level of utilization declined by 26.6 per cent per annum during the 1990s. Disaggregating into combined straight fertilizers and combined NPK complex fertilizers, the utilization rates declined by 20.1 and 32 per cent per annum, respectively, for the two groups of fertilizers during the 1990s. Apart from urea, 23-23-0 and 20-20-20, the utilization levels of all fertilizer types employed declined significantly during the 1990s. Notably, the use of urea declined by 30 per cent per annum between 1993 and 1994. Total straight fertilizer use in 1990 was 12 297 metric tons, but by 1994 it had declined steeply, to 4210 metric tons. Similarly, total NPK use was 15 777 metric tons in 1990, but by 1994 it had declined to 1612 metric tons. In 1990, the total metric tons of all fertilizers used was equal to 28 067; by 1994 it had declined to 5822 metric tons.

The average rates of fertilizer consumption, in kilograms per hectare, increased from the 1960s to the 1980s; however, they fell from the 1980s to the 1990s (Table 17.4). For example, whereas the average potash fertilizer consumption rate was 0.5 kg/ha in the 1990s, the corresponding rate averaged 1.32 kg/ha during the previous decade (1980s). For combined nutrients NPK, the rate of consumption increased from 0.48 kg/ha in the

Table 17.2 Growth of fertilizer use in Ghana, 1960s–80s (%)

Period	Nitrogen fertilizer	Phosphate fertilizer	Potash fertilizer
1960s	5.42	33.64	−5.25
1970s	92.93	33.50	45.77
1980s	10.40	67.00	15.90

Source: Computation based on data from FAO and the Crop Services Department of Ministry of Food and Agriculture, Accra, Ghana.

1960s to 5.22 kg/ha in the 1980s, but declined to 3.1 kg/ha in the 1990s. Ghana's current fertilizer consumption rate is very low compared with the 8 kg/ha for Sub-Saharan Africa as a whole, 43 kg/ha in South America, 54 kg/ha in South Africa, 65 kg/ha in North Africa, 84 kg/ha in North America, 116 kg/ha in East Asia and 241 kg/ha in Western Europe.

A 1995 survey of two major food-producing areas in Ghana indicates that the use of fertilizer has recently declined dramatically, as have the application rates. For example, in the Semi-Deciduous Zone, farmers have reduced fertilizer application rates from the recommended one bag of 20-20-0 NPK per acre plus one bag of sulphate of ammonia per acre to one bag of 20-20-0 NPK per acre plus one half bag of urea in maize–cassava systems. The survey further indicated that, in the Forest Savannah Transitional Zone, most farmers who used inorganic fertilizer before the 1990s reduced fertilizer application rates from the recommended two bags of 20-20-0 NPK starter per acre plus two bags of urea side dressing per acre in maize–cowpea systems to one bag of urea per acre with no 20-20-0 NPK,

Table 17.3 Growth in fertilizer utilization during the 1990s[a] in Ghana (%)

Fertilizer type	Growth	Fertilizer type	Growth
Straight fertilizers	−20.1	17-17-17	−47.2
Ammonium sulphate	−41.5	25-15-15	−17.6
Muriate of potash	−27.3	23-15-5	−17.7
Urea	10.6	23-23-0	7.5
Other straight fertilizers	−2.1	20-20-20	13.3
NPK complex fertilizers	−32.0	Other complexes	−14.5
15-15-15	−17.0	Total fertilizers	−26.6
20-20-0	−52.5		

Note: [a] Covers the period 1990–94.

Source: Computations based on data from the Crop Services Department of the Ministry of Food and Agriculture, Accra, Ghana.

Table 17.4   Average annual rate of fertilizer use in Ghana (kg/ha of agricultural land[a]), 1960s–90s

Period	Nitrogen fertilizer	Phosphatic fertilizer	Potash fertilizer	Combined nutrients (N+P+K)
1960s	0.16	0.14	0.18	0.48
1970s	2.06	1.47	1.03	4.56
1980s	2.60	1.30	1.32	5.22
1990s[b]	2.00	0.6	0.5	3.1
1983-94[c]	2.2	0.9	0.8	3.9

Notes:
[a] Agricultural land includes arable land and land under permanent crops.
[b] Covers the period 1990–94.
[c] 1983–94 covers the entire structural adjustment period.

Source: *FAO Fertiliser Yearbook* (various issues) and *FAO Production Yearbook* (various issues).

whereas some farmers reduced application to one bag of 20-20-0 NPK per acre plus one bag of urea per acre in 1995. The yields of maize declined from 3800 kg/ha before the 1990s to 1000 to 1250 kg/ha in 1995.

Studies on Ghana by Fosu (1989b, 1993a and 1993b, 1994a and 1994b), Obeng *et al.* (1990), Badiane *et al.* (1992) and Bonsu *et al.* (1995) show that fertilizer demand is influenced by fertilizer–crop terms of trade, access to crop markets, the degree of commercialization of crop production, the degree of crop response to fertilizer, availability and access to crop marketing services such as transport and storage, availability and access to information on the benefits of fertilizer, application rates, timing of application and method of application, availability and access to irrigation services, and farmer access to credit. Factors that limit crop response to fertilizer include poor rainfall distribution, poor timing of field preparations, disease and insect infestation, poor weed control, inadequate land preparation, specific nutrient deficiencies and suboptimal plant population. Adequate levels of soil moisture improve crop response to fertilizer; hence farmers tend to use fertilizer when their expectations concerning rainfall are highest.

As observed earlier, the levels of utilization of inorganic fertilizer generally increased during the decades of the 1960s to the 1980s. This could be due to a number of factors. First, the fertilizer–crop price ratio was not prohibitive, because of the public delivery and subsidy policies implemented during the period. Second, there was marked improvement in availability and access to irrigation services that were publicly delivered at subsidized rates. In addition, there tended to be relatively less uncertainty concerning the amount, frequency and distribution of rainfall. Of course, there was acute drought in 1982 and 1983, after which marked uncertainty in rainfall patterns began to be experienced. Third, extension service delivery by the public sector stimulated a fair increase in farmer access to information on fertilizer use, although the coverage of the services remained limited. Finally, farmer access to credit on concessionary terms improved significantly.

Contrary to the preceding period, the 1990s brought about steep declines in the levels and rates of utilization of inorganic fertilizer in Ghana. This was due to the sectoral and macroeconomic policies implemented during the period. First, the policies of agricultural product market deregulation, agricultural input delivery privatization and subsidy withdrawal resulted in increases in both agricultural product prices and agricultural input prices. However, the magnitudes of the agricultural input price increases far outweighed those of the agricultural product price increases, leading to a significant adverse farmer cost–price squeeze during the period. Table 17.5 illustrates this phenomenon with respect to specific major agricultural commodities and various inorganic fertilizers. The unit prices of the inorganic fertilizers NPK, ammonium sulphate, urea, muriate of potash, single superphosphate and potassium nitrogen phosphate grew at annual rates of 35.5 per cent, 48.1 per cent, 22.3 per cent, 66.6 per cent, 22.2 per cent and 112.9 per cent, respectively. These tended to exceed the magnitudes of increases in the unit prices of the major agricultural commodities, which ranged between 10 per cent and 40.4 per cent per annum. The steep increases in the unit prices of fertilizer during the 1990s are due to the depreciation of the domestic currency, as Ghana relies on imported fertilizer: the nominal exchange rate, which averaged 326.33 cedis per dollar in 1990, jumped to 1000 cedis by 1995; it is currently 1600 cedis. Higher transport costs also played a role. As a result, fertilizer–crop price ratios have increased remarkably: the magnitudes of the increases have been particularly large in the cases of potassium nitrogen phosphate, muriate of potash and ammonium sulphate. The increase in the fertilizer–crop price ratio has been relatively slight in the case of urea. Notably, the corresponding ratios for NPK and urea tended to favour cocoa production, as the ratios declined during the period (see Table 17.5).

Another factor that has contributed to the decline in the utilization of inorganic fertilizers during the 1990s has been the decline in the availability and farmer access to institutionalized credit during the period. Indeed, during the period the stance of monetary policy and government domestic borrowing tended to crowd out agricultural producers in the domestic credit market. The share of agriculture in commercial bank loans and advances, and in secondary bank loans and advances, declined during the period (Table 17.6). Furthermore, farmer access to credit declined as agricultural lending rates increased because of the withdrawal of the earlier concession enjoyed by farmers: the agricultural lending rate averaged 26 per cent in 1990 and rose to 31.5 per cent and 28.75 per cent in 1993 and 1994, respectively. The real volume of agricultural credit declined by 0.4 per cent per annum. Financial institutions now prefer to invest in government treasury bills rather than lend to agriculture, which is seen as risky. During the 1990s, the treasury bill rate was higher than the average agricultural lending rate for all years except 1991. This trend has hampered financial intermediation in the economy.

Third, the uncertainty about the amount, timing, frequency and distribution of rainfall during the 1990s, coupled with limited farmer access to irrigation, was an important factor precipitating decline in the demand for fertilizer during the period. During the 1990s, irrigation water charges were rationalized, with the result that they increased significantly. Consequently, the levels of availability and utilization of irrigation declined. The area of agricultural land under irrigation and the proportion of agricultural land under irrigation declined. The level and proportion of land under irrigation had also declined during the 1980s (Fosu, 1993a, 1993b). Public expenditure on public agriculture goods and services, such as irrigation, and meteorological and agricultural extension services, declined significantly. For example, the share of agriculture in total development expenditure, which stood at 17.1 per cent during the immediate pre-Structural Adjustment era (specifically, 1980–82), declined to 11 per cent in the 1980s and to 4 per cent in the 1990s. During the period, public agricultural development expenditure grew by 17.3 per cent per annum, whereas total public development expenditure grew by 16.7 per cent, implying that the share of

Table 17.5   Growth in wholesale prices of agricultural products and fertilizer–crop price ratio in Ghana, 1990–94 (%)

	Product price	NPK	AS	Urea	MOP	KNP
Cocoa	40.4	−4.9	6.7	−18.1	26.2	72.5
Maize	12.8	22.7	34.3	9.5	53.8	100.1
Rice (local)	17.9	17.6	29.2	4.4	48.7	95.0
Millet	14.3	21.2	32.8	8.0	52.3	98.6
Sorghum	14.6	20.9	32.5	7.7	52.0	98.3
Cowpea	16.2	19.3	30.9	6.1	50.4	96.7
Groundnut	19.5	16.0	27.6	2.8	7.1	93.4
Cassava	10.0	25.5	37.1	12.3	56.6	102.9
Yam	16.8	18.7	30.3	5.5	49.8	96.1
Onion	19.2	16.3	27.9	3.1	47.4	93.7
Tomatoes	20.5	15.0	26.6	1.8	46.1	92.4
Oil palm	21.0	14.5	26.1	1.3	45.6	91.9

Table 17.6   **Percentage annual share of agriculture in total credit in Ghana, 1990-94**

Year	Commercial banks	Secondary banks	Total
1990	15.8	16.1	15.9
1991	13.6	13.0	13.2
1992	11.1	8.7	9.7
1993	9.6	7.5	8.33
1994	6.6	9.3	8.27

Source: Calculation based on data from *Quarterly Digest of Statistics* (various issues) published by the Ghana Statistical Service.

agriculture in total development expenditure increased by only 0.6 per cent per annum. To the contrary, the share of agriculture in total government expenditure declined by 28.2 per cent per annum, since total government expenditure grew by 45.7 per cent per year whereas total public agriculture expenditure grew by only 17.5 per cent per annum.

Finally, during the 1990s the prices of other inputs, specifically those relating to improved crop seeds, agro-chemicals, spraying machines and agricultural labour, increased; this may have contributed to the decline in fertilizer demand.

Recommendations

The results of this study suggest a number of policy recommendations. First, in order to stimulate sustained increased levels and rates of fertilizer use, small and medium-scale irrigation schemes should be established and properly maintained. Existing irrigation schemes that are not functioning should be rehabilitated as a matter of urgency. Second, the current tendency of the government to crowd out agriculture in total public expenditure and in development expenditure needs to be reversed. This is true also with respect to credit, where government has crowded out agricultural producers. Third, an effective extension service is required in Ghana. The dissemination of fertilizer technology should be part of an agricultural technology package that should also include technologies such as improved seeds and improved cultural practices that in turn improve crop response to fertilizer. Fourth, the formation and operation of viable farmer associations managed by farmers should be encouraged. Farmers could benefit from discounts on bulk purchases of fertilizer and other inputs which the associations could undertake on behalf of the farmers. In addition, credit could be obtained in bulk at concessionary rates through such associations; the cost of recovery of loans could be minimized. Finally, a scheme could be formulated whereby a proportion of the taxes paid by private fertilizer dealers could be deposited in a fertilizer revolving fund. This could be used to support economic activities related to sustained increased fertilizer utilization.

Note

1   The author wishes to thank the International Development Research Centre (IDRC), Ottawa, for funding the research project from which this chapter was derived.

References

Badiane, O., V. Nyanten and A. Seni (1992), *Food Security, Comparative Advantage and Fertilizer Use in Ghana*, IFPRI/ISSER, Washington, DC.

Bonsu, K.M., K.Y. Fosu and P.K. Kwakye (1995), 'Soil Productivity Management in Ghana', research report prepared for the World Bank, Washington, DC.

Fosu, K.Y. (1989a), 'Agriculture in Ghana's Post-1970 Development Process', paper submitted to the West African Economics Association Conference, Lomé, Togo.

Fosu, K.Y. (1989b), 'Structural Adjustment Policies' Effects on Agricultural Productivity and Production in Ghana', invited paper presented to the African Centre for Agricultural Credit Training Workshop on Effects of The Economic Recovery Programme on Agriculture, Accra, Ghana.

Fosu, K.Y. (1993a), 'Domestic Public Policy and Ghana's Agriculture, 1982–89', in E. Gyimah-Boadi (ed.), *Ghana Under PNDC Rule*, CODESRIA Book Series, Antony Rowe, Chippenham, UK.

Fosu, K.Y. (1993b), 'Effects of Privatisation of Input Delivery and Subsidy Withdrawal Policy on the Demand for Agricultural Inputs in Ghana', interim research report for the International Development Research Centre (IDRC), Ottawa, Canada.

Fosu, K.Y. (1994a), 'Determinants and Effectiveness of Government Expenditure Policy in Ghana's Agricultural Sector', *Issues in African Rural Development*, **2**, Winrock International Institute for Agricultural Development, Arlington.

Fosu, K.Y. (1994b), 'Public Private Financing Under Uncertainty: An Ophelimity-Theoretic Model for ECOWAS Agriculture', *West African Economic Journal*, **7**: 1–18.

Obeng, B., K.G. Erbynn and E.O. Asante (1990), 'Fertiliser Requirements and Use in Ghana', report submitted to the Government of Ghana, Accra.

World Bank (1984), *Ghana: Policies and Programmes for Adjustment*, World Bank, Washington, DC.

18 Consequences for Agricultural Policies of Analysing Economic and Political Factors of Pesticide Use in Developing Countries

G. Fleischer and H. Waibel [a]

Introduction

The use of chemical pesticides was widely introduced and promoted in developing countries as an essential part of modernized farming systems in the course of agricultural modernization, the so-called 'green revolution'. In the perceived need to increase food production and national self-sufficiency for a growing population, research and development as well as rapid expansion of yield-increasing technology packages were favoured. Since adoption of external technologies by smallholders was seen as a major problem, national governments, supported by international funding agencies, opted for pricing, marketing, extension and other intervention strategies that influenced farmers' decisions towards the use of these kinds of input. The success of this strategy is underlined by available market forecasts for the period 1992–6, which show high growth rates of pesticide use in major developing countries, while markets in developed countries stagnated or declined (Woodburn, 1992).

Although major successes in terms of achieving national production and

[a] University of Hanover, Institute of Economics in the Faculty of Horticulture, Herrenhäuser Str.2, D-30419 Hanover, Germany.

food security objectives, especially in Asian countries, cannot be denied, green revolution strategies have been heavily criticized. On the one hand, pesticides played an essential part as a means of securing the utilization of the yield potential of the newly introduced seed varieties, but, on the other hand, overuse and misuse led to unexpected adverse effects. Occupational health hazards of farmers and farmworkers, water pollution, loss of natural enemies and biodiversity, resistance and food residue problems were increasingly recognized.

Externalities lead to social costs that are often neglected since they are hidden and may occur with a time lag. Frequently, groups concerned with environmental and health damage interests are not effectively represented in the political process, leading to suboptimal situations for the society as a whole. In contrast to these hidden costs, the benefits of chemical pesticide use are taken for granted. With growing use trends in developing countries, both the potential future costs of damage to natural resources and the misallocation of resources that is caused by the amount of direct and indirect subsidies provided to pesticide users come increasingly into consideration.

It has become obvious that governments' pesticide policies were at least partly responsible for overuse and misuse. The role of direct and indirect subsidies on national pesticide use was analysed by Repetto (1985) for nine developing countries; subsidies had grown in major agricultural production systems and now placed a heavy burden on governments' budgets. With the onset of structural adjustment programmes, conditions for pesticide use changed in many countries. State-controlled input delivery to farmers at subsidized prices was mostly abolished. It was expected that market prices instead of artificially lower administered prices would allow a more efficient use of agricultural inputs, including fertilizer and pesticides.

Still to be assessed is whether the structural adjustment programmes and the integrated pest management (IPM) extension and training programmes introduced in some countries are able to restore the balance in favour of chemical crop protection. Pesticide use trends have to be analysed in order to determine the driving economic and political forces and to indicate those areas where price distortions and institutional constraints hamper the adoption of rational crop protection practices.

The objective of this chapter is to provide an overview of the scope of pesticide policy studies at the individual country level. These types of studies are aimed at analysing national pesticide use trends, developments in major farming systems, and patterns of political and institutional conditions influencing farm-level decision making. Additionally, evidence of external costs are collected from secondary sources. The analysis identifies and evaluates factors influencing the level of chemical pesticide use. The theoretical concept follows a welfare economic approach incorporating private and social benefits and costs. Factors identified are then weighted according to their relative importance by an expert panel. Initial results from country studies lead to policy conclusions regarding future needs for government intervention.

Framework for Policy Analysis

Methodological problems are often found in the analysis of economic and political forces that influence pesticide use. Economic justification of the current level of pesticide use in many farming systems is doubtful. The economics of pesticide use under conditions of developing countries has not yet commanded as much attention as would be expected, in view of the high priority that is placed on its adoption by farmers. Comprehensive analyses of the benefits and costs, both at the level of individual decision making and from the perspective of the society as a whole, are seldom found.

At the field level, empirical and anecdotal evidence has reported frequent overuse and misuse of chemical pesticides in many areas. However, economic evaluations of productivity have been mostly derived from research station data which indicate high potential crop loss without chemicals and high productivity of chemical pesticide use. The gap between these results may be explained by problems in crop loss assessment resulting from difficulties in establishing cause and effect relationships and from monocausal effectiveness trials. Potential long-term effects of agricultural resource degradation such as resistance of pests, secondary pest outbreaks and destruction of the natural anti-phytopathogenic potential are often overlooked. Productivity estimates have shown diverging results, leading to the conclusion that a reliable functional approach may not easily be found (Carrasco-Tauber and Moffitt, 1992, see also Chapter 26 of the present volume).

Policy analysis is often sector-oriented. Plant protection policy is planned almost exclusively with the objective of raising production levels and the producers' income. In view of the dichotomic role of pesticides as a means of safeguarding agricultural production and a potential cause of natural resource damage, an integration of economic and policy analysis is particularly useful. Since the institutional reasons for the deviation of pesticide use from its social optimal are market and government failure, a separation is less meaningful (Table 18.1). From the viewpoint of welfare economic theory, the reference system for economic and policy analysis should be the social optimum (Figure 18.1).

In Figure 18.1, benefits and costs of pesticide use are plotted against units of prevented crop loss. Benefits are equal to prevented crop loss times the

Table 18.1   **Reasons for institutional failure**

Market failure	Example in the case of pesticide use
Performance failure	(a) asymmetric information on product characteristics
	(b) chemical pesticide use causes externalities, thus leading to suboptimal allocation
Market absence	public goods (e.g., water, natural environment, biodiversity) are affected by pesticide damage
Government failure	
Lack of intervention	(a) property rights for natural resources are not assigned
	(b) tolerance of negative externalities
Policy failure	inappropriate market, pricing, subsidy/tax, trade policies
Administrative failure	lack of enforcement of legal stipulations

product price. Each unit of prevented crop loss is determined by a specific level of pesticide use costs. Costs increase exponentially because the marginal rate of crop loss prevention per unit of pesticide use is decreasing in Figure 18.1. In economic theory, the optimal level of input use is reached when marginal costs equal marginal benefits. In Figure 18.1, three optimal levels of pesticide use are distinguished:

1   Taking into account private costs as perceived by the user leads to A as the optimal level of crop protection. *Perceived private costs* include expenses for pesticides, spraying equipment and labour.
2   Considering, in addition to the perceived private costs, on-site externalities such as health problems of the user and overestimates of prevented crop loss causes an increase of costs at the farm level. This corresponds to the *actual private costs*, and B represents the optimal use of pesticides from the private user's viewpoint.
3   Because off-site externalities such as pollution of drinking water occur, *social costs* of pesticide use are still higher than actual private costs: C represents the level of chemical crop protection that is optimal from society's viewpoint.

The internalizing of external effects matches the demand of allocative efficiency by applying the full-cost principle to the use of resources (Tietenberg, 1992). A major drawback in using this framework is the problem that, in most cases, there may be considerable uncertainty in the available data as regards exactly determining the shapes of the curves of marginal damages and private net benefits (Oskam, 1994). In practical policy, there is scope to derive the level of pesticide use that is acceptable to the society in an open political process between the different interest groups

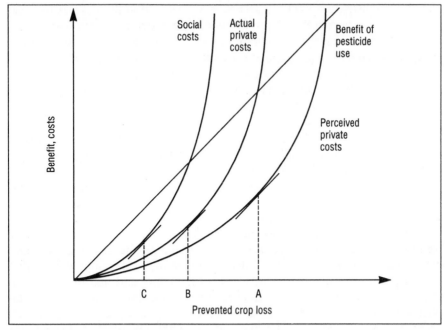

Source: Waibel (1994).

Figure 18.1 Private and social optimum of pesticide use

and government agencies concerned, as experience with the formulation of pesticide use reduction programmes in some European countries showed. However, economic assessment of use patterns and associated externalities can at least determine the extent of the deviation of current social costs from perceived private costs. An example for evaluating occupational health impacts has been provided in the study of rice insecticide use by Rola and Pingali (1993). This kind of data provides information on the direction of necessary change.

Allocative efficiency has no lobby to represent it in the real world of policy making. Government's regulatory intervention may help to remedy the situation of market failure, although intervention comes with no assurance of optimality. An explanation for the political process of capturing the regulatory decision making by agricultural interests has been given in several studies in industrialized countries. Noll and Owen (1983) pointed out that the regulatory agency is required to consider arguments of the different groups concerned, but depends heavily on the information provided by the different stakeholders. Agricultural interests, and especially those of the chemical industry, are likely to be better represented in the process because of better access to data. Small groups tend to be better organized with access to larger financial resources than groups with a low degree of organization, such as consumers and taxpayers (Becker, 1983). Cropper *et al.* (1992) showed in an empirical analysis of regulatory decisions by the US Environmental Protection Agency (EPA) that interest group lobbying had a significant influence on the final decision.

In his analysis of the historical development of US pesticide policies, Bosso (1987) identified the 'iron triangle' of agricultural interests which dominated throughout the 1950s and 1960s in the formulation of pesticide-related policies in the United States. Developing countries tend to duplicate the traditional focus on command and control approaches, especially with respect to registration requirements, which are sensitive to influence by pro-pesticide interests in industrialized countries.

A considerable step forward in analysing the reasons for deviation of pesticide use levels from their social optimum is the identification and evaluation of institutional factors that contribute to this development. Waibel (1990) provided a distinction between price factors and non-price factors. *Price factors* are those that influence directly the farm gate price of the chemical pesticide and the ratio between output and input prices, at which point the user decides on the application of the chemical. Subsidies are provided by lowering the market price either through state marketing agencies or through import duty and sales tax exemptions for pesticides and complementary inputs. Hidden subsidies occur in the case of governments refunding pesticide companies' production costs. There are inappropriate rules for outbreak budgets of plant protection services that lead to the provision of pesticides for users at lower prices or free of cost. *Non-price factors* can predominantly be found in institutional regulations and in the information environment that affects farmers' pesticide use decisions. Priorities in government-financed research and extension activities, as well as education and training curricula and industry advertisements that are biased against non-chemical alternatives, can lead to a lack of information at the users' level on appropriate control options. Chemicals often appear as the only solution to a perceived problem. Externalities are imperfectly considered in policy decision making, either by total neglect of damage costs or by inappropriate investment in mitigation strategies.

Results from Country Studies

As a literature overview compiled by the World Bank revealed, a large number of price and non-price factors still exist (Farah, 1993). Whether the cut in explicit direct subsidies in many countries in the course of structural adjustment programmes improved the situation remains uncertain. A survey among officials of plant protection services from 22 countries concluded that in each country several indirect subsidises still favour chemical pesticide use over its alternatives (Fleischer and Waibel, 1993).

Since empirical studies at the level of individual countries were needed, a joint framework for conducting this research was developed by a group of economists and policy specialists (Agne *et al.*, 1994). The application of the theoretical framework on pesticide use and policies is carried out in four countries in the course of a study project of the University of Hanover and GTZ (Deutsche Gesellschaft für Technische Zusammenarbeit). The major objective is to improve the information base on pesticide use and its influencing policy factors. Since pesticide issues were frequently narrowed down to the choice of the most effective means of pest control rather than analysing linkages to the state of the agro-ecosystem and other sectors of the economy, raising awareness of the scope of problem analysis and policy evaluation is a major outcome.

Results were obtained from a review of available reports from various disciplines: statistics on import, marketing and use of pesticides, data on occupational poisoning cases and interviews with key players in governmental and non-governmental organizations. Identification and evaluation of price and non-price factors that were found currently to influence chemical pesticide use levels are undertaken in a comparative analysis to a free-market, undistorted situation. Ranking of the relative importance of these factors is done according to expert opinion. Whereas price factors can be quantified, institutional factors are weighted according to their relative importance. Finally, a committee of national experts comprising members from different government agencies and relevant interest groups discussed and evaluated the policy matrix.

Results from Costa Rica and Thailand suggest that there is a far higher number of factors located in the institutional environment than those influencing directly the market prices that push pesticide use away from its optimal use (Agne, 1995; Jungbluth, 1995). These factors are more hidden from policy makers than the price factors. In both countries, import duty and sales tax exemptions play a major role in lowering market prices of pesticides to the user. These preferential arrangements clearly distort the price ratio of farm inputs. For example, in the case of herbicides, the price of family or hired labour is increased relative to that of herbicides. Tax exemptions for external inputs that are complementary to chemical pesticides, such as spraying equipment and nitrogen fertilizer, act in the same direction.

Non-price factors in governments' agricultural policies have a significant impact on chemical pesticide use. Governments' promotion of production systems that are highly pesticide consuming plays a major role in the development of banana production in Costa Rica and of fruit tree cropping in Thailand. Neither occurrence of external effects (Castillo, 1995) nor doubtful long-run profitability caused by the resistance phenomenon (Waibel and Setboronsarng, 1993; Agne, 1995) have yet been considered in programme design. Credit requirements of agricultural development banks that mandate chemical pesticide use are another factor that distorts the optimal choice of pest control options.

Among the effects of biases in the institutional setting governing the availability, distribution and use of crop protection measures, the information environment of users' decision making plays a crucial role. Research and extension priorities as well as educational and agricultural training curricula are heavily biased towards chemical solutions for perceived pest problems. Therefore information on non-chemical alternatives and consideration of agro-ecosystem linkages lowering pest infestation levels are lacking. Farmers lack adequate information on realistically expected crop losses and on alternative crop protection strategies. Furthermore, information by industry sources plays a significant role in influencing farmers' crop protection decisions for major cash crops. IPM extension and training efforts have had a rather limited impact in view of the small number of farmers involved.

Negative externalities have been recognized in Thailand and Costa Rica, especially in the health sector. Although considerable underreporting, especially in remote rural areas, is assumed, pesticide poisoning cases show a high level of occupational health hazards. Thailand has started to fund a safe use programme on health risk reduction. Such mitigative strategies generally violate the 'polluter pays principle' as long as costs are born by taxpayers. Government risk-reduction activities are oriented to current pesticide use levels rather than the optimal level, so they fail to act as an incentive for internalizing the social costs of pesticide damage. Effects on the natural environment have not yet been systematically monitored and may only be detected in the long run.

Consequences for Policy Formulation

Case studies of pesticide use and policy at the individual country level provide an information basis that is suitable for identifying important areas for policy intervention. The aim to reverse the policy development away from explicit and implicit subsidies should be approached from a multi-sector perspective. Consequences for policy formulation arise at two levels.

National Policies

In order to counterbalance the predominant impact on pesticide use of import duty and sales tax exemptions, domestic trade policy should be revised (Agne, 1995). The example of Costa Rica shows that expected negative consequences on growers of pesticide-intensive crops will likely be offset by a number of positive effects: (1) the amount of foreign exchange needed for imported formulations and technical materials will be reduced (given a negative price elasticity of pesticide demand, which is likely); (2) the underutilization of domestic resources for pesticide control will be alleviated; (3) budgetary expenses for mitigation of pesticide damage (health care, water treatment) will be reduced; and (4) the increase in government revenues can be used to finance research and development activities on sustainable crop protection practices. These effects are, to a large extent, directly measurable and quite obvious for political decision makers.

Reversing the impact of non-price factors on pesticide use patterns demands institutional changes, especially those related to human resources. Approaches have to be process-oriented since success can only be expected in the long term. Strengthening of participatory elements in plant protection systems appears as a major element for such strategies. Farmers should be strengthened in their capacity to make appropriate decisions that reduce potential pest infestation, relying more on the on-farm regulation factors. Education and training curricula should be freed from their bias towards chemical solutions. Another area of institutional adaptation is the regulatory framework. Considering social cost–benefit assessment in registration and regulatory intervention decisions would enhance the incorporation of all relevant impacts, including those in non-agricultural sectors. Relevant interest groups, such as consumer and environmental groups, should be included in the decision-making process. A rational policy mix may include especially economic instruments.

In the case of chemical pesticides, there are interdependencies between policies directed at agriculture and those related to health, labour, trade and environment. Pesticide policies have to be reformulated in a consistent approach.

International Policies

Agenda 21 of the United Nations Conference on Environment and Development (UNCED) conference is demanding a paradigm shift at the global level, mainly focusing on the sustainability of agricultural production. IPM has been declared as a suitable technology for achieving this objective.

However, it is still lacking concrete implementation on a large scale. Current pesticide policies have been identified as a major constraint.

Institutional reform and structural adjustment in developing countries can be supported by global developments and by support from international and bilateral agencies. The example of food residue limits, which were imposed by industrialized countries on third world countries' imports and which had a significant impact on pesticide use patterns in some locations, show that developments in international trade have high impacts. Global phase-out programmes (such as the one on ozone-depleting substances) are another example of restrictions at the international level. Donor support of pesticide policy reform may contribute to both matching the demands of the agricultural export sector and reducing overall pesticide use.

Conclusions

Despite increasing popularity of the Integrated Pest Management (IPM) concept in developing countries, there is growing awareness on the part of government and private decision makers concerning the negative externalities caused by chemical pesticides and their use in developing countries. While benefits of a pesticide-based strategy tend to be overestimated, costs tend to be underestimated because of methodological and data problems. As a consequence, excessive pesticide use is being stimulated by a number of hidden and indirect subsidies. Country case studies are a means of trying to assess the state of a country in terms of the extent to which policies are in place that drive pesticide use towards or away from its social optimum. Preliminary results of the country case studies which are under way indicate that non-price factors are influential in causing excessive pesticide use. The political economy of pest management decision making results in decisions that reflect the imbalance of power among the various interest groups. The current and expected world food situation, together with the declining support for agriculture-based development, bears the danger of a further increase in the dominance of the private sector. The induced perception that more pesticides will help to avert an expected world food crisis is being systematically nourished by the chemical industry through well-directed studies and research.

Independent research has failed to demonstrate that IPM has the potential not only to reduce chemical pesticide use, but at the same time to increase production. As a result of IPM training, farmers are in a position to reallocate some of the money saved on pesticides to more productive inputs and to become better crop and ecosystems managers. There is a need to design economic studies that are able to capture the human capital effects in terms of stimulating the learning processes and innovative capacities of small-scale farm communities induced by IPM training. Furthermore, it is not yet fully understood in which way policy factors constrain a more rapid implementation of IPM. Finally, there is a need for effective mechanisms of policy dialogue that reduce the existing imbalance among interest groups. Pesticide use decision making will then move towards greater reliance on non-chemical strategies.

References

Agne, S. (1995), 'Economic Analysis of Crop Protection Policy in Costa Rica', draft paper, GTZ/Hanover University Pesticide Policy Project, Hanover.

Agne, S., G. Fleischer and H. Waibel (eds) (1994), *Proceedings of the Göttingen Workshop on Pesticide Policies, Göttinger Schriften zur Agrarökonomie, Vol. 66*, Institute of Agricultural Economics, University of Göttingen, Göttingen.

Becker, G.S. (1983), 'A Theory of Competition Among Pressure Groups for Political Influence', *Quarterly Journal of Economics*, 3(98): 371–400.

Bosso, C.J. (1987), 'Pesticides and Politics: The Life Cycle of a Public Issue', University of Pittsburgh Press, Pittsburgh.

Carrasco-Tauber, C. and L.J. Moffitt (1992), 'Damage Control Econometrics: Functional Specification and Pesticide Productivity', *American Journal of Agricultural Economics*, 74(1): 158–62.

Castillo, L. (1995), 'Sustainability Requires a Necessary Change in the Banana Plantain Industry', paper presented at the 13th International Plant Protection Congress, The Hague, 2–7 July.

Cropper, M.L., N.N. Evans, S.J. Bernard, M.M. Ducla-Soares and P.R. Portney (1992), 'The Determinants of Pesticide Regulation: A Statistical Analysis of EPA Decision Making', *Journal of Political Economy*, 100: 175–97.

Farah, J. (1993), 'Pesticide Policies in Developing Countries: Do They Encourage Excessive Pesticide Use?', World Bank Technical Paper Series 238, World Bank, Washington, DC.

Fleischer, G. and H. Waibel (1993), 'Survey Among Plant Protection Officers During the Global IPM Conference, Bangkok, August 1993', report to the FAO/UNEP Panel of Experts on Integrated Pest Control, Göttingen/Rome.

Jungbluth, F. (1995), 'Aspects of Pesticide Policies in Thailand', draft paper, GTZ/Hanover University Pesticide Policy Project, Hanover.

Noll, R.G. and B.M. Owen (1983), *The Political Economy of Deregulation: Interest Groups in the Regulatory Process*, American Enterprise Institute for Public Policy Research, Washington, DC.

Oskam, A. (1994), 'Pesticides: Issues at Stake for Economists', in J. Michalek and C.H. Hanf (eds), *The Economic Consequences of a Drastic Reduction in Pesticide Use in the European Union*, revised papers of a workshop held in Tannenfelde (Schleswig-Holstein), 13–14 November 1993, Vauk Kiel.

Repetto, R. (1985), *Paying the Price: Pesticide Subsidies in Developing Countries*,

World Resources Institute, Washington, DC.

Rola, A. and P. Pingali (1993), *Pesticides, Rice Productivity, and Farmers' Health: An Economic Assessment*, International Rice Research Institute (IRRI), Los Baños, Philippines.

Tietenberg, T. (1992), *Environmental and Natural Resource Economics*, 3rd edn, Harper Collins College, New York.

Waibel, H. (1990), 'Pesticide Subsidies and the Diffusion of IPM in Rice in Southeast Asia: The Case of Thailand', *FAO Plant Protection Bulletin*, **38**(2): 105–11.

Waibel, H. and S. Setboronsarng (1993), 'Resource Degradation Due to Chemical Inputs in Vegetable-Based Farming Systems in Thailand', *Journal of the Asian Farming Systems Association*, **2**(1): 107–20.

Waibel, H. (1994), 'Towards an Economic Framework of Pesticide Policy Studies', in S. Agne, G. Fleischer and H. Waibel (eds), *Proceedings of the Göttingen Workshop on Pesticide Policies, Göttinger Schriften zur Agrarökonomie, Vol. 66*, Institute of Agricultural Economics, University of Göttingen, Göttingen.

Woodburn, A. (1992), *Future Pesticide Market Trends*, unpublished consultancy report, Allan Woodburn Associates Ltd., Edinburgh.

19 Financial and Economic Evaluation of Phosphate Rock Use to Enhance Soil Fertility in West Africa: Is there a Role for Government?[1]

A. Kuyvenhoven[a]*, J.A. Becht*[b] *and R. Ruben*[c]

Introduction

The problem regarding sustainability of agriculture in the Sahel (that is, the West African countries of Burkina Faso, Chad, Mali, Mauritania and Niger) urgently calls for a solution: the livelihood of large segments of the population is in jeopardy. Therefore attempts to solve this problem through the development and introduction of agricultural techniques preventing soil degradation are appropriate (Cornelisse, 1993).

Research has shown that the limited rainfall in the Sahel is not the most constraining factor on agriculture. Fertilization is one of the best means to enhance water utilization because improved soil fertility could increase the efficiency of water use by 50 per cent. At present, only 10–15 per cent of the rainfall is used for vegetative growth; the rest is lost through evaporation, drainage and run-off. Intensification of Sahelian agriculture by means of

[a] Department of Development Economics, Wageningen Agricultural University, P.O. Box 8130, 6700 EW, Wageningen, The Netherlands.
[b] Tinbergen Institute, Erasmus University Rotterdam, The Netherlands.
[c] Department of Development Economics, Wageningen Agricultural University, P.O. Box 8130, 6700 EW, Wageningen, The Netherlands.

phosphate rock (PR) application will improve and maintain soil fertility (Koster, 1994).

After 25 years of agricultural research in the Sahel, international research institutes have reached a consensus that sustainability should be based on sensible management of the agricultural resource base, with soil fertility as a criterion for sustainable land use. Besides a combination of erosion-reduction and farm management measures, three aspects are of crucial importance to sustainability: (1) organic material, (2) use of nitrogen (N) fixers and (3) nutrients, of which phosphate is the most important.

Foreign exchange shortages and debt crises have constrained fertilizer use by restricting fertilizer imports and supply in many African countries (see Chapter 17 of the present volume). Consequently, these countries have relied excessively on fertilizer aid. As most bilateral donors are reluctant to make long-term commitments for fertilizer, dependence on aid introduces a high degree of uncertainty and prevents the development of efficient input supply and marketing systems. It also discourages fertilizer use because farmers do not feel secure in adopting fertilizer-intensive cropping practices when access to fertilizer is uncertain. Another disadvantage of fertilizer aid is that cheap subsidized fertilizer aid reduces incentives to develop domestic resources, especially PR for direct application.

After the 1994 franc FCFA devaluation, the real price of imported fertilizer increased substantially, further constraining its use, but it also provided an incentive to develop domestic substitutes. Coupled with general donor fatigue with project and commodity aid, the restoration of soil fertility through programme aid is increasingly considered a lasting and more cost-effective substitute for food aid.

Investment in the application of phosphorus sources, especially those with a significant content of less soluble phosphorus (P) such as ground PR, can be considered as a restoration of the natural resource base, because it augments and maintains the stock of natural capital embodied in soil resources. Both farmers and society benefit from increasing agricultural output and reduced nutrient depletion in agricultural production (Gerner and Baanante, 1995). Defined in this way, PR application can be considered a capital investment.

Phosphate as a capital investment raises various issues regarding the financing of phosphate fertilizers. First, investment is lumpy, requiring an initial investment of large doses of PR that yields returns over a long period of time. Farmers often do not have adequate financial resources to make such investments, nor are commercial banks willing to lend because of poor collateral. Second, it rebuilds the natural fertility of soils that have been depleted. Investment in soils is comparable to land reclamation or land improvement projects. This chapter presents a financial and economic analysis of capital investment to improve soil fertility in the Sahel by means of PR. More specifically, it deals with micro and other economic criteria for the evaluation of such a capital investment in soil fertility, making use of a case study on the prospects for PR application.

Agrarian Policies and Public Investment

Available options to address soil degradation and decreasing soil productivity can be divided into soil productivity *management*, based on intensification of mineral fertilizer consumption, and soil productivity *enhancement*, through recapitalization of soil fertility through capital investment (MacMillan, 1995). Both strategies are to be combined with technical measures that guarantee the highest possible efficiency of input use, basically depending on soil organic matter status, soil acidity, soil moisture storage capacity and the phosphate fixing capacity of soils. The structure of farming systems and practices also needs to be taken into account to evaluate feasible and appropriate alternatives for resource use intensification. Adjustment of farming systems and adoption of new technologies that intensify the use of land, labour or capital will take place when factor proportions become more constrained (Hayami and Ruttan, 1985). Government efforts to accelerate this intensification process often meet with limited success owing to market and/or institutional failures (Sadoulet and de Janvry, 1995). The most important market and institutional factors likely to limit the process of intensification of farming systems are reviewed in the following paragraphs.

A wide range of price policies affect factor use: deficiency payments, production subsidies, floor prices, taxes, import or export levies and investment grants. In addition, governments employ quantitative limits on inputs and outputs. The impact of price policies on adjustment in factor use depends on such things as the market environment, trade characteristics of the product and internal factor availability. With respect to the market environment, price policies tend to be less effective in a small, closed economy facing less elastic supply and demand conditions. Infrastructure investments may, however, reduce marketing costs and thus increase price responsiveness. Price policies directed at producers, and commodities that are only marginally integrated into markets, are likely to be less successful. Price and marketing controls usually discourage farmers from attaining a marketable surplus, but are also difficult to enforce. Otherwise, the complementarity between externally supplied production factors and internally available resources requires serious consideration. External inputs are normally used to increase the productivity of scarce factors. Labour and investment capital are usually scarce in West Africa, while access to land is less pressing. Therefore farmers tend to be reluctant to use cash- or labour-intensive methods of enhancing soil productivity.

Institutional limitations may also hamper the process of agricultural intensification. Lack of clearly defined property rights, limited access to financial resources and risk aversion have a direct impact on the farmers' willingness to invest and/or adopt technological innovations. With respect to property rights of land, it is important for capital investment that there be guaranteed access to resource *flows* and that the investment is reflected in the value of the resource *stock*. Secure access to income streams can be safeguarded, even under conditions of common property, if boundaries and use rights are sufficiently defined (Runge, 1981). However, incentives for capital investment to improve the quality of fixed resources can only be expected where appropriate land markets emerge (Feder *et al.*, 1988). Expenditures on land improvement and soil conservation practices that have a positive long-term effect on the productive capacity of soils can be considered capital investments. They occur at a given time, but result in a flow of benefits over several cropping seasons and years. Because these capital investments are embodied in the soil, reverse conversion into monetary capital requires that the land market recognize these investments. However, public investment to enhance the production capacity of common property resources is likely to be considered an income transfer that cannot be maintained.

There exists a close relationship between access to external financial resources and attitudes towards risk. Extensive land use (mainly of range lands) is strongly related to savings objectives (for consumption smoothing), and intensification can only be expected if rural financial markets develop (Udry, 1994) and/or there exists income diversification through off-farm employment or migration (Reardon *et al.*, 1994). Both mechanisms permit the creation of alternative savings that can be mobilized to enhance on-farm investment.

Prospects for on-farm investment also depend on the availability of external infrastructure and services. Public investment in infrastructure and transport networks is critical in determining input costs at the farm level. Spillover effects of these investments are generally high, through farmers' supply response and adoption of new technologies.

Finally, the discount rate is important. If options for borrowing are limited, farm households will rely on risk-coping strategies to reduce income variability. Diversification of production systems, storage facilities for cereals, off-farm employment and risk-sharing contracts can be used to spread income risks temporarily. In the case of liquidity constraints, most investment will be directed towards portfolio diversification, while in-depth investment to improve the resource base is likely to receive less attention (Sadoulet and de Janvry, 1995). In these circumstances, public investment in the resource base may enhance prospects for more stable future incomes.

Framework for Appraisal

From the point of view of society, investment choices regarding the application of PR should be based on all economic and environmental benefits, including externalities that are usually ignored in the traditional analysis of private investment decisions. Investment in applications relates in principle to four sectors: (1) agriculture production and market supply, (2) infrastructure development, (3) mining operations, and (4) government finance. In the agricultural production sector, the supply curve shifts to the right as the result of increasing yields, in the mining sector because of an increased scale of production. Higher demand for PR requires corresponding adjustments in marketing facilities and infrastructure. Land rents will increase because of increased productivity in farming.

Partial equilibrium indicators or criteria to assess the impact of an intervention that shifts the demand and/or the supply curve are changes in consumer and producer surplus, land rent effects and government budget effects. These constitute the efficiency effects. The full farm-level benefits concern higher revenues and/or increased food security, both of which are closely related to increased yields. The latter also increase costs at the farm level: higher labour costs due to the extra labour needed for harvesting and applying of PR, and equipment costs. Costs in the mining sector are related to the extra equipment and labour costs necessary to meet the increased demand for PR. Costs in infrastructure are related to the construction of new and improved roads and to the improvement of extension services. External effects on the environment may be known, but do not enter into the financial considerations of private decision makers, although they are important to society. In addition to these efficiency-related goals, redistribution and environmental criteria are usually introduced. PR application generates extra employment in agriculture, mining and the infrastructure sector. The impact on government budgets (over and above direct project costs) and balance of payments is also a consideration, but not necessarily an efficiency consideration.

Intensification, new varieties, better fertilizers or reduced transport costs all shift the agricultural supply curve to the right. Welfare gains differ sharply when the good is a non-tradable (sorghum, millet) versus a tradable (cotton) or a commodity subject to government price support. In the case of a non-tradable good, increased production results in decreases in price, with consumers being the main beneficiaries. The effects on farmers are positive, but small. For a tradable good, no price change may occur. Then farmers gain, resulting in increased land rents, while the gain to consumers is small or negligible (see Sadoulet and de Janvry, 1995).

The remainder of this section focuses on the constraints upon fertilizer use at both the farm and national levels. These can be classified in two general categories: constraints that restrict the demand for fertilizer and are associated with agricultural production technology, the resource endowment of farmers, and socioeconomic factors affecting attitudes and behaviour of farmers; and constraints that restrict the supply of fertilizer and are associated with import, production and marketing of fertilizers (Thompson and Baanante, 1988).

Farm-level Constraints on Phosphate Rock Use

Investments in phosphate rock are determined by the following (Green and Ng'ong'ola, 1993; Herdt and Mandac, 1980): (1) ownership/property rights (or continuous possession) in order to guarantee access to income flows, (2) farm size, (3) share of land under cropping and stocking rate (indicators for resource pressure), (4) access to credit, (5) off-farm income available for on-farm investment, (6) farming system, (7) access to timely and adequate supplies of fertilizers and other variable inputs and their prices, (8) decision makers' risk preferences, and (9) knowledge of and access to information about the use of fertilizers and agricultural production technology in general. Farmers in the Sahel often do not own their land and so are not willing to invest in long-term land improvement. Farmers with well-established land access rights obtain all of the short- and long-term added revenues associated with the application of PR. Farmers who have use of land on a long-term basis through land-leasing arrangements, such as sharecropping, will share these benefits with landowners who may be private landlords or with the community as a whole. Tenant farmers who sharecrop the land for only one season will not obtain any of the long-term benefits and only a part of the short-term benefits (Gerner and Baanante, 1995). *Ownership/property rights* in the Sahel can be characterized as a traditional communal type of land tenure and land use with the following characteristics: (1) low property concentration, with sovereign rights vested in the community, (2) decentralized cultivation, with use rights for group members; and (3) subsistence production (World Bank, 1975). Hence investment in PR should be paid by the community as a whole and not by individual farmers.

As noted above, the nature of investments in PR (high 'up-front' costs) means farmers lack the ability to make such investments. Access to credit is limited, although off-farm income can help to overcome a capital constraint and finance the purchase of a fixed-investment type of innovation (Feder *et al.*, 1985). *Farm size* can affect the rate of adoption of new technologies such as PR use, depending on the characteristics of the technology and the institutional setting. The relationship between farm size and adoption depends on such factors as fixed adoption costs, risk preferences, human capital, credit constraints, labour requirements and tenure arrangements. An often mentioned constraint on adoption of new technology by smaller farms relates to fixed costs of implementation. In the case of PR, these costs are of considerable importance. Large fixed costs reduce the tendency to adopt and slow the rate of adoption by smaller farms (Feder *et al.*, 1985).

Most farmers willing to invest in PR have a relatively intensive *farming system*; animal traction is employed and manure is applied. Timing of PR applications is important for both short-term and long-term viability. *Labour availability*, particularly important in Africa (Helleiner, 1975), is another variable affecting farmers' decisions about adoption of new agricultural practices. Applying PR increases the seasonal demand for labour, so that adoption is less attractive for those with limited family labour or those operating in areas with less access to labour markets. Labour shortages are mainly caused by lack of animal power, male labour migration and women's excess burden, resulting in late ploughing and planting, late weeding and harvesting, and low yields (Harrison, 1987).

Finally, lack of education and extension services can be an obstacle to the adoption of PR. The inability to read and understand fertilizer packages and instructions restricts the effectiveness of using written information as a means of disseminating knowledge about fertilizers. Field research experience has shown at least one unique constraint, that using the product in windy conditions forces the product into the eyes and causes a burning sensation. Surely, these types of constraints can be overcome by extension education.

National Constraints on Phosphate Rock Use

In the Sahel, a wide gap between production and use of phosphate fertilizers has increased reliance on imports, but the lack of foreign exchange is a major problem. Termination of fertilizer subsidies helps rectify this problem. As locally produced PR is cheaper than imported fertilizer, subsidies can be abolished, thereby relieving pressure on government budgets.

Lack of infrastructure also constrains PR use. Transport costs are high because (1) roads from the mine to the factory where the ore is crushed are in poor condition, (2) consumption areas are a long way from the factory, (3) limited scale of operation reduces the bargaining power of phosphate companies for transport rates; and (4) transport is poorly organized (Dahoui, 1995; World Bank, 1994). Further, inefficiency in the mining sector increases costs.

Financial and Economic Evaluation of Phosphate Rock Application

The economic costs determining the farm gate price of PR for direct application are location-specific. These costs are the retail price of PR, transport of PR to farm sites and administration costs. The production costs of PR consists of the following elements (with their contribution to 1994 production costs): mine operating costs (7 per cent), rock transport (22 per cent), mill operating costs (58 per cent) and capital recovery (13 per cent) (Dahoui, 1995). In addition to the inherent characteristics of the PR, the costs of transporting PR to farm sites will be critical in determining the feasibility of using indigenous resources of PR in the Sahel. In 1994, for Mali and after the depreciation of the FCFA, the farm gate prices of imported phosphate fertilizer (TSP) and PR, and the elements comprising price, are provided in Table 19.1.

The costs of purchasing PR are not the only costs related to the application of PR. PR needs to be applied, which will cost labour and traction time. The annual depreciation costs for a plough are FCFA1670, based on one plough for every 7.5 ha (van Duivenboden *et al.*, 1991). Cost for one day of labour is FCFA600. Application of PR will increase yields and farmers need extra labour, depending on the crops planted. Maize is a labour-intensive crop that requires more labour to apply PR than does, for example, millet (World Bank, 1994). Labour may be more expensive in some regions than others, and particularly during the peak season. Therefore not enough labour may be available to harvest all of the extra yield. In that case, the farmer is not able to profit fully from the PR application. Similar costs are incurred when other (imported) fertilizers are used.

Table 19.1   Phosphate fertilizer price in Mali, 1994 (FCFA kg^{-1}P$_2$O$_5$)

	TSP	PR
Import price/production cost	317.4	91.9
Administration and margins	19.0	38.3
Transport (include taxes for TSP)	137.3	113.2
Total	473.7	243.4

Source: Dahoui (1995).

The cost–benefit analysis is performed for one hectare of arable land in Mali that is successively grown with maize and groundnut during a time frame of 10 years. The annual yields are based on data from the World Bank (1994). The average farm gate price of maize and groundnut are assumed to amount to 35 and 80 FCFA kg⁻¹, respectively. In order to estimate labour costs, labour demand is calculated on the basis of coefficients provided by van Duivenboden *et al.* (1991). Two types of PR application are distinguished. In case 1, PR is only applied during year 1 (120kg P_2O_5) and no 'maintenance' PR is applied in the following years. In case 2, the same amount of PR is applied in year 1 as in the first case, but in successive years 25kg P_2O_5 is applied annually as 'maintenance'.

Five alternative scenarios for PR application are examined. For each a financial and an economic return is calculated. The base scenario, (a), refers to a situation with sufficient labour and average rainfall in each year of the time frame. Under scenario (b), the shadow price for labour is 800FCFA man day⁻¹ in peak season periods (fertilizer application and the post-harvest period) versus 600FCFA in the other periods under scenario (a). Scenario (c) differs from (a) with respect to rainfall: years 3, 6 and 9 are assumed to be years with limited rainfall, which reduces the yield to one half of the realized yield in years with average rainfall. Under scenario (d), the price for the non-tradable good maize decreases to 85 per cent of the initial price of 35FCFA per kilogram. Under scenario (e), the three changes in assumptions are combined. The discount rate equals 30 per cent in the financial analysis.

External effects that need to be taken into account in a broader social economic context concern the prevention of soil mining. Calculations by van der Pol (1992) before the devaluation of the FCFA show that soil mining contributes, on average, to a loss of 44 per cent of the total agricultural productive value. Since this estimate is based on replacement cost of nutrients lost, the present estimate may be higher because relative nutrient prices have risen. As PR application is not the only means to prevent soil mining, the contribution of PR is assumed to be 50 per cent (World Bank, 1994). Expressed as a percentage of the total agricultural production value and taking into account price increases after the devaluation, the prevention of soil mining due to PR application is assumed to equal 40 per cent of the agricultural production value. The discount rate for the social economic analysis is 10 per cent.

The results are presented in Table 19.2. They show that the financial NPV of the PR application investment is positive and, assuming that physical yields are correctly estimated and fully realized, should pose no constraint on adoption by farmers. With a 10 per cent discount rate, the economic NPVs are highly attractive. For case 1(e), the financial internal rate of return equals

36.2 per cent; for case 2(e), it equals 30.9 per cent. As the values for NPVs and IRRs indicate, the outcome in the different cases and conditions is highly sensitive to the time pattern of PR application.

A good financial profit is not the only condition for adoption of a PR investment by the farmers. Farmers are primarily interested in the income effects. In order to calculate income effects, financial operations are introduced. Their cost corresponds to a five-year loan at an interest rate of 15 per cent needed to finance the first PR application. In case 1, the annual income effects under scenario (e) show that, in years 3 and 5, the farmer is not able to meet his loan obligations from current revenues. The risk of such a situation occurring may prevent farmers from investing in PR. In years 7 and 9, the farmer also has a negative income if he or she applies PR, which is slightly more negative than the income the farmer receives in the situation without PR. The same is true for case 2: the farmer is not able to meet his loan obligations in years 3 and 5, and is unable to pay for his annual PR application. In these years, the farmer's income is even lower.

Despite the generally more profitable outlook of an initial annual PR investment (case 2), credit institutions might still not lend to the farmer because of fears that he will not apply the PR annually (referred to as 'moral hazard') or because the farmers do not have sufficient collateral. In this case, public intervention to guarantee farmer loans might be an appropriate policy response.

Table 19.2   **Financial and economic net present values (in FCFA) and internal rates of return (%) of PR application for different scenarios**

(1) One-time PR application	Financial NPV	Financial IRR	Economic NPV	Economic IRR
(a) base scenario (see text)	36 512	69.4	89 159	271.5
(b) higher labour costs	23 016	54.3	67 043	159.5
(c) 3 dry years	25 747	60.7	67 142	254.2
(d) lower price for maize	21 385	52.0	65 665	145.9
(e) combination of (b), (c) and (d)	5 738	36.2	37 173	75.9
(2) Initial and annual PR applications	Financial NPV	Financial IRR	Economic NPV	Economic IRR
(a) base scenario (see text)	43 029	50.9	149 324	144.0
(b) higher labour costs	24 289	45.5	113 290	80.3
(c) 3 dry years	28 676	50.8	113 877	120.8
(d) lower price for maize	24 215	45.3	114 391	78.6
(e) combination of (b), (c) and (d)	1 334	30.9	65 198	42.9

Source: Calculated on the basis of World Bank (1994) data.

Distributional and Other Impacts

At the macro level, effects on the government's budget, employment and the balance of payments need to be considered. In both the mining and infrastructure sectors, extra employment is generated. Based on information for the mining industry in Niger, the number of people employed in PR mining has been estimated at 3.1 persons per tonne (ILO, 1994). Additional employment is also generated in transport and extension, although this depends on the availability of skilled individuals and, perhaps, government funding.

PR investment will also increase food security. Even in a year with lower rainfall, the PR influence on production will still be present, and the lower production level is likely to exceed the production in the case of a normal year without the application of PR. An increase in the overall availability of domestic food supply will have a positive effect on the balance of trade. Reliance on imports of both fertilizer and food will decline.

Investments in the construction of new roads and improvements in existing roads, along with the expansion of the extension service (and possibly research and development in agriculture), will increase the budget costs to government. To the extent that mining of PR remains a government activity, an expansion of this activity will increase the budget, but revenues might also increase. However, such mining might best be privatized. Both mining and transport of PR could have adverse impacts on the environment which should be taken into account in the evaluation of the feasibility of PR use, but has not been done here. For example, estimates for Sub-Saharan Africa based on the cost of reclaiming land after mining show that this cost will amount to about US$3–4 per tonne of PR produced.[2]

Conclusions

Recent devaluation has resulted in considerable increases in the nominal and real prices of fertilizers in many African countries. In those FCFA countries where PR is available and suitable for direct application, the 1994 downward adjustment in the value of their domestic currency creates a favourable environment for the use of PR by making imported fertilizers more costly. In this respect, PR as a capital investment becomes financially attractive.

What is the role of government, if any, in the adoption of phosphate rock? Government plays an important role in several ways. First, it provides extension services to farmers, showing them how they can benefit from investments in PR, and conducts continuing research into optimal application, crop rotation and so on that help farmers maximize net returns while preventing soil degradation. Second, government can enhance access to credit, perhaps by providing loan guarantees. Third, policies that result in improvements to public infrastructure will reduce costs of PR and raise farm gate output prices. Finally, marketing and distribution of both farm inputs and outputs is important, and governments should reduce any institutional or other barriers that stand in the way of efficient operation of markets, including land markets. In this regard, fertilizer subsidies or food subsidies (or taxes on domestic farm products) to help those in urban areas need to be eliminated. The role for donor agencies is to help governments in West Africa achieve these objectives.

Notes

1 The authors gratefully acknowledge the assistance and information provided by Hans Jansen of WAU Atlantic Zone Programme, Herman van Keulen of WAU/AB-DLO, Keffing Sissoko of IER-PSS, Hamady Djouar of IER-RSPGRN, Eric Smailing of SC-DLO and Nico Heerink of WAU during the process of writing this chapter.
2 The exchange rate since the devaluation of the FCFA in January 1994 is 525 FCFA to one US dollar.

References

Cornelisse, P. (1993), 'The Purpose of Soil Protection in the Sahel', *Agriculture, Economics and Sustainability in the Sahel, Papers Presented at the Third Sahel Seminar, May 1992*, KIT, Amsterdam.
Dahoui, K.P. (1995), 'Costs Determinants of Phosphate Rock in Some West African Countries', in H. Gerner and A. Uzo Mokwunye (eds), *Use of Phosphate Rock for Sustainable Agriculture in West Africa*, International Fertiliser Development Centre – Africa, Lomé, Togo.
Feder, G., R.E. Just and D. Zilberman (1985), 'Adoption of Agricultural Innovations in Developing Countries: A Survey', *Economic Development and Cultural Change*, **33**: 255–98.
Feder, G., T. Onchan, Y. Chalamwong and C. Hongladarom (1988), *Land Policies and Farm Productivity in Thailand*, Johns Hopkins University Press, Baltimore.
Gerner, H. and C.A. Baanante (1995), 'Economic Aspects of Phosphate Rock Application for Sustainable Agriculture in West Africa', in H. Gerner and A. Uzo Mokwunye (eds), *Use of Phosphate Rock for Sustainable Agriculture in West Africa*, International Fertiliser Development Centre – Africa, Lomé, Togo.
Green, D.A.G. and D.H. Ng'ong'ola (1993), 'Factors Affecting Fertilizer Adoption in Less Developed Countries: An Application of Multivariate Logistic Analysis in Malawi', *Journal of Agricultural Economics*, **44**(1): 99–109.
Harrison, P. (1987), *The Greening of Africa: Breaking Through in the Battle for Land*

and Food, International Institute for Environment and Development, Earthscan, London.

Hayami, Y. and V.W. Ruttan (1985), *Agricultural Development: An International Perspective*, 2nd edn, Johns Hopkins University Press, Baltimore.

Helleiner, G.K. (1975), 'Smallholder Decision Making: Tropical African Evidence', in L.G. Reynolds (ed.), *Agriculture in Development Theory*, Yale University Press, New Haven, Conn.

Herdt, R.W. and A.M. Mandac (1980), 'Modern Technology and Economic Efficiency of Philippine Rice Farmers', *Economic Development and Cultural Change*, **29**: 375–99.

ILO (1994), *Yearbook of Labour Statistics*, 53rd issue, International Labour Office, Geneva.

Koster, J. (1994), *Plattelandsontwikkeling en duurzaamheid – wat heeft dat concreet te betekenen?*, Beleidsnotitie DGIS, Ministerie van Buitenlandse Zaken, The Hague.

MacMillan, A. (1995), 'Recapitalization of Soil Productivity in Sub-Saharan Africa', draft initiating memorandum, FAO Investment Centre, Rome.

Reardon, T., C. Delgado and P. Matlon (1994), 'Determinants and Effects of Income Diversification amongst Farm Households in Burkina Faso', *The Journal of Development Studies*, **28**(2): 264–96.

Runge, C.F. (1981), 'Common Property Externalities, Isolation and Resource Depletion in a Traditional Grazing Context', *American Journal of Agricultural Economics*, **63**(4): 595–606.

Sadoulet, E. and de Janvry, A. (1995), *Quantitative Development Policy Analysis*, Johns Hopkins University Press, Baltimore.

Thompson, T.P. and C.A. Baanante (1988), *A Socio-economic Study of Farm-Level Constraints to Fertiliser Use in Western Niger*, International Fertiliser Development Center, Muscle Shoals, Alabama.

Udry, C. (1994), 'Risk and Insurance in a Rural Credit Market: an Empirical Investigation in Northern Nigeria', *Review of Economic Studies*, **61**(3): 495–526.

van Duivenboden, N., P.A. Gosseye and H. van Keulen (eds) (1991), *Competing for Limited Resources: The case of the fifth region of Mali. Report 2: Plant, Animal and Fish Production*, Centre for Agrobiological Research (CABO-DLO), Wageningen.

van der Pol, F. (1992), *Soil Mining: An Unseen Contributor to Farm Income in Southern Mali*, Royal Tropical Institute, Amsterdam.

World Bank (1975), 'Land Reform', Sector Policy Paper, World Bank, Washington, DC.

World Bank (1994), *Feasibility of Phosphate Rock Use as a Capital Investment in Sub-Saharan Africa: Issues and Opportunities*, World Bank, Washington, DC.

PART VI
POLICY INSTRUMENTS AND POLICY ANALYSIS: INDUSTRIALIZED COUNTRIES

20 External Effects of Agro-chemicals: Are they Important and How do we Cope with them?

A.J. Oskam[a]

Introduction

The importance of agro-chemicals might be characterized by their contribution to the value of agricultural production, with estimates of the contribution varying widely (Pimentel, 1993; Oerke *et al.*, 1994; Zadoks, 1980). According to Oerke *et al.* (1994: 749–53), crop protection products prevented the loss of 48 per cent of the actual yield of eight principal food and cash crops during the period 1988–90 (see Chapter 1 of the present volume). These crops covered 47 per cent of the total crop area in the world. Damage averted amounted to $160 billion, while expenditure on all crop protection products amounted to $26 billion, providing benefits of $134 billion. However, this does not consider external effects, which some think are large, thus fuelling pleas for organic farming and a total ban on agro-chemicals.

A ban on all agro-chemicals would cause a large increase in agricultural product prices with (on average) positive income effects for farmers and negative income effects for the chemical industry, processing industries and consumers. On average, the gross national products of countries would diminish, even though environmental effects are often assumed to be positive (Michalek and Hanf, 1994). Sudden and large reductions of food production and substantial increases in food prices could disrupt social structures and

[a] Department of Economics and Management, Wageningen Agricultural University, Hollandseweg 1, 6706 KN, Wageningen, The Netherlands.

the environment. Therefore those advocating a switch from a chemical-based to a biology-based agriculture likely think about the long term. Others advocate a switch to integrated farming, with strong reductions in the use of agro-chemicals, but without banning them (Wijnands and Vereijken, 1992).

Economists often think less radically. In the Pigouvian tradition, they argue in favour of balancing the net private benefits of agro-chemicals with their external effects. According to economists, environmental goals are best achieved by economic incentives or instruments of economic policy (Tietenberg, 1985; Baumol and Oates, 1988; Opschoor and Pearce, 1991; Pearce and Turner, 1990). Divergence between social and private costs and benefits in private decision making is the main reason for the existence of environmental problems. Compensating for the difference between private and social costs/benefits with levies/subsidies would solve the problem, because economic agents would make their decisions according to real costs and benefits to society. There are several factors that make it less easy to apply such strict reasoning in practice: a lack of information about private and especially social costs/benefits; a difference between the distribution of income and resources that result from the market process (whether or not levies and subsidies for the environment are included) and the preferred distribution; the existence of several distorting elements within the economy and the difficulty of levying and subsidizing them without distorting the economic process; and non-rational behaviour. Therefore it is questionable whether economic instruments always form the best option in practice.

Measuring the External Effects of Agro-chemicals Use

Negative external effects of fertilizer and pesticides are mostly related to soil, groundwater and surface water pollution. Indirect effects might be impacts on biodiversity and the (related) effects on flora and fauna. As Pearce (1993) and Smith (1992) suggest, measurement of external effects in agriculture is not easy. Several authors have recommended general methodologies to measure external effects or their prevention (Antle and Capalbo, 1995; Bingham, 1995; Bergland, 1996), but there are few applications.

External effects consist of a quantity and a price component. Quantities are measurable, although uncertainties exist. The price component (shadow prices) is more difficult to determine. Different methods are available, each with related uncertainties. Consider the marginal environmental cost (MEC) of a negative external effect (such as an emission), as illustrated by the MEC curve in Figure 20.1, which shows a situation with increasing external effects per unit of additional emission. Interest focuses on the level of MEC at a

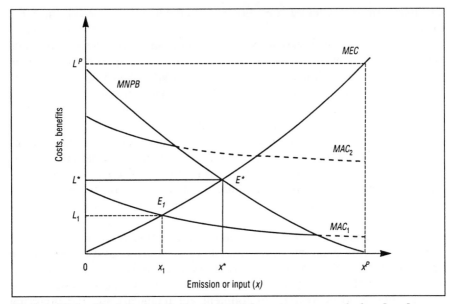

Figure 20.1   Deriving socially optimal input use or emission levels

particular level of emission, say x^p. Direct observation of the MEC curve would be useful, but is often not available. Therefore indirect methods are used to quantify the MEC curve. The applied methodology will try to find at least two points of the MEC curve and extend that curve on the basis of its assumed functional characteristics.

The marginal net private benefit (MNPB) of emissions and the marginal abatement cost (MAC) are also indicated in Figure 20.1. In an equilibrium situation, without charging for emissions, MNPB = 0. This holds because producers are assumed to produce where marginal (private) cost equals marginal revenue. The position of the MAC curve needs elaboration. If we assume cost-efficient abatement is used, the MAC curve will never be above the MNPB curve, because emissions can always be reduced by decreasing input use and production. In Figure 20.1, two different MAC curves, MAC_1 and MAC_2, are illustrated. The relevant part of each curve is below MNPB. If marginal external damages are given by the MEC curve as indicated, a low level of abatement costs (MAC_1) would imply optimal social emissions of x_1. An emission levy of L_1 could be used to attain this optimal level. Issuing tradable emission permits of amount x_1 would result in a price level per unit of emissions equal to L_1. E_1 is on both MAC_1 and MEC. Assuming the higher abatement costs, optimal emissions are x^*, which could be obtained using tradable permits or a levy L^*. E^* lies on both the MNPB curve and the MEC curve.

If the MEC curve passes through the origin and a particular functional form for MEC is assumed, we can generate MEC if we are provided with an *optimal* levy or emission level. It is possible to obtain the MEC at input level x^p, which equals L^p. At this level of emission (x^p) the marginal environmental cost can be measured. The total external effects of using/emitting x^p instead of x_1 or x^* is equal to the area between MEC and min{MNPB, MAC} over the interval $x_1 - x^p$ or $x^* - x^p$, respectively. The marginal external effect of producing at input/emission level x^p equals L^p. Since the total curve is the integral of the marginal curve, and vice versa, the MEC curve can be found. This is *one* method of deriving marginal environmental costs within a market economy and under the assumption of consistent decision making by government.

The second method of deriving a point on the MEC curve is based on the opportunity cost principle. We assume that two processes generate an identical external effect and include two processes in the same set of figures. Process 1, with its related $MNPB_1$ curve and MAC_h curve, reflects the 'agricultural process' (Figure 20.2a). The reference process is production process 2 (Figure 20.2b). Observe that the reference process already uses abatement at the present level of x. Figure 20.2c provides the summation of the two processes over the horizontal axis with increasing costs of emission reduction to the left of the reference point x^p (= $x_1^p + x_2^p$). Assuming a MEC

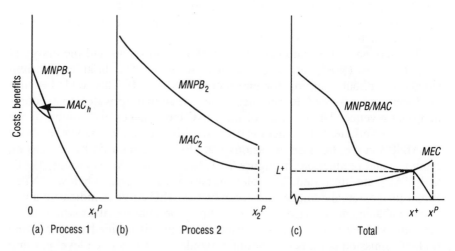

Figure 20.2   Deriving socially optimal emissions or input use when two processes are available

curve, the optimal level of emission is x^+. This level might be achieved by levy L^+ or tradable emission permits x^+.

Assuming that process 2 generates greater emissions and the abatement of process 2 is at the optimal level, the MEC curve in Figure 20.2c is the relevant curve. The marginal environmental costs of process 1, at its present level of emission x_1^p, is only slightly higher than L^+, which is equal to MAC_2 at x_2^p (Figure 20.2c). Under these limiting conditions, the shadow price of emission x_1^p might be derived from abatement costs of the other process. This illustrates the *second* method.

As illustrated in Figure 20.1, sometimes abatement costs help determine optimal emission levels, but under other conditions the MNPB curve is relevant. Agro-chemicals belong to the category of non-point pollutants, where abatement costs are high, unless they are limited to point pollution in relation to packaging material and cleaning of equipment or cleaning drinking water at resource areas. Then a MAC curve might be relevant for determining optimal levels of input use.

Deriving a MNPB Curve

The derived input demand functions for fertilizer and pesticides generate the relevant information to derive the MNPB curve. Assuming a linear demand function for a particular input that generates external effects, the MNPB curve is reflected in the part of the demand curve above current market clearing price, say p_1. If a levy is already paid (or input use is restricted), a correction would need to be made to derive MNPB. Assume the following demand function:

$$x = \beta_1 + \beta_2 p \quad \beta_1 > 0, \ \beta_2 < 0$$

where x is input quantity and p is input price. This relation is depicted in Figure 20.3 by the line DD'.

The computation of the two parameters β_1 and β_2 is straightforward when information is available on the average price elasticity ($\bar{e}$), the average amount of an input ($\bar{x}$) and the average price of an input ($\bar{p}$): $\beta_1 = \bar{x}(1-e)$ and $\beta_2 = e \bar{x}/\bar{p}$.

The effect of an input price change, say from p_1 to p_2, assuming that output prices are constant, reduces the rent of quasi-fixed inputs (for example, labour, land, buildings, machinery) by the area $a + b$ (Boadway and Bruce, 1984: 220–23). Moreover, a restriction on input use at x_2 for environmental reasons indicates that the MEC equals $p_2 - p_1$. A levy on the input x, assuming no transaction costs and a lump sum redistribution of levy, reduces the rent of quasi-fixed inputs by area b.

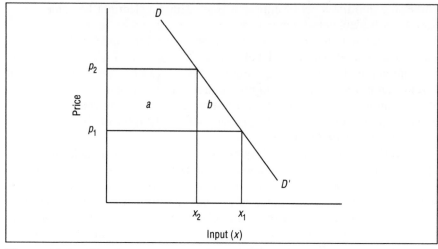

Figure 20.3   The demand curve for an input

This methodology provides a framework for calculating shadow prices of external effects caused by agro-chemicals. It should be realized, however, that these shadow prices are not constant in time and depend also on the extent of the external effects.

The Marginal Environmental Costs of an External Effect at Different Levels and in the Course of Time

Deriving one point of the MEC curve is insufficient. A rather general function has been selected to represent marginal environmental costs. We call this the shadow price of external effects. This shadow price depends on the quantity of an external effect, population, income per capita and individual preferences. Such a functional relation is similar to an inverted demand function in demand theory. Because we focus on the relation between external effect and shadow price, population and income per capita are amalgamated in the product of these two variables. Applying a log-linear specification gives:

$$v_t = z_t \, (x_t - c)^b \, y_t^{\ F} \qquad \text{if } x \geq c \tag{20.1}$$

$$v_t = 0 \qquad \text{if } 0 < x < c \tag{20.2}$$

v = the real shadow price of a particular external effect
x = the quantity of the external effect (as represented by fertilizer use, say)
c = a particular threshold: external effects cannot be observed (or no damage occurs) below this threshold
y = the real net product of a country
b = (shadow) price flexibility of the external effect
F = (shadow) price flexibility with respect to real net product
z = preference variable
t = time

The functional relation between v and x is the MEC curve in Figures 20.1 and 20.2c. The above equations might be considered a flexible specification of a MEC. This curve is influenced by real net production of a country (y), preferences (z) and use of the input causing the externality (x). In the base year, z equalizes the shadow price and the right-hand side of the above equation. If $c = 0$, MEC = 0, as indicated by the origin in Figure 20.1.

The implicit 'income elasticity' of an external effect (e_y) can be derived from equations (20.1) and 20.2):

$$e_y = -(F/b)[(x_t - c)/x_t] \qquad (20.3)$$

This income elasticity reflects the percentage reduction of the negative externality required to compensate for a 1 per cent increase in real net national product. The price flexibility is $b[x_t/(x_t - c)]$.

Equations (20.1) and (20.2) illustrate the opportunity to introduce a threshold for an external effect. If parameter c is negative, the MEC curve cuts the vertical axis above zero and already the first unit of emission causes marginal environmental damage. Specification of the MEC curve according to equations (20.1) and (20.2) is illustrated in Figure 20.4. Assume an emission level x_0 in period 0 causing marginal environmental costs equal to v_0. A shift of the MEC curve, either because of a change of preferences or because of a change of the real net product, causes, at the same emission level, an increase of marginal emission costs to v_1. To keep marginal emission costs at the same level, emissions should be reduced to x_1. Clearly, the function requires three parameters to be specified: c, F and b.

Estimates of External Effects Caused by Agro-chemicals

Negative external effects of agriculture in the Netherlands have been estimated by Oskam (1993). Here we provide the figures with respect to pesticides and minerals (Table 20.1). Estimates of the external effects of

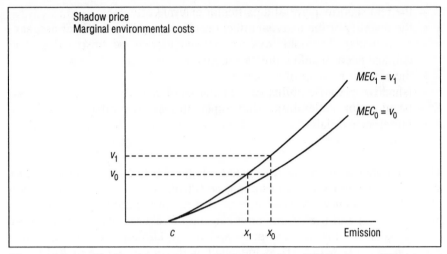

Figure 20.4   Shadow prices of emissions under different conditions

pesticides, ammonia and nitrate are based on method 1; those of phosphate are based on method 2. Although estimates are uncertain, they are at least indicative. Calculations have been made under the assumption that emissions directly affect the environment. The results illustrate that the effects of pesticides are less important than the effects of minerals (ammonia, nitrate, phosphate fertilizer) in the Netherlands. Further, the importance of negative external effects of pesticides and minerals in the Netherlands appears to be declining over time.

Research by Adger and Whitby (1993) for the UK gave quite different results. Their results are point estimates for 1988, showing negative external effects due to minerals of 1.4 per cent of net value added in UK agriculture.

Table 20.1   Negative external effects of pesticides and minerals in The Netherlands; monetary value and percentage of gross value added in agriculture

Year	Pesticides Value (m.Dfl.)	%	Minerals Value (m.Dfl.)	%
1960	11	0.3	95	2.6
1970	45	0.7	362	5.6
1980	319	2.8	1 311	11.6
1986	468	2.6	1 732	9.8
1990	453	2.5	1 532	8.3
1994	272	1.6	1 480	8.8

Source: Own calculation.

They did not consider pesticides. Research by Heinz (1995) indicated that the annual costs of cleaning drinking water because of pesticides amount to ECU 30 million (Dfl. 60 million) for the Netherlands and ECU 140 million for the UK (Table 20.2). Figures for the Netherlands are substantially lower than in Table 20.1.

Existing information illustrates the size of negative external effects. According to the general specification of the shadow price function, the value of negative external effects will increase over the course of time, unless substantial reductions in use and/or emissions are realized.

Table 20.2   Estimated costs of complying with (0.1 µg/l) pesticide levels in drinking water and prices of drinking water (ECU/m³)

Country	Cost of cleaning (ECU/m³)	Water price (ECU/m³)	Annual use of drinking water (m.m³)	Estimated amount of raw water (m.m³) exceeding 0.1 µg/l
Austria	0.02	0.78	450	33
France	0.04	1.22	6 080	2 888
Germany	0.03	1.33	6 502	975
Italy	0.03	0.46	8 465	2 649
Netherlands	0.05	1.06	1 227	593
United Kingdom	0.07	0.77	7 620	1 966

Source: Heinz (1995; 70, 211–12).

Instruments for Dealing with Negative External Effects

According to the Scientific Council of the Netherlands (WRR, 1992), four groups of instruments can be identified to deal with negative external effects (see Table 20.3):

1   Rules and regulations, which are especially popular among governments and lobby groups outside farming (D in Table 20.3);
2   Covenants and other forms of contracts between governments and producers' organizations, which are accepted under the threat of 'rules and regulations' or 'economic instruments' (S in Table 20.3);
3   Economic instruments, which are most popular among professional economists, some government officials and groups of farmers who either expect important property rights or redistribution of income (F in Table 20.3); and
4   Legislation that gives individuals or organizations the right to charge individuals, firms or organizations causing negative external effects (C in Table 20.3).

Table 20.3 Classification of policy instruments to address negative external environmental effects according to situation

Ability to measure emissions	Number of sources/ agents	Cost differences of technologies; technological options	Problem category	Primary instrument[a]
Good	Small	Small	1 Conveniently arranged	D
		Large	2 Distribution problem	F C
	Large	Small	3 Controllable	F C S
		Large	4 Heterogeneous	F C
Difficult	Small	Not important	5 Not observable	D
	Large	Small	6 Diffuse	S
		Large	7 Unclear	?

Note: [a] D = direct regulation; F = financial instruments; C = civil law; S = social rules.

Source: WRR (1992).

The characteristics of the environmental problem determine which type of policy instrument is suitable. A link between the various characteristics of environmental externalities and the appropriate instrument to use is provided in Table 20.3.

Opschoor and Vos (1989) and OECD (1993) identify five different categories of economic instruments: (1) charges or taxes; (2) subsidies for environmental services or reductions in pollution; (3) deposit refund systems; (4) tradable permits; and (5) enforcement incentives, which might be considered as a mixture of legal and economic instruments (for example, penalty fines related to environmental damage, compensations on the basis of court decisions). Each instrument affects the income distribution and the distribution of property rights. The same is true of other policy instruments (rules and regulations, extension, and so on), but the effects on income are less clear. Charges and taxes are often seen by producers as increasing their costs. Even incentive charges that are returned on a lump sum basis to the same sector (after deduction of administrative costs) are perceived as cost-increasing. Economic reasoning on the grounds of economic efficiency is not generally accepted. Are economic/financial instruments often used to mitigate the negative external effects of agro-chemicals?

Pesticides

According to the criteria of the Scientific Council of the Netherlands (WRR, 1992), pesticides belong to the category of controllable (3) or heterogeneous (4) problems (Table 20.3). Here the assumption is made that emissions are equal to the application of pesticides. In both situations, financial instruments are considered to be the first choice (Table 20.3). Table 20.4 gives an overview of the different policy instruments in a large number of OECD countries. It is quite clear that economic incentive policies are used only to a very limited extent. Table 20.5 provides a more detailed overview of policy targets in three countries with an active policy of reducing pesticide applications.

Target reductions have been achieved in Sweden using different measures, including economic incentives (Table 20.4). Sweden applied two different

Table 20.4   Economic incentive policies for pesticides in several OECD countries (circa 1992)

Country	Estimated level of pesticide use[a]	Type of policy[b]	Policy includes an economics incentive
Belgium	10.7	Pest warning system	No
Denmark	2.2	Volume reduction policy, treatment reduction policy	Financial levy (about 3%)
France	4.4	Good agricultural practice	No
Germany	4.4	Restricting and banning particular pesticides	No
Greece	6.0	None	No
Ireland	2.2	None	No
Italy	7.6	Extension, quality improvement agricultural products	No
Luxembourg	3.1	None	No
Netherlands	17.5	Volume reduction policy, compound policy[c]	No
Portugal	1.9	None	No
Spain	2.6	Pesticide residue policy (food)	No
UK	3.6	Safe use of pesticide policy	No
Japan	17.7	Pesticide residue policy (food)	No
Sweden	1.3	Several measures to reduce pesticide use	Financial levies (about 40%)
USA	2.4	Pesticide residue policy (food), individual accounting for farmers with regard to some pesticides	No

Notes:
[a] In kilograms active ingredient per hectare of arable and horticulture area.
[b] Nearly all countries operate a registration policy; Ireland, Luxembourg and Portugal might be exceptions.
[c] Policies about specific ingredients to reduce the environmental burden of pesticides.

Source: Oskam (1995); based on Brouwer *et al.* (1994) and Reus *et al.* (1994).

levies, one on active ingredients and the other on a 'standard' application of pesticides per hectare. The separate effect of economic incentives is difficult to determine (Oskam *et al.*, 1992: 48–54). Reductions in the use of active ingredients in Denmark have been achieved without substantial economic incentives. Here the 1990 target of a 25 per cent reduction was, with 18 per cent actual reduction, only partly reached, moreover the intended reduction in the number of applications actually showed an increase (ibid.: 56). The percentage reduction in Sweden is much larger than in Denmark; it is difficult to say whether this is due to the higher levies in Sweden. Implementation of levies in Sweden has been much easier than in Denmark, however, because Sweden had its own agricultural policy before joining the EU.

Targets for reduction of pesticide applications in The Netherlands have been achieved at an aggregate level without applying financial instruments. A covenant between the Agricultural Board and the government puts most responsibility on the agricultural sector, without using any financial instrument (Vijftigschild and Oskam, 1994). Part of this agreement concerns the cancellation of an intended financial levy on pesticides.

Fertilizer/Minerals

According to the classification of the WRR, fertilizer belongs to category 3 environmental problems (Table 20.3). This implies that financial and civil law instruments would be suitable. Measurement of the emission of minerals (and especially ammonia, nitrate and phosphate) is not easy. In The Netherlands, feed and fertilizer provide roughly the same amount of

Table 20.5   **Pesticide policy in three countries with an active volume reduction policy**

Variable	Denmark	Sweden	Netherlands
Reference period	1981–5	1981–5	1984–8
Kg active ingredient per hectare in reference period	2.9	2.3	21
First target year	1990	1990	1995
Target reduction (%)[a]	25	50	37
Realized reduction (%)[a]	18	48	40
Second target year	1997	1996	2000
Target reduction %[a]	50	75	56

Note: [a] % of active ingredient during the reference period.

Source: Oskam *et al.* (1992) and Nederlandse Stichting voor Fytofarmacie (Netherlands Foundation for Phytopharmacy) (NEFYTO).

ingredients (Mulder and Poppe, 1993: 122). Part of the minerals are included in agricultural products. Moreover, there are standards/thresholds regarding the quantity of ammonia, nitrate and phosphate per hectare that may be emitted without substantial damage, but these critical levels are subject to change. Because of such problems, minerals might also be included in category 6 of Table 20.3.

Tables 20.6 and 20.7 present an overview of existing policies in several

Table 20.6   Type of policies and economic incentive measures with respect to minerals in EU countries

Country	Type of policy	Economic incentive policy	Estimated level of N and P fertilizer use kg per hectare
Austria	Vulnerable zones	Levy on fertilizer (abolished 1/1/95)	N = 55 (1989/90)
Belgium	Code of good agricultural practice; manure regulation	None	N = 163 (1990/91)
Denmark	Prohibition of a number of agricultural practices; compulsory fertilizer management plans and balance sheets; green cover	Subsidy scheme of environmental investments; fines for excessive use of minerals	N = 125 P = 12 (1992)
Finland	Upper limits for the use of fertilizer and manure; green cover	Nutrient taxes on P and N	N = 94 P = 19 (1993/94)
France	Defining vulnerable zones	Lump sum charge for some farms	N = 98 (1990/91)
Germany	Fertilizer law; water balance law (water protection zones); application of 2078/92	Financial compensations in water protection zones	N = 106 P = 32 (1991/92)
Greece	None	Support to reduce prices of agro-chemicals	N = 46 (1990/91)
Ireland	None	None	N = 60 (1990/91)
Italy	None	None	N = 46 (1990/91)
Netherlands	Manure regulation; no specific regulation with respect to fertilizer	None	N = 218 (1990/91)
Portugal	None	None	N = 32 (1990/91)
Spain	None; some regional initiatives	None	N = 38 (1990/91)
Sweden	Rules on animal density; crop cover in winter time	Levy/tax on N and P (abolished 1/1/95)	N = 73 P = 8 (1994)
United Kingdom	Good agricultural practices; designating protected areas and compensating farmers	Premiums on reduced fertilizer use in certain areas	N = 92 (1991/92)

Source: Simonsen (1996), Brouwer *et al.* (1995).

countries. A limited number of countries apply financial instruments, which concern two different types of fertilizer ingredients (Table 20.7). Finland in particular has a high tax on nitrogen fertilizer. This tax is, as in Sweden, mainly used to finance agricultural exports. There is no indication that fertilizer use in Finland increased less than in the Netherlands. Moreover, the influence of the N fertilizer price on application rates is not very clear. Other causes, such as technological change (including better information) and the availability of nitrogen from manure, can play a larger role. In many EC countries there is a reduction of N fertilizer use, together with decreasing fertilizer prices.

The implementation of economic incentive measures to reduce the emission of minerals requires a lot of information (see OECD, 1993: 9–10). According to recent experiences in the Netherlands, this information helps farmers achieve a lower emission level. This does not imply, however, that bringing about a further reduction of fertilizer use by economic incentive measures or other policy instruments would not be justified. Several studies, including Burrell (1989), Laurila (1992) and de Wit (1992), make clear that fertilizer price has only a small influence on application rates.

Reflections

Given this overview of policy measures with respect to pesticides and minerals, it should be stressed that economic incentive measures are only used in some cases. Moreover, the application of economic instruments with

Table 20.7 **Type of economic incentive policies for three countries with an active policy for fertilizer**

Variable	Finland	Norway	Sweden
Start of policy	1979	1988	1982/84
Type of policy	Excise duty on fertilizer	Levy of fertilizer	Price regulation levy (1982) and financial levy (1984)
Level of economic incentives (1991)	2.9 FIM/kgN 1.7 FIM/kgP	1.17 NOK/kgN 2.23 NOK/kgP	0.60 SEK/kgN 1.20 SEK/kgP
Financial instruments[a] (% of <u>Dutch</u> price of fertilizer ingredients, 1991)	104 (N) 35 (P)	29 (N) 32 (P)	16 (N) 19 (P)

Note: [a] FIM = 0.42 Dfl.; 1 NOK = 0.29 Dfl.; 1 SEK = 0.32 Dfl.; Prices N = 1.17 Dfl./kg; P = 2.02 Dfl./kg; the results of the calculations show large differences from OECD (1993, p. 4).

Source: Vos *et al.* (1992, 57-8); LEI/CBS, *Landbouwcijfers*, 1993; own calculations.

respect to minerals was stopped by Austria, Finland and Sweden after entering the European Union in 1995. This is a clear illustration that those measures were mainly to prevent excessive use of fertilizer and pesticides under a high price regime of agricultural products. Direct regulation and soft instruments (such as 'good agricultural practice') is more popular now. What might be the reasons?

1   The value of the external effects in agriculture is unknown or uncertain. Even if economists could quantify external effects within reasonable uncertainty limits, policy makers still have to be convinced about the usefulness of those results. This implies a substantial reduction of the available economic incentive instruments, because instruments based on the (price) level of external effects cannot be used.
2   External effects caused by pesticides are local and specific. This implies that tradable emission permits are not attractive. This seems to be less important for fertilizer.
3   It is impossible to operate marketable permits without defining property rights. If permits are distributed according to historical emission levels for one particular pollutant, producers of other negative external effects are tempted to increase emissions. The Dutch government has been reluctant to introduce a transferable manure quota, for example. Here we could also learn from the introduction, distribution and operation of a milk quota in Europe.
4   Often future target levels of negative and positive external effects are defined by means of policy decision making with incomplete information. Those targets/standards are used by economic researchers to derive necessary levels of incentive charges or subsidies to reach those targets. Governments and economic agents are often reluctant to determine charges and subsidies by trial and error.
5   There are indications that targets may be reached without applying economic incentive mechanisms, although it could be that the threat of charges or other measures plays an important role in preparing agreements between governments and representatives of the agricultural sector. Because technological changes seem to be most important, policies should promote efficient development and application of new technologies. If economic incentive mechanisms generate high transaction costs, other types of measures might be more suitable.
6   If targets for negative external effects are reached without any long-lasting incentive mechanism, the final result is suboptimal because economic agents are assumed to produce at a level where private marginal costs and revenues are equal.
7   It is difficult to find *ex post* quantifications of the consequences of

economic incentive measures with respect to environmental policy in agriculture. This implies that we really cannot convince the policy maker of the usefulness of our results, except that clear economic arguments might help them in their reasoning.

Many economists have overestimated the acceptability of economic measures in practice. It is strange that, even after 20 years of environmental policy, the number of economic incentives instruments in agriculture is still limited. This holds for various types of pollution.

Concluding Remarks

Upon reviewing the literature on environmental economics in agriculture, one observes that agricultural economists often study the consequences of output restrictions or emission reductions. Numerous models have been developed to answer such questions (see Berentsen *et al.*, 1992; Dubgaard and Nielsen, 1989; Fontein *et al.*, 1994; Komen *et al.*, 1995; Oskam *et al.*, 1992; Oude Lansink, 1994; Schmitz and Hartmann, 1993). This is the easy way to find answers to questions. The results, however, are not sufficient for the implementation and the performance of economic incentive measures. First of all, good quantitative information on external effects is missing. Moreover, *ex post* analyses of economic incentive measures, also in comparison with other approaches, are not available. And, last but not least, economists focus on charges, taxes, subsidies and tradable permits, but technological development, information and extension seem to be more important. The influence of economic incentive measures on technology, information and extension is a particularly important research area.

References

Adger, W.N. and M. Whitby (1993), 'Natural-Resource Accounting in the Land-Use Sector: Theory and Practice', *European Review of Agricultural Economics*, **20**: 77–97.
Antle, J.M. and S.M. Capalbo (1995), 'Measurement and Evaluation of the Impacts of Agricultural Chemical Use: A Framework for Analysis', in P.L. Pingali and P.A. Roger (eds), *Impact of Pesticides on Farmers' Health and the Rice Environment*, Kluwer, Boston.
Baumol, W.J. and W.E. Oates (1988), *The Theory of Environmental Policy*, Cambridge University Press, Cambridge.
Berentsen, P.M.B., G.W.J. Giesen and S.C. Verduyn (1992), 'Manure Legislation

Effects on Income and on N, P, and K Losses in Dairy Farming', *Livestock Production Science*, **31**: 43–56.

Bergland, O. (1996), 'Assessing Environmental Benefits from Agricultural Pollution Control: Concepts, Methods and Challenges'. Proceedings of the Workshop on Mineral Emissions From Agriculture, Concerted Action AIR3-CT93-1164, Oslo, 25–8 January.

Bingham, G. (1995), 'Issues in Ecosystem Valuation: Improving Information for Decision Making', *Ecological Economics*, **14**: 73–90.

Boadway, R.W. and N. Bruce (1984), *Welfare Economics*, Basil Blackwell, Oxford.

Brouwer, F.M., J.J. Terluin and F.E. Godeschalk (1994), 'Pesticides in the EC', *Onderzoekverslag 121*, LEI-DLO, The Hague.

Brouwer, F.M., F.E. Godeschalk, P. Hellegers and H.J. Kelholt (1995), 'Mineral Balances at Farm Level in the European Union', *Onderzoekverslag 137*, LEI-DLO, The Hague.

Burrell, A. (1989), 'The Demand for Fertilizer in the United Kingdom', *Journal of Agricultural Economics*, **40**: 1–20.

De Wit, C.T. (1992), 'Resource Use Efficiency in Agriculture', *Agricultural Systems*, **40**: 125–51.

Dubgaard, A. and A.H. Nielsen (eds) (1989), *Economic Aspects of Environmental Regulations in Agriculture*, Vauk, Kiel.

Fontein, P.F., G.J. Thijssen, J.R. Magnus and J. Dijk (1994), 'On Levies to Reduce the Nitrogen Surplus: The Case of the Dutch Pig Farms', *Environmental and Resource Economics*, **4**: 455–78.

Heinz, I. (1995), 'Economic Efficiency Calculations in Conjunction with the Drinking Water Directive (Directive 80/778/EEC)', Part III, Dortmund, Institut für Umweltschutz.

Komen, R., A.J. Oskam and J. Peerlings (1995), 'Effects of Reduced Pesticide Application for the Dutch Economy', Workshop on Pesticides, Concerted Action AIR3-CT93-1164, Wageningen, 24–7 August.

Laurila, I. (1992), 'Economics of Nitrogen: Application to Cereal Crop Production in Finland in the 1990s' (in Finnish with English summary), Publication No. 1, University of Helsinki, Department of Economics and Management, Helsinki.

Michalek, J. and C-H. Hanf (eds) (1994), *The Economic Consequences of a Drastic Reduction in Pesticide Use in the EU*, Vauk, Kiel.

Mulder, M. and K.J. Poppe (1993), 'Landbouw, Milieu en Economie', *Periodieke Rapportage 68–89*, LEI-DLO, The Hague.

OECD (1993), *Economic Instruments for Achieving Environmental Goals in the Agriculture Sector*, Environment Directorate, Paris.

Oerke, E-C., H-W. Dehne, F. Schönbeck and A. Weber (1994), *Crop Production and Crop Protection: estimated losses in major food and cash crops*, Elsevier, Amsterdam.

Opschoor, J.B. and D.W. Pearce (eds) (1991), *Persistent Pollutants: Economics and Policy*, Kluwer, Dordrecht.

Opschoor, J.B. and J.B. Vos (1989), *Economic Instruments for Environmental Protection*, OECD, Paris.

Oskam, A.J. (1993), *External Effects of Agricultural Production in the Netherlands: Environment and Global Warming*, Poster abstract, Proceedings 7th EAAE Congress, September 1993, Stresa, Italy.

Oskam, A.J. (1995), 'Economics of Pesticides: An Overview of the Issues', Workshop on Pesticides, Concerted Action AIR3-CT93-1164, Wageningen, 24–7 August.

Oskam, A.J., H. van Zeijts, G.J. Thijssen, G.A.A. Wossink and R. Vijftigschild (1992), 'Pesticide Use and Pesticide Policy in the Netherlands, *Wageningen Economic Studies*, 26, PUDOC, Wageningen.

Oude Lansink, A. (1994), 'Effects of Input Quotas in Dutch Arable Farming', *Tijdschrift voor Sociaalwetenschappelijk onderzoek van de Landbouw*, 9: 197–217.

Pearce, D. (1993), *Economic Values and The Natural World*, Earthscan, London.

Pearce, D.W. and R.K. Turner (1990), *Economics of Natural Resources and the Environment*, Harvester Wheatsheaf, New York.

Pimentel, D. (1993), 'Assessment of Environmental and Economic Impacts of Pesticide Use', in D. Pimentel and H. Lehman (eds), *The Pesticide Question*, Chapman & Hall, New York.

Reus, J.A.W.A., H.J. Weckseler and G.A. Pak (1994), 'Towards a Future EC Pesticide Policy: An Inventory of Risks of Pesticide Use, Possible Solutions and Policy Instruments', CLM-Report, Utrecht, The Netherlands.

Schmitz, P.M. and M. Hartmann (1993), *Landwirtschaft und Chemie*, Vauk, Kiel.

Simonsen, J.W. (ed.) (1996), 'Inventory on Mineral Pollution from Agriculture', Country Reports of the Workshop on Mineral Emissions From Agriculture, Concerted Action AIR3 CT93-1164, Oslo, 25–8 January.

Smith, V.K. (1992), 'Environmental Costing for Agriculture', *American Journal of Agricultural Economics*, **74**: 1076–88.

Tietenberg, T.H. (1985), *Emissions Trading: An Exercise in Reforming Pollution Policy*, Resources for the Future, Washington, DC.

Vijftigschild, R.A.N. and A.J. Oskam (1994), Pesticide Use in the Netherlands: Extent, Problems and Policy', in J. Michalek and C-H. Hanf (eds), *The Economic Consequences of a Drastic Reduction in Pesticide Use in The EU*, Vauk, Kiel.

Vos, J.B., J.H. Leopold and H.J. Sterk (1992), 'De mogelijkheid van regulerende heffingen voor de vermindering van het minderalenoverschot van de Nederlandse landbouw', DHV Consultants, Amersfoort, The Netherlands.

Wetenschappelijke Raad voor het Regeringsbeleid (WRR) (1992), 'Milieubeleid: Strategie, Instrumenten en Handhaafbaarheid', WRR-Rapport 41, SDU, The Hague.

Wijnands, F.G. and P. Vereijken (1992), 'Region-Wise Development of Prototypes of Integrated Arable Farming and Outdoor Horticulture, *Netherlands Journal of Agricultural Science*, **40**: 225–38.

Zadoks, J.C. (1980), 'Economische aspecten van gewasbescherming; een verkenning', *Landbouwkundig Tijdschrift/pt*, **92**: 313–23.

21 Economic Policy and Water Pollution

G. Flichman[a] *and D. Jourdain*[b]

Introduction

Since the 1980s there has been growing public concern about water quality. Water pollutants are often classified as *point source* or *non-point source* pollutants. Point source pollutants are those that can be traced to a precise source, such as a pipe, ditch or container. In agriculture there are relatively few point sources of water pollution although certain types of confinement livestock facilities and greenhouse facilities could qualify as point sources. Environmental policies initially concentrated on point source industrial pollution, but then attention shifted to non-point sources of surface and groundwater pollution. Agriculture is now perceived as the main polluter of the water supply. Hence governments seek to counter ecological damage from agricultural practices, and questions arise as to the types of policies to be implemented. One of the difficulties is that agriculture has its own specificities. First, prices are often subsidized (The Common Agricultural Policy (CAP) is an example for Europe) and stimulate production intensification. It is difficult to suggest a tax on agricultural products otherwise subsidized without having contradictory effects. Moreover, a tax on agricultural products has inevitable effects on the redistribution of revenues. Taxes applied on inputs related to pollution (fertilizers and pesticides) also have a strong income effect. Land is a fixed input, with price subsidies inducing intensification and a consequent higher price of land (rent). Higher prices induce an increasing use of chemical inputs.

[a] Centre International des Hautes Etudes Agronomiques Méditerranéennes, Institut de Montpellier, France.
[b] Centre de coopération internationale en recherche pour le développement (CIRAD), Département des Cultures Annuelles, B.P. 5053, 34032 Montpellier, Cédex 1, France.

Second, pollution created by chemicals cannot be linked directly to the level of intensification, as in the case of industrial pollution, where increases in production induce an increase in pollutants. The link between agricultural practices and pollution is stochastic in nature since weather situations and many other parameters, such as soils and the shape of the watershed, are involved in the process (see Chapter 23 of the present volume). Furthermore, chemical losses through leaching or runoff vary across crops and seasons. For example, risks of nitrates leaching are highest when rainfall is high, evaporation is low and crop demands are low (Hanley, 1990). Finally, movements of groundwater are difficult to monitor, and there is a time lag between emissions and detection of chemical residues. Once the aquifer is contaminated, the residues may remain in the groundwater for a long period, and it is then technically difficult and costly to treat the aquifer.

Assessment of the effects of agricultural and environmental policies requires the understanding of the relations between production practices, related net returns and environmental impacts. Non-point agricultural pollution has previously been studied at the regional or watershed level (Anderson *et al.*, 1985; Baudry, 1989; Oglethorpe and O'Callaghan, 1995; Vreke, 1990; see also Chapter 23 of the present volume) and at the farm level (Fernandez-Santos *et al.*, 1993; Hornsby *et al.*, 1993; Turvey, 1991; Wossink and Renkema, 1994). Farm-level studies incorporate environmental indices into economic analyses to evaluate income and environmental trade-offs.

In this chapter, these relations are examined for a small agricultural region (Vallées et terrasses, South-west France), using a farm model based on the characteristics of a typical farm in the region.

The POLEN Model

The production process can be studied as a joint production of two outputs, crops and pollution, assumed to be separable. Two transformation functions are then considered $y = f(x)$ and $z = h(x)$, where f describes the relationship between crop outputs and the vector x of inputs employed by the farmer, z the flow of non-point pollution and $h(.)$ the transformation function of inputs into pollution. The problem is then one of maximization of the farmers' revenue, subject to a maximum contaminant level in the groundwater (Anderson *et al.*, 1985; Howitt and Taylor, 1993).

Specific production and transformation of the chemical functions need to be developed and tested. However, a certain number of methodological problems arise when using functions taken from econometric studies. First, there is not always a direct link between use of inputs and crop productivity. This is particularly the case of the use of pesticides used to abate damages.

A problem arises then on the choice and justification of a functional form (Lichtenberg and Zilberman, 1986).

Another problem with the supply/response function is the availability of data. Usually, there are not enough degrees of freedom in time series data to evaluate cross-supply elasticities. Data are therefore aggregated, and agricultural inputs will be, at best, aggregated as fertilizers or pesticides. This is difficult to accept when working on the environmental effects of chemicals where each chemical will have a different behaviour in each environmental compartment.

Finally, econometric functions should be used in the case of minor changes. In cases of radical changes, or when studying the effects of agricultural policies, we may need to take options and values lying outside the range of values observed historically (Boussemart *et al.*, 1995; Hazell and Norton, 1986).

With the development of plant growth simulators in recent years, an alternative has become available for analysis of agricultural policies. Crop yields and indicators of potential pollution are obtained for different management systems under various weather conditions. These input/output coefficients are then integrated into the farm programming model, giving indications on the production choices, farmers revenues and environmental impact of the management systems chosen by farmers. The POLEN model is such a model.

General Characteristics

The POLEN model is a farm linear programming model, with special characteristics.

● It uses simulated data obtained from the agronomic erosion–productivity impact calculator (EPIC) model. The crop yield and pollution indicator technical coefficients are derived from simulations of EPIC. The pollution index used is the summation of all nitrate losses (leaching, subsurface flow and runoff).
● POLEN is a recursive model. Optimization is annual, with the results of one year having an influence on the following year. This is true of yields associated with different rotation schemes, the availability of capital goods, financial flows, and so on.
● Economic risk is treated in the model using a method that combines Freund's approach with the Target MOTAD method (see Hazell and Norton, 1986).

We consider different 'states of nature': (a) those determined by climatic conditions that will affect yields and nitrate pollution; (b) those determined by future price variations; and (c) those determined by future expectations on subsidies variation. The complete set that defines the states of nature is built upon a series of climatic inputs obtained using historical long-term climatic data and their influence on yields. In addition, future variations of prices and subsidies are developed according to commonsense criteria and the results of farmers' and policy makers' expectations. A gradual reduction in prices is foreseen both by farmers and policy analysts after the McSharry–reform of the CAP, but the level of subsidies paid cannot be considered a sure event. Thus, in our model, we attach different subjective probabilities to expected future subsidies based on the current year's level.

POLEN permits an analysis of the technical, socioeconomic and environmental aspects of the problem within a unified framework. The integrated use of a comprehensive agronomic simulation calculator with a mathematical programming model makes it possible to associate yields and potential levels of pollution, for specific soil and weather situations. The same level of irrigation and fertilization may have quite different effects in terms of nitrate pollution according to weather and soil conditions. EPIC makes the calculation on a hectare basis. Information from EPIC enters the linear programming model. When we obtain the optimal solutions from the economic point of view (for different scenarios), it is possible to observe the associated results in terms of potential pollution. The model evaluates the 'cost' in terms of farmers' revenue losses caused by a reduction in the pollution level and calculates the results concerning production and land use patterns.

Crop Production Activities

We define the dimensions of the crop production activities to correspond with the information provided by EPIC. The dimensions are the crop, agronomic techniques and soil type. A large number of technical coefficients are associated with each cropping activity, all defined *ex ante* and incorporated principally in auxiliary external files to make the core of the model as 'clean' as possible.

Some of these technical coefficients come from input and output EPIC files: (1) yields; (2) environmental results (nitrate leaching, runoff and subsurface flow), or 'nitrate loss'/potential nitrate pollution; (3) tillage, fertilizer application, irrigation, pesticide application, supervision, seeding and other operations that are part of the technical schedule; (4) quantities of other inputs applied. Coefficients mentioned in points 1 and 2 come from EPIC output. These data are obtained out of simulations of five typical climatic years that are a representative sample of a long-period climatic series (25 years).

Principal Equations of the POLEN Model

The objective is to maximize expected utility: where $U(.)$ is the utility level; X_t the set of farming decisions in period t, including allocated surface to crops, techniques, use of inputs, and so on; Y_t represents the set of financial variables, as monthly cash flow, interest payments and investment level; E is the expectations operator; $NETINCOME$, is net income; ϕ is the risk-aversion coefficient; and $\lambda(X_t, Y_t)$ is the sum of negative deviations from $E[NETINCOME(X_t,Y_t)]$. Yields considered for the calculation are the average of the five years' simulations. The optimization process is annual. Capital goods (irrigation equipment, tillage equipment) may be increased on an annual rental basis.

$$MAX\ U(X_t, Y_t) = E[NETINCOME(X_t, Y_t)] - \phi.\lambda(X_t, Y_t) \qquad (21.1)$$

$NETINCOME$ (.) is composed of the following elements:

$$NETINCOME(X_t, Y_t) = REVENUE(X_t; P_t) + SUBSIDY(X_t) - \\ VARCOST(X_t) - FINANCOST(Y_t, Y_{t-1}) - FIXEDCOSTS \qquad (21.2)$$

where P_t is the vector of prices for year t; $REVENUE(X_t; P_t)$ represents the crop revenues resulting from the multiplication of EPIC yields by crop prices and hectares allocated to each crop; $SUBSIDY(X_t)$ is the sum of all subsidies under CAP reform; $VARCOST(X_t)$ is the sum of all variable costs; $FINANCOST(Y_t, Y_{t-1})$ are the net financial costs dependent on financial decisions in years t and $t-1$.

The constraints are as follows: *Rotational constraints* ensure that all available land is subject to the set-aside provisions of the CAP reform, and land allocated to a particular crop i over crop j in year t, has to be less than the area of crop j grown in year $t-1$; its purpose is to model rotational constraints.

$$\Sigma X_t \leq \Sigma X_{t-1} - SETASIDE(X_t) \qquad (21.3)$$

Labour constraints are represented by a farm labour balance equation:

$$\Sigma(X_t * LABOR(X_t)) \leq FARMLAB + SEASON_t \qquad (21.4)$$

Equation (21.4) requires that the sum of all labour is less than the amount of permanent labour available to the farm ($FARMLAB$), plus the amount of hired seasonal labour $SEASON_t$, $FARMLAB$ is an exogenous parameter. According to the characteristics of the labour markets in the different regions, labour constraints have been expressed differently, as in Spain for example.

As regards *risk constraints*, risk is considered according to the following equations:

$$NETINCOME(X_t, Y_t; e, q, n) + DEV(e, q, n)$$
$$\geq E[NETINCOME(X_t, Y_t)] \tag{21.5}$$

$$\sum_{e}\sum_{t}\sum_{n}DEV(e, t, n) \leq \lambda(X_t, Y_t)*30 \tag{21.6}$$

Equation (21.5) computes for each combination of states of nature the negative deviations of actual net income from the expected value of net income. Parameters (e, q, n) represent three different sources of instability. Subsidy instability is represented by e, and can take three values for each crop within the CAP reform ($e1, e2, e3$). Yield instability is accounted for by parameter q, which in turn can take on five values, one for each year of the five years considered in the EPIC model simulations, q is high in good years and low in bad years (These five years are a representative sample of the climatic conditions of the regions, obtained from data of long-period climatic data (between 25 and 35 years). Lastly, price instability is reflected by the parameter n, which can take two values ($n1, n2$), with one optimistic and the other pessimistic. In sum, constraint (21.5) is represented by ($3*5*2 = 30$) equations, one for each combination 'states of nature'.

Equation (21.6) sums all the negative deviations and makes them less to or equal than $\lambda(X_t, Y_t)*30$, where 30 represents combinations of states of nature. The right-hand side in this equation is multiplied by the risk-aversion coefficient, and appears in the objective function, equation (21.1) with a negative sign.

Other equations, not written here, deal with other specific constraints, technical and economical, applicable to each region. In the cases where irrigation activities are incorporated, additional constraints related to variable water availability are taken into account.

Environmental Criteria

Environmental simulation models provide information on the amount of chemicals (pesticides, fertilizers) found in the different environmental compartments under different management systems. For pesticides, complex indices are usually used, to better represent the difference in toxicity between active ingredients. Verhoeven *et al.* (1994) integrated an environmental yardstick for pesticides in an economic farm model to monitor effects of two environmental control systems for arable farming in the Netherlands, while Teague *et al.* (1995) developed complex environmental indices for pesticides and nitrates in the different environmental compartments. Pollution is estimated here in terms of total nitrate losses from the farm. EPIC calculates the losses for each crop activity, and these values are incorporated as associated parameters of the production activities. It is then possible to 'count' the potential nitrate pollution that is related to each specific optimal solution of the model.

Deterministic versus Stochastic Approaches for Environmental Criteria

Two approaches are possible when environmental criteria are considered. The first approach considers the average environmental criteria over a large number of years. The effects of different policies are then tested on this index. One of these policies can be the establishment of a maximum limit in the chemical loading of groundwater due to agricultural practices. Teague *et al.* (1995) showed that, although the deterministic solution constrained the expected value of the chemical loading below the given target level, there was still a large probability that the chemical loading exceeds this target. Therefore there is a need to develop a stochastic approach for the study of agroenvironmental studies.

Analysis of environmental risk can be done in the same manner as for economic risk. The idea developed here is to use the concept of Target MOTAD to study risk of pollution by agro-chemicals (Flichman, 1995a, 1995b; Jourdain, 1995a and 1995b; Teague *et al.*, 1995). An important difference concerning the interpretation of risk in the case of environmental issues is that this interpretation has a more 'objective' and general meaning that when we incorporate economic risk into a model. It is more objective because the limit put on an environmental variable is obtained from some criteria related to a clearly specified objective. This can also be done in economic models, when they are strictly normative. But in models built for policy analysis, risk is usually used as a means of calibrating the model (nobody really knows the risk aversion of farmers and, even if it is known, there is always the problem of aggregation). Limited risk methods, such as Target MOTAD, appear very suitable for analysing environmental risk, because what we are limiting and why is known.

The POLEN model allows us to explore the possibilities of applying two types of policies in order to reduce nitrate pollution: (1) the adoption of production plans that limit potential pollution, without affecting price structures; and (2) introduction of a tax on nitrogen fertilizer. We use the model built for the region of Toulouse to simulate the possible effect of these policies.

The initial model results correspond to the production plans that maximize the objective function and limit pollution in two different ways: by imposing a limit to average pollution with respect to climatic influence, and by limiting the level of pollution for each type of climatic year, with three levels of tolerance for the non-respecting of the imposed limit. The levels of potential pollution correspond to an average farm, but actual pollution may vary strongly, depending on soil type, crop and technique. The database used for nitrate losses has approximately 5000 values for each region, obtained from EPIC simulations. The initial model is represented by:

$$NITLOSS(X_t, Y_t, n) - DEV(n) \leq BUT(X_t, Y_t)$$

$$\sum_n DEV(n) \leq \lambda E(X_t, Y_t)$$

where *NITLOSS* is the total loss of nitrates, as estimated by EPIC for each production activity; *BUT* is the limit to pollution, applied for each climatic situation; and λE is the limit to the accumulation of deviations (Target MOTAD).

Results and Discussion

Five types of climatic years are considered, furthermore, we consider the results of simulating a 200 per cent tax on nitrogen, which is a necessary level to obtain a sensible reduction of pollution. Figures 21.1 and 21.2 show the effects created by imposing different levels of restrictions on pollution, or applying a 200 per cent tax on nitrate fertilization. Each set of bars comprises four elements: nitrate pollution on average (kg/ha), nitrate pollution in a climatic year when pollution would be at its highest, farm income level, and irrigated area. Income and irrigated area are measured by an index. The 'No ref' scenario reflects the situation without the CAP's reform prices and subsidies, and without any restriction on pollution; 'Avg' represents the situation where average pollution is restricted; 'But 1', 'But 2' and 'But 3' impose restrictions for all the climatic years, with three different levels of λE. In Figure 21.2, 'ReFORM' is the scenario with CAP reform and without any restriction to nitrate pollution. 'Poll.1' and 'Poll.2' refer to different levels of pollution output restrictions, while 'Surf.irr. refers to the area under irrigation and 'Revenu' to revenue. All variables are measured in index terms.

The results presented in the figures demonstrate the importance of CAP reform concerning the relations between potential pollution levels and

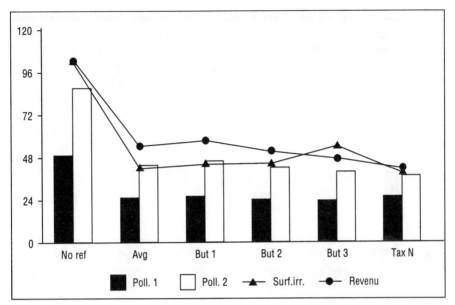

Figure 21.1   Income and pollution: non-reformed CAP

farmers' incomes. In the scenario without reform, if we impose constraints on pollution, income losses are much higher than in the 'reform' scenario. It is possible to propose to farmers production plans allowing a sensible pollution reduction with small losses in income. In these conditions, after CAP reform, implementing environmental protection policies becomes easier. The costs of imposing restrictions on pollution in terms of income losses will be lower in the post-CAP reform situation.

Two types of pollution restriction policies have been tested with the model. In the 'reform scenario', a policy for reducing nitrate pollution based on a tax on nitrogen use would cause a severe diminution of income. The alternative, which is a contractual policy ('cahier de charges'), would produce only a small reduction in farmers' income. The nitrogen tax would also produce a significant reduction in irrigation (Figure 21.2). In this region, well managed irrigation allows a better use of nitrogen by the crop. Pollution is not directly correlated to the quantity of nitrogen applied, which is why a tax to reduce pollution is inefficient.

We also calculate the budgetary cost of these two policies (in the case of the reform scenario). Table 21.1 shows quite clearly that contracting with farmers has a lower cost than a nitrogen tax. Costs of each policy are calculated by assuming complete compensation for the loss of income determined by the reduction in pollution. In the case of the tax policy, the

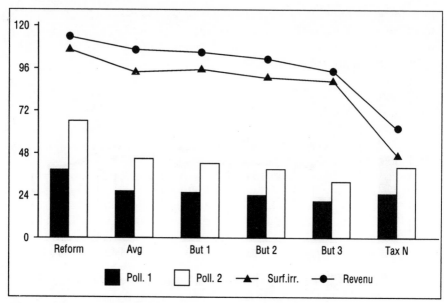

Figure 21.2   Income and pollution: reformed CAP

income from the tax is deducted from the cost. That means that the cost in Table 21.1 is the difference between income reduction and tax.

The advantages of a policy based upon a contract with the farmers, compared with a tax on nitrogen use, comes from the fact that a tax prompts the search for a production plan using less nitrogen. But pollution is not linearly determined by nitrogen use: rotations and agronomic techniques strongly influence pollution levels. An indirect way to reduce pollution using the price structure could be applied, but it would be necessary to modify more than one input price to obtain good results. A contractual policy creates the problem of additional costs for controlling the application of the established norms by farmers. This is an important problem in general terms,

Table 21.1   CAP reform scenario

	Budg. cost/ha	Poll 1	Poll 2	Irrig. surf.
But 1	89	24.69	41.31	44.83
But 2	124	23.21	38.10	42.84
But 3	199	19.98	31.55	41.84
Tax	184	24.77	39.71	22.26

but is minor in the case of the agriculture of the European Union. Farmers already provide the government with an enormous amount of information in order to qualify for subsidies, and thus contracts can be implemented at a relatively low marginal control cost.

References

Anderson, G.D., J.J. Opaluch and W.M. Sullivan (1985), 'Nonpoint Agricultural Pollution: Pesticide Contamination of Groundwater Supplies', *American Journal of Agricultural Economics*, **67**: 1238–43.

Baudry, J. (1989), 'Interactions Between Agricultural and Ecological Systems at the Landscape Level', *Agriculture, Ecosystems & Environment*, **27**: 119–30.

Boussemart, J.P., G. Flichman, F. Jacquet and H.B. Lefer (1995), 'L'apport des modèles bioéconomiques à l'analyse des politiques agricoles. Une illustration sur la Beauce et la région de Toulouse', *Journées IFRESI*, January.

Fernandez-Santos, J., S. Zekri and A.C. Herruzo (1993), 'On-farm Costs of Reducing Nitrogen Pollution Through BMP', *Agriculture, Ecosystems & Environment*, **45**: 1–11.

Flichman, G. (1995a), *Politique économique et pollution par des nappes par les nitrates en Europe*, Académie d'Agriculture de France, Paris, 7 November.

Flichman, G. (1995b), 'Impact Analysis of Different Policies in Some European Regions. Competitiveness and Environment Protection. Final Report' (Final Report of POLEN Project), Montpellier.

Hanley, N. (1990), 'The Economics of Nitrate Pollution', *European Review of Agricultural Economics*, **17**: 129–51.

Hazell, P.B.R. and R.D. Norton (1986), *Mathematical Programming for Economic Analysis in Agriculture*, Macmillan, New York.

Hornsby, A.G., T.M. Buttler and R.B. Brown (1993), 'Managing Pesticides for Crop Production and Water Quality Protection: Practical Growers Guide', *Agriculture, Ecosystems & Environment*, **46**: 187–96.

Howitt, R. and C.R. Taylor (1993), 'Some Microeconomics of Agricultural Resource Use', in G.A. Carlson, D. Zilberman and J.A. Miranowski (eds), *Agricultural and Environmental Resource Economics*, Oxford University Press, New York/Oxford.

Jourdain, D.J. (1995a), 'Utilisation des modèles bio-économiques pour l'analyse des stratégies de protection des plantes: faisabilité, problèmes théoriques', Documents de travail, CIRAD-CA, December.

Jourdain, D.J. (1995b), 'An Analysis of Pesticide Use in Vegetable Farming: The Case of Thailand (Part II)', *Agro-Chemicals News In Brief*, **28**(4): 27–30.

Lichtenberg, E. and D. Zilberman (1986), 'The Econometrics of Damage Control: Why Specification Matters', *American Journal of Agricultural Economics*, **68**: 261–73.

Oglethorpe, D.R. and J.R. O'Callaghan (1995), 'Farm-Level Economic Modelling Within a River Catchment Decision Support System', *Journal of Environmental Planning and Management*, **38**(1): 93–106.

Teague, M.L., D.J. Bernardo and H.P. Mapp (1995), 'Farm-Level Economic Analysis Incorporating Stochastic Environmental Risk Assessment', *American Journal of Agricultural Economics*, **77**: 8–19.

Turvey, C.G. (1991), 'Environmental Quality Constraints and Farm-Level Decision Making', *American Journal of Agricultural Economics*, **73**: 1399–1404.

Verhoeven, J.T., G.A.A. Wossink and J.A.W.A. Reus (1994), 'An Environmental Yardstick in Farm Economic Modelling of Future Pesticide Use: The Case of Arable Farming', *Netherlands Journal of Agricultural Science*, **42**(4): 331–41.

Vreke, J. (1990), 'Modelling Agriculture to Support Regional Water Management', *European Review of Agricultural Economics*, **17**: 317–34.

Wossink, G.A.A. and J.A. Renkema (1994), 'Farm Economic Modelling of Integrated Plant Production', in P.C. Struik, W.J. Vredenberg, J.A. Renkema and J.E. Parlevliet (eds), *Plant Production on the Threshold of a New Century*, Kluwer Academic Publishers, Boston/Dordrecht/London.

22 Benefits of Improving Water Quality in South-western British Columbia: An Application of Economic Valuation Methods[1]

G.C. van Kooten[a]

Introduction

The US Environmental Protection Agency (EPA) determined that agriculture is the largest US source of surface water contamination and a major contributor to groundwater pollution (Napier, 1983; Diebel *et al.*, 1992). Water problems include bacteria, salinity, sediment, pathogenic organisms, toxic material and nutrient (nitrate) pollution. The EPA conducted a national survey on pesticides in drinking water wells and discovered that about 52 per cent of community wells have detectable amounts of nitrate, 10 per cent of wells contain at least one pesticide, and 7 per cent may contain both nitrates and pesticides (Diebel *et al.*, 1992). Similar problems are appearing in the Abbotsford aquifer region of SW British Columbia (BC) in Canada.

The Abbotsford aquifer covers approximately 100 square km in SW BC and an additional 100 square km in NW Washington state in the USA. It is the largest of the approximately 200 aquifers in the lower Fraser River valley and is an important source of residential, industrial and agricultural water in the region. In 1981, groundwater supplied 44 per cent of the water for the

[a] Department of Agricultural Economics, University of British Columbia, Canada.

area between Surrey and Chilliwack on the south side of the Fraser River, and from Maple Ridge to the district of Kent on the north side (Dorcey and Griggs, 1991: 45). Groundwater provided almost all of the water requirements for the residents of Abbotsford, as well as a large portion of water for other uses.

The study area is increasingly subjected to the pressures of population growth. Development in all sectors is evident, and this has increased the extent and intensity of the land use. On the Canadian side of the border, the trend has been towards the loss of agricultural land to urban expansion. Approximately 20 per cent of the aquifer is now covered by urban areas, with the remainder in agriculture. Agricultural activities include row cropping (mainly raspberries, but also corn and potatoes), poultry production, dairying and pasture, and hog production. Land use on the US side of the aquifer is less intensive than in Canada; satellite imagery reveals less cultivation, more extensive dairying, and more forested land in the USA (Liebscher *et al.*, 1992). The more intensive Canadian agricultural activity reflects the increased value of the land owing to its proximity to a major urban centre and the existence of an international boundary that prevents spillover of urban expansion into the USA. Since there is potential to develop BC agricultural land for other purposes, such as housing or recreation, including golf courses, farm enterprises are more intensive in order to earn rates of return that are similar to those realized in other land uses.

There are other institutional factors that affect land use intensity. These include the BC Agricultural Land Reserve, which prohibits development of agricultural land; the land use distorting effects of national marketing boards for eggs, broilers and milk; current and historical barriers to agricultural trade between Canada and the USA; and the unique characteristics of the food processing industries on the Canadian and US sides of the border.

The Abbotsford aquifer is largely unconfined and covered with sand and gravel deposits. These features, combined with high precipitation over the winter months, explain why manure and other effluent readily percolate into the groundwater below. The aquifer's only water inflow is from a small underground stream at its northern end. Since large amounts of water are tapped by the Abbotsford municipal water system and the fish hatchery on the east side of the aquifer, and because there is no regulation on well drilling on private property, pollution levels are exacerbated (Dorcey and Griggs, 1991: 25). Further, since water from the aquifer flows south into the USA, Canadian activities related to the aquifer are subject to the Boundary Waters Treaty of 1909. This treaty states that water flowing across the boundary 'shall not be polluted on either side to the injury of health and property on the other side'; therefore water quality is an international concern.

To date, nitrates and pesticides originating from agricultural land use practices have been held largely responsible for the contaminated water (Liebscher *et al.*, 1992). Farm practices that have been identified as causes of groundwater pollution include exposed stockpiling of manure (Fullerton, 1991a, 1991b) and overapplication of chemical fertilizers and manure for fertilization and soil enhancement. Since less recognized pollution sources, such as septic field effluent, landfill leachate, leaking underground storage tanks, accidental chemical spills and airport de-icing urea formaldehyde, may also contribute to the pollution, well sampling has recently been extended to include some of these (Liebscher *et al.*, 1992; Canter and Knox, 1986).

During the summer of 1993, residents who used water from the aquifer were asked to boil their drinking water because of contamination by ecoli bacteria originating in livestock wastes. While bacterial contamination is a concern, it is related to the contamination of groundwater by nitrates originating in livestock wastes, and this has been the focus of recent research. Since 1955, the National Hydrology Research Institute and Environment Canada, along with the BC government and local municipalities, have collected over 450 domestic well and piezometer samples of groundwater in the region. Sampling locations were on a large grid but, initially, chemical analyses were confined to traditional inorganic constituents and the frequency with which the water was sampled was highly variable. In 1984, however, a noticeable increase in localized nitrate concentrations raised concern, and sampling was focused on the south Matsqui region where the problem appeared to be most severe, with sampling extended to include pesticides in 1991 (Liebscher *et al.*, 1992).

Nitrogen nitrates in drinking water pose a health risk to infants, particularly those under six months of age who are on a formula-based diet rather than breast milk (Addiscott *et al.*, 1992). When infants consume too much nitrate they may develop a blood disorder called *methaemoglobinaemia*, also known as 'blue baby syndrome'. In infants' digestive systems nitrate converts to nitrite which, when in the blood, prevents haemoglobin from carrying oxygen. The infant suffers oxygen deprivation, and in severe cases may die. In those infants who already have a respiratory or intestinal infection, the disease can be especially acute (Muia and Thomas, 1990).

Although the majority of cases of blue baby syndrome have occurred when water concentrations exceeded 100 mg/l of nitrate-nitrogen (Addiscott *et al.*, 1992), nitrate-nitrogen levels as low as 10 parts per million (ppm) in drinking water have been linked to methaemoglobinaemia (Cogger and MacConnell, 1991). Few cases of methaemoglobinaemia have been recorded in the USA in recent years, but many are never reported (Cogger and

MacConnell, 1991: 247). The long-term effect of nitrate consumption in older infants, children and adults is not known for certain at this time; however, ruminant animals such as cattle and sheep can also develop the disease.

After many years of testing, a recent report by Liebscher *et al.* (1992: 1, 35) stated that 'Approximately 60 per cent of the samples collected from the south Matsqui study area have nitrate-nitrogen concentrations that exceed the 10 mg/l maximum acceptable concentration for drinking water as defined in the Health and Welfare Canada *Canadian Drinking Water Quality Guidelines*'. Environment Canada's 1989 sampling results found 46 out of 73 sample sites with nitrate-nitrogen concentrations greater than 10 mg/l. The 'mean for these samples was 13.08 mg/l, with 0.0 mg/l and 41.5 mg/l as minimum and maximum concentrations detected'. Current water quality standards require that nitrate-nitrogen concentrations not exceed 10 mg/l, while the federal government's target is for them to be less than 1 mg/l.

Several alternatives have been proposed for handling the manure problem: constructing adequate on-farm and regional manure storage facilities; composting manure either on-farm or at large-scale regional facilities; converting poultry manure to cattle feed; transporting manure off the aquifer to regions with nutrient deficient soils; improving management of manure by raspberry producers; and combinations of these methods (Fullerton, 1991a, 1991b; Stennes, 1992). None of these methods can be considered financially feasible (see BC Ministry of Agriculture, Fisheries and Food, 1993; Stennes, 1992), while the government has ruled out penalties as these would mean that producers in the region would be disadvantaged relative to those located off the aquifer. Agricultural scientists and policy makers appear to favour composting as this results in an environmentally benign product that provides organic matter to soil. Because none of the approaches to the problem is privately profitable, public intervention by way of subsidies will be needed. To justify such intervention, it is necessary to determine that individuals value improved water quality more than the subsidy amount that would be required: that is, that the discounted social benefits of improving water quality exceed the discounted social costs. This study uses contingent methods to determine the value of improvements to water quality in the study region.

Economic Valuation Measures Used in this Study: Theory

In this study, three evaluation methods are used: willingness to pay, contingent fuzzy ranking and defence expenditures, with the latter serving primarily as a lower bound check on the former measures. The first two methods are described in this section, with both relying on a contingent valuation (CV) survey.

Willingness to Pay

Consumers are assumed to maximize their utility, which is a function of the market goods (x) they consume and water quality, Q. The household's economic problem is:

$$\text{Maximise } u(x, z, Q) \text{ subject to: } m = p\,x, \tag{22.1}$$

where m is household income, p is a vector of prices, and z is a vector of social and other factors that affect utility. The indirect utility function associated with (22.1) is $v(m, p, Q; z)$, while the expenditure function is $e(p, Q; u, z)$. The indirect utility function and the expenditure function are assumed continuous and twice differentiable in p, Q and m. The indirect utility function is non-decreasing and quasi-concave in Q; the expenditure function is non-increasing and convex in Q. Since prices remain fixed and z is a vector of characteristics (that is, used in the regression analysis), we drop these variables in the remaining theoretical analysis.

Hicksian compensated measures are used to evaluate welfare changes from increments or decrements in the availability of a public good, in this case improvements in water quality (Johansson, 1987; Hoehn, 1992). The CV method elicits the Hicksian welfare measures in the case of natural resource damages and uses these in cost–benefit analysis (Hoehn, 1992). The Hicksian compensating surplus gives the maximum amount that the household is willing to pay (WTP) for an improvement in water quality, while the Hicksian equivalent surplus is the minimum amount that the household would demand as compensation to forgo the improvement in water quality. Arrow *et al.* (1993) argue that WTP is preferred to compensation demanded and may even overstate the actual value of the change in the environmental amenity, although Knetsch (1989, 1993) argues otherwise. The difference between the two measures is determined by whether individuals have the property right to the improved water quality (equivalent surplus is to be elicited) or not (WTP is appropriate).

In this study, we elicit the respondent's WTP, thereby focusing on compensating surplus. For household k, the compensating surplus (W) of the improvement in water quality from Q^0 to Q^1 is given by:

$$W^k(Q^1, Q^0, m_k) = m_k - e(Q^1, v(Q^0, m_k)).$$

A Taylor series expansion about Q^0 and the mean income level, μ_m, gives the following expression for CV:

$$W^k = W(Q^0, Q^0, \mu_m) + (Q^1 - Q^0) \, \partial W/\partial Q + (m_k - \mu_m) \, \partial W/\partial m + \tfrac{1}{2}$$
$$(Q^1 - Q^0)^2 \, \partial^2 W/\partial^2 Q + \tfrac{1}{2} (m_k - \mu_m)^2 \, \partial^2 W/\partial^2 m + \tfrac{1}{2} (Q^1 - Q^0)$$
$$(m_k - \mu_m) \, \partial^2 W/\partial Q \partial m + R,$$

where R refers to remaining terms. Then the willingness to pay of the kth household for the improvement in water quality can be written as:

$$WTP^k = \alpha_0 + \alpha_1 \, \Delta Q + \alpha_2 \, \Delta Q^2 + \alpha_3 \, (m_k - \mu_m) + \alpha_4 \, (m_k - \mu_m)^2$$
$$+ \alpha_5 \, \Delta Q \, (m_k - \mu_m) + \epsilon,$$

where $\alpha_0 = W(Q^0, Q^0, \mu_m) = 0$ since the compensating variation of no change in water quality must be zero; $\alpha_1 = \partial W/\partial Q$; $\alpha_2 = \partial W/\partial m$; $\alpha_3 = \tfrac{1}{2}\partial^2 W/\partial^2 Q$; $\alpha_4 = \tfrac{1}{2}\partial^2 W/\partial^2 m$; $\alpha_5 = \partial^2 W/\partial Q \partial m$; and $\epsilon = R$. The empirical model is completed by adding social factors describing attitudes, age, household make-up and size, and so on.

Fuzzy Pairwise Comparisons

A second approach to valuing improvements in water quality is to ask respondents to reveal their degrees of preference between alternative goods using fuzzy pairwise comparisons. Fuzzy logic is increasingly used as a controller in everything from washing machines to cement kilns and subway systems (Klir and Folger, 1988; Kosko, 1992; Kosko and Isaka, 1993), to aggregate communities for regional analysis (Harris *et al.*, 1993), to determine optimal forest management strategies (Hof, 1993) and to estimate non-market values under uncertainty (van Kooten *et al.*, 1996). Fuzzy pairwise choice is used to provide respondents in the Abbotsford region with an alternative measure of the value of water quality.

Fuzzy pairwise comparisons were first used by van Kooten *et al.* (1986) to study farmers' goal hierarchies for use in multiple-objective decision making. The fuzzy pairwise method results in a ratio scale that can then be used to value non-market goods and services if one of the items in the set has a known market value. Fuzzy pairwise comparisons require that, if there are n items, all are compared in pairwise fashion; thus there are $n(n-1)/2$ pairwise comparisons that need to be made. Items can then be ordered.

A measure of the intensity of preference between two items, A and B, is made by marking on a line, with endpoints denoted A and B, the degree of preference for one over the other; a mark placed at the centre of the line indicates indifference. A measure of the intensity of the preference of item A over item B is determined by measuring the normalized distance from the left-hand side endpoint (where A is assumed to be located) to the respondent's mark, where the line is of unit length after normalization. Denote this distance by r_{AB}. If $r_{AB} < 0.5$, then A is preferred to B; if $r_{AB} > 0.5$, then B is preferred to A; if $r_{AB} = 0.5$, A is equally preferred to B; and $r_{AB} = 1 - r_{BA}$.

Van Kooten *et al.* (1986) developed a measure indicating the intensity of preference of one item over another. Once all of the pairwise measures r_{ij} are obtained, the measure of intensity for item j, m_j, is determined as

$$m_j = 1 - \left(\frac{\displaystyle\sum_{i=1}^{k} r_{ij}}{k-1} \right)^2$$

where the numerator in the second term on the right-hand side is the Euclidean norm and the denominator is its maximum value; k is the number of items that are ranked by the fuzzy pairwise comparison. As an example, suppose the following measures: $m_A = 0.2$; $m_B = 0.6$; $m_C = 0.3$; and $m_D = 0.75$. Further suppose that item C is valued at \$100. Then, by independence of irrelevant alternatives (one's preference between oranges and apples does not depend on whether or not a grapefruit exists in the choice set), item C is valued at \$250 (= \$100 × 0.75/0.3).

Abbotsford Water Quality Survey: Empirical Results

A survey of residents in the Abbotsford region was conducted during May 1993. The survey was sent to 343 households, with 18 returned as undeliverable. Reminder notices were sent to all those in the sample approximately three weeks after the first mail. In all, 89 completed surveys were returned, providing a response rate of 27.4 per cent for deliverable surveys. The low return rate can be explained by a number of factors. First, there has been a significant amount of migration into the region, with many new residents unfamiliar with the water quality issue or unable to communicate adequately in English, or both (see Athwal, 1994). Second, follow-up phone calls and other persistent reminders for respondents to complete and return the survey, which are now employed in most survey work of this nature, could not be used because of the UBC Ethical Review process: mail enquiries and returns had to be kept completely confidential and 'harassment' via repeated follow-up would not be permitted. Funding limitations prevented the use of an outside consultant to conduct the survey, as is now usual.

The main objective of the survey was to a elicit respondents' WTP for improvements in water quality. In addition, they were asked about purchases of bottled water and in-home water filtration systems, and to reveal their preferences for four goods using fuzzy pairwise comparisons. Background and personal information and Likert-scale responses to opinion questions were also elicited. The survey instrument was intensively pretested on a group of 20 students. Additional information is found in Hauser *et al.* (1994).

Summary Data

A summary of the personal and background information of respondents is found in Table 22.1. On average, respondents were 41.3 years old and had had an average of one year of post-secondary education, which is reasonably close to the Statistics Canada 1986 average education level of just over 12 years. Hence it can be assumed that there is no educational bias between respondents and the general populace in the study region. Statistic Canada's 1991 census indicates that average family size in the region is 2.9, which corresponds to the average of 3.0 for the current survey.[2] There was an average of only 0.385 children under age five, which is understandable considering the average age of respondents.

Respondents have lived in their homes for an average of 7.0 years and in the area for 15.2 years, so they should be aware of water quality issues. Also 89.2 per cent of respondents own their homes, and 13.8 per cent had land in the Agricultural Land Reserve. If these owners have a farm enterprise, their

Table 22.1   Summary of personal and background information

Item	Mean	Coefficient of variation (%)
Age of respondents	41.3 years	43.5
Female respondents	27.6%	163.5
Family size	3.0	44.5
Number of children under age five	0.385	182.1
Own their homes	89.2%	35.0
Length of time living in neighbourhood	15.2 years	91.8
Length of time living in current home	7.0 years	107.4
Education	13.1 years	19.3
Household income	$44 620	61.1
Scaled scores		
Concern about water quality	0.5371	61.5
Concern over externality from farming	0.3516	85.0

views towards agricultural pollution and water quality may be affected by the fact that they own farmland. Hence this variable is included in the WTP regressions.

According to the 1986 census, average household income in the study region was $46 493 in 1992 dollars, which is not too different from the average household income of survey respondents – approximately $44 620.[3] Respondents' average monthly rent or mortgage payment was $600 (assuming owners paid some property taxes).

Two scaled scores were constructed from the opinion questions. Because perceptions regarding externality might be important to individual behaviour or their stated WTP, two opinion questions dealing with perceptions of farm externality were combined into a single scaled score. The scaled score takes on a value of 1 when externality from farm operations is perceived to be high, and a score of zero when it is perceived to be low. Likewise, the opinion question regarding belief about water quality was scaled to take on values between 0 and 1. The averages for these scaled scores are also provided in Table 22.1, and these indicate that there is greater concern over water quality than over general farming externalities.

Questions pertaining to residential sewage and septic systems were included, along with those on water quality; a summary of responses is provided in Table 22.2. Sewage disposal questions are important because poorly maintained septic fields are believed to contribute to aquifer nitrate-nitrogen pollution. Of respondents, 40.6 per cent indicated that they have a septic system, while the remainder believed they were connected to municipal sewers. (One respondent admitted to not knowing anything about the sewer system.) Of those who knew they had a septic system, only 55.2 per cent had cleaned their system within the last four years (as required), 10.3 per cent cleaned it in the last 5–10 years, 3.5 per cent had not cleaned their system in 10 years, 20.7 per cent did not know when their system had last been cleaned, and 10.4 per cent had never cleaned their system. In

Table 22.2   **Water quality and sewer maintenance**

Item	Mean	Coefficient of variation (%)
Respondents with septic system	40.63%	121.8
Length of time since septic system last cleaned	approx. 8 years	49.5
Perceived drinking water source	municipal/don't know	46.1
Respondents using bottled water or filters	36.9%	131.7

conclusion, just over one-half of respondents who knew they owned a septic system maintained it according to acceptable practices.

Water filtration systems and water bottle purchases are indicative, not only of a minimum WTP for improved water quality, but also of perceived water quality. Of respondents, 37 per cent had purchased bottled water within the last year, and 27 per cent owned some type of water purification filter. This indicates that there is some concern over local water quality, but it is generally not considered to be a serious problem. Respondents paid an average of $69.59 a year on defensive expenditures.

Willingness to Pay for Improved Water Quality

Unlike standard CV questions where respondents are either asked to provide a 'yes/no' response to a stated WTP (dichotomous choice format) or are asked to simply state their maximum WTP (open-ended format), the current survey used information on composting costs (minus expected revenues) to generate a supply curve for water quality improvements, with improvements in water quality given in terms of changes in the nitrate level from 12 mg/l. Respondents simply identified their preferred combination of water quality improvement and the corresponding amount they would have to pay for that improvement (see Hauser *et al.*, 1994 for details). The average WTP of all respondents was $63.86 a year, but it was $70.85 a year for those who indicated that the source of their drinking water was groundwater or did not know whether their drinking water came from the aquifer. Because the supply curve was presented to respondents, it was not possible to include a measure of water quality in the regressions. However, income and income squared were included in the ordinary least squares (OLS) regression as required by theory. Socio-economic variables (such as education and age) were also included in the regression, as was the scaled opinion question regarding water quality. The regression results are provided in Table 22.3.

The estimated regression equations were used to predict possible values for willingness to pay. These indicate that those with land in the agricultural land reserve (ALR) are willing to pay more than those owning no agricultural land, perhaps because they see themselves as contributing to nitrate-nitrogen pollution. WTP ranges from about $78 to $90 a year for those without land in the ALR, and $114–125 a year for those with land in the ALR (ignoring regression model A3).

Fuzzy Valuation

In the questionnaire, respondents were asked to make fuzzy paired comparisons over the following four items: (1) reducing one's commuting

Table 22.3 Regression analysis of willingness to pay for improved water quality*

Item/model	WTP of all respondents			WTP of those on groundwater or who do not know their water source		
	A1	A2	A3	W1	W2	W3
Income	5.56	8.64		1.3205	4.1962	
	(1.22)	(2.50)		(0.24)	(1.06)	
Square of income	1.53		2.69	1.335		1.61
	(1.04)		(2.41)	(0.81)		(1.32)
Belief about water quality	−31.73	−28.2	−35.34	−67.66	−66.73	−68.61
	(−1.39)	(−1.25)	(−1.56)	(−2.34)	(−2.32)	(−2.43)
Own ALR land	24.10	25.81	−24.65	42.53	44.98	42.66
	(1.15)	(1.23)	(1.17)	(1.71)	(1.84)	(1.74)
Constant	69.37	73.94	66.32	96.19	101.80	95.57
	(4.76)	(5.31)	(4.60)	(4.70)	(5.315)	(4.77)
R^2	0.1646	0.1480	0.1418	0.2287	0.2142	0.2274
Predicted WTP ($/yr):						
if ALR land	114.38	114.71	55.35	123.19	125.56	120.93
no ALR land	90.28	88.90	80.00	80.66	80.58	78.27

Note: *The numbers in parenthesis are the corresponding standard errors.

time to work by one-half; (2) improving the availability and quality of one's drinking water; (3) preventing the development of a golf course on agricultural land; and, (4) a 33-inch, split-screen, stereo colour television set with remote control. For the 40th respondent, for example, the following matrix of normalized distances was constructed.

Item	1	2	3	4
1	0	0.2121	0.9697	0.1212
2	0.7879	0	0.5606	0.4242
3	0.0303	0.4394	0	0.3485
4	0.8788	0.5758	0.6515	0

The matrix indicates that 1P2, 1P4, 2P4, 3P1, 3P2 and 3P4, where P denotes 'is preferred to'. Using the above formula (section 2), the preference intensity scores are as follows: $m_1 = 0.4227$, $m_2 = 0.3904$, $m_3 = 0.6757$ and $m_4 = 0.2863$. This individual ranked 'preventing development of a golf course on agricultural land' highest, followed, in order, by a reduction in commuting time, improved water quality, and the colour television. He or she also valued improved water quality 1.36 times (0.3904/0.2863) as much as the television set.

The average scores of all respondents for these items, and their coefficients of variation, are provided in Table 22.4. These indicate that the respondents ranked the four items in the following order: improved water quality, halving commuting time, preventing golf course development on agricultural land, and the television. Improved availability or quality of drinking water was considered to be 2.1 times more important than the television by the group as a whole.

The value of the television varies according to brand and where it is purchased, with prices ranging from about $900 to almost $2000, but it is perceived prices that are important. Upon asking a number of individuals about their perception of price, we found that their average price for such an item was about $1350; answers of less than $1000 were common. Hence we employ values of $1350 and $900, and annualize these simply by dividing by 10 – the approximate useful life of a television. The subsequent values are then multiplied by 2.1 to obtain an estimate of the value of improved water quality based on fuzzy pairwise comparisons. This provides a household estimate of approximately $189–$280 a year for water quality improvements.

The fuzzy scores for the four items in Table 22.4 were regressed on a number of explanatory variables using seemingly unrelated regression, which is the same as independent OLS regression using the same regressors. The explanatory variables used in the regressions were the scaled attitudinal scores, education, income, whether or not the respondent had land in the ALR, whether or not the respondent owned their place of residence, and time spent commuting. The regression results are presented in Table 22.5. Using these results, the predicted fuzzy scores for each of the items were calculated depending on whether or not the respondent owns land in the ALR and their place of residence. The predicted preference intensities are provided in the bottom rows of the table.

From the predicted preference intensities for the ranked items, it is possible to calculate respondents' intensity of preference for water quality relative to the 33in colour television. These depend on ownership of land in

Table 22.4   Intensity of preference for fuzzy pairwise ranked items

Item	Mean	Coefficient of variation (%)
Halve commuting time	0.4605	32.1
Improve water quality	0.6528	24.1
Prevent golf course development	0.4395	39.9
33" colour television	0.3026	41.1

the ALR and ownership of their residence. Those owning both land and their residence valued improvements in water quality by a factor of 1.836 over the television, or about $248 a year. Those who owned their place of residence but did not own land in the ALR valued improvements in water quality at $193 a year, while those who owned no property whatsoever valued it at $242 a year.[4] If individuals perceive the price of the television to be lower than $1350, say only $900, then improvements in water quality are valued at $165, $128 and $161, respectively. In general, improvements in water quality are valued higher by those with ALR land, as was the case for WTP.

Defence Expenditures

A third method was used to determine the accuracy of the WTP measure. Respondents were asked to complete a table indicating the brands and

Table 22.5 Regression analysis for intensity of preferences and predicted intensities

Item fuzzy score	Halve commuting time	Improve water quality	Prevent golf course devel_opt.	33″ TV
Income	−0.0176	−0.0182	−0.0128	0.0148
	(−1.66)	(−1.65)	(−1.06)	(1.51)
Own land in ALR (=1)	0.1787	0.0164	−0.2142	−0.0700
	(2.67)	(0.14)	(−2.88)	(−1.14)
Own place of residence (=1)	0.0707	−0.0787	0.0163	0.0277
	(1.08)	(−1.16)	(0.21)	(0.45)
Quality score	−0.0536	−0.2138	0.2525	0.0671
	(−0.84)	(−3.24)	(3.48)	(1.14)
Externality score	0.0246	0.1447	−0.1916	−0.0060
	(0.36)	(2.07)	(−2.46)	(−0.09)
Open space score	−0.0992	−0.0377	0.0725	−0.0481
	(−1.04)	(−0.38)	(0.66)	(−0.54)
Time spent commuting	−0.0620	−0.0110	0.0071	−0.0036
	(0.94)	(−1.61)	(0.95)	(−0.59)
Education	0.0256	−0.0082	0.0018	−0.0230
	(2.86)	(−0.89)	(0.17)	(−2.78)
Constant	0.1247	0.9083	0.2637	0.5979
	(0.82)	(6.03)	(1.59)	(4.47)
R^2	0.3658	0.3981	0.4416	0.269
Predicted scores				
ALR land Own residence				
1 1	0.2710	0.5198	0.2088	0.2831
1 0	0.2003	0.5985	0.1925	0.2554
0 1	0.0923	0.5034	0.4230	0.3531
0 0	0.0216	0.5821	0.4067	0.3254

amounts of bottled water purchased in the previous month (April 1993), as well as to indicate the brand of any water filter they might own. Some respondents did not answer this question, although they indicated that they did purchase bottled water or own a filter; in addition, taxes on purchases of bottled water or water filters were not included in the analysis. As a result, the true stated defence expenditure is probably underestimated. Further, since some respondents purchased only small bottles of water, they can be excluded from the defence expenditure calculation, since this appears to indicate that they do not perceive their residential water quality to be a problem, but rather would purchase this water anyway, despite improvements in the aquifer's water quality. Finally, since filters are often permanent and have little or no maintenance requirements, a 25-year life was assumed unless the manufacturer indicated otherwise.

Of the 89 respondents to the Abbotsford survey, 62 are on ground water, and these are the only ones considered in the determination of defence expenditures. The calculations indicate that respondents paid an average of $69.59 a year (with standard deviation of $147.47) to avoid using well water (drawn from the aquifer) for drinking purposes. As expected, this is less than their stated WTP, as determined above. A regression of defence expenditures on income and family size is provided in Table 22.6. It indicates that households may have been more willing to purchase bottled water or water filters as the number of individuals affected by poor water quality increased. Household income levels do not appear to affect purchases, however. Defence expenditures of about $70 a year serve as a lower bound estimate of the benefits of improved water quality.

Discussion

In 1991, there were 29 840 private households in the Central Valley Regional

Table 22.6 **Regression analysis of defence expenditures in the Abbotsford region of British Columbia**

Item	Estimated coefficient	t-statistic
Constant	15.619	0.207
Income	9.935	0.629
Income squared	−8.629	−1.872
Household size	35.049	1.688
R^2	0.1489	

District. In drawing our random sample, 90 out of 343 households (or 26.24 per cent) were in regions where groundwater was used for drinking purposes, while 62 out of 89 respondents (69.66 per cent) indicated that they were on groundwater. Hence some 18.28 per cent of households, or about 5500, in the Central Valley Regional District are on groundwater. For comparison, according to the latest Census, the 1991 population of the District of Abbotsford was 18 864. Almost all residents in the District are on groundwater. Assuming three individuals per household, some 6300 households are on groundwater. Multiplying the number of households by defence expenditures of $70 a year per household results in a lower bound estimate of the benefits of improved water quality of $0.44 million. This number is very close to the average stated WTP of $70.85 per household ($0.45 million). However, on the basis of WTP estimates from Table 22.3 of $78–$90 a year per household, the estimate of benefits is somewhat higher: $0.49–$0.57 million. If WTP estimates for those who own ALR land are used ($114–$125/year), the benefits of improved water quality are $0.72–$0.79 million. Finally, using the results from the fuzzy pairwise comparisons gives benefits of $128–$284 a year per household. The total benefits of improved water quality would then be $0.81–$1.79 million, significantly higher than that provided by the other measures.

Using data from a telephone survey of Abbotsford residents (Athwal, 1994), van Kooten and Athwal (1996) estimated a logistics function for dichotomous choice responses to contingent improvements in water quality. From the logistic function, mean WTP was found to be $160 a year, while median WTP was $135 a year. The results of the fuzzy analysis embraces those of the dichotomous choice approach. Van Kooten and Athwal (1996) also found that the social benefits of improving water quality in the Abbotsford area are substantially below the amount of subsidy required to make composting feasible. It would appear, therefore, that nitrate-nitrogen pollution of groundwater in Abbotsford, BC, is not a severe social problem requiring large-scale government intervention. Rather, as demonstrated by Stennes (1992), improvements in the management of manure applications, sale of some manure to farmers in other regions and some specialized, small-scale composting, all of which make sense on the basis of their private benefits, are preferred to major government intervention to eliminate entirely the problem of nitrogen pollution of the aquifer.

Notes

1   Research support by Anke Hauser is greatly appreciated. Funding was provided by Environment Canada under Contribution Agreement No. KA 601-3-0037/01-XSB. This

chapter was written while the author was a visiting professor in the Department of Agricultural Economics and Policy at Wageningen Agricultural University.

2 Only some census data are available for 1991. Where possible, 1991 data are used; otherwise we rely on 1986 census data.

3 The 1986 income ($35 572) was converted to a 1992 basis using the index for average hourly earnings.

4 The other case was not included because there were no respondents who had land in the ALR and did not also own their place of residence.

References

Addiscott, T.M., A.P. Whitmore and D.S. Powlson (1992), *Farming, Fertilisers and the Nitrate Problem*, CAB International, Wallingford, UK.

Arrow, K., R. Solow, E. Leamer, P. Portney, R. Randner and H. Schuman (1993), 'Appendix I – Report of the NOAA Panel on Contingent Valuation', *Federal Register*, **58**(10), (15 Jan.): 4602–14.

Athwal, R.K. (1994), 'Costs and Benefits of Improving Water Quality by Composting Livestock Wastes. A Contingent Valuation Approach', Unpublished MSc. thesis, Department of Agricultural Economics, University of BC, Vancouver.

BC Ministry of Agriculture, Fisheries and Food (1993), 'Economics of Composting', *Composting Factsheet*, Agdex 537/727, Soils and Engineering Branch, January.

Canter, L.W. and R.C. Knox (1986), *Septic Tank Systems Effects on Ground Water Quality*, Lewis Publishers, Chelsea, Michigan.

Cogger, C.G. and C. McConnell (1991), 'Clean Water for Washington: Why the Concern About Agricultural Contamination in Groundwater?', Cooperative Extension Publication No. EB1632, Washington State University, August.

Diebel, P.L., D.B. Taylor, S.S. Battie and C.D. Heatwoll (1992), 'Tradeoffs Between Water Quality and the Economic Impact of Low-Input Agriculture in the Costal Plain of Virginia', Working Paper No. 92-12, Kansas State University, Manhattan.

Dorcey, A.H.J. and J.R. Griggs (1991), *Water in Sustainable Development: Exploring our Common Future in the Fraser River Basin*, Westwater Research, UBC, Vancouver.

Fullerton, D.J. (1991a), *Economic Feasibility of Alternative Composting Systems*, BC Ministry of Agriculture, Fisheries and Food, Abbotsford, July.

Fullerton, D.J. (1991b), *Economic Feasibility of Poultry Manure Treatment Systems*, BC Ministry of Agriculture, Fisheries and Food, Abbotsford.

Harris, T.R., S.W. Stoddard and J.C. Bezdek (1993), 'Application of Fuzzy-Set Clustering for Regional Typologies', *Growth and Change*, **24** (Spring): 155–65.

Hauser, A., G.C. van Kooten and L. Cain (1994), 'Water Quality and the Abbotsford Aquifer: Overview and Cost–Benefit Analysis of Livestock Waste Disposal Alternatives using Contingent Valuation Methods', Agricultural Economics Working Paper No. 94-2, University of British Columbia, Vancouver.

Hoehn, J.P. (1992), 'Natural Resource Damage Assessment and Contingent

Valuation: Issues and Research Needs', Staff Paper No. 92-36, East Lansing, Department of Agricultural Economics, Michigan State University, Michigan.

Hof, J.G. (1993), *Coactive Forest Management*, Academic Press, San Diego.

Johansson, P.O. (1987), *The Economic Theory and Measurement of Environmental Benefits*, Cambridge University Press, Cambridge.

Klir, G. and T. Folger (1988), *Fuzzy Sets, Uncertainty and Information*, Prentice-Hall, Englewood Cliffs, New Jersey.

Knetsch, J. (1989), 'The Endowment Effect and Evidence of Nonreversible Indifference Curves', *American Economic Review*, **79** (December): 1277-84.

Knetsch, J. (1993), 'Resource Economics: Persistent Conventions and Contrary Evidence', in W.L. Adamowicz, W. White and W.E. Phillips (eds), *Forestry and the Environment: Economic Perspectives*, CAB International, Wallingford, UK.

Kosko, B. (1992), *Neural Networks and Fuzzy Systems*, Prentice-Hall, Englewood Cliffs, New Jersey.

Kosko, B. and S. Isaka (1993), 'Fuzzy Logic', *Scientific American*, **269**, (1 July): 76-81.

Liebscher, H., B. Hii and D. McNaughton (1992), *Nitrates and Pesticides in the Abbotsford Aquifer*, Environment Canada, July.

Muia, M.J. and M.P. Thomas (1990), 'A Question of Nitrates', *Environmental Education and Information*, **9**: 91-100.

Napier, T.L. (1983), *Water Resource Research. Problems and Potential for Agricultural Communities*, Soil Conservation Society of America, Ankeny, Iowa.

Stennes, B. (1992), 'The Economics of Off-Farm Litter Disposal Options for South Coastal BC Poultry Farms', Stennes Consulting, Delta, BC Report prepared for BC Ministry of Agriculture, Fisheries and Food – Farm Management Branch as a part of the Canada–BC Soil Conservation Program.

van Kooten, G.C. and R. Athwal (1996), 'Costs and Benefits of Improving Water Quality by Composting Livestock Wastes: An Application of Contingent Valuation', Agricultural Economics Working Paper, Wageningen Agricultural University, Netherlands.

van Kooten, G.C., R.A. Schoney and K.A. Hayward (1986), 'An Alternative Approach to the Evaluation of Goal Hierarchies among Farmers', *Western Journal of Agricultural Economics*, **11**: 40-49.

23 Policy Instruments to Control Multi-nutrients in an Agricultural Watershed

A. Lintner[a] *and A.J. Weersink*[b]

Introduction

Nutrients, such as nitrogen and phosphorus, are applied by agricultural producers to enhance plant growth. However, costs in terms of on-farm productivity reduction (Briggs and Bos, 1990) and off-farm water pollution (Pearce *et al.*, 1985; PLUARG, 1978) can result if soil and/or the applied nutrients are lost through erosion and water infiltration. Nutrient water pollution can cause a number of health problems, upset ecosystem integrity and reduce recreational values. The health effects from excess nitrates include infantile *methaemoglobinaemia*, or 'blue baby syndrome', and stomach cancer in adults (Health and Welfare Canada, 1980; Hanley, 1990). In addition, excess nutrients can cause the growth of blue-green algae that produce toxins that are harmful to humans if ingested (Fuller and Flemming, 1990). A nutrient imbalance can affect the food web dynamic by upsetting the photoplankton community and cause excess algae growth that depletes the dissolved oxygen as it decays (Environment Canada, 1987). These ecosystem impacts may also influence the recreational enjoyment of the environment. A reduction in oxygen from eutrophication can decrease the stock of valued fish species such as trout and increase the stock of other species that require little oxygen such as sludge worms and carp (Environment Canada 1987).

Agriculture is the major contributor of nutrients in the waters of the Great

[a] Department of Economics, Wilfrid Laurier University, Waterloo, ON, Canada.
[b] Department of Agricultural Economics and Business, University of Guelph, Guelph, ON, Canada N1G 2W1.

Lakes Basin (GLWQB, 1989). Phosphorus (P) was the key nutrient in the eutrophication of Lake Erie in the late 1960s and 1970s (Environment Canada, 1987). Concern over phosphorus levels in the Basin led to the implementation of programmes such as the Soil and Water Environmental Enhancement Program (SWEEP) and Tillage 2000, which encouraged farmers to change to less erosive farming practices in order to reduce the amount of phosphorus runoff into the Great Lakes (Stonehouse and Bohl, 1990). The switch to conservation tillage from conventional tillage can raise nitrogen (N) concentration in the groundwater. Tillage stimulates mineralization and nitrification while slowing denitrification, thereby reducing nitrogen leaching into the groundwater, but it leaves the surface more susceptible to erosion and runoff (OECD, 1986). Reducing tillage results in greater infiltration (Bedient and Huber, 1992; Kachanoski and Rudra, 1992). Indeed, the level of nitrates has risen and this emphasizes the need to consider potential trade-offs in pollutants when examining how water quality objectives may be efficiently attained.

Despite the observed trade-offs among nutrient pollutants from agriculture and the joint effect these pollutants can have on water quality, previous studies have generally focused on only one type of pollution at a time. For example, the nitrogen problem was studied by Fernandez-Santos *et al.* (1993), by Johnson *et al.* (1991), by Moxey and White (1994), by Pan and Hodge (1994) and by Helfand and House (1995); the soil erosion and/or sediment-bound phosphorus problem was studied by Braden *et al.* (1989, 1991) and by Bouzaher *et al.* (1990). Teague *et al.* (1995) developed an environmental risk index for both pesticides and nitrates and examined the effects on farm income from a reduction in these indices, but did not look at alternative instruments for achieving the environmental objectives. Kramer *et al.* (1984) used a model to account for both sediment and sediment-bound phosphorus as well as soluble nitrogen, but 'no attention was made to model the delivery mechanism for agricultural nonpoint source pollution' (Kramer *et al.* 1984: 843). Another limitation of previous studies is their treatment of the watershed as a single farm unit under the control of a social planner. If the existence of actual farm units and decision makers is not incorporated into the analysis, the interdependency of individual farm decisions and emissions for the entire watershed may be ignored. Without individual farm units in the model, environmental policy instruments, such as Segerson's (1988) ambient scheme, cannot be evaluated.

The purpose of this chapter is to evaluate pollution control instruments aimed at simultaneously controlling the concentrations of sediment-bound and soluble nutrients within an agricultural watershed in Ontario. The multi-contaminant watershed management problem presented in this chapter determines the cost-effective farming and abatement activities while attempting to meet water quality objectives for three types of nutrient pollution: sediment-bound nitrogen and phosphorus in surface water and soluble nitrogen in groundwater and surface water. The least-cost solution cannot be attained through firm-specific, emission-based instruments, which are infeasible owing to monitoring problems. As a result, the efficiency and environmental effectiveness costs of four input and ambient based regulatory instruments are examined. Included is the system of taxes and subsidies based on a threshold ambient concentration proposed by Segerson (1988) in order to address the diffuse source pollution problem. The modelling of actual firms within a watershed, as opposed to the field-specific approach of previous studies, permits what is believed to be the first empirical examination of Segerson's instrument. Details on the model and data used are provided in the next section. Results of the base and cost-effective solutions to the watershed management problem are presented, followed by an evaluation of the four control instruments. The final section provides a summary and discusses possible extensions to the multi-contaminant model.

Model of Pollutant Control

Nutrients used in agricultural production are transported with surface water and groundwater through runoff and infiltration, respectively. Switching from conventional to conservation tillage increases crop residues on the soil surface. The rougher surface due to these residues allows less water to run off, thereby reducing soil erosion. While sediment-bound emissions may be reduced, soluble emissions into the groundwater may increase owing to the larger soil pores associated with conservation tillage. Concentrations of the nutrient pollutants in the surface water and groundwater are jointly determined by water volumes, emissions, transport mechanisms and pollutant pathways. A hydrological simulation model is necessary to estimate the level of the various emissions.

Social Planner

The objective of the regulator's economic model is to maximize watershed profits while meeting water quality objectives for both sediment-bound and soluble pollutants. The sediment-bound pollutants are phosphorus and nitrogen moving into the surface water. Soluble pollutants are nitrogen moving to both the surface water and groundwater. Soluble phosphorus emissions are negligible and are ignored in the analysis (Frere *et al.*, 1980). Formally, the problem is represented as:

$$\text{Maximize } x \quad \sum_{j=1}^{f} \sum_{i=1}^{A} \pi_i X_{ij} \tag{23.1a}$$

subject to

$$X_{ij} \geq 0 \ \forall \ i, j \tag{23.1b}$$

$$\sum_{i=1}^{A} X_{ij} = \overline{X}_j \ \forall \ j \tag{23.1c}$$

$$X_{lj} = X_{mj} = X_{nj} \ \forall j, \text{ and crops } l, m, n \text{ in rotation } i \tag{23.1d}$$

$$\frac{\sum_{j=1}^{f} \sum_{i=1}^{A} e_i X_{ij} t_{jo} (X_{i,j+1}, X_{i,j+2}, \cdots, X_{i,f})}{\sum_{j=1}^{f} \sum_{i=1}^{A} r_i X_{ij} + RO} * 100 \leq \overline{P} \tag{23.1e}$$

$$\frac{(\sum_{j=1}^{f} \sum_{i=1}^{A} enb_i X_{ij} t_{jo} (X_{i,j+1}, X_{i,j+2}, \cdots, X_{i,f})) + (\sum_{j=1}^{f} \sum_{i=1}^{A} ens_i X_{ij} + NSO)}{\sum_{j=1}^{f} \sum_{i=1}^{A} r_i X_{ij} + RO} * 100 \leq \overline{SN} \tag{23.1f}$$

$$\frac{\sum_{j=1}^{f} \sum_{i=1}^{A} eng_i X_{ij}}{\sum_{j=1}^{f} \sum_{i=1}^{A} d_i X_{ij} + IO} * 100 \leq \overline{GN} \tag{23.1g}$$

Profits are maximized by the amount of land allocated to farming activity i in field j (X_{ij}). Watershed profit is the sum of returns for each of the A possible activities on each of the f possible fields with net returns per hectare for activity i on field j denoted by p_{ij}. Non-negativity, land availability and rotational conditions are represented by the constraints (*1b*), (*1c*) and (*1d*), respectively. These constraints, together with the objective, make up the profit-maximising problem for the entire watershed when pollution emissions are not controlled. This is the base model.

Environmental constraints on water quality are added to the base model through equations (*1e*), (*1f*) and (*1g*). Constraint *1e* requires that the average concentration of surface water phosphorus, which is equal to total loadings divided by the total volume of runoff, be less than or equal to some level $\overline{P}$ (mg/l). Total loadings are determined by taking emissions from each field and calculating the amount that will reach the watershed outlet. Emissions originating from a particular field j depend on the farm management practices chosen for that field, $\sum_{i=1}^{A} e_i X_{ij}$, where e_i is the emission rate of sediment-bound phosphorus from activity i (kg/ha). The percentage of these emissions from field j that reaches the outlet (O) is given by the transfer coefficient t_{jo}. The transport mechanism depends on activities chosen for all fields downstream from field j, starting from the adjoining field $j + 1$ to the field closest to the water outlet f. Volume of runoff is determined using runoff depth from activity i (r_i) multiplied by area for all fields engaged in i and then adding runoff from other areas in the watershed, such as bushes and roadways (RO).

The second environmental constraint ($1f$) ensures that nitrogen concentration in surface water does not exceed some specified concentration, $\overline{SN}$. Concentration is calculated in a similar fashion to that of phosphorus discussed above, except that soluble emissions of nitrogen must be accounted for. The first term in the parentheses of total surface nitrogen loadings represents emissions of sediment-bound nitrogen. This level is found by taking emissions from each activity (enb_i), multiplied by area allocated to that activity, with the transport mechanism then used to determine the amount reaching the outlet. The second term in the numerator represents soluble nitrogen emissions. Total soluble nitrogen load for surface water is determined by adding up emissions from each activity (ens_i) and each field plus any other soluble emissions (NSO). The soluble load is in solution in the runoff water and is therefore completely transported to the outlet without any deposition. Runoff volume is calculated using the same method as for phosphorus.

The final constraint, ($1g$), provides a condition for groundwater nitrogen concentration, $\overline{GN}$. The numerator sums the total soluble nitrogen load moving further into the soil, which depends on the emissions of soluble ground pollutant from activity i (eng_i). The denominator calculates the volume of infiltration water as the sum of the depth of infiltration for each activity (d_i) multiplied by the area for each of the activities and each of the fields. Infiltration from the bushes, farmsteads and the road must be also accounted for (IO).

Individual Farm Model

The j fields in the social planner model are not generally owned and operated by j individuals. Rather, an individual producer manages a set of fields. The multi-contaminant model just developed can be extended to account for this situation by setting up h objective functions where h is the number of farm operators (h^2j). Each operator chooses the activities for fields only under his or her control independent of the activities of others. The social planner has control over all fields in the watershed.

Empirical Model

The multi-contaminant pollutant control model is applied to an Ontario agricultural watershed to determine the effectiveness of policy instruments for achieving environmental objectives. The next section describes the information used to implement the model.

Study Area

The watershed used in this study is a sub-watershed of the Lake St Clair drainage basin located in Maidstone Township, Essex County, Ontario. This 280-hectare watershed was chosen for the Pilot Watershed Study by Agriculture Canada to examine the effects of alternative farming practices on soil erosion and phosphorus contamination (Agriculture Canada, 1990). The 15 farms partly contained within the boundary of the watershed happen to possess identical physical characteristics (slope, soil type and so on) in all aspects except distance from watershed outlet. The watershed is further divided into 65 fields among these 15 farms.

Management Systems

Agricultural activities of the watershed are exclusively cash cropping, with soybean, corn and wheat grown on 56, 14 and 10 per cent, respectively, of the watershed over the period 1989 to 1991 (Deloitte and Touche, 1992a). Five three-year crop rotations based on actual rotations employed over the life of the Pilot Watershed Study are evaluated: (1) continuous corn (CCC); (2) corn followed by two years of soybean (CSS); (3) corn–soybean–wheat (CSW); (4) wheat followed by two years of soybean (WSS); and (5) an alfalfa hay pasture (HHH) (see Table 23.1, column 3). These rotations are grown using either conventional tillage (CT) or no-till (NT) (see Table 23.1, column 5). In addition, two nitrogen fertilization levels are assumed for corn (see Table 23.1, column 6). The first is the actual average application (A) given in the Pilot Watershed Study (Deloitte and Touche, 1992b). The second is the efficient use (M) defined where the marginal value product of nitrogen is equal to its cost. Yield response curves from Beauchamp *et al.* (1987) were used to determine marginal product. Actual average applications of fertilizer were used where possible for the remaining crops; otherwise, suggested

Table 23.1   Farm management practices and pollutant parameters

Practice	Activity (i)	Rotation	Crop	Tillage	Fertil.	Annual profits ($/ha)	3 yr av. profits ($/ha)	Sed P (e)	Sed N (enb)	Sol N (ens)	Ground Sol N (eng)	Runoff (r) (mm)	Infilt. (d) (mm)
1	1	CCC	C	CT	A	93.33	93.33	1.01	2.03	1.09	2.48	47	35
2	2	CCC	C	CT	M	59.32	59.32	1.01	2.03	1.23	2.88	47	35
3	3	CCC	C	NT	A	137.25	137.25	0.30	0.61	0.64	4.67	32	50
4	4	CCC	C	NT	M	103.49	103.49	0.30	0.61	0.73	5.42	32	50
5	5	CSS	C	CT	A	214.19	172.61	1.20	2.39	1.09	2.48	47	35
	6	CSS	S	CT	A	151.83		0.95	1.91	0.08	0.06	38	44
	7	CSS	S	CT	A	151.83		1.12	2.24	0.95	2.17	47	35
6	8	CSS	C	CT	M	214.85	172.84	1.20	2.39	0.08	0.06	38	44
	9	CSS	S	CT	A	151.83		0.95	1.91	0.08	0.06	38	44
	10	CSS	S	CT	A	151.83		1.12	2.24	0.08	0.06	32	50
7	11	CSS	C	NT	A	253.10	144.70	0.57	1.13	0.64	4.67	25	57
	12	CSS	S	NT	A	90.50		0.54	1.07	0.06	0.08	25	57
	13	CSS	S	NT	A	90.50		0.52	1.02	0.57	4.08	32	50
8	14	CSS	C	NT	M	255.90	145.63	0.57	1.13	0.06	0.08	25	57
	15	CSS	S	NT	A	90.50		0.54	1.07	0.06	0.08	25	57
	16	CSS	S	NT	A	90.50		1.01	2.03	1.09	2.48	47	35
9	17	CSW	C	CT	A	204.26	161.53	0.95	1.91	0.08	0.06	38	44
	18	CSW	S	CT	A	151.83		0.63	1.26	0.42	1.52	39	43
	19	CSW	W	CT	A	128.50		1.01	2.03	1.39	3.24	47	35
10	20	CSW	C	CT	M	223.43	167.92	0.95	1.91	0.08	0.06	38	44
	21	CSW	S	CT	A	151.83		0.63	1.26	0.42	1.52	39	43
	22	CSW	W	CT	A	128.50		0.56	1.11	0.64	4.67	32	44
11	23	CSW	C	NT	A	244.28	154.87	0.54	1.07	0.06	0.08	25	57
	24	CSW	S	NT	A	90.50		0.37	0.74	0.30	3.20	27	50
	25	CSW	W	NT	A	129.82		0.56	1.11	0.82	6.11	32	55
12	26	CSW	C	NT	M	264.69	161.67	0.54	1.07	0.06	0.08	25	57
	27	CSW	S	NT	A	90.50		0.37	0.74	0.30	3.20	25	50
	28	CSW	W	NT	A	129.82		0.63	1.26	0.42	1.52	39	43
13	29	WSS	W	CT	A	128.50	144.05	0.79	1.57	0.08	0.06	38	44
	30	WSS	S	CT	A	151.83		1.12	2.24	0.08	0.06	38	44
	31	WSS	S	CT	A	151.83		0.37	0.74	0.30	3.20	27	55
14	32	WSS	W	NT	A	129.82	103.61	0.49	0.99	0.06	0.08	25	57
	33	WSS	S	NT	A	90.50		0.52	1.02	0.08	0.06	38	57
	34	WSS	S	NT	A	90.50		0.59	1.18	0.08	0.06	24	44
15	35	HHH	H	NT	A	70.99	70.99	0.21	0.10	0.20	0.00	40	58
–	–	Bush	–	–	–	0.00	0.00	0.00	0.00	0.00	0.00		
–	–	Farm	–	–	–	0.00	0.00	0.00	0.00	0.00	0.00		42

Note: Crops in rotation are corn (C), soybeans (S), wheat (W) and hay (H); tillage choices are conventional tillage (CT) or no-till (NT). Corn fertilization levels (Fertil.) are either efficient (M) or actual use (A).

applications given by the Ontario Ministry of Agriculture and Food (1988) were used (both are denoted A).

A total of 35 farming activities representing a combination of crop within a particular rotation, tillage practice and fertilizer application are identified. Together these annual activities define 15 farm management practices that are a specific combination of crop rotation (5), tillage method (2) and corn fertilization level (2).[1] Yield, output price and input cost for each farming activity are based on actual farm data gathered in the Pilot Watershed Study (Agriculture Canada, 1990; Deloitte and Touche, 1992a, 1992b) or, if the necessary information was not gathered, from provincial sources (OMAF, 1988, 1992). Table 23.1 lists the subsequent net revenues for each annual activity (column 7) and for each farm management practice averaged over three years (column 8). Corn is the most profitable activity provided it is in rotation with another crop. The most profitable farm management practice is corn followed by two years of soybeans. Soybeans allow for higher corn yield and a lower cost than other rotations that include corn. The least profitable farm management practice is continuous, no-till corn.

Emissions and Transport

Field characteristics, rainfall and farm management practices are all used in the hydrological simulation model to determine the level of emissions and their transport generated under alternative conditions. The Agricultural Non-Point Source Pollution (AGNPS) model was chosen for its ability to determine surface and groundwater implications for many different pollutants, including nitrogen and phosphorus, at the same time (Young *et al.*, 1994). Emissions of soluble nitrogen available to leach into the groundwater are determined through AGNPS using the Chemicals, Runoff and Erosion Agricultural Management Systems algorithm (Frere *et al.*, 1980). Infiltration and runoff volumes resulting from the different farm management practices are calculated using the Soil Conservation Service Curve Number method (Bedient and Huber, 1992). The transport mechanism for sediment-bound pollution is determined using the soil deposition output from the AGNPS model. The pathways indicate the direction of the movement of the pollutants to the watershed outlet from each of the fields. The transport mechanism determines, for each farm management practice chosen, the amount of pollutants from any given field that reach the outlet, given the farming activities chosen 'downstream'. Water volumes, emissions, transport mechanism and pollutant pathways all jointly determine the pollution concentrations in the surface water and groundwater.

Sediment-bound emissions of nitrogen (*enb*) and phosphorus (*e*) are listed for each activity in Table 23.1 (columns 9 and 10). Sediment-bound emissions for both pollutants are highest for corn in the corn–soy–soy rotations under conventional tillage (activities 5 and 8). The second year of soybeans in the same rotation with conventional tillage emits the second highest amount of sediment-bound pollutants. A switch from conventional tillage to no-till reduces sediment-bound emissions of both nitrogen and phosphorus. Emissions of soluble nitrogen (*ens*) moving to surface water (Table 23.1, column 11) are highest for corn under conventional tillage. Again, a switch to no-till reduces emissions to the surface water. Soluble groundwater nitrogen emissions (*eng*) are highest for no-till corn activities (Table 23.1, column 12). In contrast to soluble nitrogen moving to surface water, a switch from conventional tillage to no-till will increase emissions of soluble nitrogen moving to the groundwater. In general, a movement to no-till farming will decrease runoff and increase infiltration, as indicated by the levels of runoff (*r*) and infiltration (*d*) (Table 23.1, columns 13 and 14).

Results

Base Model

The profit maximization solution for the entire watershed when pollution emissions are not controlled is for all farms to grow a rotation of corn followed by two years of soybean using conventional tillage with efficient nitrogen use on corn (farm management practice 6). Average profits for the entire watershed over the three years are $47 129.10 per year and each farm will earn annually per hectare average profits of $172.84. Average emissions, runoff and infiltration per hectare are also the same for every farm. These values, combined with the transport mechanism, determine the concentrations of the three pollutants. At the outlet of the watershed, the phosphorus concentration is 0.8 milligrams of phosphorus per litre (mg P/l) with yearly concentrations ranging from 0.67mg P/l in the year corn is grown to 1.28mg P/l in the second year of soybeans owing to the higher erosion caused by the latter crop. Nitrogen concentrations are 2.4 and 1.7 milligrams of nitrogen per litre (mg N/l) in the surface water and groundwater, respectively. Yearly concentrations in the surface water are 3.30mg N/l when corn is grown, 2.36mg N/l in the first soybean year, increasing to 2.77mg N/l when the second soybean crop is planted. In this case, the erosivity of the soybean crop is counterbalanced by the low soluble nitrogen emissions associated with soybeans. Groundwater nitrogen concentrations are much higher when corn is grown in the rotation (5.31mg N/l vs. 0.16mg N/l for soybeans) owing to the high application levels of nitrogen fertilizer required for corn.

The results suggest there is no groundwater quality problem since the soluble nitrogen concentration (1.7mg N/l) is below the Canadian drinking water quality guideline of 10mg N/l. The surface water phosphorus concentration of 0.8mg P/l would indicate a potential eutrophication problem since the surface phosphorus concentration is greater than 0.01mg P/l (Mengel and Kirkby, 1987: 342). However, the emissions that reach the Belle River will depend upon whether or not the land use between the watershed and the river serves to further reduce or to enhance the transport of emissions. For example, if farmland between the watershed outlet and the Belle River is under no-till, emissions originating from the watershed may be reduced to a negligible amount. Although these issues are important to the amount of pollution reaching the Belle River, and eventually Lake St Clair, for the purposes of this chapter the surface water quality is considered at the watershed outlet.

Cost-effective Abatement

Since water quality objectives are only violated with respect to the level of phosphorus in surface water, the cost-effective allocation of farming activities is determined for reducing the phosphorus concentration, while at the same time maintaining the nitrogen water quality objectives that the surface nitrogen concentration be no more that 10 times the phosphorus concentration and that watershed groundwater concentration of nitrogen be no more than 10mg N/l. The optimal allocation of farming and abatement activities is determined where the marginal benefit of abatement is equal to the marginal abatement cost (Field and Olewiler, 1995). Since the marginal benefits of phosphorus abatement are unknown and a phosphorus concentration level less than the eutrophication threshold of 0.01mg P/l cannot be achieved with any farming activities, the 'optimal level' of abatement is assessed by arbitrarily setting the water quality goal at a surface water phosphorus concentration of 0.64mg P/l, which represents a 20 per cent reduction in the concentration.

The cost-effective solution to this environmental goal requires only two downstream farms to change from their base solution practice of growing a corn–soy–soy rotation under conventional tillage. These two farms each switch one field to conventionally tilled corn–soy–wheat (management practice 10) and one field to no-till corn–soy–wheat (management practice 12) (see Table 23.2). Initial restrictions on phosphorus prompt a change in the last crop grown in the rotation because of the lower emissions of sediment-bound pollutants and lower transport coefficients associated with growing wheat as compared to soybeans. Further constraints on phosphorus up to the 20 per cent level cause no-till continuous corn to be grown on one field by the two affected farms.

Annual watershed profits are reduced by \$113.15 to \$47 015.95 or \$172.42/ha.[2] Profits of the two farms are reduced by 1.5 per cent and 3.3 per cent, respectively, relative to the base solution. The shadow value of this 20 per cent reduction in phosphorus concentration is \$1415.90 per mg/l, which can be used as the marginal abatement cost for the purpose of setting emission taxes.[3] Despite the restrictions on the phosphorus concentrations, water quality objectives on nitrogen concentrations are still met. Surface water nitrogen concentration of 2.2mg N/l fell as a result of the switch in management practices, but groundwater nitrogen concentration rose from 1.8mg N/l on both affected farms to 2.9mg N/l and 4.1mg N/l. The result illustrates the trade-off between nutrient pollutant levels that motivated development of the multi-contaminant model. Other empirical examples may lead to situations where all excess nutrient levels exceed optimal levels.

Evaluation of Control Instruments

The socially optimal instrument would achieve the environmental goal(s) at least cost. The cost-effective solution above involves firm-specific standards on emission levels (performance base).[4] However, firm-specific standards or taxes on relatively homogeneous farms may be administratively difficult for the regulator to implement, and politically infeasible. Uniform instruments on emissions[5] may then be an alternative, but both firm-specific and uniform performance-based instruments require emissions to be observable. Without the ability to measure or proxy the instruments, the regulator may need to resort to input-based or ambient-based instruments.

Since the cost-effective abatement cannot be attained with any policy instrument under present technology, the environmental objectives can only be met by imperfect regulatory instruments. The cost of these instruments relative to the least-cost solution depends upon the degree of heterogeneity in marginal abatement costs among firms and is an empirical question (Helfand and House, 1995). These costs are evaluated for four second-best control instruments: (1) a mandatory switch in farming practices; (2) a ceiling on nitrogen fertilizer applications; (3) a uniform nitrogen fertilizer tax; and (4) an ambient tax/subsidy scheme. Efficiency in meeting the water quality objectives is determined by comparing the outcome of the behaviour of individual farms with the cost-effective allocation of abatement. Efficiency of the instruments relative to the cost-effective allocation is independent of whether or not the specific water quality goal was determined to be efficient in the first place. Not all instruments are able to achieve the desired water quality goal for phosphorus. In those cases, a comparison will be made in terms of the total cost to the farmers of the instrument and how close the phosphorus concentration is to the desired concentration. In the

Table 23.2   **Effects of instruments on farm management practices, profit and water quality**[a]

Instrument	Farm management practice (% of watershed area)					Farm profit before tax ($/ha)	Water quality		
	CSS-CT (6)	CSW-CT (10)	CSW-NT (12)	WSS-CT (13)	HHH (15)		Surface P (mg/l)	Surface N (mg/l)	Ground N (mg/l)
Base	1.00					172.84	0.80	2.4	1.7
Cost-effective abatement	0.94	0.04	0.02			172.42	0.64	2.2	1.9
Mandatory switch to no-till			1.00			161.67	0.43[b]	2.2	5.5
N ceiling									
(0 kg N/ha)					1.00	70.99	0.64	1.5	0.1
(29 kg N/ha)				1.00		144.05	0.75	2.0	1.2
Ambient tax/subsidy ($1415.9/mg P/l)	0.94	0.04	0.02			172.42	0.64	2.2	1.9

Notes: [a] Dollar values and concentrations are averaged over the duration of a rotation (3 years); practices: CSS = corn–soy–soy, CSW = corn–soy–wheat, WSS = wheat–soy–soy, HHH = continuous hay, CT = conventional tillage, NT = no till; (.) = farm management practice from Table 23.1.
[b] Instrument exceeds P goal by 33%.

cases that do achieve the desired goal for the phosphorus concentration, they may have varying impacts on the other water quality measures as well as potential differences in efficiency. Because the dollar values of the damages done by the different pollutants are not known, the impact of the instrument on other water quality measures is merely noted. Each of the instruments is discussed in turn. All results are summarized in Table 23.2.

The regulator could require a mandatory switch to no-till practices in an effort to reduce erosion and subsequently surface water concentrations of the nutrient pollutants. Imposing such a best management practice would be relatively easy to observe with a trip in a small plane over the watershed or through the use of satellite remote sensing. In response to the regulation on tillage, the entire watershed would switch to no-till corn–soy–wheat (practice 12) since this is the most profitable no-till practice. Groundwater nitrogen concentrations increase to 5.5mg N/l (which is still lower than the drinking water guideline) since more nitrogen is applied with wheat now included in rotation and more is infiltrating the soil with the use of no-till. Annual watershed profits are reduced to $161.67/ha/yr, a 6.5 per cent decrease from the cost-effective solution.[6]

Since the cost-effective outcome induces a reduction in surface water nitrogen concentrations along with the change in the phosphorus concentration, perhaps it is possible to achieve the desired water quality goals using controls based on nitrogen fertilizer applications. Because corn yield response to nitrogen is the same for both tillage practices, the desired reduction in loadings has to occur through a change in crop choice rather than through a switch from conventional tillage to no-till. The only means by which the surface water phosphorus concentration of the cost-effective solution can be met is by entirely restricting nitrogen fertilizer use. All nutrient emissions will be lowered, as the optimal solution would be to plant the entire watershed to hay. Since profits will be reduced by 59 per cent, this instrument is inefficient and overly effective. A nitrogen fertilizer tax of 300 per cent would induce the same outcome as the ceiling of zero kg N/ha. The crop rotation with the next lowest fertilizer requirements is the wheat–soy–soy rotation. Either imposing a restriction equal to the amount of nitrogen used, or requirement that this rotation be grown, results in a decrease in profits of 17 per cent if conventionally tilled. While the nitrogen emissions are reduced, the surface water concentration of phosphorus is increased relative to the cost-effective solution.

Segerson (1988) demonstrated that, when many firms contribute to the ambient concentration, the tax/subsidy on ambient concentrations above/below a threshold level should be equal to the full marginal damage for all farms. This will lead to a situation where the marginal taxes received, when only the tax is applied, will be larger than the marginal damage of the concentration. This must be done to avoid free-riding when individual emissions are unobservable. The diffuse nature of the sediment-bound pollution analysed in this chapter lends itself to the application of the ambient tax suggested by Segerson. If the value of the marginal damages at the cost-effective solution ($1415.90 per mg P/l, or shadow value of a 20 per cent reduction in phosphorus loadings) is shared among the 15 farms in the watershed, the Pigouvian tax would be $94.39 per mg P/l (1415.90/15). Such a tax would lead to free-riding by the downstream farms, who are supposed to change behaviour from the base model in order to achieve the cost-effective abatement level. To avoid free-riding, the regulator should implement a tax/subsidy equal to the marginal damage of $1415.90 per mg P/l. If the rest of the watershed engages in their base profit-maximizing choice (conventionally tilled corn–soy–soy), one of the two affected downstream farms will choose to change practices to that of the regulator's cost-effective solution. Given the high costs of ambient concentration, profit-maximizing choice for this specific farm is to change practices regardless of the practices chosen by the other farm. This farm will change to the regulator's cost-effective solution even if the other affected farm engages in the regulator's cost-effective activities which will be the profit-maximizing choice for the latter farm as predicted by Segerson (1988). Thus the efficient solution is reached.

If an ambient tax only is applied, all farms share in paying the total tax, which is 15 times the marginal damage, and there is no longer a balanced budget (Segerson, 1988). The same result, however, can be achieved with the tax/subsidy scheme that pays the marginal damage ($1415.90 per mg P/l) under the threshold of 0.64mg P/l and charges the same over the threshold. The profit-maximizing choice for the two affected downstream farms will exactly meet the threshold and no taxes (or subsidies) will be paid. Farmers would prefer the ambient tax to a firm-specific emission tax, if feasible, since no taxes are actually paid. However, it should be noted that this instrument transfers the burden of information from the planner to the farmers. For the ambient scheme, the planner needs to observe only the concentration and apply the tax/subsidy to every farmer equally. Farmers need to have full information about other farmers' activities and the transport mechanism. The increase in informational requirements may lead farmers to believe that another, perhaps inefficient, instrument may be better.

Conclusions

A multi-contaminant management model of an actual Ontario watershed was developed to examine the cost-effective farming and abatement activities while meeting water quality objectives for four types of nutrient pollution: sediment-bound and soluble nitrogen and sediment-bound phosphorus in surface water, along with soluble nitrogen in groundwater. Not only is more than one type of pollution considered, but the actual farms in the watershed are recognized, rather than the watershed being treated as a single unit with differing fields. The emissions originating from any particular farm are dependent upon the abatement activities of the farmer and the abatement activities of other farmers within the watershed. This interdependence of emissions will lead to a more complicated efficiency condition for incentive control instruments, because a farm's transport coefficients are no longer fixed values.

Four control instruments were evaluated in terms of their cost efficiency and effectiveness in meeting the environmental objectives. Although the farms in the watershed examined are nearly homogeneous, the farms are heterogeneous in terms of abatement for surface water nutrients. The interdependence of emissions created a situation where the cost-efficient solution involved only two farms changing their behaviour to meet the desired water quality goals. The only instrument that achieved the same pattern of farming and abatement activities as the cost-effective allocation, as well as the desired water quality goals, was the ambient tax scheme which has not been previously tested in an empirical application. Provided the marginal damages can be estimated, the tax/subsidy scheme would be preferred over a firm-specific emission instrument by the farmers because of the smaller impact on profitability and by the regulator because of the relative ease of enforcement. However, the transfer of informational requirements on other farm activities and the transport mechanism from the planner to the farmer may lead farmers to prefer another, less efficient instrument.

The hydrological simulation used in this model is based on a single storm that occurs at the same time in each of the three years. When the uncertainty in rainfall is taken into account in the creation of nutrient pollution, the most severe storms will lead to the greatest concentrations of nutrient pollution. If the instrument is set sufficiently high to ensure that the cost-effective concentrations of pollution are met in the worst-case storm event, the concentrations in other less severe events will be much lower than the desired concentrations. This will put a huge financial burden on the firms involved and lead to 'overregulation' in all but the most severe (and least probable) case. Baumol and Oates (1988) suggest a two-part instrument of a standard and a penalty which will only be applied if the standard is violated. Segerson (1988) also suggests that the combination tax/subsidy for ambient concentrations is effective in the face of this type of uncertainty. These instruments could quite easily be tested empirically in the framework of the multi-contaminant model developed in this chapter.

Uncertainty in the timing, duration and intensity of rainfall will influence not only the concentrations of pollutants but also the yields that farmers realize. Risk-averse behaviour may cause reactions to control instruments to differ, particularly if no-till and other practices have more variability than conventional till counterparts. Along the same lines, farm management practices could be extended to include more farm choices, giving farmers more flexibility and perhaps decreasing the inefficiency of some of the control instruments. With or without these extensions, the model developed in this chapter can be applied to other economic problems where the joint outcomes of individual actions are interdependent in creating an outcome that the regulator desires to control.

Notes

1   We define 15 rather than 20 (5*2*2) farm management practices since the pasture rotation involves only one tillage choice and, along with the WSS rotation, does not include corn and subsequently has one fertilization level.

2   Reduction in phosphorus concentrations can be attained for relatively small changes in overall watershed profitability. However, the loss in profit from the environmental restrictions is borne largely by downstream farms, such as in the example. A 10 per cent (60 per cent) reduction in phosphorus concentrations at the outlet requires a switch of farming on only 3 per cent (29 per cent) of the watershed. Many farms not near the watershed outlet need not change farming practices at all. As the fields around the watershed outlet change cropping choice and tillage practice, the amount of sediment-bound pollution which reaches the pollution receptor from farms further away also declines.

3   A constant marginal benefit of phosphorus abatement of \$1415.90 per mg P/l would result in the same 20 per cent reduction in phosphorus concentrations at the outlet. The cost-effective level of abatement (0.80−0.64), would cost \$113.20 for abatement and provide \$226.54 in benefits (\$1415.90 per mg P/l × 0.16 mg P/l). The net benefits would thus be \$113.34 (\$226.54 − \$113.20).

4   A firm-specific tax of \$18.62/kgP on the two farms concerned will induce those farms to change from the base practice 6 to growing the corn–soy–wheat rotation using no-till (practice 12) on their entire farms. This corner solution is the result of the risk neutrality and lumpy abatement technology assumptions made in the modelling of individual farm management decisions.

5   Water quality objectives can also be met if a 22 per cent reduction in phosphorus emissions is imposed on all firms. The uniform reduction in emissions requires that all but one farm must lower emissions relative to the firm-specific standard. The reduction is achieved by all farms switching 40 per cent of their area to the no-till corn–soy–wheat rotation (practice 12). Profits for each farm and for the watershed decrease by 2.6 per cent relative to the base solution.

6   Abatement activity for the mandatory switch to no-till is the same as with the uniform phosphorus emissions tax. However, actions are observable and farmers pay no taxes, so

that the reduction in profits is 6.5 per cent as opposed to 11.7 per cent with the uniform emission tax.

References

Agriculture Canada (1990), *Soil Survey of the Pilot Watersheds Southwestern Ontario Soil and Water Environmental Enhancement Program*, Ecological Services for Planning, Guelph.

Baumol, W.J. and W.E. Oates (1988), *The Theory of Environmental Policy*, 2nd edn, Cambridge University Press, New York.

Beauchamp, E.G., P.G. Nedwick and R.W. Sheard (1987), *Nitrogen Requirements for Corn in Southwestern Ontario, 1987*, Dept of Land Resource Science, University of Guelph, Guelph.

Bedient, P.B. and W.C. Huber (1992), *Hydrology and Floodplain Analysis*, 2nd edn, Addison-Wesley, Don Mills, Ontario.

Bouzaher, A., J.B. Braden and G.V. Johnson (1990), 'A Dynamic Programming Approach to a Class of Nonpoint Source Pollution Problems', *Management Science*, **36**: 1-15.

Braden, J.B., R.S. Larson and E.E. Herricks (1991), 'Impact Targets Versus Discharge Standards in Agricultural Pollution Management', *American Journal of Agricultural Economics*, **73**: 388-97.

Braden, J.B., G.V. Johnson, A. Bouzaher and D. Miltz (1989), 'Optimal Spatial Management of Agricultural Pollution', *American Journal of Agricultural Economics*, **71**: 404-13.

Briggs, T. and A.W. Bos (1990), 'The Benefits of Good Water Quality', ENVIR AGFACTS, No. 02-1990, Upper Thames River Conservation Authority, London, Ontario.

Deloitte and Touche Management Consultants (1992a), *An Economic Evaluation of Soil Tillage Techniques: Volume II, Collection and Analysis of Field Data in the Pilot Watershed Study*, Soil and Water Environmental Enhancement Program, Guelph, Ontario.

Deloitte and Touche Management Consultants (1992b), *An Economic Evaluation of Soil Tillage Techniques: Volume III, Field Level Economic Analysis of Changing Tillage Practices in Southwestern Ontario*, Soil and Water Environmental Enhancement Program, Guelph, Ontario.

Environment Canada (1987), *The Great Lakes: An Environmental Atlas and Resource Book*, Government of Canada, Ottawa.

Fernandez-Santos, J., S. Zekri and A.C. Herruzo (1993), 'On-Farm Costs of Reducing Nitrogen Pollution through BMP', *Agriculture Ecosystems & Environment*, **45**: 1-11.

Field, B.O. and N.D. Olewiler (1995) *Environmental Economics*, McGraw-Hill Ryerson, Toronto.

Frere, M.H., J.D. Ross and L.J. Lane (1980), 'Chapter 4: The nutrient submodel. CREAMS. A field scale model for chemicals, runoff and erosion from agricultural management systems', Conservation Research Report No. 26, USDA,

Washington, DC.

Fuller, B. and R. Flemming (1990), 'Managing Liquid Manure Runoff from Manure Stacks and Feedlots', ENVIR AGFACTS, No. 09-1990, Upper Thames River Conservation Authority, London, Ontario.

Great Lakes Water Quality Board (GLWQB) (1989), *1989 Report on Great Lakes Water Quality*, International Joint Commission, Windsor, Ontario.

Hanley, N. (1990), 'The Economics of Nitrate Pollution', *European Review of Agricultural Economics*, **17**: 129–51.

Health and Welfare Canada (1980), *Guidelines for Canadian Drinking Water Quality – 1978 – Supporting Documentation*, Government of Canada, Ottawa.

Helfand, G.E. and B.W. House (1995), 'Regulating Nonpoint Source Pollution Under Heterogeneous Conditions', *American Journal of Agricultural Economics*, **77**: 1024–32.

Johnson, S.L., R.M. Adams and G.M. Perry (1991), 'The On Farm Costs of Reducing Groundwater Pollution', *American Journal of Agricultural Economics*, **73**: 1063–73.

Kachanoski, R.G. and R. Rudra (1992), *Technology and Evaluation Development Sub-Program – Effects of Tillage on the Quality and Quantity of Surface and Subsurface Drainage Water*, University of Guelph, Guelph, Ontario.

Kramer, R.A., W.T. McSweeny, W.R. Kerns and R.W. Stavros (1984), 'An Evaluation of Alternative Policies for Controlling Agricultural Nonpoint Source Pollution', *Water Resources Bulletin*, **20**: 841–6.

Mengel, K. and E.A. Kirkby (1987), *Principles of Plant Nutrition*, International Potash Institute, Bern, Switzerland.

Moxey, A. and B. White (1994), Efficient Compliance with Agricultural Nitrate Pollution Standards', *Journal of Agricultural Economics*, **45**: 27–37.

OECD (Organization for Economic Cooperation and Development) (1986), *Water Pollution by Fertilizers and Pesticides*, OECD, Paris.

Ontario Ministry of Agriculture and Food (1988), '1988 Crop Budgets', Publication 60, OMAF, Toronto.

Ontario Ministry of Agriculture and Food (1992), 'Agricultural Statistics for Ontario 1991', Publication 20, OMAF, Toronto.

Pan, J.H. and I. Hodge (1994), 'Land Use Permits as an Alternative to Fertiliser and Leaching Taxes for the Control on Nitrate Pollution', *Journal of Agricultural Economics*, **45**: 102–12.

Pearce, P.H., F. Bertrand and J.W. Maclaren (1985), *Currents of Change – Final Report: Inquiry on Federal Water Policy*, Inquiry on Federal Water Policy, Ottawa.

PLUARG (1978), *Contribution of Phosphorus to the Great Lakes from Agricultural Land in the Canadian Great Lakes Basin*, International Joint Commission, Windsor, Ontario.

Segerson, K. (1988), 'Uncertainty and Incentives for Nonpoint Pollution Control', *Journal of Environmental Economics Management*, **15**: 87–98.

Stonehouse, D.P. and M. Bohl (1990), 'Land Degradation Issues in Canadian Agriculture', *Canadian Public Policy*, **16**: 418–31.

Teague, M.L., D.J. Bernardo and H.P. Mapp (1995), 'Farm-level Economic Analysis

Incorporating Stochastic Environmental Risk Assessment', *American Journal of Agricultural Economics*, **77**: 8–19.

Young, R.A, C.A. Onstad, D.D. Bosch and W.P. Anderson (1994), *AGNPS, Agricultural Non-Point-Source Pollution Model, Version 4.03, AGNPS User's Guide*, USDA, Washington, DC.

24 Costs and Benefits of Pesticide Reduction in Agriculture: Best Solutions[1]

I. Heinz[a]

Introduction

At the present time there are few empirical studies that deal with the costs and benefits of pesticide use and environmental damage (Williams, 1990; Ruttan, 1994; Zilberman and Marra, 1993; Midmore and Lamkin, 1994; Oskam, 1994; Carlson, 1996). One reason is that the economic approach has not been adopted in the fields of human toxicology and ecotoxicology. Another lies in the number of unsolved methodological problems that stand in the way of widespread application of cost–benefit analysis. This is particularly apparent in political discussions regarding government restrictions on pesticide use and environmental limits; there is an increasing need for scientific evaluative criteria if statutory controls are to be legitimized. Economic investigations of environmental problems show that the cause of ecological damage is frequently to be found in the lack of compensation for damage. The problem is that damage compensation is generally possible only when the party causing the environmental damage, the damaged parties and the environmental damage can be identified. With regard to pesticides, these conditions are frequently not met. An approach to solving this problem is provided in this chapter.

Economic Assessment of Pesticide Environmental Damage

An extensive literature deals with the human toxicological and ecotoxicological risks of pesticide use (Hollis, 1991; Maroni and Fait, 1993; DFG,

[a] Institute for Environment Research, University of Dortmund, D-44221 Dortmund, Germany.

1994; Swanson and Lloyd, 1994; Zimmermann and Dieter, 1994; Lingk, 1995), but much remains to be done. If the ecological and economic consequences of environmental damage could be understood *in their entirety* then it would be possible to weigh the advantages and disadvantages of application bans or restrictions on pesticide use. One part of the environmental effects eludes economic assessment, however, above all because of possible long-term damage and because certain environmental damage is irreversible and cannot adequately be expressed in monetary terms. Environmental damage cannot now be assessed economically, but what information exists regarding its human toxicological and ecotoxicological risks should not fail to be included as physical variables in cost–benefit analysis. Even though it is not now possible to identify all environmental damage caused by pesticides or to evaluate this damage economically, cost–benefit analysis can be a great help in determining the maximum tolerable concentrations of pesticides (for example, in foodstuffs or drinking water), or bans or restrictions aimed at protecting rare plants or animals (National Research Council, 1989; San Juan, 1995).

Environmental standards can prevent a great deal of human toxicological and ecotoxicological damage and ameliorate the damage that has already occurred. The economic assessment of this environmental damage does face methodological problems, but, in contrast, it is a relatively simple matter to determine the costs of *correcting* the damage. Accordingly, water supply companies in areas under intensive farming frequently incur additional costs for water-conditioning measures and other precautions (such as shutting down drawing shafts, or prospecting for uncontaminated water resources) in order to comply with the applicable drinking water maximum concentration values for pesticides. Owing to the complex nature of transport processes in the soil and to diffusion of pollutants, it is possible in only a few cases to identify individual farmers as having caused contamination of the groundwater with their pesticides (for example, see Chapter 23 of the present volume). For this reason, alternative regulatory instruments will be required if water resources and the drinking water supply are to be protected from harmful pesticides. On the other hand, there are still gaps in our knowledge regarding the sensitivity of the human organism and of ecosystems. Although governments are endeavouring to prevent damage to health by implementing, for example, limit values for foodstuffs and drinking water, there is still the matter of residual hazards, small as they may be. For this reason, some recommend dispensing with the use of chemical plant treatment agents altogether.

Most industrial countries regard their environmental standards as providing more or less generous safety margins aimed at minimizing the (in part unknown) residual hazards. In these countries, costs (such as for the treatment of illnesses due to pesticides) would be difficult to determine. This may not be the case in developing countries which have less strict environmental standards.

There is little dispute regarding the benefits of using pesticides (Beach and Carlson, 1993; Zadoks, 1996). These include yields and lower costs obtained with plant treatment and pest control. Bans or restrictions on the use of pesticides, particularly in drinking water catchment areas and conservation areas, lead to lower yields and cost increases for the farmers, thereby impairing profitability.

Applying Cost–Benefit Analysis to External Costs of Pesticide Use

As part of a cost–benefit analysis, the advantages of using pesticides together with the environmental dangers mentioned and their consequential costs are confronted by the goal of finding a rational basis for the public decisions regarding environmental standards or restrictions on pesticide use.

In cost-benefit analysis, additional criteria are also taken into consideration, criteria that are ignored in the optimization decisions taken by individual pesticide users. The farmer is primarily concerned with maximizing the profitability of his business, often ignoring external costs on society (Beach and Carlson, 1993). In order to be able to make decisions regarding application bans or restrictions that are optimal for society as a whole, it is necessary to find out, if possible, what the additional costs are that the farmers incur. After all, what we are talking about here are the social costs of human toxicological and ecotoxicological limit values. As part of the process, a decision will have to be made concerning the political extent to which society is prepared to accept increased costs of health care and protection of wildlife species, for example. In the extreme case, the decision may involve the banning of a pesticide. In such a case, the social benefits should clearly be higher than the costs of banning pesticides.

There is no doubt that the political process, which should lead to *social* optimization of pesticide use, is not free of conflicts, particularly as opposing interests – pesticide manufacturers, the agriculture industry, the foodstuffs industry, the water supply companies, the conservation movement and consumers – are involved. It is important, therefore, to include in this process scientifically based findings regarding the costs and benefits of the government regulation of pesticide use. On the benefits side, *monetary* factors should be included as well, some of which are determined by using stated preference approaches (see Chapter 22 of the present volume). The stated preference approach can be used to determine the extent to which society is prepared to bear the costs for reducing pesticide use. Possible cost savings resulting from reducing pesticide use should be taken into account in political decisions regarding the application of bans or restrictions, say for drinking water (Heinz *et al.*, 1995; van Kooten, Chapter 22 of the present volume). In addition to the pesticide contamination of untreated water and local conditions (for example, the proportion of groundwater or surface water, the water resources available, climatic factors), factors influencing costs are the applicable drinking water limit values for the individual pesticides and their metabolites.

As can be seen from Table 24.1, there are wide variations in the pesticide contamination of water resources in individual countries. In France, Greece, Italy, Portugal and Spain, pesticide contamination of water is comparatively unfavourable. In Europe as a whole, approximately 30 per cent of water supply exceeds the maximum concentration value for pesticides. The proportion of human populations affected is about the same order of magnitude.

Water suppliers' companies will have to make extra costs if they are to comply with the maximum concentration value currently in force: in the member states of the European Community $0.1\mu g/l$ for individual pesticides is prescribed as a strict precautionary limit. The maximum concentration value is frequently criticized, particularly on the grounds that it does not take into consideration the varying toxicological significance of individual pesticides and thus forces pesticide users to incur unnecessary expenses (EUREAU, 1989, 1993, 1994; Parliamentary Office of Science and Technology, 1993; ECPA, 1994; Martijn, 1995; Johnen, 1996). Countries such as the USA, Canada and the former Soviet Union apply differentiated limit values for pesticides, as do the WHO *Guidelines* (WHO, 1993).

Table 24.1   Water contamination from pesticides, 1995

	Total delivery	Groundwater*	Proportion > 0.1 $\mu g/l$ total	Proportion > 0.1 $\mu g/l$ groundwater	Proportion > 0.1 $\mu g/l$ surface water
	mil. m^3	%	%	%	%
Austria	450	49	7	15	0
Denmark	348	99	5	5	n.a.
France	6 080	62	48	40	60
Germany	6 052	64	15	15	15
Greece	950	68	12	n.a.	50
Italy	8 465	48	31	50	50
Netherlands	1 227	69	48	25	100
United Kingdom	7 620	28	26	15	30

Note: *Relatively high deliveries of spring water in Austria and Italy (50% and 37%, respectively).

However, many toxicologists argue that this precautionary maximum concentration value should be retained, since our knowledge of the environmental risks is incomplete, particularly concerning synergistic or interaction effects.

These discussions caused the European Commission to order an investigation into not only the toxicological grounds for the uniform 0.1 μg/l maximum concentration value, but also its economic effects. The results show that the consequential costs of the precautionary limit value vary considerably in the individual EC member states (Heinz *et al.*, 1995). The reason for this is the differing initial conditions in the individual countries with regard to drinking water production. While waterworks in Germany and Austria, for instance, can predominantly make use of groundwater and spring water, in countries such as the United Kingdom drinking water is primarily obtained from surface water. Since surface waters are at higher risk in areas used by agriculture, these countries will incur relatively higher costs in drinking water production.

Also when groundwater makes up a higher proportion of the drinking water source, drinking water production tends to be organized in a more distributed fashion. At the local level, this means that it is considerably easier for negotiations to occur between water supplies and farmers than is the case with large superregional water supply systems, such as those found in France and the United Kingdom. As the study has shown, negotiations of this type usually lead to optimal (as far as costs are concerned) solutions regarding compliance with the maximum pesticides concentration value in force.

In Germany, Austria and The Netherlands, there are numerous examples of water suppliers preferring to finance measures for reducing the pesticide contamination of water resources. Such measures frequently enable them to save many times more in water-conditioning costs. In contradiction to the 'polluter pays' principle, these companies make compensation payments to farmers when the latter cut back on the use of pesticides or dispense with them altogether. They also buy up agricultural land which they then lease back to farmers with conditions such as compulsory organic farming. Further measures include financing not only agricultural advisers but also a series of experiments aimed at the development of environmentally friendly plant protection. But there are also examples of such agreements failing because the costs of preventative measures are too high. In such cases the water suppliers install additional water-conditioning facilities for eliminating pesticides or they acquire new and as yet unpolluted water resources.

Staunch advocates of the polluter pay principle do, however, oppose the situation of water suppliers financing preventative measures. While they support regulations on the pesticide user, these do little to keep farmers from using plant protection products in a way that does harm water resources

(Mapp, 1990). One major reason for this is the complicated transportation processes in the soil, and the numerous and diffuse pesticides, particularly released into surface waters, that make implementation and enforcement of official requirements more difficult. The consequences are failure to comply with the maximum pesticide concentration values in raw water and in drinking water. In many regions of Europe, the authorities actually tolerate (at least for a transitional period) the exceeding of the 0.1 μg/l limit. This is mostly the case when installation of costly water preparation facilities is economically unacceptable (as is particularly the case with smaller groundwater plants that cannot be shut down as no possibility exists of changing over to other and as yet uncontaminated water reserves).

Compared to regulation, approaches involving cooperation between pesticide users and water suppliers are considerably more effective, owing to the fact that they are based on voluntary agreements. Farmers are motivated to change over to farming methods which are protective of water resources. Monitoring and control expenses are a lot lower, especially at the pumping stations where the water suppliers can immediately detect excessive pesticide use. In addition, the parties to these agreements will always choose the *cheapest* combination of measures aimed at ensuring compliance with maximum pesticide concentrations.

As the EC study showed, 10 of the 12 water supply companies investigated in Germany took on some of the costs of conversion in the agricultural section to plant treatment methods which do not harm water resources. These cooperative agreements led to eight water supply companies not needing to apply any additional water-conditioning measures whatsoever. The cost savings they achieved in this way exceeded what would have been spent on preventative measures. Successes of this type will never be achieved by taking the path of officially imposed requirements. Cooperative agreements at the local level, such as are found in Germany and in Austria, are less widespread in other EC countries, and should be considered an exception. In France, the United Kingdom, Italy and The Netherlands, water suppliers employ water-conditioning measures. Cooperative agreements at the local level are hardly possible in vast water catchment areas that cover several thousand square kilometres, particularly when, as is the case in the United Kingdom, pesticide inputs originate to a considerable degree outside agricultural areas. Then the possibilities of buying up land will also be limited. The catchment areas of groundwater plants may be smaller, but they are frequently located in close proximity to road and rail traffic routes where pesticides are employed for weed control. In many places the use of other water resources located away from agricultural areas cannot be considered since the water resources in question are exhausted and also because, as is the case in The Netherlands, no more water extraction rights will be granted. Table 24.2 provides a summary comparison of costs at the European level.

As the EU study showed, all over Europe water-conditioning measures dominate compared with preventative measures (Table 24.3) and this is an indication of the fact that in many countries the changeover to plant protection methods that do not harm water resources is still linked with high costs. Presumably in these countries the financial outlay (transaction costs) required to set up cooperative agreements between pesticide users and water supply companies is prohibitively high. It is therefore understandable when, in countries such as France and the United Kingdom, governments, and sometimes water suppliers, argue in favour of introducing differentiated maximum concentration values for pesticides.

According to information from British water experts, with a maximum concentration for pesticides of 1.0μg/l, water-conditioning measures will no longer be required in many waterworks. For three large water supply companies (Thames Water, Severn Trent Water and Anglian Water) that together supply water to 18.5 million people, 89 per cent of the investment outlay of the total of ECU 730 million required for securing compliance with the 0.1μg/l limit would be unnecessary. On the basis of four major surface water waterworks in the United Kingdom together supplying a total of 527.5 million cubic metres per year, it would be possible to save ECU 35.9 million in water preparation costs every year. For a small groundwater waterworks that delivers 260 000 cubic metres per year, a maximum concentration value of 0.5μg/l would already remove any need for water conditioning and lead to annual savings of ECU 109 000. In a groundwater catchment area in northern Italy that supplies 22.7 million cubic metres of drinking water per year, it would have been possible with limit values of 0.2μg/l, 0.4μg/l and

Table 24.2   **Costs of current maximum pesticide drinking water guidelines, 1995**

	Cost of the 0.1μg/l limit value ECU/m³	Average price of water ECU/m³	Proportion of the costs of the 0.1μg/l limit included in the average price of water %
Austria	0.02	0.78	1
France	0.04	1.22	3
Germany	0.02	1.33	2
Italy	0.04	0.46	6
Netherlands	0.05	1.06	4
United Kingdom	0.07	0.77	8

Source: Heinz *et al.* (1995).

Table 24.3   Cost of achieving EU pesticide drinking water guidelines, 1995

	Average costs at the EU level (weighted average) ECU/m³	Most frequent values at the EU level ECU/m³
Water analysis	0.005	<0.005
Drinking water preparation	0.05	0.05–0.10
Rehabilitation/prevention	0.02	0.02–0.06

0.6μg/l to avoid 31 per cent, 68 per cent and 94 per cent, respectively, of the water preparation and acquisition costs, amounting to a total of ECU 669 000 per year. In the case of one groundwater waterworks in north-eastern Austria that pumps 2.2 million cubic metres each year, a limit value of 1.0μg/l would render unnecessary water preparation costs currently running to ECU 157 000 per year. Even if these figures are really more or less hypothetical cost estimates, they still provide an idea of the economic consequences of changing the current 0.1μg/l maximum concentration value. It is fairly safe to assume that, with a maximum pesticide concentration value of 2.0μg/l, which is the WHO's guideline value for atrazine, drinking water preparation costs in Europe would be negligible. According to British water experts, a similar effect could be achieved in many waterworks by replacing the uniform 0.1μg/l limit value currently in force with differentiated maximum concentration values based on the WHO *Guidelines* (Heinz *et al.*, 1995).

The proponents of 'toxicological' limits for individual pesticides point out that it is possible to make savings in the drinking water supply and to avoid passing on increased costs to private households without additional risks to health. They also stress that it may be the case that chemical compounds are created during water treatment that could be more dangerous than the pesticides which the water-conditioning facilities were installed to eliminate. The opponents of a change in the current maximum concentrations emphasize the need for a precautionary limit considering existing gaps in our knowledge about human toxicological and ecotoxicological effects. They point to the health risks of which the first symptoms have already appeared: increased male infertility, cancers and damage to the nervous and immune systems.

Conclusions

Decision makers who set environmental standards are in a difficult position since scientifically backed knowledge is simply not available regarding either the toxicological effects or the economic effects of pesticide application restrictions or limit values for the maximum tolerable pesticide concentrations in foodstuffs or drinking water. Yet there is ample research making a contribution to a continuing growth in knowledge regarding the environmental risks of pesticides. Even the application of cost–benefit analysis is improving. As the Heinz *et al.* (1995) study for the European Commission concluded, it is in principle possible to determine the costs of changing to plant protection methods that do not harm water resources but benefit the drinking water supply.

Among the most important advantages of a reduction in the use of pesticides we may cite the reduction in the human and ecotoxicological risks. If cases of environmental damage can be identified clearly and unambiguously, it will basically be possible to determine the economic benefits of risk reduction. Here it is primarily a matter of taking up the possible costs that may be saved in the health sector (for example, costs of treatment) and in protection of natural resources (for example, outlay on restoring or replacing biotopes). However, since the environmental risks cannot be completely evaluated using *damage rectification costs*, the advantages of using alternative plant protection methods will have to be taken into consideration in the cost–benefit analysis of the *physical* variables.

An attempt will also need to be made to obtain an economic evaluation of the benefits of reduced environmental risks with the aid of the contingent valuation or stated preference method (Misra *et al.*, 1991; Mitchell and Carson, 1989; Riera, 1995). Of particular interest is the question whether the costs of ensuring compliance with the $0.1\mu g/l$ maximum concentration for pesticides in drinking water will be accepted by the public (Söderqvist, 1994; also Chapter 22 of the present volume). Should this not be the case, this would mean that the benefits of the reduction in risks brought about with this limit value are less than associated costs, so that raising the maximum concentration for pesticides would increase social well-being. Clearly, it does seem important to determine the priorities of the public if we are to achieve an approximate social optimal when deciding on limit values. The decisive question here is to what extent the public is prepared to accept higher water prices or higher prices for food (Mitchell and Carson, 1986; Kramer, 1990; Mapp, 1990; Misra *et al.*, 1991; Weaver *et al.*, 1992; Antinelli *et al.*, 1996; also Chapter 22 of the present volume).

Note

1   As part of the amendment of the Drinking Water Directive, the European Commission, DG XI initiated and financed the study 'Economic efficiency calculations in conjunction

with the Drinking Water Directive (8/778/EEC), Part III: The parameter for pesticides and related products (Annex I of the Directive, Parameter No. 55)'. The study was produced by a German consortium of four research institutes in collaboration with partners from Austria, France, Greece, Italy, The Netherlands, Spain and the United Kingdom. Special thanks are due to my colleagues of the consortium: Arne Flessau at the Institute for Environment Research of the University Dortmund, Ninette Zullei-Seibert, Birgit Kuhlmann and Ulf Schulte-Ebbert at the Institute for Water Research GmbH, Dortmund, Monika Michels and Jochen Simbrey at the Institute for Risk Management, Dortmund and Gerd Fleischer at the Institute for Horticulture Economy of the University of Hanover. Responsibility for errors and views stated in this chapter remains only with the author.

References

Antinelli, A., A. Coletta, and C. Pucci (1996), 'Economic comparison of traditional, guided and biological control of Leptinotarsa Decemlineata Say (*Coleoptera Chrisomelydae*) in Italian potato production', in A. Oskam (ed.), *Policy Measures to Control Environmental Impacts from Agriculture*, Proceedings, International Symposium, Wageningen Agricultural University, 24–7 August 1995.

Beach, E.D. and G.A. Carlson (1993), 'A Hedonic Analysis of Herbicides: Do User Safety and Water Quality Matter?', *American Journal of Agricultural Economics*, **75**: 612–23.

Beitz, H.H.H. Schmidt and F. Herzel (1994), 'Occurrence, Toxicological and Ecotoxicological Significance of Pesticides in Groundwater and Surface Water', in H. Börner (ed.), *Pesticides in Ground and Surface Water*, Springer, Berlin/Heidelberg.

Carlson, G.A. (1996), 'Benefit studies for US pesticide regulation', in A. Oskam (ed.), *Policy Measures to Control Environmental Impacts from Agriculture*, Proceedings, International Symposium, Wageningen Agricultural University, 24–7 August 1995.

DFG (1994), *Ökotoxikologie von Pflanzenschutzmitteln*, Sachstandsbericht, VCH, Weinheim.

ECPA (1994), 'ECPA Proposal for the Revision of Parameter 55 of the Drinking Water Directive (80/778/EEC)', European Crop Protection Association, Brussels.

EUREAU (1989), 'Advice of EUREAU on the respect of Parameter 55 "Pesticides and related products" of Directive 80/778 concerning the quality of water intended for human consumption', Brussels.

EUREAU (1993), *Updated Comments by Eureau on the Revision of the Drinking Water Directive 80/778/EEC*, Brussels.

EUREAU (1994), *Implications for Water Suppliers and Householders of the New WHO Guidelines for Drinking Water Quality*, Brussels.

Heinz, I., N. Zullei-Seibert, G. Fleischer, U. Schulte-Ebbert, and J. Simbrey (1995), *Economic Efficiency Calculations in Conjunction with the Drinking Water Directive (80/778/EEC), Part III: The Parameter for Pesticides and Related Products*, study on behalf of the European Commission, DG XI, Brussels.

Hollis, J.M. (1991), 'Mapping The Vulnerabilty of Aquifers and Surface Waters to

Pesticide Contamination at the National/Regional Scale', in A. Walker (ed.), *Pesticides in Soils and Water: Current Perspectives*, The British Crop Protection Council, Farnham.

Johnen, B.G. (1996), 'Risk Assessment and Crop Protection Products Use Reduction', in A. Oskam (ed.), *Policy Measures to Control Environmental Impacts from Agriculture*, Proceedings, International Symposium, Wageningen Agricultural University, 24-7 August 1995.

Kramer, C.S. (1990), 'Food Safety: The Consumer Side of the Environmental Issue', *Southern Journal of Agricultural Economics*, 22(1): 33-40.

Lingk, W. (1995), 'Gesundheitliche Bedeutung von Pflanzenschutzmittel-Rückständen im Trinkwasser', in Industrieverband Agrar e.V. (ed.), *Forum Gewässerschutz und Pflanzenschutz*, Frankfurt.

Mapp, H.P. (1990), 'A Discussion of Water Quality and Food Safety, *Southern Journal of Agricultural Economics*, 22(1): 41-6.

Maroni, M. and A. Fait (1993), 'Health Effects in Man from Long-Term Exposure to Pesticides: A Review of the 1975-1991 Literature', *Toxicology*, 78: 1-180.

Martijn, T.G. (1995), *The Integration of Water Policy with Other Policy Areas and the Role of Research and Development*, Club de Bruxelles, Brussels.

Midmore, P. and N.H. Lamkin (1994), 'Modelling the Impact of Widespread Conversion to Organic Farming: An Overview', in N.H. Lamkin and S. Padel (eds), *The Economics of Organic Farming*, CAB International, Wallingford.

Misra, S.K., C.L. Huang and S.L. Ott (1991), 'Consumer Willingness to Pay for Pesticide-Free Produce', *Western Journal of Agricultural Economics*, 16(2): 219-27.

Mitchell, R.C. and R.T. Carson (1986), *Valuing Drinking Water Risk Reductions Using the Contingent Valuation Method: A Methodological Study of Risks from THM and Giardia*, Resources for the Future, Washington, DC.

Mitchell, R.C. and R.T. Carson (1989), *Using Surveys to Value Public Goods: The Contingent Valuation Method*, Resources for the Future, Washington, DC.

National Research Council (1989), *Alternative Agriculture*, Academy Press, Washington, DC.

Oskam, A.J. (1994), 'Pesticides; The Issues at Stake for Agricultural Economists', in J. Michalek and C.H. Hanf (eds), *The Economic Consequences of a Drastic Reduction in Pesticide Use in the EU*, Vauk, Kiel.

Parliamentary Office of Science and Technology (1993), *Drinking Water Quality. Balancing Safety and Costs*, HMSO, London.

Riera, P. (1995), 'The Social Value of Areas of Special Environmental Interest in Mediterranean Countries', in L.M. Albisu and C. Romero (eds), *Environmental and Land Use Issues. An Economic Perspective*, Vauk, Kiel.

Ruttan, V.W. (1994), 'Constraints on the Design of Sustainable Systems of Agricultural Production', *Ecological Economics*, 10: 209-19.

San Juan, C. (1995), 'Environmental Strategies and Farm Production Function', in L.M. Albisu and C. Romero (eds), *Environmental and Land Use Issues. An Economic Perspective*, Vauk, Kiel.

Söderqvist, T. (1994), 'The Costs of Meeting a Drinking Water Quality Standard: The Case of Atrazine in Italy', in L. Bergmann and D.M. Pugh (eds),

Environmental Toxicology, Economics and Institutions. The Atrazine Case Study, Kluwer Academic Publishers, Dordrecht/Boston/London.

Swanson, T.M. and R. Lloyd (1994), 'The Regulation of Chemicals in Agricultural Production: A Joint Economic and Toxicological Framework', in L. Bergmann and D.M. Pugh (eds), *Environmental Toxicology, Economics and Institutions. The Atrazine Case Study,* Kluwer Academic Publishers, Dordrecht/Boston/London.

Weaver, R.D., D.J. Evans and A.E. Luloff (1992), 'Pesticide Use in Tomato Production: Consumer Concerns and Willingness-To-Pay', *Agribusiness,* **8**(2): 131–42.

WHO (1993), *Guidelines for Drinking Water Quality,* Geneva.

Williams, A.J. (1990), 'Using a Modelling Approach to Demonstrate and Quantify Trade Offs in the Nitrate Issue as an Aid to Making Policy Decisions', in P.C. van den Noort (ed.), *Costs and Benefits of Agricultural Policies and Projects,* Vauk, Kiel.

Zadoks, J.C. (1996), 'Future Crop Protection by Pesticides and Genetic Modification: A Challenge to Economists?', in A. Oskam (ed.), *Policy Measures to Control Environmental Impacts from Agriculture,* Proceedings, International Symposium, Wageningen Agricultural University, 24–7 August 1995.

Zilberman, D. and M. Marra (1993), 'Agricultural Externalities', in G.A. Carlson, D. Zilbermann and J.A. Miranowski (eds), *Agricultural and Environmental Economics,* Oxford University Press, New York/Oxford.

Zimmermann, G.M. and H.H. Dieter (1994), 'Wie problemgerecht ist die humantoxikologische Bewertung von Pestiziden (PBSM) im Trinkwasser? UWSF-Z.Umweltchem', *Ökotox,* **6**(6): 341–9.

PART VII
PERSPECTIVES FOR
THE 21st CENTURY

25 Transformation and Environment: Perspectives for Central and Eastern European Countries

A. Lütteken and K. Hagedorn[a]

Introduction

In the countries of Central and Eastern Europe (CEEC) agriculture is subject to fundamental changes during the process of transition to a market economy. Under such circumstances agricultural policies, as well as the impacts of agricultural practices, assume new dimensions. This is interesting for both industrialized and so-called 'developing' countries. The main questions raised by this transition process focus on structural changes in CEEC agriculture – changes from different types of state or collective farming to various forms of private farms, changes in farm size and regional distribution of agricultural production – and changes in the contribution of agriculture to the general economy and towards the new agricultural policies.

Since 1989–90 the scale of agricultural input and output prices has changed considerably, affecting agricultural practices at every level of primary production. This has influenced the use of agro-chemicals, drastically reducing them in the first years, but then increasing them step by step, according to new stabilization processes and new agricultural policies in each country. In the near future there may be a strong relationship between the application of agricultural inputs, the intensity of political protection of agriculture and the success of the transformation process.

This chapter focuses on the use of agro-chemicals in the first years of

[a] Humboldt-University of Berlin, Department of Agricultural Policy, Marketing and Agricultural Development, Luisenstrasse 56, D-10099 Berlin, Germany.

transition and tries to outline a perspective for the future of Central and Eastern European agriculture. By illustrating some national examples from Central and Eastern European countries, we want to give an impression of the special situation in this part of the world.

Agriculture in the Countries in Transition

During the socialist era, agriculture was more important in the CEECs than in the EU, in terms of cultivated area, contribution to GDP and, particularly, total employment. In some countries of CEEC, its importance was similar to that in developing countries. Agricultural products were very important for national exports of some countries such as Hungary, where their contribution to total commodity exports was about 22.7 per cent in 1989 and still 22 per cent in 1993. In Bulgaria, the contribution of agricultural products even increased from 11.3 per cent in 1989 to 20 per cent in 1993 (FAO, 1994: 16). Although the economic weight of agriculture in terms of contribution to GDP and total employment has decreased rapidly in recent years, it is still important to the economy in every CEE country (Table 25.1).

Table 25.1   General economy and agriculture in CEEC10, 1993

	Pop. (m.)	Agric. area (m. ha)	(% tot. area)	Arable area (m. ha)	Agric. production* (b. ECU)	(% GDP)	Agric. employment (000)	(% tot. empl.)
Poland	38.5	18.6	59	14.3	4 648	6.3	3 661	25.6
Hungary	10.3	6.1	66	4.7	2 068	6.4	392	10.1
Czech Rep.	10.3	4.3	54	3.2	0 871	3.3	271	5.6
Slovak Rep.	5.3	2.4	49	1.5	0 512	5.8	178	8.4
Slovenia	1.9	0.9	43	0.2	0 250	4.9	90	10.7
Romania	22.7	14.7	62	9.3	4 500	20.2	3 537	35.2
Bulgaria	8.5	6.2	55	4.0	1 131	10.0	694	21.2
Lithuania	3.8	3.5	54	2.3	0 259	11.0	399	22.4
Latvia	2.6	2.5	39	1.7	0 232	10.6	229	18.4
Estonia	1.6	1.4	31	1.0	0 266	10.4	89	8.2
CEEC10	105.5	60.6	56	42.3	14.7	7.8	9 540	26.7
EU15	369.7	138.1	43	77.1	208.8	2.5	8 190	5.7
CEEC/EU	29%	44%	–	55%	–	–	–	–

Note: *As measured by gross agricultural product (GAP).

Source: European Commission (1995a:1–5).

Total agricultural output decreased in most of the CEECs (except Slovenia) as the result of various developments such as a drop in both domestic and external demand, general inflation, natural fluctuations and changes in agricultural policies. Domestically, demand prices for agricultural products rose after abolishment of the formerly high subsidies for food. At the same time, income fell owing to the economic crisis of the first years of transition. Furthermore, a considerable part of the export markets, in the former Soviet Union in particular, was lost, with the consequences of agricultural surpluses and low output prices. In this way, the agricultural sector was a loser because of price liberalization in the first years (Schneider, 1995: 3).

The decline in agricultural production was particularly pronounced in the animal sector, where output decreased by more than 30 per cent on average in the 10 countries (European Commission, 1995a, see Table 25.2). The reason for this can be seen in two facts: the former low consumer prices, for meat in particular, due to food subsidies; and the problems of adaptation caused by liberalization and privatization in the mostly large-scale and ineffective production units for animal breeding as they previously existed. Crop production decreased by more than 13 per cent, but it gained in relative importance in the first years of transition and will certainly be the first sector to be stabilized under the new conditions of a market economy.

At the beginning of the 1990s, agricultural policies in the CEECs were generally characterized by liberalization of agricultural markets, the abolishment of nearly all input and food subsidies and the first steps towards land reform. (The emergence of land markets is still one of the most difficult problems in most of the countries). In the following years market interventions, minimum prices, export subsidies and interest reductions for credit, that is, policies more or less comparable to instruments of the Common Agricultural Policy (CAP), were introduced. Some countries also started direct income subsidies for farmers, and some began to support environmentally sound production systems. Only in Slovenia are subsidies for inputs like fertilizers still an important part of agricultural policies. The behaviour towards former state and collective farms differs considerably among countries (DBV, 1996: 12ff).

Use of Agro-Chemicals in the Transition Countries

Generally, it is said that agriculture in the former socialist countries produced at a high degree of input intensity. Except for Poland and Slovenia, where private and more or less small-scale farming dominated, the former

Table 25.2   **Change in real gross agricultural output,[a] 1990 and 1994 (1989 = 100)**

Country	Total gross agric. output		Crops		Livestock	
	1990	1994	1990	1994	1990	1994
Poland	94.5	78.6	95.1	74.1	94.2	81.6
Hungary	95.3	65.6	90.7	69.6	99.8	60.0
Czech Rep.	97.7	72.2	99.3	78.7	96.6	67.6
Slovak Rep.	92.8	74.6	88.4	89.7	96.2	62.6
Slovenia	104.2	118.2	98.6	133.3	102.2	96.5
Romania	97.1	101.0	92.8	107.4	102.1	91.3
Bulgaria	94.0	70.2	92.6	93.1	95.4	48.3
Lithuania	91.1	47.7	82.2	47.6	95.6	50.7
Latvia	n.a.	n.a.	n.a.	n.a.	n.a.	n.a.
Estonia	86.9	56.4	75.3	n.a.	92.0	n.a.

Note: [a] Value of sold production plus own producer consumption at constant prices.

Source: European Commission (1995a: 7).

agricultural structure can also be described as industrialized and subsidized in all countries by governments to stimulate production and to reach a high degree of national self-sufficiency and export surpluses. This policy was a part of the politics of quantitative growth at any price, typical of the former COMECON countries. Until 1989, subsidies on inputs constituted a high proportion of total budgetary expenditure on agriculture. In Poland, for example, 15.6 per cent of the total budget went to agriculture in 1989, with 49 per cent of that for fertilizers and 7 per cent for pesticides (OECD, 1995a: 121). Input prices were fixed by the state at a low level, and state subsidies were paid directly to manufacturers of fertilizers, pesticides, machinery and so on.

The result of this policy was an increasing use of fertilizers and pesticides during the last decades of the socialist era, even at a time when western use of these inputs started to decrease, in the mid-1980s. In the COMECON6[1] and the former Soviet Union, the total amount of mineral fertilizer use increased by 18 per cent from 1980 to 1989, while it decreased by 5 per cent in the comparable group of 19 western industrialized countries (Fey, 1993).[2] But the level of fertilizer use per hectare of arable land in the socialist countries was still below the level in the western part of the industrialized world, in particular much lower than in former West Germany: 220kg NPK/ha arable land on average in the COMECON6 and the Soviet Union, 294kg/ha on average in the above-mentioned 19 western countries, and 384kg/ha in West Germany (Fey, 1993: 98).

Different observations can be made regarding the pesticide sector. The use of pesticides per unit of agricultural output was about 25 per cent higher in the COMECON6 than in the EU12 (Pearce and Warford, 1993). In Hungary during the mid-1980s, for example, the amount of active ingredients of pesticides was about 5kg/ha. At the same time it was 4kg in the mainly intensive agriculture of the EU12.

After the political upheavals of 1989/90 the situation changed radically. During the first years of transition, in 1990/91, most governments abolished most of the input subsidies for fertilizers and pesticides. As a consequence, input prices increased dramatically and nearly reached world market levels (Schneider, 1995: 4). Simultaneous with the decrease in output prices, this development resulted in an unfavourable input–output–ratio (for example, see Figure 25.1 for the Czech Republic), which was partly responsible for the decline in total agricultural production caused by reduced rentability of most farms. As a consequence, fertilizer and pesticide use declined in the period 1989–93, but this happened at a different rate in each country (Figure 25.2). In Hungary, it collapsed completely, particularly fertilizer use, and increased only in 1994. In Poland, a 64 per cent reduction occurred between 1989 and 1993 (OECD, 1995b: 269).

If we differentiate between the types of nutrients applied as fertilizer, a general observation is the reduction of phosphate and potassium, which have more long-term effects, there has been a preference for nitrogen fertilizer to support short-term yield potential. Accordingly, nitrogen fertilizer use fell less than the others (for example, see Figure 25.3 for Hungary). This can be seen as one of the reasons why the decline in agricultural production has

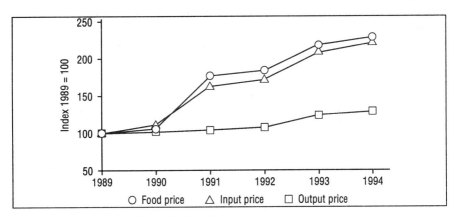

Source: European Commission (1995a: 9).

Figure 25.1   Spread between input and output prices, Czech Republic (1989 = 100)

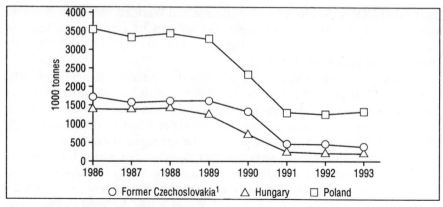

Note: [1]Since 1993, two independent states.

Source: OECD (1995b: 269).

Figure 25.2 **Consumption of commercial fertilizers (NPK) in former Czechoslovakia, Hungary and Poland (000s tonnes)**

been less severe than the fall in fertilizer use. But the lack of phosphate and potassium use in the first years of transition may lead to a loss of fertility of the soils in the years ahead, affecting yields and increasing sensitivity to climate hazards (European Commission, 1995b: 31; 1995c: 31).

The use of pesticides has also fallen since 1989. However, the level of pesticide use has differed considerably between countries. In Poland, pesticide use was traditionally low (European Commission, 1995c); it was, and is, still much higher in Hungary, where the total use of pesticides dropped by about 67 per cent from 1989 to 1992. The production of pesticides – Hungary is one of the most important producers of pesticides and fertilizers among the East European Countries – dropped by 40 per cent in the period 1990–93 (European Commission, 1995b: 30). Concerning the different types of pesticides, insecticides were reduced most (by 76 per cent from 1986 to 1992), while herbicides were 'only' reduced by about 53 per cent (Figure 25.4).

Apart from the reduction or abolishment of input subsidies, lack of capital on the farms during the first years of transformation may be seen as an additional reason for decreasing rates of input use. With increasing stability in the agricultural sector, however, the input–output ratio will improve. First efforts can be observed in Poland, Hungary and Romania. In addition, the above-mentioned establishment of new systems of price and income support will stimulate intensity of crop production. It seems realistic to say that the

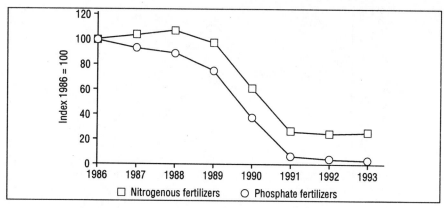

Source: OECD (1995b: 265–7).

Figure 25.3 Reduction in nitrogen and phosphate fertilizers use, Hungary (1986 = 100)

decrease in input use has bottomed out, and application of inputs will start to increase again. This may improve rentability and returns in the future, for crop production in particular.

The Impact of Agro-Chemicals Use on the Environment

Although the total use of agro-chemicals per hectare of arable land never did reach the amount used in western industrialized countries (see above), more environmental problems arose with the way they were applied in practice. The results of different studies seem to allow the conclusion that harmful pollution of the environment was not caused by the amount of fertilizer and pesticides itself, but by so-called 'improper agricultural practices' (Stoklasa, 1994: 132). As early as 1981, the Polish Academy of Science published a study in which the improper use of chemicals was held responsible for the reduction of biodiversity.

Another reason for higher pollution by use of agro-chemicals in Eastern Europe can be seen in the types of chemicals used, particularly pesticides, where the use in the west differed greatly. Some active pesticide substances, such as DDT, played a more important role in Eastern European countries only because they were produced mainly out of domestic raw materials, and no foreign currency had to be used (Heinisch *et al.*, 1994).

Environmental pollution by agro-chemicals occurred in the former socialist countries from storage and from distribution of chemicals to the

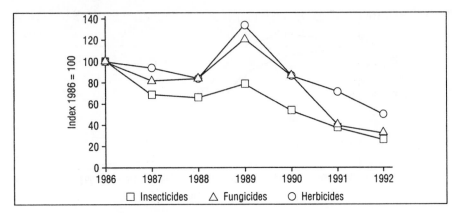

Source: OECD (1995b: 273).

Figure 25.4   Trends in consumption of pesticides, Hungary (1986=100)

farms. In the former GDR, for example, from the agro-chemical production and distribution centres, from the removal of chemical residues, and from application practices. In the Czech Republic, 50 per cent of total surface water contamination resulted from 'planar pollution' by large-scale application of agro-chemicals and small dispersed sources. Also groundwater was mainly contaminated by these sources, particularly nitrogen, which has increased by two to four times in the last 30 years (Cerná *et al.*, 1994: 7).

During the socialist era it was difficult to get information on the use and environmental impacts of agro-chemicals. In the former GDR, secrecy of such data was among the strongest in the Eastern Bloc, while in Poland, Hungary and the former Czechoslovakia, studies were published even during this time. However, many studies on regional contamination and the causal connection between chemical use and impacts on nature and food have recently been initiated (Heinisch *et al.*, 1994). They could provide evidence for regional cases of soil and food contamination.

One characteristic attitude of the former centrally planned economies facilitates present studies: the bureaucracy and the correct documentation of production, delivery and use of inputs, including pesticides. For this reason, chemists and ecotoxicologists can now refer to voluminous data, never accessible before but now open to researchers. Also careful but formerly secret studies on food contamination, mostly by pesticides, especially in the former GDR, make it possible to get new results about the impact of agro-chemical use on nature and humans regionally, under the circumstances of real production rather than under experimental conditions (Heinisch *et al.*, 1994).

It should also be noted that the majority of environmental problems caused by chemical contamination in agriculture seem to be an issue of accumulation during the last three decades. Since the mid-1980s, including the socialist countries, the most dangerous pesticides such as DDT have been reduced and replaced by other products, though this did not happen on an environmentally sound and desirable level.

Conclusions and Outlook

If we try to find a reasonable interpretation of the relationship between agricultural production and environmental pollution in the transition countries, a pattern of development may be outlined that is more or less applicable to each of them (see Figure 25.5). It comprises four periods: (1) the period of the centrally planned economy as it existed prior to the radical political changes; (2) the time of political upheavals; (3) the period of transition; and (4) the period of an established market economy, which is the main political objective in Central and Eastern Europe. From the point of view of institutional economics, the period of political changes was accompanied by destruction of marketing channels, both for inputs and outputs, and the development of legislation and structures needed for economic activity. After the political upheavals and during the transition process, new rules have to be institutionalised and norms and property rights have to be redefined. These new structures are missing to a large extent in the first years, because establishing new institutions seems to be rather difficult owing to complex networks of different political and private interests and barriers of every imaginable form. In a market economy, however, such rules and norms are important for daily politics and decision making. The process of institutional innovation will depend on the specific conditions in each country and will influence the intensity of agricultural production as well as the introduction of national environmental policies.

The political changes in 1989/90 and the collapse of the economy reduced the pressure on the environment. They gave nature a 'chance' to rest, and at the same time offered the possibility of exercising the real natural damages of the previous 40 years. The countries in transition are at present being confronted by the need to stabilize the democratic process and the economic situation, while improving the environmental situation as a basic need for sound development. This seems to be well-nigh impossible. Simultaneously, the economic changes and a mentality of 'economic growth at all costs', caused by recession and unemployment, create an atmosphere in which environmental improvements are often sacrificed.

The reduction of potentially harmful agro-chemicals in agriculture, as a

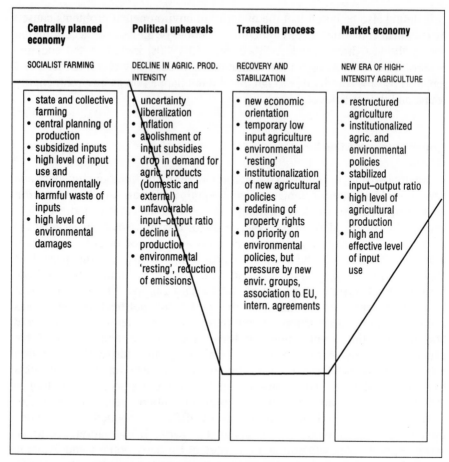

Centrally planned economy	Political upheavals	Transition process	Market economy
SOCIALIST FARMING	DECLINE IN AGRIC. PROD. INTENSITY	RECOVERY AND STABILIZATION	NEW ERA OF HIGH-INTENSITY AGRICULTURE
• state and collective farming • central planning of production • subsidized inputs • high level of input use and environmentally harmful waste of inputs • high level of environmental damages	• uncertainty • liberalization • inflation • abolishment of input subsidies • drop in demand for agric. products (domestic and external) • unfavourable input–output ratio • decline in production • environmental 'resting', reduction of emissions	• new economic orientation • temporary low input agriculture • environmental 'resting' • institutionalization of new agricultural policies • redefining of property rights • no priority on environmental policies, but pressure by new envir. groups, association to EU, intern. agreements	• restructured agriculture • institutionalized agric. and environmental policies • stabilized input–output ratio • high level of agricultural production • high and effective level of input use

Figure 25.5   Political development and development of production intensity in transition countries

consequence of the abolishment of input subsidies, is one example of the 'third period' (Figure 25.5). Now the countries in transition to a market economy have to establish new rules for economic activities and must redefine agricultural policies. Environmental considerations have not had priority status in this process during the last few years, but it is obvious that they will play a more important role in the future.

Environmental policies during the transition process require a high budgetary input, but provide large returns to society, compared to western countries (Bartel, 1994). However, the possibility of implementing environmental policy instruments seems to be rather slight at a time when the population is suffering from adapting to new economic conditions and unsatisfied needs of consumption. In addition to this, Bartel points out that the confidence of the people is very low, and especially the confidence of economic actors, in an efficient collective organization of the common natural capital. Furthermore, the pressure of fast economic growth and liberalization in the economic sector may cause new market failures as regards the environment. This will be aggravated by the lack of institutions for efficient environmental policies.

Agriculture in the Central and Eastern European countries is currently involved in such a difficult process of change that the possibilities of environmental protection are reduced. The goal of some of them, the so-called 'visegrad states', to achieve access to the EU in the future, stimulates the agricultural policies to organize this sector in a way that makes it adaptable to the CAP. This motivation certainly affects environmental policies in the agricultural sector. However, low use of potentially harmful inputs will actually reduce the motivation to implement strong environmental regulations.

Rules for sustainability and corresponding environmental policies appear to be unnecessary in the short run, but they will be urgently needed in the long run. Does the environment find itself in a 'transformation trap'? After the period of institutional innovation has passed, it may be very difficult to change the rules again in favour of the environment. This hypothesis seems to be realistic if we look at the next phase of development, when the agricultural sector will be stabilized. As we can observe now, without being restricted by adequate economic instruments and incentives to limit it, the use of energy, fertilizer and pesticides may increase at a higher rate, resulting in new damage to natural resources. For this reason, future protection of the environment from contamination by agriculture is also a question of agricultural extension, and therefore it is necessary to establish adequate extension systems during the transition process.

For the future, it should be a goal of agricultural and environmental policies to 'control' possible increases of input use in a way that will be less harmful to the environment. For this reason an interesting aspect of the transition process is the redefining of property rights concerning the use of natural resources. While in western industrialized countries property rights have developed over decades or centuries, it seems politically difficult to change new property rights and regimes in the transition countries to bring environmental rights into the bundle of property rights, although such rights could, theoretically, be defined in a more 'environmentally sound' way in the transition countries. However, redefined property rights do not give any guarantee of less contamination as long as institutionalized mechanisms for controlling implementation are not established.

Notes

1   Bulgaria, former Czechoslovakia, former GDR, Hungary, Poland and Romania.
2   Austria, Belgium, Luxembourg (together with Belgium), Canada, Switzerland, former West Germany, Denmark, Great Britain, France, Italy, Ireland, Japan, Norway, The Netherlands, Portugal, Sweden, Finland, USA.

References

Bartel, R. (1994), 'Umweltpolitik in den Reformländern Mittel- und Osteuropas', in R. Bartel and F. Hackl (eds), *Einführung in die Umweltpolitik*, Verlag Vahlen, Munich.

Cerná, A., E. Tosovská and P. Cetkovský (1994), 'Economic Transformation and the Environment', Working Paper Series, CERGE-EI, Prague.

DBV (1996), *EU-Landwirtschaft und Osterweiterung. Kriterien-Probleme-Analysen*, Schriftenreihe des Deutschen Bauernverbandes 2/1996, Bonn.

European Commission (1995a), 'Agricultural Situation and Prospects in the Central and Eastern European Countries: Summary Report', Working Document, Directorate-General for Agriculture, Brussels.

European Commission (1995b), 'Agricultural Situation and Prospects in the Central and Eastern European Countries: Hungary', Working Document, Directorate-General for Agriculture, Brussels.

European Commission (1995c), 'Agricultural Situation and Prospects in the Central and Eastern European Countries: Poland', Working Document, Directorate-General for Agriculture, Brussels.

Fey, A. (1993), 'Umweltsituation und Umweltpolitik in der ausgehenden Sowjetunion: Eine vergleichende Fallstudie', *Berliner Schriften zur Politik und Gesellschaft im Sozialismus und Kommunismus*, Bd. 8, Frankfurt a.M./Bern/New York/Paris, Verlag Peter Lang.

Food and Agriculture Organization of the United Nations (1994), 'FAO Trade Yearbook 1993', *FAO Statistics Series*, 47(121).

Heinisch, E., A. Kettup and S. Wenzel-Klein (1994), 'Schadstoffatlas Osteuropa', in J. Vogel (ed.), *Handbuch des Umweltschutzes, Landsberg*, 74: Ch. VI-1.

Organization for Economic Cooperation and Development (1995a), *Review of Agricultural Policies: Poland*, OECD, Paris.

Organization for Economic Cooperation and Development (1995b), *OECD Environmental Data Compendium 1995*, OECD, Paris.

Pearce, D.W. and J.J. Warford (1993), *World Without End: Economics, Environment and Sustainable Development*, World Bank, Washington, DC.

Schneider, M. (1995), 'Lage und Perspektiven der Landwirtschaft in den Mittel- und Osteuropäischen Ländern', *Agrarische Rundschau*, 4(95): 1–18.

Stoklasa, J. (1994), 'Environmental Problems in Central and Eastern Europe: The Possible Role of International Policy and Market-Oriented Instruments', in S.S. Nagel and V. Rukavishnikov (eds), *Eastern European Development and Public Policy*, St Martin's' Press, New York.

26 Less is More: Why Agro-chemicals Use Will Decline in Industrialized Countries

S.M. Swinton[a]

Introduction

Over the past four decades, scientists and the public at large have become increasingly aware of the risks that balance the benefits from agro-chemicals (van Ravenswaay, 1995). With accelerating momentum, policy makers have responded by enacting measures to protect citizens. Agricultural researchers have followed, seeking to develop non-chemical substitutes for agro-chemicals while industry has sought to develop safer chemicals, more narrowly aimed at augmenting agricultural productivity with minimal unwanted side-effects. Agricultural economists have been pushed to abandon some convenient assumptions and to explore how to develop optimal policies and evaluate new technologies when multiple criteria come into play.

This chapter explores three strands of thinking about the value of chemical pesticides and fertilizers to farmers and society in North America and Europe over the past 40 years. It begins by tracing how economic analysis of agrochemical costs and benefits has evolved. Next it examines recent research and development of management technologies for agricultural nutrients and pests. Finally, it touches on changing public policies regarding agro-chemicals. Focusing primarily on the United States, it identifies a

[a] Department of Agricultural Economics, Michigan State University, East Lansing, Michigan 48823-1039, USA.

pattern of scientific learning and public policy that is leading agro-chemical application to become more sparing and judicious.

Early Agro-chemical Production Analysis

With the explosive rates of adoption of synthetic fertilizers and pesticides following World War II, early economic analyses sought to recommend how best to apply them. The early economic studies on agro-chemicals identified profit-maximizing rates and measured the contribution of agro-chemicals to the value of agricultural production:

$$\max_x \quad E[\pi] = pY - w\mathbf{x} - FC$$
$$s.t. \quad Y = f(x^p, x^f, x^o)$$

Models typically maximized expected net revenue (profit), $E[\pi]$, subject to the production function constraint: where p = output price, Y = output, w = input price, $\mathbf{x}$ = vector of production inputs, including x^p = pesticide input, x^f = fertilizer input and x^o = other inputs, and FC = fixed costs. Typical assumptions included the following: (1) profits are a suitable proxy for producer utility; (2) no economic externalities accompany agro-chemicals use; (3) no significant dynamic effects result from agro-chemicals use; and (4) agro-chemicals contribute directly to production. This approach was exemplified by the fertilizer response research of Heady and his associates (for example, Hexem and Heady, 1978; Heady and Dillon, 1961) and the pesticide productivity research of Headley (1968). The production function research of Heady and associates explored biologically and economically suitable functional forms and estimated economic relationships and decision rules associated with profit-maximizing input use, cost-minimizing input combinations and revenue-maximizing product mixes. Subsequent research explored technical and allocative efficiency in agricultural input use.

Getting the Biology Right

More than a decade after Stern *et al.* (1959) introduced economic injury levels – the key threshold concept of integrated pest management (IPM) – agricultural economists began to formulate decision rules for pesticide use in terms of a pest damage function (Talpaz and Borosh, 1974; Feder, 1979). From this perspective, pesticides became *indirect* contributors to productivity, their contribution dependent on pests being present. While the objective function of these models was unchanged from the earlier approach, their characterization of yield as a multiplicative product of potential yield and the proportion that survives pest damage made the presence of pests a necessary condition for pesticide productivity. Models typically took the form:

$$\max_x \quad E[\pi] = pY - wx - FC$$
$$s.t. \quad Y = f(x^f, x^o)[1 - D(pest, x^p)]$$

where $D(.)$ is a damage function of pest pressure and control inputs applied.

Lichtenberg and Zilberman (1986) used the damage function approach econometrically to make an influential critique of Headley's pesticide productivity estimates. Their claim was not fully substantiated in empirical tests by Carrasco-Tauber and Moffitt (1992) that continued to find the marginal productivity of pesticides to be over five times their price. However, subsequent econometric analysis suggests that potential pest damage and hence pesticide productivity may, in fact, be less (Chambers and Lichtenberg, 1994). From a policy perspective, the reduced estimate of pesticide productivity suggests that the social cost of reducing pesticide use might be less than previously believed.

A second vein of research explored the effects of pest management on the financial risk faced by agricultural producers. Recognizing the drawbacks of yield function specifications that forced variance to rise with input use, Just and Pope (1978) proposed an econometric specification that separated the mean production function from a heteroskedastic error term that could explicitly model non-constant variance. This model is distinct from the previous ones in two respects. First, instead of expected profit maximization alone, the objective function is a multi-attribute utility function, with utility based on both expected net returns and risk (written below as variance). Second, the random process generating the variance is explicitly modelled as an additive heteroskedastic term; this allows it to test whether or not a production input increases the riskiness (variance) of output. A version of the Just–Pope model that combines it with the damage function model above is:

$$\max_x \quad U(E[\pi], Var[\pi])$$
$$s.t. \quad \pi = pY - wx - FC$$
$$\cdot \quad Y = f(x^f, x^o)[1 - D(pest, x^p)] + h(x^f, x^o, x^p, pest)\epsilon$$

where ϵ is a random disturbance term.

Drawing on this specification of the pest damage function, researchers tested the hypothesis that pesticides reduce yield risk and generally found that they did (although this need not necessarily be true: see, for example, Pannell, 1990). For policy design, this research implied that crop insurance might substitute for agro-chemicals use. While it has been argued that moral hazard can induce crop-insured farmers to use more agro-chemicals (Horowitz and Lichtenberg, 1993), new research supports the conventional view that crop insurance tends to reduce agro-chemical use (Smith and Goodwin, 1996).

Beyond Profitability

In the 1990s, evidence of private environmental benefits from reduced agro-chemicals use that was previously lacking (Fox *et al.*, 1991) suggested that profitability alone is not a valid proxy for farmer utility. Apart from economic externalities, farmers appear to care about agrochemical effects on their health and environmental quality. Using contingent valuation, entomologists and economists demonstrated that Midwestern US field crop farmers value health and environmental quality, and are willing to pay for it (Higley and Wintersteen, 1992; Owens *et al.*, 1996). Higley and Wintersteen inferred that 'environmental thresholds' would result in IPM decision rules that called for pesticide applications less often than conventional economic injury levels. Beach and Carlson's (1993) hedonic analysis showed that actual herbicide prices reveal that water quality and user safety are valued attributes.

Householder willingness to pay for reduced nitrate contamination of groundwater has been demonstrated through averting expenditure studies (Abdalla, 1990; Abdalla *et al.*, 1992; Abdalla, 1994; see also Chapter 22 of the present volume) as well as contingent valuation research (Poe and Bishop, 1992; also Chapter 22 of the present volume) and fuzzy logic methods (see Chapter 22). These rural household studies, and others that focused specifically on farmers, all documented the fact that respondents value water quality.

Related research in developing countries has shown that the cost of illness due to pesticide exposure can be very high. Results indicate that prior awareness of morbidity costs could have induced farmers to choose different pest management practices – for example, for insect control in Filipino rice (Rola and Pingali, 1993; Antle and Pingali, 1994; Pingali *et al.*, 1994) – or else confront a painful trade-off between yield protection and probable medical costs, as with disease control in Ecuadorian potato (Crissman *et al.*, 1994).

Collectively, these studies measuring the value of health and environmental consequences of agricultural production have highlighted the fact that farmers do care and should care about non-market environmental values. From an analytical standpoint, this implies that a multi-attribute utility function guides the selection of agricultural inputs, so non-financial objectives carry weight that may cause the 'best' input mix to be one that does not maximize net returns. For simplicity, the model below focuses on expected outcomes, omitting concerns about variability of outcomes:

$$\max_x \quad U(\pi, H, E)$$
$$s.t. \quad \pi = pY - w\mathbf{x} - FC$$
$$Y = f(x^f, x^o)[1 - D(pest, \mathbf{x}^p)]$$
$$H = h(\bar{H}, x^p, x^f)$$
$$E = e(\bar{E}, \mathbf{x}^p, \mathbf{x}^f)$$

where $H(.)$ = health production function, $\bar{H}$ = health endowment, $E(.)$ = environment quality function, and $\bar{E}$ = environmental quality endowment.

Where agrochemical inputs increase yield but depress health and environmental quality, this suggests that 'optimal' choice of agrochemical inputs will result in lower levels of their application. This results from solving a decision rule that is based, not simply on equating marginal value product with marginal input cost, but rather on equating marginal value product on both marginal input cost and marginal health and environmental cost (disutility) as well. From a policy standpoint, evidence of farmer willingness to reduce agro-chemicals use in enlightened self-interest suggests that further research and outreach are needed on the health and environmental consequences of agricultural production.

An alternative to measuring health and environmental costs in monetary units is to use an efficiency frontier approach to illustrate trade-offs between financial and non-market utility attributes of agro-chemicals use (Hoag and Hornsby, 1992; Bouzaher *et al.*, 1992; Chu *et al.*, 1996; see also Chapter 13 of the present volume). This allows them to identify inefficient strategies (such as those that increase both costs and use of hazardous agro-chemicals) that are not on the efficient trade-off frontier. The optimal choice of agro-chemicals strategy is determined by the preferences of the decision maker. Studies have shown that marginal gains in environmental quality can be achieved at fairly low cost (Hoag and Hornsby, 1992; Bouzaher *et al.*, 1992; Chu *et al.*, 1996; see also Chapter 13 of the present volume).

The Evolving Technological Environment

Advances in crop pest and fertility management technology and biological knowledge have proceeded at least as rapidly as economic knowledge. In pest management, there are several important developments. First, the new generation of pesticides involves dramatically lower rates than the post-World War II generation. The newer pesticides tend to have more specific biochemical modes of action and therefore to be more selective in their use. This means that non-target species, including humans, wildlife and beneficial insects, are less likely to be at risk. Second, the first generation of genetically engineered crops are coming to market. Many of the new cultivars are either pest- or pesticide-tolerant. A new cotton variety naturally produces the toxin secreted by the *Bacillus thuringiensis* (Bt) bacterium that kills key insect pests. A new variety of soybeans can tolerate the spraying of glyphosate, normally a non-selective herbicide. The Bt cotton will require less insecticide use, while the new soybeans will allow low-dose, low-mammalian toxicity, rapidly decomposing glyphosate to substitute for alternative herbicides.

Advances in information technology are making it more feasible to evaluate the benefits of agro-chemicals use – both financial and environmental – and to use that information to prescribe (and justify) suitable levels. Over the past 20 years, researchers have developed a set of IPM decision aid computer programs to identify economic injury levels for management of insects (Reichelderfer and Bender, 1979; Moffitt *et al.*, 1984) and weeds (Wilkerson *et al.*, 1991; Wiles *et al.*, 1996; Swinton and King, 1994; Lybecker *et al.*, 1994). These models predict crop yield loss from pest damage, and represent an advance over the earlier generation of pesticide decision aids which simply ranked pesticides on their efficacy at killing the target species. Although they are driven by expected-profit-maximization decision rules, they tend to recommend less agro-chemicals use than the prior efficacy owing to their explicit incorporation of pest population data and yield projections.

A newer generation of computer programs allows producers to make multi-objective comparisons between profitability and environmental criteria such as erosion and leaching (for example, PLANETOR (Hawkins *et al.*, 1995) or to factor environmental costs from the non-market valuation studies discussed above into the IPM decision aid models.

The advent of site-specific crop management (SSM) technology in North America and Europe offers rich opportunities to manage agro-chemicals spatially. SSM uses either field sensing technology (such as yield monitors, soil probes or electric eyes) or mapping and guidance technologies (that is, computerized geographic information systems linked to in-field positioning systems and variable rate input controllers) to tailor input application or monitor productivity referenced to landscape characteristics (see Chapter 12 of the present volume). Initially tested for yield monitoring and fertilizer applications, SSM is now being applied to applications of lime, seeding density and variable rate herbicides (Pierce *et al.*, 1996). Although its performance to date is not well documented at the farm level, SSM is widely expected to boost farm profitability by saving unnecessary input applications and augmenting yields where that is worthwhile, and to reduce environmental contamination by reducing agrochemical applications that exceed predicted crop needs. It also has potential for incorporation of fertilizer and pesticide decision aid programmes adapted at a subfield level to tailor threshold agrochemical applications site-specifically (Oriade and King, 1994).

Public concern about health and environmental risk from agro-chemicals use in the industrialized countries appears to have induced agro-chemicals-saving technological change. In this respect, the nature of induced innovation differs slightly from the form introduced by Hayami and Ruttan (1985), whose hypothesis contended that an increase in the relative price of one production factor induces biased technological change that reduces the relative need for that factor. In the recent case of agro-chemicals, it would appear that induced innovation may have taken place in response to a *perceived* increase in the relative cost of agro-chemicals due to perceptions of health and environmental risk. Information is the production factor that appears to be substituting for agro-chemicals in the form of integrated pest management, soil nutrient testing, SSM and other information-intensive technologies that reduce agro-chemicals use while maintaining quantity and quality of output.

Enhancing the efficiency of nutrient uptake is a key area for crop fertility research, especially for nitrogen fertilizers that leach into groundwater or are lost to the atmosphere owing to their volatility. Soil and plant tissue nitrate tests have been developed to improve the accuracy of nitrogen applications to growing crops (Binford *et al.*, 1990; Follett *et al.*, 1991).

Beyond efficiency improvements in existing agro-chemicals management practices, there are a new set of systems approaches to ecological management of agricultural systems. In crop fertility research, recent research has examined the role of crop rotation and cover crops, highlighting the role of microflora and microfauna in enhancing soil quality (Doran *et al.*, 1986; Harwood, 1985; Reganold *et al.*, 1993). With the emerging recognition that reduced reliance on agro-chemicals may mean discontinuous changes in agricultural systems, new research has examined discontinuous jumps to farming systems that are no longer nested subsets of existing systems (Luna *et al.*, 1994; Stute and Posner, 1993).

Pest management research is also shifting towards manipulation of the ecology in which crops are raised. This may mean identifying landscape characteristics that favour beneficial parasitoids and wildlife (Landis and Haas, 1992), creating environmental niches for beneficial wildlife, propagating diseases that afflict certain weed species, or otherwise disrupting the life or reproductive cycle of a pest species. A narrower but important ecological research field is the study of how to avert pesticide resistance in agricultural pests. In general, the ecological management approach calls for much more detailed knowledge of pest and crop ecology than has been necessary for agrochemically based pest management.

Policy and Social Environment

Public concerns about agro-chemicals have induced policy makers to raise the direct cost of agro-chemicals use, to remove subsidy incentives to overuse agro-chemicals and to change research funding patterns to steer scientific research towards reducing environmental risks from agro-chemicals use. In shifting the social costs of non-point agricultural pollution to farmers, the Dutch government has pioneered nutrient accounting law (Breembroek *et al.*, 1996). Financial penalties are levied on farmers whose audited nutrient accounts indicate that they have exceeded permissible levels of nitrogen, phosphorus or potassium contributions to the farm environment. While costly to enforce, this law directly addresses expected pollution outcomes. No other countries have attempted effluent taxes. There are, however, examples of agro-chemical input taxes in some US states. For example, Iowa and Michigan have imposed taxes on agro-chemicals purchases, allocating revenues for research and extension to encourage reduced agro-chemicals use.

In the United States, water quality and farmworker safety concerns led the US Congress in 1988 to require reregistration by 1997 of all pesticides registered by the Environmental Protection Agency under the less exigent standards existing before 1985. The high cost of toxicology tests and environmental fate and transport research, borne by chemical companies registering or reregistering their compounds for each agricultural use, has reduced the number of new pesticides that companies attempt to register in the United States. This will likely induce more non-chemical pest management methods simply because of the dearth of chemical alternatives. However, the associated shortage of legal pesticide choices may also foster among agricultural pests genetic resistance to specific pesticides, which tends to accelerate with increased reliance on a given compound.

Recent moves to remove agricultural subsidies and trade protection is reducing the value of crop yield gained or saved thanks to agro-chemicals. The 1994 General Agreement on Tariffs and Trade (GATT) converted most forms of agricultural protection and subsidy to tariff equivalents, which are gradually reduced, with accompanying reductions in incentives for agro-chemicals use that would be unjustified at world prices. In the United States, the Federal Agriculture Improvement and Reform (FAIR) Act of 1996 has removed US target prices and deficiency payments in wheat, maize, rice and feed grains, eliminating these incentives for excess chemical use (although such incentives will continue in quota-protected sugar and peanuts). Economic research played a role, having documented empirically that agricultural subsidies induce increased agro-chemicals use (Ribaudo and Shoemaker, 1995).

Legal liability for environmental damage is an area of risk management that is of greater concern to US farms and agribusiness. For the time being, the concerns are about point pollution sources such as pesticide spills or leaky storage. The US federal government has begun requiring applicator certification for restricted-use pesticides and detailed pesticide record keeping in all instances. Many US states have passed 'right to farm' laws that implicitly acknowledge the legal liability threat by identifying acceptable farm management practices which, if followed, will exempt the farmer of legal liability in 'nuisance' lawsuits by neighbours who are displeased with farming practices (Hamilton, 1990).

Finally, research is branching out into market-driven methods of reducing agro-chemicals use. The intense competitive pressure to cut costs in vertically coordinated agricultural businesses such as confinement livestock operations can lead to reduced agro-chemicals use (Dijkhuizen and Rougoor, 1996). Against a backdrop of proliferating contract production of US agricultural commodities, efforts have begun to define contract terms that could be used by a processing firm to induce farmers to moderate their agro-chemicals use in the interests of protecting the processor's reputation or reducing liability risk (Chu *et al.*, 1995, 1996). Agricultural nutrient trading is a market-driven public policy solution that can induce an economically efficient level of pollution (Hahn and Stavins, 1991). It entails designating sustainable levels of water pollution and issuing tradable nutrient emission permits. To date this has been used in the United States on an experimental basis only (for example, in the Tar-Pamlico River Basin in North Carolina, see Rader, 1994).

Caveats and Conclusions

Although the forces leading North American and European agriculture to use less agro-chemical input are strong and widespread, there will, of course, be some exceptions. The pattern is quite apparent among large-scale field crops, but it may be less pronounced in high-value agricultural goods such as horticultural crops where (1) quality plays a big part in determining crop price, (2) yields are quite risky, and (3) pest management in particular may hold few affordable alternative practices. Similarly, as Dijkhuizen and Rougoor (1996) observed, pharmaceutical use in livestock makes a major contribution to reduced mortality and increased rate of weight gain, making reductions in pharmaceutical inputs potentially costly to attain.

Another exception is developing countries where levels of agro-chemicals use have been low. This chapter has focused on the industrialized parts of Europe and North America where agro-chemicals use has been 'technically and allocatively efficient' in the sense of using agro-chemicals up to the point where increased use would yield no economic gain. Because markets and transport systems are well developed in these areas, the farm-level costs of agro-chemicals have been low relative to many developing countries, so it has been allocatively efficient for farmers to use them at higher rates. In parts of the world where farm-level costs of agro-chemicals are high (or agro-chemicals are unavailable when needed), public investments in infrastructure and farmer education will likely more than offset the forces described here as inducing reduced agro-chemical use. For example, where such changes persuade farmers that fertilizer use can reliably yield significant gains in output value, rates of use should rise. Indeed, the threat of nutrient depletion in some regions suggests a need for more fertilizer use. Similarly, where pest and disease protection is minimal, potential gains from pesticides and pharmaceuticals can be important.

The net contribution of agro-chemicals depends on the relative value of the output they add or save. In rich countries, where food costs are a small share of household expenditures, citizens may be willing to accept higher food prices for the sake of lower agrochemical risks to health and environmental quality. Comparable rises in food prices may be unacceptable in less affluent economies, where food security is at issue and food costs account for a big share of household budgets.

In North America and Europe, the distinct forces of research, technology and policy innovation described here are overwhelmingly propelling agro-chemicals use in the same direction. Whether by pushing or pulling, they are inducing agricultural producers to reduce agro-chemicals use from recent levels. Push forces include new legal requirements, liability risks and diminished agrochemical alternatives. Parallel pull forces include cost reduction, producer health concerns and opportunities to engage in profitable contracts and to meet consumer demand in health-conscious niche markets. The combined prognosis is for a mix of pest and nutrient management practices where agro-chemicals use will become less overall but more precisely directed in time and space.

References

Abdalla, C.W. (1990), 'Measuring Economic Losses from Ground Water Contamination: An Investigation of Household Avoidance Costs', *Water Resources Bulletin*, **26**: 451–63.

Abdalla, C.W. (1994), 'Groundwater Values from Avoidance Cost Studies: Implications for Policy and Future Research', *American Journal of Agricultural Economics*, **76** (December): 1062–7.

Abdalla, C.W., B.A. Roach and D.J. Epp (1992), 'Valuing Environmental Quality Changes Using Averting Expenditures: An Application to Groundwater Contamination', *Land Economics*, **68** (May): 163–9.

Antle, J.M. and P.L. Pingali (1994), 'Pesticides, Productivity and Farmer Health: A Philippino Case Study', *American Journal of Agricultural Economics*, **76** (August): 418–30.

Beach, E.D. and G.A. Carlson (1993), 'Hedonic Analysis of Herbicides: Do User Safety and Water Quality Matter?', *American Journal of Agricultural Economics*, **75** (August): 612–23.

Binford, G.D., A.M. Blackmer and N.M. El-Hout (1990), 'Tissue Test for Excess Nitrogen during Corn Production', *Agronomy Journal*, **82** (January): 124–9.

Bouzaher, A., D. Archer, R. Cabe, A. Carriquiry and J.F. Shogren (1992), 'Effects of Environmental Policy on Trade-offs in Agri-Chemical Management', *Journal of Environmental Management*, **36** (September): 69–80.

Breembroek, J.A., B. Koole, K.J. Poppe and G.A.A. Wossink (1996), 'Environmental Farm Accounting: The Case of the Dutch Nutrient Accounting System', *Agricultural Systems*, **51**: 29–40.

Carrasco-Tauber, C. and L.J. Moffit (1992), 'Damage Control Econometrics: Functional Specification and Pesticide Productivity, *American Journal of Agricultural Economics*, **74** (February): 158–62.

Chambers, R.G. and E. Lichtenberg (1994), 'Simple Econometrics of Pesticide Productivity', *American Journal of Agricultural Economics*, **76** (August): 407–17.

Chu, M., S.M. Swinton and S.S. Batie (1995), 'Designing Contracts to Reduce Agricultural Non-point Source Pollution', Staff Paper No. 95-44, Department of Agricultural Economics, Michigan State University, East Lansing, MN.

Chu, M., S.M. Swinton and S.S. Batie (1996), 'Agricultural Production Contracts to Reduce Nitrate Leaching: A Whole-Farm Analysis', paper presented at the annual meeting of the American Agricultural Economics Association, San Antonio, Texas, 28–31 July.

Crissman, C.C., D.C. Cole and F. Carpio (1994), 'Pesticide Use and Farm Worker Health in Ecuadorian Potato Production', *American Journal of Agricultural Economics*, **76** (August): 593–7.

Dijkhuizen, A.A. and C.W. Rougoor (1996), 'Extent and Profitability of Pharmaceutical Use in Livestock Farming', paper presented at the International Agricultural Economists' symposium on 'Economics of Agro-Chemicals', Wageningen Agricultural University, Netherlands, 24–7 April.

Doran, J.W., D.G. Fraser, M.N. Culik and W.C. Liebhardt (1986), 'Influence of

Alternative and Conventional Agricultural Management on Soil Microbial Processes and Nitrogen Availability', *American Journal of Alternative Agriculture*, **2** (Summer): 99–104.

Feder, G. (1979), 'Pesticides, Information and Pest Management under Uncertainty', *American Journal of Agricultural Economics*, **61** (February): 97–103.

Follett, R.F., D.R. Kenney and R.M. Cruse (eds) (1991), *Managing Nitrogen for Groundwater Quality and Farm Profitability*, Soil Science Society of America, Madison, WI.

Fox, G., A. Weersink, G. Sarwar, S. Duff and B. Deen (1991), 'Comparative Economics of Alternative Agricultural Production Systems: A Review', *Northeastern Journal of Agricultural and Resource Economics*, **20**: 124–42.

Hahn, R.W. and R.N. Stavins (1991), 'Incentive-based Environmental Regulation: A New Era from an Old Idea?', *Ecology Law Quarterly*, **18**: 1–42.

Hamilton, N.D. (1990), *What Farmers Need to Know about Environmental Law: Iowa Edition*, Drake University Agricultural Law Center, Des Moines.

Harwood, R.R. (1985), 'The Integration Efficiencies of Cropping Systems', in T.C. Edens, C. Fridgen and S.L. Battenfield (eds), *Sustainable Agriculture and Integrated Farming Systems,* Michigan State University Press, East Lansing, MN.

Hawkins, R., R.O. Hawkins, D.W. Nordquist and others (1995), *PLANETOR User's Manual*, Version 2.0 edn, Center for Farm Financial Management, University of Minnesota, St Paul, MN.

Hayami, Y. and V.W. Ruttan (1985), *Agricultural Development: An International Perspective*, 2nd edn, Johns Hopkins University Press, Baltimore.

Headley, J.C. (1968), 'Estimating the Productivity of Agricultural Pesticides', *American Journal of Agricultural Economics*, **50** (February): 13–23.

Heady, E.O. and J.L. Dillon (1961), *Agricultural Production Functions*, Iowa State University Press, Ames, IA.

Hexem, R. and E.O. Heady (1978), *Water Production Functions for Irrigated Agriculture*, Iowa State University Press, Ames, IA.

Higley, L.G. and W.K. Wintersteen (1992), 'A Novel Approach to Environmental Risk Assessment of Pesticides as a Basis for Incorporating Environmental Costs into Economic Injury Level', *American Entomologist*, **38**: 34–9.

Hoag, D.L. and A.G. Hornsby (1992), 'Coupling Groundwater Contamination with Economic Returns When Applying Farm Pesticides', *Journal of Environmental Quality*, **21** (October–December): 579–86.

Horowitz, J.K. and E. Lichtenberg (1993), 'Insurance, Moral Hazard and Agricultural Chemical Use', *American Journal of Agricultural Economics*, **75** (November): 926–35.

Just, R.E. and R.D. Pope (1978), 'Stochastic Specification of Production Functions and Economic Implications', *Journal of Econometrics*, **7**: 67–86.

Landis, D.A. and M.J. Haas (1992), 'Influence of Landscape Structure on Abundance and Within-Field Distribution of European Corn Borer (Lepidoptera: Pyralidae) Larval Parasitoids in Michigan', *Environmental Entomology*, **21** (April): 409–16.

Lichtenberg, E. and D. Zilberman (1986), 'The Econometrics of Damage Control:

Why Specification Matters', *American Journal of Agricultural Economics*, **68** (May): 261–73.

Luna, J., V. Allen, J. Fontenot and others (1994), 'Whole Farm Systems Research: An Integrated Crop and Livestock Systems Comparison Study', *American Journal of Alternative Agriculture*, **9** (Winter/Spring): 57–63.

Lybecker, D.W., E.E. Schweizer and P. Westra (1994), *WEEDCAM Manual*, Department of Agricultural Economics, Colorado State University, Ft Collins, CO.

Moffitt, L.J., D.C. Hall and C.D. Osteen (1984), 'Economic Thresholds under Uncertainty with Application to Corn Nematode Management', *Southern Journal of Agricultural Economics*, **16**: 151–7.

Oriade, C.A. and R.P. King (1994), 'An Economic Analysis of Site-Specific Management and Delayed Planting Strategies for Weed Control', paper presented at the annual meeting of the American Agricultural Economics Association, 7–10 August, San Diego, CA, Department of Agricultural and Applied Economics, University of Minnesota, St Paul, MN.

Owens, N., S. Swinton and E. van Ravenswaay (1996), 'A New Way to Measure Farmer Willingness to Pay for Safer Herbicides', paper presented at the Third National IPM Symposium/Workshop, Washington, DC, 27 February–1 March.

Pannell, D.J. (1990), 'Responses to Risk in Weed Control Decisions under Expected Profit Maximization', *Journal of Agricultural Economics*, **41** (September): 391–403.

Pierce, F.J., P.C. Robert and J.D. Sadler (eds) (1996), *The State of Site-Specific Management in Agriculture*, Agronomy Society of America, Madison, WI.

Pingali, P.L., C.B. Marquez and F.G. Palis (1994), 'Pesticides and Philippine Rice Farmer Health: A Medical and Economic Analysis', *American Journal of Agricultural Economics*, **76** (August): 587–92.

Poe, G.L. and R.C. Bishop (1992), 'Measuring the Benefits of Groundwater Protection from Agricultural Contamination: Results from a Two-Stage Contingent Valuation Study', Staff Paper No. 341, Department of Agricultural Economics, University of Wisconsin, Madison, WI.

Rader, D.N. (1994), 'Nutrient Trading as a Management Option: The Tar-Pamlico Experiment', in P.E. Norris and L.E. Danielson (eds), *Economic Issues Associated with Nutrient Management Policy: Proceedings of a Regional Workshop*, Report SRDC No. 180, Mississippi State, MS: Southern Rural Development Center, Mississippi State University.

Reganold, J.P., A.S. Palmer, J.C. Lockhart and A.N. MacGregor (1993), 'Soil Quality and Financial Performance of Biodynamic and Conventional Farms in New Zealand', *Science*, **260** (16 April: 344–9.

Reichelderfer, K.H. and F.E. Bender (1979), 'Application of a Simulative Approach to Evaluating Alternative Methods for the Control of Agricultural Pests', *American Journal of Agricultural Economics*, **61** (February): 258–67.

Ribaudo, M.O. and R.A. Shoemaker (1995), 'The Effect of Feedgrain Program Participation on Chemical Use', *Agricultural and Resource Economics Review*, **24** (October): 211–20.

Rola, A. and P. Pingali (1993), Pesticides, Rice Productivity and Health Impacts in the Philippines', in P. Faeth (ed.), *Agricultural Policy and Sustainability: Case Studies from India, Chile, the Philippines and the United States*, World Resources Institute, Washington, DC.

Smith, V.H. and B.K. Goodwin (1996), 'Crop Insurance, Moral Hazard and Agricultural Chemical Use', *American Journal of Agricultural Economics*, **78** (May): 428–38.

Stern, V.M., R.F. Smith, R. van den Bosch and K.S. Hagen (1959), 'The Integrated Control Concept', *Hilgardia*, **29**: 81–101.

Stute, J.K. and J.L. Posner (1993), 'Legume Cover Crop Options for Grain Rotations in Wisconsin', *Agronomy Journal*, **85** (November/December): 1128–32.

Swinton, S. and R.P. King (1994), 'Bioeconomic Model for Weed Management in Corn and Soybean', *Agricultural Systems*, **44**: 313–35.

Talpaz, H. and I. Borosh (1974), Strategy for Pesticide Use: Frequency and Applications', *American Journal of Agricultural Economics*, **56** (November): 769–75.

Van Ravenswaay, E.O. (1995), 'Public Perceptions of Agrichemicals', Task Force Report No. 123, Council for Agricultural Science and Technology (CAST), Ames, IA.

Wiles, L.J., R.P. King, E.E. Schweizer, D.W. Lybecker and S.M. Swinton (1996), 'GWM: General Weed Management Model', *Agricultural Systems*, **50**: 355–76.

Wilkerson, G.G., S.A. Modena and H.D. Coble (1991), 'HERB: Decision Model for Postemergence Weed Control in Soybean', *Agronomy Journal*, **83** (March): 413–17.

Author Index

Abdalla, C.W., 362, 369
Abrol, I.P., 118, 125
Acharya, S.S., 54, 56
Ackello-Ogutu, Ch., 13, 17, 168, 178
Adams, R.M., 330
Adamowicz, W.L. 311
Addiscott, T.M., 297, 310
Adesina, A.A., 182, 191
Adger, W.N., 272, 280
Agne, S., 243, 245, 247
Agricultural Finance Corporation
    (AFC), 109, 116
Agriculture Canada, 318, 320, 329
Ahmed, R., 42, 57
Akakpo-Drah, A., 160, 164
Alagh, Y.K., 100, 105
Albisu, L.M., 343
Ali, M., 128, 142
Allen, J., 69, 72
Allen, V. 371
Almekinders, C.J.M., 168, 178
Anderson, G.D., 284, 293
Anderson, J.R., 131, 142
Anderson, R.E., 192
Anderson, W.P., 331
Andriesse, A., 61, 73
Antinelli, A., 341, 342
Antle, J.M., 266, 280, 362, 369
Archer, D., 369
Arrow, K., 299, 310
Asante, E.O., 236
Athwal, R.K., 301, 310

Baanante, C.A., 250, 254, 260, 261
Babcock, B.A., 13, 14, 17
Babu, S.C., 100, 106

Badiane, O. 232, 236
Baidu-Forson, J., 182, 191
Baltussen, W.H.M., 215–221
Bartel, R., 356, 358
Batie, S.S., 369
Battenfield, S.L., 370
Baudry, J., 284, 293
Baumol, W.J., 266, 280, 327, 329
BC Ministry of Agriculture, Fisheries,
    and Food, 298, 310
Beach, E.D., 335, 342, 362, 369
Beattie, B.R., 178
Beauchamp, E.G., 318, 329
Becht, J.A., 249–261
Becker, G.S., 242, 247
Bedient, P.B., 314, 320, 329
Bender, F.E., 364, 371
Berck, P., 13, 17, 168, 178
Berentsen, P.M.B., 280
Bergland, O., 266, 281
Bergmann, L., 344
Bernard, S.J., 247
Bernardo, D.J., 293, 330
Bertelsen, M., 213
Bertrand, F., 330
Bezdek, J.C., 310
Bhagwati, J., 54, 56
Binford, G.D., 365, 369
Bingham, G., 266, 280
Bishop, J., 69, 72
Bishop, R.C., 362, 371
Blackmer, A.M, 369
Blackwell, M., 13, 17
Boadway, R.W., 281
Bohl, M., 314, 330
Bojö, J., 69, 72

Bonsu, K.M., 232, 236
Booltink, H.W.G., 169, 178, 179
Borlaug, N.E., 21, 39
Börner, H. 342
Borosh, I.P., 360, 372
Bos, A.W., 313, 329
Bosso, C.J., 242, 247
Bosch, D.D., 331
Bouma, J., 179, 193
Boussemart, J-P., 285, 293
Boussemart, J-Ph., 14, 17
Bouzaher, A., 314, 329, 363, 369
Braden, J.B., 314, 329
Breembroek, J.A., 366, 369
Breman, H., 62, 72, 130, 143
Briggs, T., 313, 329
Brouwer, F.M., 75–91, 221, 275, 277, 281
Brouwer, J. 61, 72
Brown, L.R. 31, 36, 39
Brown, R.B., 293
Bruce, N., 281
Burrell, A., 278, 281
Burrows, T.M., 53, 56
Buttler, T.M., 293
Buurma, J.S., 215–221
Byerlee, D., 128, 142

Cabe, R., 369
Cain, L., 310
Campbell, C.L., 10, 17
Canter, L.W., 297, 310
Capalbo, S.M., 266, 280
Carlson, G.A, 10, 17, 335, 333, 362, 369
Carpentier, A., 13, 17
Carpio, F., 369
Carrasco-Tauber, C., 13, 17, 239, 247, 361, 369
Carriquiry, A., 369
Carson, R.T., 341, 343
Castillo, L., 244, 247
Centre for Monitoring Indian Economy (CMIE) 99, 106
Cerná, A., 354, 358
Cetkovský, P., 358

Chadha, K.L., 96, 106
Chalamwong, Y., 260
Chambers, R.G., 13, 17, 361, 369
Chen, K., 39
Chen, L., 28, 39
Cheng, X., 152, 147
Chopra, K.L., 100, 106
Chu, M., 363, 369
Coble, H.D., 372
Coetzee, G.K., 158, 164
Cogger, C.G., 297, 310
Cole, D.C., 369
Coletta, A., 342
Commission of the European Communities (CEC), 76, 77, 91
Cornelisse, P., 249, 260
Council Regulation (EEC), 89, 91
CountyNatWest WoodMac, 7, 18, 75, 91
Crissman, C.C., 362, 369
Cropper, M.L., 242, 247
Cruse, R.M., 370
Cruz, P., 170
Culik, M.N., 369

Dahoui, K.P., 256, 260
Dai, Q., 125
Danielson, L.E., 371
Das, G., 54, 56
David, B.V., 41, 44, 48, 51, 56, 58
DBV, 349, 358
Debertin, D.L., 97, 106
Deen, B., 370
de Buck, A.J., 181–192
de Haan, T., 204
Dehne, H-W., 7, 18, 281
de Jager, A., 59–73
De Janvry, A., 139, 140, 142, 251, 253, 254, 261
de Koeijer, T.J., 18, 69, 72, 167–179
Delgado, C.L., 64, 72, 261
Deloitte and Touche Management Consultants, 318, 320, 329
Dervaux, B., 14, 17
Desai, G.M., 42, 43, 56, 100, 106
de Snoo, G.R., 192

de Steenhuijzen Piters, C.B., 61, 72
de Veer, J., 197, 204
de Wit, C.T., 167, 178, 204, 278, 281
DFG, 333, 342
Dholakia, B.H., 54, 56
Dhrymes, P.J., 137, 142
Diebel, P.L., 295, 310
Dieter, H.H., 334, 344
Dijk, J., 195–205, 281
Dijkhuizen, A.A., 367, 368, 369
Dillon, J.L., 260, 370
Direction des Enquêtes et Statistiques
    Agricoles (DESA), 159, 163, 164
Djiteye, M.A., 62, 73
Dommen, A.J., 139, 142
Doran, J.W., 365, 369
Dorcey, A.H.J., 296, 310
Draycott, A., 178
Dyke, P.T., 125
Dubgaard, A., 280, 281
Ducla-Soarcs, M.M., 247
Duff, S., 370

ECPA, 336, 342
Edens, T.C., 370
Edwards, C.A., 152
Ehlers, H., 196, 205
Eicher, C.K., 158, 164
Ekbom, A., 69, 72
El-Hout, N.M., 369
Embleton, M.E., 178
Environment Canada, 313, 314, 329
Epp, D.J., 369
Erbynn, K.G., 236
EUREAU, 336, 342
European Commission, 348–352, 358
Evans, D.J., 247, 344

Faasen, R., 77, 91
Faeth, P., 120, 125, 259
Fafchamps, M., 142
Fait, A., 333, 343
Fang, S., 39
FAO, 2, 4, 358
Farah, J., 56, 242, 247
Farber, S., 132, 136, 142

Feder, G., 252, 255, 260, 360, 370
Fernandez-Santos, J., 284, 293, 314,
    329
Fey, A., 350, 358
Field, B.O., 329
Fleischer, G., 237–248
Flemming, R., 313, 330
Flichman, G., 283–294
Folger, T., 300, 311
Follett, R.F., 365, 370
Fontein, P.F., 280, 281
Fontenot, J., 371
Fosu, K.Y., 255–236
Fox, G., 13, 18, 362, 370
Frank, D.F., 168, 178
Fraser, D.G., 369
Frere, M.H., 315, 320, 329
Fresco, L.O., 73, 143, 170
Fridgen, C., 370
Fuchs, C., 205
Fuller, B., 313, 330
Fullerton, D.J., 298, 310
Fussell, L.K., 72

Gandhi, V.P., 41–58
Gautam, K.C., 52, 57
Gerner, H., 64, 68, 72, 250, 254,
    260
Giesen, G.W.J., 280
Gilad, B., 182, 191
Godeschalk, F.E., 91, 281
Goodwin, B.K., 362, 372
Gopal, M., 52, 57
Gosse, G., 178
Gosseye, P.A., 261
Goudriaan, J., 168, 178
Government of Karnataka, 110, 116
Governor's Soil Resources Study
    Commission, 119, 125
Great Lakes Water Quality Board
    (GLWQB), 314, 330
Green, D.A.G., 254, 260
Greenwood, D.J., 170, 172, 178
Griggs, J.R., 296, 310
Groenwold, J.G., 200, 201, 205
Gulati, A., 54, 57, 96, 106

Haas, M.J., 365, 370
Habets, A.S.J., 170, 178
Hackl, F., 358
Hagedorn, K., 347–358
Hagen, K.S., 372
Hahn, R.W., 370
Hair, J.F., 182, 192
Hall, D.C., 371
Hamilton, N.D., 367, 370
Han, C., 146, 153
Hanf, C-H., 265, 281
Hanley, N., 284, 293, 313, 330
Hanumantha, R.C.H., 96, 106
Hanumappa, H.G., 107–116
Harris, T.R., 160, 164, 300, 310
Harrison, P., 255, 260
Hartmann, M., 280, 282
Harwood, R.R., 146, 152, 365, 370
Hassink, J., 178
Hauser, A., 302, 310
Haverkamp, H.C.M., 184, 192
Haverkort, B., 143
Hawkins, R., 364, 370
Hawkins, R.O., 370
Hayami, Y., 132, 140, 142, 251, 261,
    365, 370
Hayward, K.A., 311
Hazell, P.B.R., 285, 293
Headley, J.C., 360, 370
Heady, E.O., 360, 370
Health and Welfare Canada, 313, 330
Heatwoll, C.D., 310
Heerink, N.B.M., 127–143, 153
Heidhues, F., 142
Heinisch, E., 353, 358
Heinz, I., 273, 281, 333–344
Helfand, G.E., 13, 17, 168, 178, 314,
    323, 330
Hellegers, P.J.G.J., 75–91, 281
Helleiner, G.K., 255, 261
Hengsdijk, H., 143
Herdt, R.W., 254, 261
Hermann, L., 72
Herricks, E.E., 329
Herruzo, A.C., 293, 329
Hexem, R., 360, 370

Hiemstra, W., 127, 142
Higley, L.G., 362, 370
Hii, B., 311
Hiremath, B.N., 95–106
Hoag, D.L., 363, 370
Hodge, I., 314, 330
Hoehn, J.P., 299, 311
Hof, J.G., 300, 311
Hoger, R., 97, 106
Hollis, J.M., 333, 343
Hongladarom, C., 260
Hoogeveen, M.W., 195, 205
Hornsby, A.G., 284, 293, 363, 370
Horowitz, J.K., 362, 370
House, B.W., 314, 323, 330
Howitt, R., 284, 293
Huang, C.L., 343
Huber, W.C., 314, 320, 329
Hufnagel, J., 205
Hutten, T., 197, 204

IFDC Africa, 160, 164
IKC at, 173, 178
ILO, 259, 261
Ippel, B.M., 183, 192
Isaka, S., 300, 311

Jacquet, F., 293
Jager, J.H., 199, 203, 204
Janssens, R.B.M., 200, 203, 204
Johansson, P.O., 299, 311
Johnen, B.G., 336, 343
Johnson, G.V., 329
Johnson, S.L., 314, 330
Jones, C.A., 125
Jorritsma, J., 184, 192
Jourdain, D., 283–294
Jungbluth, F., 243, 247
Just, R.E., 13, 18, 260, 361, 370

Kachanoski, R.G., 314, 330
Kaish, S., 182, 192
Keddeman, W., 69, 73
Kelholt, H.J., 91, 281
Kennedy, P., 137, 142
Kenney, D.R., 370

Kerns, W.R., 330
Kettup, A., 358
King, R.P., 364, 365, 371, 372
Kirkby, E.A., 322, 330
Klir, G., 300, 311
Knapp, K., 13, 18
Knerr, B., 142
Knetsch, J., 299, 311
Knox, R.C., 297, 310
Koffi-Tessio, E.M., 157-165
Komen. R., 280, 281
Koole, B., 369
Kosko, B., 300, 311
Koster, J., 250, 261
Kramer, C.S., 341, 343
Kramer, R.A., 314, 330
Kroll, K., 125
Kruseman, G., 143
Kuhlmann, F., 168, 178
Kumar, P., 53, 57
Kuyvenhoven, A., 249-261
Kwakye, P.K., 236

Lal, R., 152
Lamkin, N.H., 333, 343
Landis, D.A., 365, 370
Lane, L.J., 329
Larson, R.S., 329
Laurila, I., 278, 281
Leamer, E., 310
Lefer, H.B., 293
Leferink, J., 171, 179
Leischer, G., 342
Lemaire, G., 178
Leopold, J.H., 282
Li, W., 27, 39
Li, X., 39
Lichtenberg, E., 13, 17, 18, 285, 293,
    361, 362, 369, 370
Liebhardt, W.C., 369
Liebscher, H., 297, 311
Lin, B., 21, 26, 27, 39
Lingk, W., 334, 343
Lintner, A., 313-331
Liu, S., 153
Lloyd, R., 334, 344

Lockhart, J.C., 371
Lu, G., 23, 24, 39
Lu, L., 152
Luloff, A.E., 344
Luna, J., 365, 371
Luo, S., 146, 153
Luo, Y., 29, 39
Lütteken, A., 347-358
Lutz, E., 69, 73
Lybecker, D.W., 364, 371, 372

Ma, X., 39
MacGregor, A.N., 371
Maclaren, J.W., 330
MacMillan, A., 251, 261
Madden, L.V., 10, 17
Madden, P., 152
Magnus, J.R., 281
Malik, R.P.S., 117-125
Mandac, A.M., 254, 261
Mapp, H.P., 293, 330, 341, 343
Maroni, M., 333, 343
Marquez, C.B., 371
Marra, M., 333, 344
Martijn, T.G., 336, 343
Mathur, S.C., 46, 57
Matlon, P., 261
Mausolff, C., 132, 136, 142
McConnell, C., 297, 310
McNaughton, D., 311
McSweeny, W.T., 330
Mehrotra, K.N., 44, 57
Mellor, J.W., 42, 57
Mengel, K., 322, 330
Meyer, R.E., 153
Michalek, J., 265, 281
Midmore, P., 333, 343
Miltz, D., 329
Ministry of Agriculture of China
    (MOA), 22-24, 39
Ministry of Agriculture, Nature
    Management and Fisheries, 215,
    221
Ministry of Finance of India, 54, 57
Miranowski, J.A., 17, 344
Mishra, J.S., 341, 343

Misra, S.K., 341, 343
Mitchell, R.C., 341, 343
Modena, S.A., 372
Moffitt, L.J., 13, 17, 239, 247, 361,
    369, 371
Mokwunye, A.U., 59–73, 163, 164,
    260
Mol, E., 127–143
Moxey, A., 314, 330
Muia, M.J., 297, 311
Mulder, M., 277, 281

Nachane, D.M., 54, 57
Nadkarni, M.V., 55, 57
Nagel, S.S., 358
Nambiar, K.K.M., 118, 125
Napier, T.L., 295, 311
National Research Council, 334, 343
Naylor, R., 52, 57
Nedwick, P.G., 329
Neeteson, J.J., 178
Ng'ong'ola, D.H., 254, 260
Niangado, O., 62, 72
Nielsen, A.H., 280, 281
Noll, R.G., 241, 247
Noordam, W.P., 183, 192
Nordquist, D.W., 370
Norris, P.E., 371
Norton, R.D., 285, 293
Nyanten, V., 236

Oates, W.E., 266, 280, 327, 329
Obeng, B., 232, 236
O'Callaghan, J.R., 284, 293
Ochan, T., 260
OECD (Organization for Economic
    Cooperation and Development)
    278, 281, 314, 330, 350, 358
Oerke, E-C., 8–10, 18, 265, 281
Oglethorpe, D.R., 284, 293
Olewiler, N.D., 329
Onchan, T., 260
Onstad, C.A., 331
Ontario Ministry of Agriculture and
    Food, 320, 330
Oomen, G.J.M., 170, 177, 178

Opaluch, J.J., 293
Opschoor, J.B., 266, 281
Oriade, C.A., 365, 371
Oskam, A.J., 11, 18, 240, 247,
    265–282, 333, 343, 344
Osteen, C.D., 371
Otsuka, K., 140, 142
Ott, S.L., 343
Oude Lansink, A., 280, 282
Ouedraogo, S., 213
Owen, B.M., 241, 247
Owens, N., 362, 371
Oza, A.N., 54, 57

Pagiola, S., 73
Pagoulatos, A., 13, 17
PAGV, 173, 178
Pak, G.A., 282
Palis, F.G., 371
Palmer, A.S., 371
Pan, J.H., 314, 330
Pandey, S., 13, 18
Pandurangadu, K., 52, 57
Pannell, D.J., 361, 371
Papendick, R.I., 153
Paris, Q., 13, 17, 18, 167, 168, 178
Parlevliet, J.E., 178, 294
Parliamentary Office of Science and
    Technology, 336, 343
Parr, J.F., 146, 153
Pastakia, A.R., 56, 57
Patel, N.T., 41, 47, 50, 58
PAU, 120, 121, 125
Pearce, D.W., 351, 358
Pearce, P.H., 266, 281, 313, 330
Peerlings, J.H.M., 281
Penning de Vries, F.W.T., 62, 73
Perrin, R.K., 167, 178
Perry, G.M., 330
Peters, G.H., 1–18
Phillips, W.E., 311
Phokela, Amrit, 44, 57
Pierce, F.J., 364, 371
Pimentel, D., 11, 18, 265, 282
Pingali, P., 241, 248, 362, 369, 371
Pinto-Toyi, A.K., 163, 164

Plant Protection Service, 215, 221
PLUARG, 313, 330
Poe, G.L., 362, 371
Pope, R.D., 361, 370
Poppe, K.J., 83, 91, 215, 221, 277, 281, 369
Portney, P., 247
Portney, P. 310
Posner, J.L., 365, 372
Pouzet, D., 160, 164
Powlson, D.S., 310
Prabhu, K.S., 52, 57
Pretty, J.N., 72, 73, 127, 142
Prudencio, C.Y., 61, 73
Pucci, C., 342
Pugh, D.M., 344

Qu, F., 145–153
Quedraogo, S., 213

Rabbinge, R., 128, 143
Rader, D.N., 367, 371
Rajasekaran, B., 106
Rajasekhar, D., 107–116
Raju, V.T., 52, 57
Randner, R., 310
Rao, C.H.H., 56, 57
Rao, J.M., 55, 57
Rask, N., 157, 164
Reardon, T., 129, 131, 143, 252, 261
Reddy, R.Y., 96, 106
Reddy, V.R., 55, 58
Reganold, J.P., 365, 371
Reiche, C., 73
Reichelderfer, K.H., 181, 192, 364, 371
Reijntjes, C., 127, 142, 143
Renkema, J.A., 18, 72, 178, 284, 294
Repetto, R., 125, 238, 247
Reus, J.A.W.A., 275, 282, 294
Reynolds, L.G., 261
Ribaudo, M.O., 367, 371
Riera, P., 341, 343
RIVM, 72, 91
RIZA, 77, 91
Roach, B.A., 369

Robert, P.C., 371
Roger, P.A., 280
Rogers, E.M., 68, 73, 182, 192
Rola, 241, 248, 362, 371
Romero, C., 343
Rosegrant, M.W., 53, 57
Ross, J.D., 329
Rougoor, C.W., 367, 368, 369
Roy, S., 107, 116
Ruben, R., 127, 143, 249–261
Rudra, R., 314, 330
Rukavishnikov, V., 358
Runge, C.F., 252, 261
Ruttan, V.W., 132, 142, 251, 261, 333, 343, 365, 370
Rutten, H., 197, 204

Sadler, J.D., 371
Sadoulet, E., 139, 142, 251, 253, 254, 261
Sah, D.C., 96, 106
San Juan, C., 334, 343
Sarma, J.S., 54, 55, 58
Sarwar, G., 370
Schmitz, P.M., 280, 282
Schneider, M., 349, 351, 358
Schönbeck, F., 7, 18, 281
Schoney, R.A., 311
Schoorlemmer, H.B., 181, 192
Schröder, J.J., 168, 171, 179
Schueller, J.K., 169, 179
Schulte-Ebbert, U., 342
Schuman, H., 310
Schweizer, E.E., 371, 372
Segerson, K., 314, 315, 325, 330
Seni, A., 236
Sere, Y., 207–213
Setboronsarng, S., 244, 247
Shah, A., 96, 106
Sharma, A., 54, 57
Sharma, P.K., 54, 57
Sheard, R.W., 329
Shetty, P.K., 96, 106
Shoemaker, R.A., 367, 371
Shogren, J.F., 369
Shylendra, H.S., 105, 106

Sidibé, A., 207–213
Simbrey, J., 342
Simonsen, J.W., 277, 282
Singh, K., 95–106
Smaling, E.M.A., 59–73, 163, 165
Smit, A.L., 171, 179
Smith, R.F., 372
Smith, V.H., 362, 372
Smith, V.K., 266, 282
Söderqvist, T., 341, 343
Solow, R., 310
SPAAR, 65, 73
Spiertz, J.H.J., 179
Srinivasan, T.N., 54, 56
Srivastava, U.K., 41, 47, 50, 58
Staatz, J.M., 158, 164
Stavins, R.N., 370
Stavros, R.W., 330
Stennes, B., 298, 309, 311
Sterk, H.J., 282
Stern, V.M., 360, 372
Stocking, M.A., 69, 73
Stoddard, S.W., 310
Stoklasa, J., 353, 358
Stone, B., 42, 43, 56
Stonehouse, D.P., 314, 330
Stoorvogel, J.J., 62, 73, 163, 165
Stouthart, F., 171, 179
Stroosnijder, L., 143
Struik, P.C., 178, 294
Stute, J.K., 365, 372
Subramanian, S.R., 106
Sullivan, W.M., 293
Swanson, T.M., 334, 344
Swinton, S.M., 359–372

Talpaz, H., 360, 372
Tatham, R.L., 192
Taylor, C.R., 284, 293
Taylor, D.B., 310
Taylor, D.C., 147, 152
Teague, M.L., 289, 293, 314, 330
Teboh, J.F., 157, 165
Terluin, I.J., 91
Thijssen, G.J., 18, 281, 282
Thomas, P., 105, 108

Thomas, M.P., 297, 311
Thompson, R.L., xvii–xx
Thompson, T.P, 254, 261
Tian, Z., 39
Tietenberg, T.H., 240, 248, 266, 282
Tosovská, E., 358
Turner, R.K., 266, 282
Turvey, C.G., 284, 294

Udry, C., 252, 261
UNDP, 130, 143
Upender, M., 53, 58
Uzo Mokwunye, A., 59–73, 163, 164, 260

van Asperen, P., 179
van Berkum, S., 76, 90
van den Bosch, R., 372
van Dongen, G.J.M., 179
van der Meer, H.G., 179
van der Meulen, H.A.B., 182, 192
van den Noort, P.C., 344
van der Pol, F., 62, 66, 73, 143, 257, 261
van der Werf, A., 171, 179
van der Werf, E., 142
van der Werf, H.M.G., 11, 18
van Dongen, G.J.M., 179
van Duivenboden, N., 256, 261
van Ittersum, M.K., 128, 143
van Keulen, H., 130, 143
van Klaveren, J.D, 12, 18
van Kooten, G.C., 1–18, 295–311
van Mensvoort, J.J.M., 72
van Niejenhuis, J.H., 181–192
van Noordwijk, M., 169, 176, 179
van Ravenswaay, E.O., 359, 371, 372
van Rheenen, T., 134, 143
van Zeijts, H., 18, 282
Van Zyl, J., 158, 164
Venugopal, P., 50, 58
Verduyn, S.C., 280
Vereijken, P., 129, 143, 181, 192, 266, 282
Verhagen, A. (J.), 169, 173, 178, 179
Verhees, F.J.H.M., 167–179

Verhoeven, J.T., 288, 294
Verma, J.S., 46, 53, 58
Vernooy, C.J.M., 83, 91
Vidya, S., 96, 106
Vijftigschild, R.A.N., 108, 276, 282
Vishwanathan, A., 100, 106
Vogel, J., 358
Vos, J.B., 274, 278, 281, 282
Vosti, S., 129, 143
Vredenberg, W.J., 178, 294
Vreke, J., 284, 294
Vyas, S.C., 100, 106

Wadman, W.P., 169, 176, 179
Waibel, H., 237–248
Walker, A., 343
Walther, J., 205
Wang, W., 153
Wang, Z., 153
Wanmali, S., 56
Warford, J.J., 351, 358
Waters-Bayer, A., 143
Weaver, R.D., 13, 17, 341, 344
Weber, A., 181, 196, 205, 281
Weckseler, H.J., 282
Weersink, A., 13, 18, 313–331, 370
Welten, J.P.P.J., 91, 221
Wenzel-Klein, S. 358
Westra, P., 371
Wetenschappelijke Raad voor het
    Regeringsbeleid (WRR), 273,
    282
Wetzstein, M.E., 10, 17
Whitby, M., 272, 280
White, B., 314, 330
White, W., 311
Whitmore, A.P., 310
WHO, 336, 344

Wijnands, F.G., 181, 192, 221, 266,
    282
Wijnands, J.H.M., 91
Wiles, L.J., 364, 372
Wilkerson, G.G., 364, 372
Williams, A.J., 333, 344
Williams, J.R., 119, 125
Williams, W.A., 17, 178
Windmeijer, P.N., 61, 73
Wintersteen, W.K., 362, 370
Woodburn, A., 237, 247
World Bank, 158, 165, 236, 254,
    256–258, 261
Wossink, G.A.A., 1–18, 167–179,
    181–192, 282, 284, 294, 369
Wu, J., 145–153
Wu, S., 39

Xia, Z., 39
Xin, Naiquan, 31, 39

Young, R.A, 320, 331
Youngberg, I.G., 153

Zamchiya, J.M., 56
Zadoks, J.C., 265, 282, 335, 344
Zeddies, J., 202, 205
Zekri, S., 293, 329
Zhang, N., 40
Zhang, R., 145–153
Zhang, W., 35, 39
Zhou, Z., 39
Zilberman, D., 13, 18, 260, 285, 293,
    333, 344, 361, 370
Zimmermann, G.M., 334, 344
Zinnah, M.M., 182, 191
Zullei-Seibert, N., 342

Subject Index

ADI (Acceptable Daily Intake), 12
Africa
    fertilizer use in, 3–4
    pesticide use in, 7–10
America, North, Central and South
    fertilizer use in, 3–4
    pesticide use in, 7–10, 275
American Cyanamid, 49–50
Asia
    fertilizer use in, 3–4
    pesticide use in, 7–10
Australia
    low tillage farming in, xix
    see also Oceania
Austria, 336–339

BASF, 49–50
Bayer, 49, 50
Belgium, 77–86, 275
BHC (benzene hexochloride), 45–42
biotechnology, xix
blue baby syndrome, 11, 297
Brazil
    low tillage farming in, xix
    see also America, South
British Columbia, 295–312
Burkina Faso, 207–214
    see also Sub-Saharan Africa

CAP, 283, 349, 357
Central and Eastern Europe (CEEC),
    347–349
China
    agro-chemicals use in, 21–26
    economic reform and fertilizer use
        in, 25–26

food security, 30–33
    intensive farming systems in,
        146–147
    see also Asia
Ciba-Geigy, 49
contingent valuation (CV), 299
Costa Rica, 243

DDT, 45–47, 355
Denmark, 77–86, 275
depletion, 15, 60–62, 119–123,
    157–165, 207–208
distribution see fertiliser use and
    pesticide use
Du Pont, 49

econometric analysis
    of production functions, 13–14,
        361–362
    of soil depletion in Togo, 157–165
effectiveness of crop protection, 9–10
efficiency
    frontier, 183–186
    of agro-chemicals use, 3–4, 9–10
    of fertilizer use in China, 25–28
    of fertilizer use in India, 116
    of fertilizer use in Togo, 157–165
    of nutrient uptake, 176
environmental effects
    and price responses, 202
    and technological change, 363–364
    data and methodological problems,
        244
    economic assessment of, 266–273,
        335–340
    of agro-chemicals use defined,

10–13
of fertilizer use in China, 34–35
of fertilizer use in India, 96
of intensive farming systems in
    China, 146
of nitrogen use in The Netherlands,
    77
EPIC, 119–121, 285–286
erosion, 119–123, 313–315
Europe, Western and Eastern
    fertilizer use in, 3–4
    pesticide use in, 7–10
European guidelines for drinking
    water, 12, 336
extension
    and farmers' perceptions, 182
    and sustainable agriculture, 14, 16,
        101, 244, 280
    in Sub-Saharan Africa, 72, 235

FADN (Farm Accountancy Data
    Network), 76–85
farmers' perceptions, 101, 181–182,
    220, 244
FCFA devaluation, 63, 163, 250
fertilizer use
    and infrastructure and services, 260
    and marketing, 28, 48
    defined, 7
    development by continent, 1–5
    efficiency in China, 25–28
    in Central and Eastern Europe,
        347–349
    in Europe, 77–86
    in Ghana, 225–236
    in India, 44
    in India, Karnataka, 109
    in Sub-Saharan Africa, 62–72
FMC, 53
food supply–demand balance
    and the chemical industry, 242
    in Asia, 238
    in China, 30–33
    in India, 56
    in Sub-Saharan Africa, 59
    world projections, xvii

France, 77–86, 284–293, 275
fuzzy pairwise comparison, 300–301

GATT, 54, 62
Germany, 77–86, 336–339, 275
Ghana, 225–236
    see also Sub-Saharan Africa
Greece, 77–86, 275

health effects
    and technological change, 363–364
    of agro-chemicals defined, 10–13
    of nitrogen emission, 297, 313
HEIA (high external input
    agriculture), 127–144
HEISA see HEIA
Hoechst, 53

IAFS (Integrated Arable Farming
    Systems), 101
IFDC, 60
India
    fertilizer use in, 116
    pesticide use in, 44–48
    see also Asia
indicators, 14
    of environmental risks, 288–289,
        314
Indonesia
    low and high input systems in,
        126–144
    low tillage farming in, xix
    see also Asia
institutional failure, 233, 238–240
IPM, 238–245
Ireland, 77–86, 275
Italy, 77–86, 275

Japan, 77
    see also Asia
knowledge see extension

LEIA (low external input
    agriculture), 127–144

Mali see Sub-Saharan Africa

marginal abatement costs (MAC), 266
marginal environmental cost
    (MEC), 266
marginal net private benefit (MNPB),
    267
marketing *see* fertilizer use and
    pesticide use
Monsanto, 53

Netherlands, 77, 86, 181–182,
    195–200, 215–216, 275
non-price factors, 242, 246
NPK ratio, 26
nutrient depletion *see* depletion

Oceania
    fertilizer use in, 3–4
    pesticide use in, 7–10

perceptions *see* farmers' perceptions
pesticide use
    and marketing and distribution,
        44–54
    defined, 2
    development by continent, 6–8
    in Europe, 77–86
    in India, 44–48
    in tulip farming systems, 215–221
phosphate rock use, 66–67, 249–261
phytotoxicity, 11
PLANETOR, 364
POLEN model, 285–286
policy
    analysis and policy formulation,
        239–242, 266–273
    development and fertilizer demand
        in Ghana, 225–236
    summary of economic analyses,
        13–14
policy instruments, 235, 274, 283, 309
    and ambient schemes, 314–315
    nutrient accounting law, 366
    tradable permits, 367
    used in European countries, 275
Portugal, 77–86, 275
precision agriculture, 129, 168, 364

price responses
    and non-price factors, 242–244
    of pesticide and fertilizer use in
        the Netherlands, 79–83
    of pesticide use in India, 44–48
production functions, 130–134,
    167–170, 200, 359–363
productivity
    and application of nutrients, xix
    and erosion in India, 117
    and fertilizers in Sub-Saharan
        Africa, 52
    of agro-chemicals use, 2–10

residues of pesticides *see* health
    effects
returns of agro-chemicals use *see*
    productivity
Rhône-Poulenc, 53
risks *see* farmers' perceptions

Sahel,
    see also Sub-Saharan Africa
Sandoz, 53
Schering, 53
sediment runoff, 297
    see also depletion
Shell, 53
site-specific agriculture *see* precision
    agriculture
soil erosion and fertility *see*
    depletion
Soviet Union *see* Central and Eastern
    Europe
Spain, 77–86, 275
Structural Adjustment Programmes
    (SAP), 62, 63, 70, 225
Sub-Saharan Africa
    depletion in, 60–62
    fertilizer use in, 60–62
    value–cost ratios in, 63, 160–162
Sumitomo, 53
sustainable agriculture
    and agro-chemicals use, 7
    in China defined, 146–147
    in India defined, 56

Thailand, 243
Togo, 157–165
  see also Sub-Sahara Africa
transition
  Central and Eastern Europe, 16,
    347–349

United Kingdom, 275
United States
  low tillage farming in, xixi
  see also America

urea and manure use 209

value–cost ratios, 63, 160–162

West Africa *see* Sub-Saharan Africa,
    59–73
Western Germany *see* Germany
Willingness to Pay (WTP), 299
WTO agreements, xviii, 54

Zeneca, 53